The EC, Eastern Europe and European Unity

For Margriet

The EC, Eastern Europe and European Unity
Discord, Collaboration and Integration Since 1947

PETER VAN HAM

PINTER
London an
Distributed exclu.

PINTER
A Cassell imprint
Wellington House, 125 Strand, London WC2R 0BB, England

First published in 1993

Paperback published in 1995

Distrubuted exclusively in the USA by St. Martin's Press, Inc., Room 400, 175 Fifth Avenue, New York, NY10010, USA

Peter van Ham is hereby identified as the author of this work as provided under Section 77 of the Copyright, Designs and Patents Act, 1988.

British Library Cataloguing in Publication Data

A CIP catalogue record for this book is available from the British Library

ISBN 1 85567 124 7 (Hbk)
ISBN 1 85567 336 3 (Pbk)

Library of Congress Cataloguing-in-Publication Data
Ham, Peter van, 1963-
    The Eastern Europe and European unity : discord, collaboration
and integration since 1947/Peter van Ham
        p. cm.
    Includes bibliographical references and index.
    ISBN 1-85567-124-7
        1. Europe-Economics integration. 2. European Economic Community.
    3. East-West trade (1945-   ) I. Title.
HC241.H346 1993
337. 1'4-de20
                                                                    92-43975
                                                                        CIP

Typeset by Saxon Graphics, Derby
Printed and bound in Great Britain by SRP Ltd, Exeter

Contents

Preface and acknowledgements

The purpose of this book is twofold. First, to provide an historical *tour d'horizon* of the economic and political relations between the European Community and the East. The book begins with the impact of the Marshall Plan on the genesis of West European integration, and ends with the year following the draft-Maastricht Treaty on European Union. A period of some 45 years is thereby covered. Second, it examines EC-East European relations from a specific, theoretical perspective. It is argued that the process of West European integration has been encouraged and facilitated by the rigid structure of the Cold War, in which the threat posed by the Soviet Union temporarily inhibited internal conflicts, and in which American hegemony provided the relatively stable and secure economic, political and military framework in which the major West European countries were able to cooperate and take major steps towards the ultimate ideal of a European Union. One of the questions this book addresses is whether the passing of the Soviet threat and the relative decline of American hegemony (in short: the return to multipolarity), will thwart the current process of further economic, monetary and political integration among the EC member states, and how this will affect the EC's relations with its eastern neighbours.

The following people have offered valuable comments on all or parts of the manuscript: Barry Buzan, Peter Ludlow, John Maslen, Alfred Pijpers, John Pinder, Alfred van Staden, Edmund Wellenstein and Wolfgang Wessels. I am very grateful to all of them. Generous financial support has been provided by the Royal Netherlands Academy of Arts and Sciences, which gave me the opportunity to study this subject as a Research Fellow within the Department of Political Science of Leiden University. Finally, but foremost of those deserving acknowledgement, are my family. My parents have always been a source of encouragement. My wife, Margriet Schoorl, has been unconditionally supportive and remains an intellectual companion as well as best friend. One could say that the main reason for writing this book was to dedicate it to her.

Peter van Ham
Leiden, Autumn 1992

1. Introduction

Virtuosos transcend the limits of their instruments and break the constraints of systems that bind lesser performers.

Kenneth N. Waltz, 'Reflections on *Theory of International Politics*: A Response to my Critics', in Robert O. Keohane (ed.), *Neorealism and Its Critics* (New York: Columbia University Press, 1986), p.344.

1.1 'Things could have been different'

It is always tempting to adopt a linear view on history. It is comforting to believe that mankind will learn from its mistakes and that nations and governments will grow wiser and more pacific as centuries go by, along similar lines as technology and the natural sciences have developed over the ages. It is also attractive to assume – as the French philosopher Joseph de Maistre did – that 'nothing great has great beginnings', and that gradual historical processes will one day bear fruit. In the light of the considerable achievements of West European economic and political integration and the recent demise of Soviet-style Communism, it is appealing to argue – as Francis Fukuyama did a few years ago[1] – that capitalism and liberalism have won an overwhelming victory over their main ideological competitors.

The development of the European Community (EC) towards a European Union, as well as Brussels' congenial relationship with the countries of Central Europe and the former Soviet Union, seem to affirm this rather optimistic reading of history. Within some forty years, the nature of European politics has changed considerably. Under the aegis of the United States and during the height of the Cold War, six West European countries had set some guarded steps towards the integration of two sectors of their economies, which eventually resulted in the establishment of the EEC in 1957. During large parts of the Cold War, the European Community had played only a modest role. But now that bipolarity has given way to a considerably looser international structure, the EC has become one of the major architects of the 'New Europe' of the next millennium. This calls for an explanation. There is a wide, be it tacit, consensus that the success of the European Community embodies the superiority of market-oriented economies *vis-à-vis* centrally planned economic systems. Whereas the Soviet-style systems were still able to compete with the West during the 1950s and much of the 1960s, they have failed to keep track with the West when the superpower competition shifted into areas like microelectronics and other sophisticated technologies where the USSR and Eastern Europe knew a serious disadvantage. What was more, since the 1970s, the United States, Japan and the members of the EC have economically outperformed the USSR and Eastern Europe. Both have been major factors contributing to the recent demise of the Soviet-type systems. Now that the West has won the Cold War, it is widely assumed that only political liberalism provides a sound basis on which innovative new ideas will flourish and mature, and that only high levels of education, the free movement of ideas, people, finance and trade will provide the essential dynamic for capitalist systems to sustain economic growth. It is therefore also no coincidence that ever since Soviet-style economics and totalitarianism lost the historical battle with capitalism and political liberalism, the European Community has become the focal point for many Central European countries and former Soviet Republics. Most countries of the former Soviet bloc now aspire to join the EC, which unquestionably illustrates the validity of the well-known maxim 'when you can't beat them, join them'.

In this book we will analyse the process of West European integration in the light of the European Community's economic and political relations with the 'other Europe' under Communist rule. We will start with the period directly after World War II, in which the main ideas and plans concerning West European economic integration have matured. Our analysis will also include the last months of 1991, when the Soviet Union gave way to the Commonwealth of Independent States and when the Maastricht Treaty on an Economic and Monetary Union (EMU) and a European Political Union (EPU) was initialled. Both have to be considered as historical events which seemed once more to indicate the vitality of West European economic and political integration, as well as the final collapse of Communism as we know it. Much has transpired between the Marshall Plan and the Maastricht Treaty. Although we will certainly not play down the significance of the successes of the Common Market experiment, our inquiry of post-war European history will *not* start from the above-mentioned Fukuyama thesis. Instead, Stanley Hoffmann's recent admonition will be kept in mind: 'In explaining why the division of Europe and communist rule in much of Central and Eastern Europe came to a sudden end, we should not too easily assert the necessity of the transformation. Things could have been different.'[2]

In this book we will therefore maintain that the formation of the European Coal and Steel Community (ECSC) and the EC can *not* be simply explained as a logical and rational linear process from economic conflict and political discord to a peaceful and prosperous European Union. The course from the Marshall Plan to the Maastricht Treaty has been complicated and hazardous, with many detours and without distinct road markings. What is more, the considerable successes of the EC may at times overshadow the haphazard nature of West European integration. Since the mid-1980s, the ambitious plan for the construction of a free internal market and political integration within the EC in 1993 has generated a remarkable integrationist momentum. With the series of Intergovernmental Conferences and the hectic developments in Brussels over the last few years, it is therefore all too easy to forget that only a decade ago the European Community was in the doldrums; for many years a feeling of 'Europessimism' permeated the atmosphere in the EC's Berlaymont Headquarters. It has to be acknowledged that West European integration has evolved joltingly with many temporary successes, Pyrrhic victories, disappointments and set-backs, as well as a number of major achievements and triumphs. Little wonder, therefore, that the formation of the European Community has at times closely resembled the well-known Echternach procession: making three hops forward and two hops back.

In section 1.2 of this introductory chapter we will provide a sketch of the analytical assumptions on which our examination of EC-East European relations will be built. There we will present an overview of the major International Relations theories which have sought to explain the EC phenomenon. Since the EC's relations with the East are central to this book, we will examine whether, and how, these theories have related to the East-West conflict and EC-East European relations in general. In analysing the ties between the European Community and the Communist East, this book will deal with two major developments. On the one hand it will study the process of integration within the EC; on the other hand it will examine the *dis*integration of the economic, political and military structures in the East. We have already indicated that we will not assume any directionality or inevitability in these two processes. However, our study of the EC-East European relationship will have to come to grips with these two opposite developments. One of the more interesting questions which we will examine is whether, and how, these two processes relate to one another.

Until a few years ago, European politics was characterized by two confronting coalitions of states. Both the members of the European Community and the members of the Council for Mutual Economic Assistance (CMEA) were firmly entrenched in military alliances. Despite the not always overlapping membership rolls, the EC and NATO, as well as the CMEA and the Warsaw Pact, clearly comprised two antithetical military-political and economic blocs.[3] In the Manichean world of the Cold War, East-West relations were perceived as a zero-sum game in which the achievements and gains of one alliance were *ipso facto* considered a loss for the other. To some extent, this mechanism has also operated in the relations between the EC and the CMEA. Communist leaders have always staunchly criticized all West European efforts to further the process of economic and political integration within the European Community framework. In turn, American and West European policy-makers have discouraged cooperation within the CMEA under the assumption that further Communist collaboration would reinforce Soviet hegemony in the region. Each economic coalition has therefore tried to halt the process of economic and political unification of its antipode, in the mean time trying to maintain the momentum of its own integrational efforts. In this respect, the East-West conflict has provided several major incentives for both coalitions to sustain integration in order to close their ranks. It will therefore be argued that the Austrian Count Coudenhove-Kalergi was making a good point when he observed – in 1922 – that Europe would be faced with two alternatives: 'either to overcome all national hostilities and consolidate in a federal union, or sooner or later succumb to a Russian conquest'.[4] All in all, the bipolarity of the Cold War era has resulted in an interesting and sometimes symbiotic relationship between the West and East European processes of economic and political integration.

Now that the traditional Soviet threat has abated and bipolarity has given way to multipolarity, the question has arisen as to the EC's new role in world politics. Since the Community has been established and developed within the rigid structure of the Cold War, it is an appropriate question to ask whether the EC has now acquired sufficient dynamic to sustain the present integrationist momentum and to attain the aspirations of European unity? Will cooperation among the EC members endure now that several major external incentives are gone? Or have several decades of cooperation among the West European nations bolstered the EC's authority and influence sufficiently to sustain integration? These are important questions which cannot be answered without reference to some portentous theoretical debates which have engaged many scholars over the past decades. In order to answer these far-ranging questions, this book will try to go beyond a simple chronicle of the EC's ties with the East, but will apply one of the most powerful theories in order to explain EC-East European relations in a more profound manner.

In an effort to analyse the EC's ties with the East, this book will therefore aspire to two things. First, it seeks to provide an analytical *tour d'horizon* of the economic, political and ideological conflicts and battles between these two parts of the European continent. Second, by examining these events within a specific theoretical framework, it hopes to generate a more profound understanding of the development of European politics.

1.2 The approach of this book

Analysing the political and economic developments in Argentina or India seems relatively uncomplicated in comparison to making some useful statements about Europe now which still make some sense after a year or so. It is beyond doubt that European history has been moving at great speed during the late-1980s and early-1990s; many a scholar seems to have severe difficulties in keeping track with it. In an effort at overcoming some of these predicaments, the approach of this book will be both historical and theoretical. One level of analysis will be predominantly descriptive, examining the major developments in the relationship between the EC and the East; our theoretical focus will provide a more conceptual perspective on these relations.

Most studies on Europe explore its uncertain future, and rightly so. For many years, East-West affairs have only changed marginally. Most Communist leaders have managed to stay in power for quite a long time, doing their utmost to maintain the *status quo* within their socio-economic system; often successfully. With the revolutions of the late-1980s, however, the nature of Europe's political scene, as well as its balance of power, have altered significantly. For most policy-makers and most analysts these changes have come unexpectedly. Drafting scenarios for the post-Cold War era has therefore become essential in order to provide plans and concepts for Europe's future architecture. Despite this dire need for strategic thinking about Europe's prospects, a large part of this book will have its back turned to the future and will provide an historical account of the European Community's relations with the East. There are a number of quite compelling reasons for doing this. First of all, the tale of EC-East European relations – however interesting – still remains largely untold. Some aspects have gained considerably more attention from academics than others; in particular, the ties between the European Community and the CMEA have been relatively well documented and analysed. However, several large white spots still await examination. Second, it would be short-sighted to assume that the relations between the Community and its Eastern neighbours only started when the EC and the CMEA took up official contacts in June 1988, after several decades of disengagement. Many of the challenges and dilemmas which the European Community will face in the years to come, in its policy towards the East, have their roots in the recent past. This makes it all the more necessary to extend our knowledge of the ways in which West European integration has been influenced by the East and how the European Community in turn has swayed Communist policy. By providing some of the historical backcloth against which European politics is currently unfolding, we will be able to put a number of important theoretical and policy-oriented problems into their proper perspective.

As said, this book will not analyse EC-East European relations in a theoretical vacuum. As Robert O. Keohane and Stanley Hoffmann have reminded us recently: 'Attempts to avoid theory ... not only miss interesting questions but rely implicitly on a framework for analysis that remains unexamined precisely because it is implicit'.[5] Our examination of the development of the EC will therefore start from an explicit theoretical position by applying the paradigms of the Neo-realist theory of International Relations. In later chapters we will also examine several of the theoretical concepts which have recently been formulated as extensions of Neo-realism.

We will specifically examine the explanatory power of the theory of Neo-liberal institutionalism, a theory which has recently been advanced by scholars like Robert Keohane and Jack Snyder.[6] We will argue that both Neo-realism and Neo-liberal institutionalism go a long way in explaining the development of post-war politics, but that the former theory can best be applied to the period in which the European Community has been established, whereas the latter may be more powerful in explaining the EC's further development. Keohane's argument that the institutionalist approach constitutes both a critique and a modification of Neo-realism, that it has supplemented Neo-realism but not replaced it, seems to be confirmed by this study.[7] By adopting these specific theoretical frameworks for analysis we will make an effort at providing more penetrating insights in the post-war relations between the European Community and the East. In this book we will, however, not make an attempt to test or to sharpen these Neo-realist concepts. We will – quite modestly – apply them as the most useful theoretical tools available to get some grip on one of the major developments in post-war European politics.

Before examining the specifics of Neo-realist theory, let us first introduce the two principal antithetical perspectives on world politics: Realism and Functionalism. Realists have seen world politics as 'a state of war', whereas Functionalists (also sometimes called Institutionalists) have considered cooperation as essential to world affairs due to the growing economic interdependence among states. Both theories have provided powerful arguments explaining the alternation of discord and collaboration among the member states of the EC. Realist academics (like Bernard Brodie, Inis L. Claude, Hans J. Morgenthau, Arnold Wolfers and Stanley Hoffmann), have all aired the view that events in world politics can best be understood as a continuous struggle for power among states who are guided by a rational understanding of their national interests. Since Realists assume that states conduct their foreign policies in a so-called 'anarchical environment' – in the sense that there is no central authority which can impose limits upon a state's pursuit of its sovereign interests – it has been argued that (the increase or the consolidation of) state power will always be the immediate political aim of nations. Realist thinkers have argued that cooperation will not come easy, since states cannot trust each other. In such a competitive environment, states will be more concerned with relative than with absolute gains which is likely to hamper the collective action necessary to accomplish integration. For similar reasons, states will only establish an alliance under the circumstances of an acute external threat or other powerful external pressures. In this Realist view, cooperation and stability are the products of antagonism and confrontation, whereby political order and cooperation among states can never be based upon something as woolly as the 'harmony of interests'. Any form of cooperation could therefore only be temporary.

Whereas Realists stress the inevitability of discord among nations, Functionalists focus upon the conditions which may stimulate cooperation. Little wonder, therefore, that the genesis of West European economic integration – in the early-1950s – has traditionally received most attention from scholars applying Functionalist theories. From a Functionalist perspective, the development of the ECSC and the EEC can be explained by the mechanism of 'spill-over', which implies that cooperation in specific economic fields will lead to cooperation on trade and monetary issues, as well as foreign policy. Initially, Functionalists propagated their ideas as a method of overcoming the opposition of politicians to solving international problems by supranational decision-making. The so-called Neo-functionalist offshoot of this theory thereafter maintained that economic integration could only be achieved when politicians become actively involved in the integration process. Neo-functionalists also argued that policy-makers in Western Europe would have no other choice than to cooperate, since this would be the logical and inescapable consequence of earlier decisions. Due to their growing economic and financial interdependence, West European nations could only achieve major national interests through close cooperation within a supranational framework of decision-making. The original formulations of these Neo-functionalist concepts can be found in the earlier work of scholars like Ernst B. Haas and Leon N. Lindberg.[8] Haas has maintained that integration would be a 'process whereby political actors in several distinct national settings are persuaded to shift their loyalties, expectations and political activities toward a new centre, whose institutions possess or demand jurisdiction over the pre-existing national states. The end result of a process of political integration is a new political community, superimposed over the pre-existing one'.[9]

The Founding Fathers of West European integration (Paul-Henri Spaak and Jean Monnet) did indeed hope that such a process would start off with the pooling of coal and steel within the ECSC. In this respect, Neo-functionalist concepts have, *post hoc*, provided a theory which has reflected sympathy with the development of West European unification, assuming that the member states of the Community would be inclined to give up parts of their national sovereignty in exchange for economic efficiency, prosperity and security. Since economic integration would call for political and military cooperation, unification in these fields was expected to follow suit. In this respect, the optimistic and teleological tenet of Neo-functionalism fits the argument made by Fukuyama that economic and technological progress will eventually result in the increasing homogenization of all human societies. It is also closely linked with the notion that market-oriented societies and liberal democracies will not behave imperialistically towards each other.[10] However, the 1960s seemed to disprove most Functionalist assumptions, since West European leaders were reluctant to relinquish their decision-making autonomy on foreign trade, let alone on issues of high politics such as foreign policy. After being discarded for over a decade, Neo-functionalism has received renewed attention due to the current success of the 1992 initiative.[11]

In our effort to explain the relations between the EC and the East, we will, however, not return to Neo-functionalism but to Neo-realism. Neo-realism has provided several concepts which will prove useful in analysing this relationship. One of the main starting-points of Neo-realism is that in order to understand world politics one should not exclusively examine the aims, policies and actions of states. Starting with *Man, the State and War. A Theoretical Analysis* (1959) by Kenneth N. Waltz, Neo-realists have argued that international politics should be considered as a system, whereby the internal attributes of the actors (states) are given by assumption and are not treated as variables. This so-called 'systemic theory' of international relations treats the unit's characteristics as known and tries to explain political changes as the result of modifications of the structure of the system and not so much on the basis of changes within the units. Waltz has argued that 'Systems theories explain why different units behave similarly and, despite their variations, produce outcomes that fall within expected ranges. Conversely, theories at the unit level tell us why different units behave differently despite their similar placement in a system.'[12]

Neo-realism further maintains that the behaviour of states can best be explained by the distribution of power within the international system. Waltz has argued that 'Each state arrives at policies and decides on actions according to its own internal processes, but its decisions are shaped by the very presence of other states as well as by interactions with them. When and how internal forces find expression, if they do, cannot be explained in terms of the interacting parties if the situation in which they act and interact constrains them from some actions, disposes them towards others, and affects the outcomes of their interactions.'[13] Under conditions of anarchy, states can only survive when they adapt themselves to changing circumstances and do their utmost to achieve a high level of economic and technological competitiveness. Waltz refers to this process as the 'shoving and shaping' influence of continuous competition among states, which tends to result in units (i.e. states) that are functionally alike. Countries who show low growth rates, not just for a few years but continuously, or who lose out under outside pressures for technological innovation, will have to adapt or must give way to stronger states. This has happened in very different ways over the centuries, but the basic mechanism applies to this very day. The Greek historian Thucydides is often quoted to the effect that 'the strong do what they can, the weak suffer what they must'.

The structure of the post-war system of world politics has been clear and simple. For decades, international politics has been dominated by the two superpowers which emerged after World War II; the United States and the Soviet Union controlled most economic and military assets and capabilities in the international system, which in turn resulted in the construction of two opposite regional security complexes. The threat perceptions and political and economic concerns of the states comprising these complexes (be it NATO and the Warsaw Pact for military security, or the EC and the CMEA for economics), were so closely linked with each other that 'their national security problems cannot reasonably be analyzed apart from one another'.[14] Waltz has maintained that this bipolar system has significantly contributed to the establishment of the EC:

> So long as European states were the world's great powers, unity among them could only be dreamt of. Politics among the European great powers tended toward the model of a zero-sum game ... The emergence of the Russian and American superpowers created a situation that permitted wider ranging and more effective cooperation among the states of Western Europe. They became consumers of security ... The new circumstances made possible the famous 'upgrading' of the common interests ... Not all impediments to cooperation were removed, but one important one was – the fear that the greater advantage of one would be translated into military force to be used against the others ... The removal of worries about security among the states of Western Europe does not mean the termination of conflict; it does produce a change in its content ... Politics among European states became different in quality after World War II because the international system changed from a multipolar to a bipolar one. The limited progress made in economic and other ways towards the unity of Western Europe cannot be understood without considering the effects that followed from the changed structure of international politics.[15]

In short, the bipolar structure of post-war world politics has provided two crucial endogenous pressures for West European states to cooperate. First, the acuteness of the Soviet threat temporarily overshadowed principal conflicts among West European states. Second, the predominance of the United States has worked as a catalyst of West European integration since the major burden of military and economic security was now shouldered by Washington. Both external factors have facilitated West European states to overcome their collective actions problems.[16] The EC's relations with the East should therefore be studied in this context, keeping in mind that the integrationist tendencies in Western Europe can in large part be brought back to these structural causes. On the basis of this Neo-realist analysis, several important theoretical concepts have been developed, most notably regime theory and the theory of hegemonic stability. We will briefly discuss the relevance of these theories to our examination of EC-East European relations.

Hegemonic stability theory argues that cooperation among states depends upon the existence of a hegemonic power. Hegemonic powers have the capabilities to establish and maintain so-called 'regimes', which can be defined as 'sets of implicit or explicit principles, norms, rules, and decision-making procedures around which actors' expectations converge in a given area of international relations. Principles are beliefs of fact, causation, and rectitude. Norms are standards of behavior defined in terms of rights and obligations.

Rules are specific prescriptions or proscriptions for action. Decision-making procedures are prevailing practices for making and implementing collective action.'[17] Post-war American hegemony has resulted in several of these regimes, most notably within the liberal world economy. Institutions like the General Agreement on Tariffs and Trade (GATT) and the International Monetary Fund (IMF) have provided a forum for cooperation and have monitored the implementation of the free-market rules in the international economy. Much of post-war European politics has been shaped in the context of an extreme bipolar European order, which, according to some analysts, has been responsible for the 'long peace' of more than forty-five years in this region.[18] Hegemonic stability theory also suggests that with the demise of the hegemonic power it will be increasingly difficult to sustain these regimes and that cooperation among states will become hard. Indeed, with the relative decline of American power, many post-war regimes have become under stress. It would be beyond the scope of this book to analyse the further details of these theories.

It is important to acknowledge the fact that the theory of hegemonic stability goes a long way in explaining the establishment of the European Community. The EC-'regime' has become institutionalized over the decades, and although the national interests of the EC's member states are far from harmonious, the EC has provided the institutional framework which has reduced uncertainty, facilitated communication and information, and has overcome the obstacles to collective action.[19] As Keohane has argued: 'regimes contribute to cooperation not by implementing rules that states must follow, but by changing the context within which states make decisions based on self-interest'.[20] Regimes, therefore, do not necessarily require the renunciation of states of the fundamental principle of national sovereignty; they cooperate out of self-interest since the effective pursuit of national goals generally requires collective action. Regime-theory does not therefore go 'beyond the nation state', but accepts the central role of states acting within the structure of a particular system of world politics.

For Western Europe the question arises whether the process of integration within the EC will also come to a halt now that American hegemony seems to be a thing of the past and bipolarity has given way to multipolarity. Keohane has been rather optimistic about the EC's prospects when he argues that 'Cooperation is possible after hegemony not only because shared interests can lead to the creation of regimes, but also because the conditions for maintaining existing international regimes are less demanding than those required for creating them'.[21] Keohane's hypothesis of Neo-liberal institutionalism, which we will examine more elaborately in the final chapters of this book, provides a further theoretical underpinning for this view. As Snyder has argued: 'When institutions are strong, there is order; the effects of anarchy are mitigated ... One possible solution to the contemporary dangers ... would be to recruit reformist Eastern regimes into the West's already well-developed supra-national political order, especially the European Community.'[22] Others have also maintained that the institutionalized character of the EC has significantly changed the economic and political behaviour of the European states. The profound ideational changes which have taken place – modifying the belief systems of the elites of the EC member states – is said to have resulted in a regime in which the major actors have approximately compatible views on the nature of the international order, enjoying a minimum of political solidarity.[23] This is, of course, not to say that conflicts among the EC member states are non-existent. It does, however, imply that much of the Hobbesian anarchy has been ameliorated and that the clarity of the EC rules and procedures has gone a long way in overcoming traditional collective action problems.

These theoretical questions are especially important since many certainties of the Cold War have been shattered in the late-1980s and early-1990s. After four decades of East-West conflict and American and Soviet hegemony in their respective spheres of interest, the cards of world power have been reshuffled. Germany has been united; the CMEA has ceased to exist; many borders are again under discussion; Yugoslavia is enmeshed in a civil war; the Warsaw Pact is dead and NATO is looking for new, mainly non-military tasks; the European Community is playing an increasingly active role in the formulation of foreign and security policy of its member states; many former Communist countries have applied for EC membership; the Soviet Union has been replaced by the Commonwealth; and the military presence of the United States in Western Europe is more uncertain than ever before. This list can be lengthened without difficulty, and with every month new problems will place themselves upon the already overcrowded agendas of European policy-makers. Liberals like Fukuyama have cheered these developments; liberal institutionalists like Keohane have been guardedly optimistic. But lacking a hegemonic power and having replaced bipolarity with a very volatile form of multipolarity, will Europe not become prone to civil wars and overall chaos? Will the members of the EC now again be confronted with the traditional collective action problems on a similar scale as before World War II? Some scholars have not been very confident that the EC will be strong enough to contain post-Cold War conflicts, both within and outside the EC-area. In a provocative article, John J. Mearsheimer has maintained that 'the prospects for major crisis and war in Europe are likely to increase markedly ... If the present Soviet threat to Western Europe is removed, and American forces depart for home, relations among EC states will be fundamentally altered. Without a common Soviet threat and without the American night watchman, Western European states will begin viewing each other with greater fear and suspicion, as they did for centuries before the onset of the Cold War ... there are good reasons for looking with skepticism upon the claim that peace can be maintained in a multipolar Europe on the basis of a more powerful EC.'[24]

This book will examine both the Neo-realist and the Neo-liberal institutionalist perspectives. As Buzan *et al.* have maintained: 'The evolution of the European Community provides a fascinating case study of the contending logics of anarchy and interdependence at play. On issues ranging from defence to currencies, the states within the EC are torn between their tradition-driven, self-regarding, anarchic imperative of "look after yourself", and the contemporary interdependence imperatives to specialize and harmonize.'[25] We will argue that the peril of multipolar instability might be best offset by the strengthening of the European Community, which will not result in the liberal utopia of peace through economic interdependence, but which might go a long way in compensating for the disciplining influence of American hegemony and the multitude of external pressures for alliance building which has existed under bipolarity. In 1959, Waltz wrote that 'Wars occur because there is nothing to prevent them'.[26] The civil war in Yugoslavia and the conflicts within the former Soviet Union are a case in point. How far the European Community has become a force and institution strong enough to prevent similar things to happen in the EC-region, is still unclear.

The last four chapters of this book will be directly concerned with these recent changes in European politics. Chapters 2 to 7 will examine the establishment of the EC during the Cold War and analyse EC-East European relations. Knowing how the drama of the Cold War controversy has ended, it would be foolish – and very difficult – not to make use of the available benefits from hindsight. However, no *post hoc* wisdom will be applied, since 'What was unpredicted by analysts with established theories, cannot, in general, be adequately explained post hoc through the use of such theories'.[27]

1.3 The structure of this book

Without exaggeration one can label the relationship between the EC and Eastern Europe before 1989 as embryonic. In most textbooks on the European Community there is hardly any mention of Brussels' relations with the East. Prior to 1989, the EC lacked a fully-fledged policy *vis-à-vis* the East European countries, mainly because institutional relations with the CMEA were non-existent. This book will show that underneath this lack of official ties an intriguing and complex pattern of relations has been hidden.

As mentioned above, the book will begin with the Marshall Plan and the division of Europe after World War II. Chapter 2 will provide an historical account of how the process of West European integration had started off without the countries of Central Europe. It explores how and why these countries have been excluded from the earliest stages of integration. It will examine the ways in which Cold War bipolarity has influenced the behaviour of states in Europe and it will discuss how the process of West European economic and political integration has been encouraged by US hegemony and the menace of Communist power. Chapter 3 will continue this historical account for the period 1950-7. It will argue, among others, that the political developments in the East (i.e. the Korean War and Stalinist terror) have influenced the ECSC experiment. Chapter 4 will focus especially on the way in which the Soviet Union has responded to the West European integration efforts. We will see that Moscow has done its utmost to hamper West European integration, but that it had to acknowledge that the Common Market was achieving some noteworthy successes.

Chapter 5 will look at the strained relationship between the EC and the East after Brussels initiated its Common Commercial Policy. It will mainly focus upon the economic relations between the EC and the State-trading countries. We will argue that the Soviet Union and Eastern Europe have only made concessions *vis-à-vis* Brussels when the EC was able to close its ranks and to provide a unified front in its economic dealings with the East. When West European collaboration within the EC framework proved impossible, as has been the case with export credits for East-West trade, no CMEA member has been willing to make compromises. Chapter 6 takes up the problem of the Community's dire lack of a coordinated political strategy towards the East. We will discuss the distinct policies of the major EC member states, analyse the role of the EC in the Conference on Security and Co-operation in Europe (CSCE) – both before and after the Helsinki Accords were signed in 1975 – and examine Brussels' position during the inter-Alliance conflicts on East-West trade issues during the early-1980s.

Chapter 7 will mainly deal with the uneasy relationship between the EC and the CMEA. Chapter 8 will examine the two parallel revolutions which took place between 1989 and 1992. In 1989 the post-war system collapsed together with the fall of the Berlin Wall; in 1992 the countries of the EC will take some significant steps towards a positive integration of Western Europe. Both processes have major implications for the future architecture of Europe, and both processes cannot be analysed separately from one other. Chapter 9 will deal with the question of how the West can assist Central Europe and the former Soviet Republics in their transformation into market-based and democratic systems. It will examine Brussels' new role as the central institution coordinating western assistance to the East, turning the EC into the proverbial lighthouse for the former Communist countries to focus their hopes and to steer a steady course towards their final goal of fully fledged EC membership. This brings us to Chapter 10, which will take up the question of how Brussels can and should deal with the aspirations of Central European EC membership. This chapter will spell out the options for the Community and focus upon Brussels' dilemma of 'deepening' versus 'widening' the EC. The epilogue to this book will draw all arguments of the previous chapters together, and it will address the utility of the Neo-realist and Neo-liberal institutionalist assumptions in our effort to provide analytical clarity on the relations between the European Community and Central Europe over the decades. We will argue that the structure of multipolarity will not *necessarily* have to result into discord and conflict in Europe, although the chances for major conflicts have certainly increased. Even Neo-realists like Waltz have refused to accept the inevitability of discord under conditions of multi-polarity. As Waltz has argued: 'Structures condition behaviors and outcomes, yet explanations of behaviors and outcomes are indeterminate because both unit-level and structural causes are in play ... Structures shape and shove. They do not determine behaviors and outcomes, not only because unit-level and structural causes interact, but also because the shaping and shoving of structures may be successfully resisted ... With skill and determination structural constraints can sometimes be countered. Virtuosos transcend the limits of their instruments and break the constraints of systems that bind lesser performers.'[28] Whether the EC has acquired such expert skills remains a moot point.

2. European Integration Without the East, 1945-1950

Every right-thinking person will end by being convinced on this point, however little he reflects on an axiom equally striking for its importance and universality. This is that *nothing great has great beginnings*. No exception to this law will be found in the whole of history.

Joseph de Maistre, in *The Works of Joseph de Maistre* (New York: Schocken Books, 1971), p.158.

2.1 Introduction

Even before World War II came to a close, Europe had already been divided into a Soviet and a western sphere of influence. This did not come as a surprise, since United States President Franklin D. Roosevelt had envisaged a post-war world in which Great Britain would take up its role as the policeman of the Middle East and the Mediterranean, wherein France would again be dominant in Western Europe and the Soviet Union would be the major force in Central Europe. In his memoirs, Winston Churchill recalls his nocturnal discussions with Soviet dictator Joseph Stalin at the Kremlin on 9 October 1944. On that evening, Churchill wrote on a piece of paper the degree of influence of London and Moscow over several Central European countries. His estimation came strikingly close to post-war European reality: Romania, 90 per cent for the USSR; Bulgaria, 75 per cent for the USSR; Greece, 90 per cent for Great Britain; Hungary and Yugoslavia, a neat 50-50 split.[1]

In February 1945, in the Crimean resort of Yalta, the Big Three came to several concrete arrangements concerning the post-war settlement. A lofty 'Declaration on Liberated Europe' was signed (11 February 1945), promising free elections and democracy for each European country.[2] This coincided with the American plans, which had already been laid down in the Atlantic Charter agreement, signed by Washington and London in August 1941 (to which the Soviet Union later acceded). In this Atlantic Charter, a commitment was made to 'respect the right of all peoples to choose the form of government under which they will live'. And, as the historian Bennett Kovrig has remarked, 'Despite the public and private reservations of its signatories, the Atlantic Charter was taken by East Europeans of all origins, at home and in exile, as a genuine commitment to an equitable and popularly based settlement of Europe's postwar configuration'.[3]

In spite of all these paper declarations (which Stalin had already denounced as declaratory algebra), it did not come as much of a surprise that Stalin considered Central Europe a necessary buffer zone to guarantee Soviet security. Stalin had already indicated that he wanted control over Central Europe, since 'throughout history Poland has always been a corridor for attack on Russia'.[4] One can therefore certainly argue that immediately after the cease-fire, two different Europes had already come into existence, both parts being liberated by different tanks. Stalin had already observed to the Yugoslav partisan leader Milovan Djilas that 'This war is not as in the past; whoever occupies a territory also imposes on it his own social system. Everyone imposes his own system as far as his army can reach. It cannot be otherwise.'[5] In spite of all Pan-European ideas which were aired simultaneously, this was the political reality confronting Europeans in 1945.

2.2 The first preparatory years

But, of course, this did not put an end to the constant flow of proposals and recommendations concerning the unification of Europe. European integration has always been regarded as one of the major antidotes against another military confrontation in this already conflict-ridden and now also war-stricken continent. After 1945, West European cooperation was considered of vital importance in order to achieve regional security. It was, however, also acknowledged that cooperation and institution-building had to be based on less 'utopian' principles than was attempted after World War I.[6] The experience of the interbellum, economic depression and Nazism had taught that collaboration and international organizations had to start from the 'bottom up' with cooperation on concrete issues, and not so much from the 'top down' with high-minded declarations alone. It was argued that structures of cooperation and integration had to be built upon a realistic assessment of the national interests of the participating West European states; these frameworks should take into account the peculiarities of post-war Europe and should find a form in which the diverging national interests could be merged. A wide range of scholars and politicians (e.g. Paul-Henri Spaak, Charles de Gaulle and J. M. Keynes), had already during wartime planned for West European economic cooperation. Now that nationalism was discredited in most European capitals, the time was considered ripe to implement these schemes. Germany especially was well aware of the fact that its national identity should look for a more internationally acceptable outlet; Europe – and more concrete: European integration – could be just that.

In order to avoid the mistakes made by the economic and political settlement after World War I with the Treaty of Versailles, great effort was now made to create an open-door, multilateral economy. In 1944, the International Monetary Fund (IMF) and the International Bank for Reconstruction and Development (generally known as the World Bank), were set up at a conference in Bretton Woods, the United States. These organizations were created in order to provide the institutional infrastructure to maintain stable exchange rates and to finance construction and development. The subscribing countries participated on a share basis, whereby the United States was to provide 28 per cent, the USSR 12.5 per cent and Europe only 16 per cent of the IMF funds; voting power was determined by the size of the share of the countries. American dominance in the World Bank was even more evident since Washington provided 38 per cent of its capital. Economic cooperation in these institutions was considered necessary in order to avoid the creation of bilateral trade-blocs which had pestered the interbellum and which were thought to have contributed to the economic malaise which had given rise to World War II. Efforts to coordinate multilaterally the world's problems culminated in the creation of the United Nations and its various affiliated and related organizations,[7] and the General Agreement on Tariffs and Trade (GATT). GATT, established in October 1947, was especially concerned with customs and commercial policy. In general, one could say that after decades of economic mercantilism, the spirit of economic liberalism was dominant in these post-war years. One of the most popular aphorisms of that time was: 'If goods can't cross borders, soldiers will'.

These ideas were, however, not shared by the USSR. Whereas Moscow had accepted the Bretton Woods accords in 1944, it refused to ratify them one year later. Although this did not directly result in the collapse of post-war Great Power collaboration, the Soviet Union's reluctance to participate in these international organizations did not spell much good for the years to come. Early in 1946, 'the Soviets rejected membership in the World Bank and the International Monetary Fund, announced the start of a new five-year plan designed to make Russia self-sufficient in the event of another war, built up the pressure on Iran, and mounted an intense ideological effort to eliminate all western influence within the Soviet Union'.[8] It was none the less evident that Moscow's opinion and attitude concerning several issues dealing with the future of Europe could not be ignored. Since the USSR was a member of the Big Three – together with Great Britain and the United States – European unity could not be achieved without taking into account Moscow's viewpoints on several important problems which were still awaiting settlement. The German question was still open and Soviet cooperation on this issue was necessary in order to arrive at a post-war arrangement. The Soviet army had occupied large parts of the former Third Reich, which provided Moscow with an undeniable *de facto* influence over Germany's future. At the Yalta (February 1945) and Potsdam (July-August 1945) Conferences, the issue of

German reparations to the USSR had been discussed, but had not been settled. The USSR and Great Britain were in agreement that Germany should be kept under constraint and that it should remain a single unit. Mainly for this reason, no 'spheres of influence' were defined: 'the various clauses of the Potsdam Protocol furnished guarantees that the Soviets would be able to control their own occupation zone for their own purposes. Yet, the treaty provisions also provided opportunities for extending Soviet influence throughout the entire German territory.'[9] Germany soon became the focal point for the ensuing East-West conflict, where the Soviets milked their German zone of almost all manufactures and agricultural production, eventually at American expense. Disagreements about the future political structure of Germany led to further friction and enmity. Within a few years, the German question evolved from a collaborative into a competitive issue.

The American attitude towards Europe also changed markedly over the first post-war years.[10] In the beginning, United States policy-makers were suspicious of the ideas of West European union. Washington's attitude was rooted in the experiences of the interbellum, a period in which the United States had feared European integration as a thinly disguised attempt to exclude American commerce. After 1945, the United States was especially wary of the prospect of European union since it was determined that 'the basis of postwar policy must rest on a firm agreement with the Soviet Union. It was already clear that the government of the Soviet Union would look with deep suspicion on any European union, whether of a general or a particular kind.'[11] These ideas about the post-war order were based upon the Rooseveltian concept of Great Power collaboration, in which the USSR would play an important role on the European continent. Roosevelt's attitude was clearly exposed when Count Coudenhove-Kalergi handed a memorandum on Allied war aims to the American President (March 1943), pleading for some form of federal organization of post-war Europe. Roosevelt brusquely rejected these proposals, being 'convinced that the United States would have to accept the Soviet demand for a sphere of influence in Eastern Europe, and that federalist suggestions could only exacerbate relations between the two governments'.[12] During these first post-war years, the central concern of most nations was to contain a possible future German threat. In this context, the USSR was seen as the wartime ally which could also play a useful role in the construction of the post-war Europe.

Washington's initial aloofness did not, however, discourage European proponents of integration. Several options were aired, all generally heavily coloured by the specific national interests of the plan's proponent. In Great Britain the notion of creating a West European coalition had become popular as a way of increasing London's influence on the continent; the coalition was expected to provide a framework in which Europe's security problems could be settled. British policy-makers considered an Anglo-French Treaty as the corner-stone of future West European cooperation. General de Gaulle also regularly voiced his long-held views of Western Europe as an independent geographical and political entity, with Paris and London at the centre. Discussions between London and Paris on cooperation were prolonged and arduous due to the basic disagreement of both countries on the most appropriate way to settle the German question. Problems also arose due to the Soviet Union's unfavourable disposition towards a possible Anglo-French treaty. Moscow considered such an accord as the beginning of an economic and political West European bloc. In order to hamper the public debate on further West European cooperation, Moscow made active use of the West European Communist parties which were subservient to its will. Strikes and labour unrest were organized, especially in Italy and France, in an attempt to impede such cooperation efforts. Moscow's helping hand in disrupting these efforts was manifest and even conspicuous. In the Summer of 1946, Britain's Foreign Secretary, Ernest Bevin, told George Bidault, the French Premier, that he could not 'carry on a conversation [on the issue of Anglo-French cooperation] with a third Great Power in the cupboard',[13] clearly referring to Soviet influence in France via the Communist Party which had gained more than a quarter of the electoral vote in the Autumn of 1945.

Despite fervid Soviet efforts to stall the integration debate, the idea of West European economic cooperation of some sort grew in appeal. Four factors had played an important role in this process. First, it was becoming increasingly clear that Western Europe had to take a more united stance against Soviet expansionist tendencies which manifested themselves more aggressively than before. The Soviets had occupied most of Central Europe and had managed to install Communist-dominated regimes there. The 'Declaration on Liberated Europe' had evidently not been worth the paper it was written on. Already during the war, the Allies had fiercely disputed the make-up of the Lublin Committee, which formed the provisional Polish Government. Moscow refused to admit the Polish political leaders exiled in London into this Committee, which was interpreted as an attempt to turn Warsaw into Moscow's vassal after the war. In 1946, Communists held the key ministries in Poland, including those of Public Security and Defence. Similar paths were followed in Bulgaria, Romania and Hungary. In the eastern part of Germany, the Socialist Unity Party (SED) was created in April 1946, which finally resulted in the destruction of alternative political parties. All in all, in 1948, the East European countries were under *de facto* Communist and Soviet control.

Second, it was argued that economic cooperation would be able to terminate the internal conflicts in (Western) Europe and would overcome nationalism. Economic nationalism especially was expected to hamper the development of foreign trade, which would be detrimental to the reconstruction of Europe's industrial production. Economic cooperation was considered in the national interest of all European countries, establishing a free trade regime regulating several concrete economic issues. The creation of the

Bretton Woods institutions and the GATT were a clear manifestation of this way of thinking. In particular regions of Western Europe, the establishment of customs unions had already been thought out during the war (e.g. the Benelux).

Third, it was expected that European integration could achieve the best of both worlds: it would forge a healthy German economy, as well as avoid the resurgence of German nationalism and possible future aggression. These were persuasive arguments, which were especially attractive in the light of the horrendous experiences of most Europeans during the war. Nationalism – especially of the German kind – could be surmounted by closer economic and political cooperation. Germany had to be checked without repeating the mistakes made with the Versailles Treaty of 1919, which had treated Germany as a pariah and a second-rate European country. Incorporating the German economy was also considered essential for the reconstruction of Western Europe at large. Without Germany's raw materials and its huge industrial production, Western Europe would be deprived of the basic materials for its own economic recuperation. Moreover, without European integration as a political framework for cooperation, Germany's economic strength would have been perceived as a major threat. All in all, economic integration was expected to go a long way in achieving these aims. Finally, some thought that Europe had to provide a viable alternative to American plans for multilateralism, in case such a global economic system might fail to emerge. This last point was probably the least pressing argument in favour of integration.

In March 1947, the Treaty of Dunkirk was signed between France and the United Kingdom. The treaty established a bilateral military alliance which was mainly aimed at opposing possible German aggression. After this Anglo-French Treaty was signed, other West European countries showed keen interest to join. The rationale of the Dunkirk Treaty – an anti-German alliance – was soon overtaken by events. Ernest Bevin in particular was intent on restructuring this bilateral alliance into a multilateral agreement in order to cope with the looming Soviet threat. It must be realized that by early 1947, most realistic hopes of post-war cooperation between France, Great Britain, the Soviet Union and the United States, had already faded. Winston Churchill had given his famous Fulton speech (5 March 1946), warning of the Iron Curtain which was descending along the European continent, and US President Harry S. Truman had enunciated his 'Truman Doctrine' (12 March 1947), which sought to contain the spread of Communism wherever possible. The famous 'Long Telegram' by George F. Kennan, and the less well-known 'Long Despatches' written by the English diplomat Frank Roberts,[14] provided American and British policy-makers with a series of similar Cassandra cries.

The Moscow Conference of the Allied Council of Foreign Ministers of the Big Four (10 March-24 April 1947), can be considered as an important watershed in the attitude of American policy-makers towards the USSR.

During this conference, bitter arguments arose over the future of Germany. Moscow demanded heavy reparations (US$ 10 billion), control over the vital industrial centre of the Ruhr and insisted on the centralization of the German state. The Soviet Union's static and stubborn behaviour during the Moscow Conference drove France closer to the Anglo-American camp and broadened the divide between East and West. Proposed Peace Treaties with Central European countries like Poland and Czechoslovakia were now postponed. Disappointment with Moscow's attitude also speeded up the drive for West European unity, which soon resulted in several additional treaties among West European countries.

2.3 The Marshall Plan

Although Washington had been questioning the desirability of European union during most of the war years, cooperation among the European nations was now strongly supported. During the Moscow Conference, the US Secretary of State, George C. Marshall, became convinced that the Soviets 'had acquired a vested interest in the devastating sickness of Western Europe: this was useful to them as pressure on the western powers to force compliance with Russian terms on Germany, and in any case, if it was aggravated, it would facilitate Communist subversion and domination in France and Italy and perhaps other countries'.[15] Marshall ordered Kennan to set up a Policy Planning Staff, which later gave birth to the so-called European Recovery Program (ERP), generally labelled 'the Marshall Plan'. The importance of the ERP for the further development of West European integration should not be underestimated. As the Dutchman Ernst van der Beugel once noted: 'The Organization for European Economic Cooperation, the North Atlantic Treaty Organization, the Western European Union, the European Coal and Steel Community, Euratom and the European Economic Community are unthinkable without the basis laid by the idea and by the implementation of the European Recovery Program'.[16]

In the Spring of 1947, the European countries were enmeshed in a serious economic crisis. Western Europe faced an immense balance of payments deficit with the United States (US$ 4.25 billion in fiscal year 1948), and production and trade had dropped sharply. Washington feared that these deteriorating economic conditions would make West European governments budge to Soviet influence. Western Europe was also likely to pursue more protectionist policies which would in turn reduce American exports and weaken the economic basis for peace. Truman's containment policy was implemented by the enunciation of the Marshall Plan (in a speech by the US Secretary of State at Harvard University on 5 June 1947), which envisaged a massive economic assistance programme for Europe. Only three weeks later, Anglo-French-Soviet talks began at the Quai d'Orsay in order to discuss the

American offer. Washington had explicitly asked for an all-embracing European plan which could serve as a basis for a well-coordinated effort at economic assistance. It came as no surprise that the Soviet delegation favoured a *bilateral* approach to Europe's economic problems and objected to a more comprehensive plan for European economic recovery. Moscow would only accept the so-called 'shopping list' approach, whereby each country would provide an inventory of its dire economic needs to Washington, without prior coordination with the other European states. The Soviet Union correctly feared a coordinated Pan-European economic recovery effort, since this was expected to spur economic and political integration and, *ipso facto*, block the Communist monopolization of power in Central Europe.

The Soviet Foreign Minister, Vyacheslav M. Molotov, remarked that French and British proposals 'to draw up a general economic programme for the European nations – which would inevitably involve the intervention of certain States – could not serve as a basis for collaboration between the countries of Europe'. The USSR, for example, was concerned that these multilateral plans could press Czechoslovakia to increase its agricultural production to the detriment of its engineering industry, whereas Poland might be forced to produce more coal and neglect other industrial sectors. In short, Molotov argued, 'American credits would serve not to facilitate the economic rehabilitation of Europe, but to make use of some European countries against other European countries in whatever way certain strong powers seeking to establish their dominion should find it profitable to do so'. A. A. Zhdanov, Stalin's special envoy at the meeting, denounced the Marshall Plan bluntly as 'an embodiment of the American design to enslave Europe'.[17] On 2 July, Molotov left the Paris meeting. After his ostentatious departure, the Marshall Plan became an American and West European effort.

Although the American invitation to participate in the ERP was also addressed to the Soviet Union and Central Europe, George Kennan had nevertheless already argued that it was 'essential' that these countries either 'excluded themselves' or, more desirably, would 'agree to abandon the exclusive orientation of their economies'.[18] Later Kennan gave a different interpretation, saying that 'the [Marshall] approach to the Europeans was addressed, and the offer made, not just to the western portion of the continent but to Europe as a whole ... Had the Communist side – the governments, that is, of the Soviet Union and of the Eastern European countries – accepted it in the spirit in which it was offered, we would have been glad to sit down with their representatives and to inquire not only into their own needs for recovery, but into the manner in which they, too, might contribute to the general revival of Europe's economic vitality.'[19] In a similar vein, the former Belgian Minister of Foreign Affairs Paul-Henri Spaak has argued in his memoirs: 'The offer [Marshall] made to the Communists was neither a diplomatic manoeuvre nor a trap'.[20] From the onset, however, it was clear that the USSR could not afford to join. Several explicit and implicit conditions made Soviet participation nigh impossible. For example, economic assistance under the Marshall Plan was only granted under the condition that the cooperating countries would provide detailed information concerning their internal economic situation. It was also clear that participating countries would have to go a long way in cooperating with American plans to construct a multilateral, free-trade world economy. However, despite the growing suspicion of Moscow's political goals in Europe, West European leaders made efforts to avoid an open East-West split. After the Molotov walk-out, Bevin and Bidault even issued a joint communiqué which said that 'This invitation to take part in the organization will remain open to all European countries'.[21]

In response to Marshall's request a Committee of European Economic Co-operation (CEEC) was set up in the western part of Europe, in mid-July. The CEEC completed a fully-fledged recovery plan within a period of two months, specifying the various economic needs of all participating West European countries. During these talks in Paris, first mention was made of a customs union between France, Germany and the Benelux, with Italy showing keen interest too. The United States was supporting these ideas since it now considered the economic union of Western Europe as one of the most important elements of providing security against the Communist threat. As one historian has stated: 'An integrated single market promised the benefits that inhered in economics of scale, with the ultimate result being a prosperous and stable European Community secure against the dangers of Communist subversion and able to join the United States in a multilateral system of world trade.'[22] As mentioned above, the Marshall Plan specifically asked for a *comprehensive* European recovery plan, *collectively* framed by the European nations, based upon the principle that all participating countries assumed *joint* responsibility for making the programme work. It also called for setting up a permanent institution for utilizing the aid according to plan. The instrument of United States assistance was thereby clearly wielded as an economic lever to promote a sense of European unity.[23]

When the subsequent meeting of the Big Four (in London, November–December 1947) failed once more, and East and West began accusing each other of seeking full control over Germany, traditional post-war Four Power cooperation became a dead letter. In 1947, much of the groundwork for the construction of a fully-fledged western 'pluralistic security community' was done. Such a security community – according to Karl Deutsch – exists when (1) the policy-makers of two or more political units, and their societies in general, cease to consider the possibility of mutual warfare; and (2) when two or more nations stop to allocate the resources for building military capabilities aimed at each other.[24] Although no institutional framework was created to sustain this security community, the shared perception of the Soviet threat and the economic and political cooperation within the CEEC clearly created a sense of a common West European interest, both among the political elites and the populace at large. In 1948, the basic ingredients for the bipolar structure of opposing blocs were amply available; only the institutions had yet to be established. West European cooperation, on economic as well as on political and military issues, was now considered crucial.

The first concrete preparations for some form of union of Western Europe were made by the British Foreign Secretary, in January 1948. Bevin sought to construct a broad union of all free – that is non-Communist – European countries. Here again, the Soviet threat functioned as one of the major catalysts of West European integration. Without the Communist menace, neither Great Britain and France, nor the United States, would have hurried their efforts to create close West European cooperation. Bevin's efforts resulted in the Treaty of Brussels, which was signed in March 1948 by Belgium, France, Luxembourg, the Netherlands and the United Kingdom. The Treaty called for 'collective self-defence' as well as for further 'economic, social and cultural collaboration'.

With the refusal of the Soviet Union and its satellites to accept the conditions of US Marshall Plan aid, a new phase in the political economy of West European integration started. Before 1947, both Great Britain and France were keen not to antagonize Moscow by forming a solid western bloc. The Treaty of Dunkirk was therefore depicted as an anti-German alliance, which had ostensibly nothing to do with the USSR. This was also the main reason why France at first decided *not* to join the United States and Great Britain in the economic fusion of their two zones in occupied Germany (so-called 'Bizonia', in 1947). But now this had all changed. In April 1949, the United States, Great Britain and France announced an agreement for merging their western occupation zones in Germany. These military governments would soon give way to a civilian German administration (except for the western section of Berlin; see Chapter 7.6).

These developments in Western Europe made the Soviet Union conclude that 'the ultimate meaning of the ERP went beyond an attempt to save Western Europe from Communism or to seduce the Russian satellites by the example of a higher standard of living. The eventual aims were military ... The real purpose of the Marshall Plan was to create large standing armies that could threaten Russia while the Americans would back them up, if necessary, with their naval strength and their atomic-armed Strategic Air Command.'[25] Moscow reacted by a marked hardening of its attitude towards Central Europe. All Central European countries were forced to decline the offer to participate in the Marshall Plan. The Polish and Czechoslovak governments were especially embarrassed since they had already accepted the invitation to take part in the scheme, without prior consultation with the USSR; now they had to reverse their decision. Prague had already re-established its trade ties with West European countries and had considered it opportune to develop economic cooperation with the West through the Marshall Plan. In an effort to counterbalance the loss of American aid, the Soviet Union hurriedly established a network of bilateral trade treaties with the Central European countries under the cover of the so-called Molotov Plan (named after Moscow's Minister of Foreign Affairs.) Within several weeks, numerous trade agreements between the USSR and Central Europe were signed, starting with Bulgaria on 10 July, Czechoslovakia on 11 July, Hungary on 14 July, Yugoslavia on 27 July, Poland on 4 August, and finally with Romania on 26 August 1947.

The seclusion of the Communist East gave rise to a multitude of economic and political problems. As late as 1948, US Secretary Marshall had argued that 'In the European Recovery Program, we regard it as very important to stimulate, so far as possible, East-West trade relations there. That would be very helpful to the situation and would have material effects on reducing costs for us.'[26] For this reason, the recovery plan of the CEEC was optimistically based upon a continuing flow of raw materials (especially steel, coal and timber) from Central Europe and the Soviet Union. The worsening of East-West relations shed a different light upon this issue and the stoppage of East-West trade was now considered as an economic lever in Moscow's hands. William Diebold, Jr., at that time painted a gloomy scenario, whereby 'the Russians will use all possible means to frustrate the Marshall Plan. The Marshall Plan depends on supplies from Central Europe. Therefore, the Russians will cut off or manipulate exports from their satellites to the countries participating in the Marshall Plan.'[27] However, it was clear that Central Europe did also depend upon the West for capital goods and manufactured products. 'Without trade with the west it would take the eastern countries much longer to carry out the programs of industrialization, and it would cost them much more in terms of lower living standards. So there is no reason to doubt that the eastern countries desire it',[28] Diebold maintained. The Soviet Union, however, was intent to frustrate these Central European desires. As a result, this part of Europe became mainly dependent upon Moscow for its economic assistance, and Central European trade relations were therefore primarily oriented towards the Soviet economy. In 1954, for example, 80 per cent of Czechoslovak foreign trade was conducted with Prague's eastern neighbours, whereas, before World War II, this had been a mere 10 per cent.[29]

In response to the ERP, Stalin called for an alternative recovery plan for the East. In September 1947, a Communist Information Bureau (generally called Cominform) was set up,[30] in which the Communist Parties of Bulgaria, Czechoslovakia, France, Hungary, Italy, Poland, Romania, the USSR and Yugoslavia were represented. During this meeting in Wilcza Gora, in Poland, Zhdanov told his audience that the USSR 'will bend every effort in order that [the Marshall Plan] be doomed to failure ... The Communist Parties of France, Italy, Great Britain and other countries ... must take up that standard in defence of the national independence and sovereignty of their countries.'[31] Stalin personally stressed the necessity of the *Gleichschaltung* of the economic and political systems of the Central European countries; no independent, national roads towards Communism were allowed. Central Europe had become 'Eastern Europe', which together with the Soviet Union now formed one, separate Communist bloc.

2.4 Two other plans: Schuman and Pleven

After the Czechoslovak *coup d'état* in February 1948, the Iron Curtain had descended for everyone to see; the formal independence of Eastern Europe was now an illusion. Even Prague, which many in the West had considered the political and cultural bridge between East and West, was now dominated by the Communist Party led by Klement Gottwald. The economic, political and cultural isolation of Eastern Europe was clearly indicated by the marked absence of representatives of these countries at international meetings and conferences where the issues of European reconstruction and integration were being discussed.

For instance, at the Congress of Europe – which was held under the inspirational aegis of Winston Churchill (The Hague, May 1948) – sixteen democratic European countries attended; Eastern Europe was only represented by refugees. The former Central European countries were now at times alluded to as 'the Slav continental bloc', dominated by Moscow. The Congress resulted in the Council of Europe, which was inaugurated in 1949 in Strasbourg. The Council of Europe was set up in order to provide a framework for consultation and cooperation among the governments of Europe. It was to be Europe's first post-war political organization. The Preamble to its Statute noted 'the spiritual and moral values which are the common heritage of their people and the true source of individual freedom, political liberty and the rule of law, principles which form the basis of all genuine democracy'. The resolution passed by the Congress:

1. Recognizes that it is the urgent duty of the nations of Europe to create an economic and political union in order to assure security and social progress;
2. Notes with approval the recent steps which have been taken by some European Governments in the direction of economic and political cooperation, but believes that in the present emergency the organizations created are by themselves insufficient to provide any lasting remedy;
3. Declares that the time has come when the European nations must transfer and merge some portion of their sovereign rights so as to secure common political and economic action for the integration and proper development of their common resources; ...
11. Declares that the creation of a United Europe is an essential element in the creation of a united world.[32]

The absence of East European members in the Council of Europe once more indicated that these countries, due to their Communist domination, had disavowed the European 'common heritage' and would take no part in the construction of the planned 'United Europe'. Over the decades, the Council would evolve into a forum of all European democracies, most notably through its European Convention of Human Rights. This had made East European and Soviet membership utterly impossible before 1989.[33]

On 16 April 1948, the Organization for European Economic Cooperation (OEEC) was established.[34] 'European' now stood for the western part of the Old Continent, excluding countries where Communist parties had monopolized political power. (Spain was not allowed to participate since the Allies considered the Fascist Franco regime an unacceptable dictatorship; Finland did not join out of fear of stepping on Moscow's sensitive toes.) It was the OEEC which coordinated the distribution of Marshall Plan aid; national plans and requirements were cross-examined by the OEEC, which thereupon worked out a programme of distribution of American aid.[35] The OEEC was strictly intergovernmental; the sovereignty of each participating country was secured and no further conditions were set. However, for the first time in European history, the domestic economic management of sovereign states had become subject to criticism and control from their neighbours. For the first time too, most West European countries began to realize that coordination of national economic policies could be beneficial and could be preferred over a soloist or autarkic course. As Leon Hurwitz has argued: 'the OEEC went beyond just finding ways to spend the American funds: the countries involved recognized the interdependence of their economies, the need to maximize trade within the area, and the necessity of improving the international payment system'.[36] Thus, the member states liberalized their mutual trade through a gradual elimination of import quotas, and set up a European Payments Union. For most countries it was nevertheless still anathema even to consider West European cooperation on high-level political issues, since this would touch upon the core sphere of national sovereignty. Of major importance was the fact that the western part of Germany was now also cooperating within the OEEC and was economically (and politically) a part of Western Europe.[37]

Several other organizations for economic cooperation had already been set up, such as the customs union between Belgium, Luxembourg and the Netherlands (under the acronym Benelux), signed in 1944 and starting in 1948.[38] Benelux countries eliminated the customs barriers among themselves and adopted a common customs tariff *vis-à-vis* others. The Benelux union carefully recognized the national sovereignty of its members. Closer political, economic and cultural cooperation was forged by the Treaty of Brussels (1948), which was extended as the military counterpart of the Marshall Plan to the North Atlantic Treaty, signed in April 1949 by the United States, Canada and the countries of the OEEC; NATO institutionalized the American commitment to play a military role in Europe. This too had everything to do with the increasing Soviet threat, which began to manifest itself not only politically, but now also militarily. Rumours spread that the USSR had already detonated its first atomic bomb in Siberia in the Summer of 1947. In

September 1949, US President Truman officially acknowledged the fact that the Soviet Union had acquired nuclear capabilities. By providing collective military security for Western Europe, NATO has contributed considerably to the economic and political cohesion of this region.

NATO itself was the direct result of the increasing tensions between East and West, which culminated in the conflict over Berlin. In response to western efforts to set up a West German state in 1947-8 (reforming its currency and restoring German political and administrative autonomy), Moscow decided to make a major issue of the status of Berlin. Between June 1948 and May 1949, the Soviet Union blockaded the western section of the city. Great Britain and the United States had to build their well-known airbridge in order to supply the city with food, fuel and other goods. After elections in August, the Federal Republic of Germany (FRG) was established on 20 September, with Konrad Adenauer as its first Chancellor. For the USSR, the FRG signified the revival of an independent and potentially aggressive German power in world affairs, which would be hostile to Soviet interests. It was clear at that time, that after more than a year of overt and covert hostilities, the Cold War had been born under punches.

In these early years of the Cold War, several factors spurred the process of West European integration. Among the most important was the Schuman Plan of May 1950, which called for the pooling of the coal and steel production between France and Germany. Robert Schuman, the French Minister of Foreign Affairs, expected such an organization to set the first steps upon the road to the federation of Europe. The other factor was the circumstance that North Korean troops – equipped with Soviet-made weaponry – crossed the 38th parallel to invade the southern part of the Korean peninsula, on 25 June 1950. This incident was generally perceived as a Soviet-inspired act, which once more confirmed Moscow's expansionist intentions. The Schuman Plan would forge another strong economic tie between the FRG and Western Europe, which was considered necessary with the experience of the Berlin blockade fresh in mind; the Korean War lifted the anti-Communist alarm to an even higher level.

Under the relatively safe umbrella of American military protection, the Schuman Plan could concentrate itself on the intensification of European economic integration. In general, two arguments were brought forward which stressed the urgency of European integration. First, it was acknowledged that 'in the economic field, the national units into which Western Europe is divided are too small to encourage the use of modern mass-production processes, such as are naturally employed in the United States, and increasingly will be employed in the U.S.S.R. and the emerging great nations of Asia. If Western Europe is to stand any chance of competing in the long run, we must find ways of breaking down the economic barriers that today split the Continent.'[39] This argument has played a major role in the debate on European unity until the present day. The second argument was political in nature: 'But today if the Russians invaded Western Europe they would bring the Communists to power everywhere ... [and] in sum, destroy western civilization', argued Paul Reynaud, in early 1950.[40] Paul-Henri Spaak also saw the Korean War as 'a solemn warning of the need of haste ... Our task is together to defend a certain civilization, a certain way of life and a certain philosophy. Each nation must contribute its share to this common task; each can do this effectively only if all our individual efforts are merged in a single effort.'[41] The incorporation of Germany in the American-European alliance and the West European economy was expected to provide security *vis-à-vis* the USSR.

The Schuman Plan was able to break the deadlock between France, Great Britain and West Germany over the preferred road to further economic cooperation. The American Government had pressed both France and Britain to make further use of the German military potential for their defence. The United States argued that it would not be willing to continue the Marshall Plan without a combined West European military effort against a looming Soviet attack. However, France had required additional safeguards against the risk of renewed German aggression before it would concede to the come-back of Germany as a partner in both the western economy and the West European military structure. In his speech for the Congress of Europe, Churchill had already maintained that the 'first step in the re-creation of the European family must be a partnership between France and Germany'. The Brussels Treaty and NATO had provided a framework for collective western defence; the Schuman Plan was expected to do the same in the economic field. The pooling of steel and coal would undercut French suspicion, since it was acknowledged that a coordinated coal and steel production would make a future war between France and Germany not only unthinkable, but – perhaps more important – materially impossible. The OEEC had already adopted a programme which would liberalize trade and payments, but the Schuman Plan went much further and opened up vistas of a common European market which would prepare the way for a united Europe strong enough to act independently between the two superpowers. Schuman argued that 'Europe will not be made all at one, or according to a single, general plan. It will be built through concrete achievements, which create a *de facto* solidarity. The gathering of the nations of Europe requires the elimination of the age-old opposition of France and Germany.'[42]

For Germany, participation within the Schuman Plan was attractive as a manner for international rehabilitation. Konrad Adenauer was convinced that German reunification could only be achieved by a strong and united Western Europe, which required close cooperation between the FRG and France, combined with a drive towards further West European economic and military collaboration. Integration therefore received wide support within the German political arena; only the German Social-Democrats argued that German participation within a Coal and Steel Community would render national reunification more difficult since the USSR would never allow a united Germany to be closely integrated within a western bloc. Be that as it may, Article 24 of the West German constitution (the Basic Law), explicitly called for the transfer of German sovereignty to international organizations. As Bulmer and Paterson have argued: 'West German integration in a supranational European Community was seen as an important aid to the new democracy. In fact its willingness to accept a federal European framework placed West Germany at the head of the supporters of European federalism.'[43] The Federal Republic of Germany had considerably less sovereignty to lose by participation in the Schuman Plan than the other West European nations; one could even argue that Bonn could *gain* in sovereignty. Since Germany's heavy industries in the Ruhr area had been put under the control of an International Ruhr Authority (in 1949), functional integration in the fields of coal and steel would enhance Bonn's command over its own resources.

After the ECSC Treaty had been signed on 18 April 1951 in Paris (see Chapter 3.3), further steps were made in the field of military cooperation. In the light of the intensifying Soviet threat, closer West European military collaboration was considered essential. The similarities between the divide between Korea and Germany were too obvious to be ignored with impunity. Here too, the inclusion of the German military turned out to be the crucial issue. Germany was doing well economically; the outbreak of the Korean War increased demand for machinery and steel, which resulted in the growth of West German productive capacity. The Germans were, on the other hand, not obliged to spend huge sums on defence. A German contribution to the defence of Western Europe (especially where manpower was concerned), was therefore considered necessary. In October 1950, the French Premier, René Pleven, argued that West Germany should form an integral part of a European army in which the much-feared resurgence of German militarism could be contained. The Pleven Plan for a so-called European Defence Community (EDC) called for a fully integrated army under the command of one European military authority. The EDC would establish a West European army without reviving an independent German *Wehrmacht*. In order to strengthen political control over this new military organization, the EDC would also establish a so-called European Political Community, which was, among others, expected to 'ensure the co-ordination of the foreign policy of Member States in questions likely to involve the existence, the security or the prosperity of the Community' (Article 2 of the draft).

The story of the attempted creation of the EDC is a complicated and long one, which falls outside the scope of this chapter (see on these issues Chapter 3.4). Here it suffices to recall that the construction of a supranational military structure incorporating the West European states was only nipped in the bud at the very last moment. The Six had signed the EDC Treaty in 1952, but the French National Assembly refused to ratify it (August 1954) during a period in which the Soviet threat seemed less acute and Stalin's aggressive policies had shortly given way to Khrushchev's course of 'peaceful coexistence'.

2.5 European integration and the Cold War

With the breakdown of the one-world concept, the increasing suspicion between the United States and the Soviet Union and the open tug of war over Germany, culminating in the Berlin blockade, the bipolar system had been established. The bipolar nature of the post-war system has provided a wide range of incentives for economic and political integration. Our analysis follows the lines of Kenneth Waltz's ideas, who has maintained that 'Politics among European states became different in quality after World War II because the international system changed from a multipolar to a bipolar one. The limited progress made in economic and other ways toward the unity of Western Europe cannot be understood without considering the effects that followed from the changed structure of international politics.'[44] Deutsch's concept of a security community also goes a long way in explaining the institutionalization of European cooperation.

In this early period, it is not difficult to detect an almost proportional relationship between the integrative tendencies in Western Europe and the political and economic antagonism and incompatibility between the two blocs. Economic assistance under the Marshall Plan was deliberately made contingent upon European cooperation, both in the field of economics and security. Stalin reacted with a clamp-down on what still remained of the national independence of Czechoslovakia and Poland. When tensions between East and West reached a new limit in June 1950 – with the onset of the Korean War – new integrative institution-building was spurred with the Schuman Plan and the plans for a European Defence Community and a European Political Community. Similar, almost mirror-image, developments could be seen in the East, where the Cominform and the Council for Mutual Economic Assistance (CMEA) were established (see Chapter 3).

In the United States and Western Europe anti-Communist feelings mounted, whereas in the Soviet Union and Eastern Europe the anti-imperialist propaganda-machine was working at full speed. As Anthony Eden declared: 'Western solidarity had been created by Stalin's policies. It was the military threat to the West, expressed in immensely superior Soviet military power and in the attempt to blockade Berlin, which brought NATO into being. As the menace of major war receded, the existing basis of Western cohesion against Soviet encroachment might be weakened.'[45] This analysis of the interplay of bipolarity and integration conforms to Waltz's own judgement: 'Communist guerrillas operating in Greece prompted the Truman Doctrine. The tightening of the Soviet Union's control over the states of Eastern Europe led to the Marshall Plan and the Atlantic Defence Treaty, and these in turn gave rise to the Cominform and the Warsaw Pact. The plan to form a West German government produced the Berlin blockade. And so on through the 1950s, '60s, and '70s. Our responses are geared to the Soviet Union's actions, and theirs to ours, which has produced an increasingly solid bipolar balance.'[46]

The argument is indeed compelling that the essential external pressures for building a West European economic and military alliance have been provided by the USSR. The Schuman Plan and the Pleven Plan envisaged the merging of German economic and military power in order to strengthen Western Europe's defence against possible Soviet aggression. With the outbreak of the Korean War the urgency of integration was even more adamant. It was even feared that the Soviet actions in the Far East were a trick to make the United States withdraw troops from Europe, which would facilitate a Soviet invasion of Western Europe. In this respect the looming Soviet threat has functioned as the irritating grain of sand in the West European oyster, which has over time produced the 'pearl' of West European integration.

But the Cold War environment did not only help establish West European integration; it also determined which actors could join and which could not. Contrary to the forced cooperation within the Soviet bloc, where Moscow was bullying its satellites around, the West European countries could decide autonomously to commit themselves to the idea of European unity. However, several countries clung to their espoused neutrality, most notably Switzerland, Austria and some Scandinavian countries. Although Austria did participate in the Marshall Plan and felt free to join the OEEC, it chose not to enter the Council of Europe, which Moscow considered an anti-Soviet organization. In the State Treaty of 1955, Vienna pledged not to enter in a 'political or economic union' with Germany. This declaration would later prove a block to future Austrian membership of the European Community. Similar barriers to closer cooperation with the EC existed for the Nordic countries. Due to its precarious geographical position, Finland felt obliged to conclude a Treaty of Friendship, Co-operation and Mutual Assistance with the USSR in 1948, which included a statement of neutrality: 'Finland endeavors not to be involved in clashes between the interests of the Great Powers'.

Great Britain also lacked the commitment to join forces with other West European countries, which has been most clearly formulated by Winston Churchill: 'We are with Europe but not of it. We are interested and associated, but not absorbed.'[47] London still considered itself part of the famous three circles, encompassing the Atlantic, the Commonwealth and the European continent. Of course, the 'European' Coal and Steel Community did not represent the whole of historical and geographical Europe, but only a small, almost peripheral part. But it was not the West which had hijacked the concept of 'Europe'; it was the East which was forced to abstain from the process of European integration. Most people living in Eastern Europe have unquestionably been aware of this fact. It was a point most forcefully driven home by the slogans of several political parties in Czechoslovakia and Hungary during the 1990-elections: 'Let's Join Europe!'[48]

3. From Paris to Rome, 1951-1957

The peace of the world can only be preserved if creative efforts are made which are commensurate, in their scope, with the dangers which threaten peace ... The uniting of the European nations requires that the age-old opposition between France and Germany be eliminated.

> Robert Schuman, 9 May 1950, in S. Patijn (ed.), *Landmarks in European Unity* (Leyden: A.W. Sijthoff, 1970), p.47.

3.1 Introduction

After having discussed the historical background of the first preliminary steps on the road towards West European integration, this chapter will focus upon the period 1951-7. We have seen how the process of West European economic integration has been generated by the peculiarities of Cold War bipolarity. Here we will first elaborate upon the countermeasures devised by Moscow, most notably the construction of its own trading bloc. The institutionalization of economic integration in Western Europe set off with the Treaty of Paris (1951), whereafter the quest for unity was temporarily dampened by the failure of the EDC and the EPC; both episodes will be analysed within the context of East-West relations. We will also examine how the ECSC has reacted upon the several crises which befell Eastern Europe after the process of destalinization was set in motion by Khrushchev. Finally we will – again – deal with the question as to how far external and systemic factors have played a role in this earlier phase of integration.

3.2 The Council for Mutual Economic Assistance (CMEA)

After 1947, the East European countries restructured their economies along Soviet-style lines. This included all the ideologically required paraphernalia of impressive long-term plans, the nationalization of key industries and agriculture and the anchoring of the exchange rates of their currencies to the

Soviet rouble. This was the economic *Gleichschaltung* which Stalin had considered necessary in order to strengthen his grip on the new members of the Communist bloc. But Moscow did not limit itself to monitoring and restricting the economic relations of its satellites, it also set up several institutions to manage its newly established empire.

In January 1949, the Soviet Union called together representatives from Bulgaria, Czechoslovakia, Hungary, Poland and Romania, in order to formulate a practical answer to the economic integration efforts which were made in Western Europe. Initially it was argued that without some framework in which the economies of Eastern Europe could be controlled, Soviet hegemony in this region would run into major difficulties. This was witnessed by Yugoslavia, which had challenged the concept of a Soviet sphere of influence by asserting a new kind of neutralism in 1948. During this meeting in January in Moscow, the Council for Mutual Economic Assistance (CMEA) was established. The term 'assistance' in its name for a long time remained a silent witness to the fact that the CMEA was set up as the counterpart of the OEEC, which was monitoring United States' economic aid to Western Europe under the Marshall Plan. Whereas the Molotov Plan of 1947 had called for a network of bilateral trade agreements between Moscow and the East European countries, the CMEA was expected to coordinate the overall trade flows of the now Communist part of Europe. One of the CMEA's tasks was to 'exchange economic experience and to render mutual technical assistance and mutual aid in raw materials, foodstuffs, machinery, equipment, etc'.[1]

From the start the CMEA has been regarded in the West as an instrument of Soviet control over Eastern Europe. The construction of the CMEA and the further moves towards economic cooperation between the Communist countries could indeed be seen as a means of administering the Soviet alliance system. Soviet hegemony was forged by making Eastern Europe politically and economically dependent upon Moscow. As one political scientist has argued: 'In so far [the CMEA] was anything more than an anti-American gesture, it was an adjunct of the Russian policy, chiefly pursued by other means, of using planning to annex the satellite economies to Russian needs and not to develop the area as a whole in the interests of all its parts'.[2] Indeed, the USSR provided its western neighbours with raw materials and energy (in the early 1970s this amounted to 90 per cent of Eastern Europe's iron ore, 96 per cent of its oil and 60 per cent of its coal), in return for manufactures and consumer articles. Since these articles were generally of too low a quality to be sold directly on the western market, the Soviet Union quickly established itself as the most important trading partner for the East Europeans.[3] Huge cooperative projects were set up over the years, bearing such names as the 'Friendship Oil Pipeline', the 'Peace Electric Power Grid' and the 'Brotherhood Gas Pipeline'. The longer the East European economies were protected from the capitalist world economy – sheltered as they were in Stalin's 'parallel socialist economy' – the more difficult it became to resist Soviet economic and political predominance in the region. As a result, most East European leaders have made vigorous attempts to increase East-West trade in order to create a more viable alternative for their economic dependence upon Moscow.

Although the CMEA has therefore been instrumental in forging Soviet-style economies in Eastern Europe, it would go too far to portray the CMEA as nothing more than the willing instrument in the Kremlin's hands. Peter Wiles has remarked that 'One of the worst misunderstandings is to present the CMEA as simply an extension of Soviet power, on the contrary it is a brake on that power'.[4] In the following chapters we will see that the CMEA was not fully and meticulously dominated by Moscow, but that the East European countries have continuously tried to use this organization for their own national objectives. Since its conception, the CMEA Secretariat has produced elaborate drafts for economic cooperation among the Member States, but it has clearly failed to serve as a multilateral platform on which the Communist countries could coordinate their economic plans. Moscow was unwilling to streamline the CMEA and the Cominform, since it preferred to deal with its satellites by means of bilateral settlements. As a result, most member states soon fell back on a rather autarchic course, only supplemented with the network of bilateral agreements with the USSR. Particularly in the first phase, the CMEA remained a rather inactive, almost dormant entity. It is, for instance, illustrative that between 1949 and 1954, the CMEA Council met only once. Its few activities were veiled in secrecy and its earlier efforts to increase intra-bloc economic integration have not been uncovered until now. It is characteristic of the CMEA's low profile that it got its constitution (or Charter) as late as 1960.

All these developments naturally put a brake on the development of East-West trade. Traditional commercial ties between countries like Hungary and Austria and between Czechoslovakia and (West) Germany were blocked. When we consider the index of trade among the East European countries, we see that it rose from 100 in 1938 to 288 in 1948, whereas the index of East-West trade fell from 100 to a mere 42.[5] This, as a matter of course, increased Eastern Europe's economic and political dependence upon Moscow. Traditional trade patterns with the West have been severely disrupted by the Soviet insistence on the so-called 'catch-up industrialization' of many East European economies. After 1950, these countries embarked upon industrialization programmes along strict Stalinist lines, which made them, *ipso facto*, reliant upon the raw materials of the USSR, and, since the sales potential of East European end-products on the world market was low, only the CMEA market remained. These developments contributed to a Europe that was clearly divided into two blocs, with only limited economic and political contact.

After the death of Soviet dictator Joseph Stalin (March 1953), the CMEA was somewhat revived. The Soviet Union and Eastern Europe now began to adopt a policy of specialization, whereby each country was expected to concentrate its efforts on several economic activities, which, in turn, would then be coordinated by the CMEA. From 1954 onwards, all national five-year plans of the member states were to be coordinated by the CMEA. In practice this meant that the economic plans of the USSR and the other People's Republics were only loosely synchronized. The CMEA Charter (adopted in 1960) clearly acknowledged that 'Socialist integration is conducted on a purely voluntary basis, is not accompanied by the creation of any supranational organs and does not affect internal planning problems or the financial and accounting activities of organizations'. The Charter also formulated the organization's prime goals: 'to promote, by uniting and coordinating the efforts of the member-countries of the Council, the planned development of the national economy, the acceleration of economic and technical progress in these countries, the raising of the level of industrialization in the industrially less developed countries, a steady increase in the productivity of labour and a constant improvement in the welfare of the peoples of the member-countries of the Council'. The ideologically sanctified principles of 'socialist internationalism' now governed the relations between Eastern Europe and the Soviet Union. As one Soviet lawyer had it in 1969: 'The principle of comradely mutual assistance includes the right of each state of the socialist world system to receive assistance from the other socialist states, and the obligation of each socialist state to render assistance to the other socialist states. This obligation concerns equally the political, economic, military and other relations.'[6]

One of the more interesting questions in this context is in how far West European economic integration has influenced the integrative developments in the Communist bloc and increased East European economic dependence on Moscow? It is beyond doubt that, after 1947, the level of East-West trade did indeed fall significantly. This drop in East-West commerce was partly caused by the autarkic tendencies of the East itself, but also partly due to the restrictions on East-West trade installed on the western side for reasons of security. (A policy most clearly crystallized in the construction of the Coordinating Committee for Multilateral Export Controls – CoCom, in short – in 1949.) As a result, the East European countries could only turn to Moscow to satisfy their industrial needs. Although this line of argument suggests that the West European countries could perhaps have done better by maintaining elaborate economic contacts with Eastern Europe, it is hard to see how this could have been a viable option in the critically strained political context of the Cold War, particularly since the US Congress had passed an amendment to the Foreign Assistance Act ('the Marshall Plan') in April 1948, which directed the ERP administrator 'to refuse delivery in so far as practicable to participating countries of commodities which go into production of any commodity for delivery to any non-participating European country which commodity would be refused export licenses to those countries by the United States in the interest of national security'.[7] Although this amendment made aid under the Marshall Plan dependent upon a West

European commitment not to re-export certain goods to Communist countries,[8] the West European countries did only very occasionally use their economic relations for political purposes. This stood in sharp contrast to the American policy of economic warfare *vis-à-vis* the East in the 1950s.[9]

During the first ten years of the CMEA's existence, the West European economic integration process had only had a marginal impact upon the economic and political developments taking place in the East. This is not to say that Moscow had not severely criticized all efforts at integration in Western Europe (see Chapter 4). However, in the 1950s the construction of the Common Market did *not* evoke a counteraction along similar lines in the East. Until 1960, relatively little attention was paid to the ECSC and the EEC by Soviet policy-makers and the Soviet media. Moscow considered these western institutions ephemeral, bound to shatter on what it liked to call 'the dangerous cliffs of imperialist contradictions'. Only in the 1960s, the construction of the EEC seemed to have triggered the East European drive towards further economic integration. As Marshall Shulman remarked in 1963: 'Since the Common Market came into being, [the CMEA] has become transformed into an instrument through which the states of eastern Europe are being absorbed into the Soviet economic complex and are being moved in the direction of political merger. Integration in western Europe is producing integration by induction in eastern Europe.'[10] Further attention to this point will be given in Chapter 4, where we will more elaborately examine Moscow's response to West European integration.

3.3 The Treaty of Paris (1951)

Shulman's concept of 'integration by induction' is an interesting one which should be kept in mind in our analysis of the developments in the 1950s. For reasons closely related to this notion, economic integration has been opposed by several West European political factions. Social-Democrats and socialists, in particular, in certain countries, notably the FRG, have initially resisted European union because they judged it an obstacle to a settlement with Eastern Europe and an impediment to German unity.[11] They have generally argued that further integration of the Six would make it less likely that Eastern Europe would ever be able to join the West; and the more the Federal Republic of Germany would become embedded in West European institutions, the smaller the chance that German unity could ever become reality. In the previous chapter we have already referred to the West German Social-Democrats who opposed German participation in the Schuman Plan since this was expected to widen the East-West divide and make the chances for national reunification even more modest. The British Labour MP Dennis Healey had argued along similar lines in 1962: 'the Continental desire to create a Common Market as a basis for the political and economic union of Western Europe reflects a desire on both sides of the Iron Curtain to stabilize the unnatural post-war *status quo* in Europe, and to render it more permanent and more secure than it has been over the last fifteen years'.[12]

These arguments have never been forceful enough to inhibit West European economic integration, which seemed by now to have acquired its own dynamic. The suggestions made in the Schuman Plan were taken up enthusiastically by the Six (the countries of the Benelux, France, West Germany and Italy). Of the major West European countries there was only one exception: Great Britain. The United Kingdom, which in 1950 produced some 50 per cent of Western Europe's coal and 30 per cent of its steel, refused to participate in this scheme. Britain's apprehensions about supranational authority over its resources were sufficiently strong not to take part in the negotiations on the ECSC. Although London's refusal to participate was generally deplored, it did not significantly hamper the implementation of Schuman's plan. Under the pressures of the Korean War, France agreed to accept German rearmament under the uncompromising condition that Germany's war-making potential (coal and steel) would be safely entrenched in a supranational organization. In April 1951, the European Coal and Steel Community (ECSC) Treaty was signed in Paris and could thereafter be presented to the national parliaments for ratification; the Treaty entered into force in July 1952.

The practical and spiritual father of the Treaty (and Head of the French Economic Planning Commission), Jean Monnet, clearly set out the far-reaching political objective of the ECSC, which was to construct an all-embracing institution of European cooperation; a fully fledged 'European Community'. German Chancellor Konrad Adenauer stated in an address to the *Bundestag* in June 1950: 'Let me make a point of declaring in so many words and in full agreement, not only with the French Government but also with M. Jean Monnet, that the importance of this [ECSC] project is above all political and not economic'.[13] From 1953 onward, the six member countries knew a common market for coal, steel, iron ore and scrap. A High Authority – which had a substantial supranational competence – was set up by the Treaty in order to direct the ECSC's activities. Decision-making in the High Authority involved majority voting, although voting only took place in order to ratify the consensus and never in order to overrule national governments on issues of vital importance. It can be doubted whether member states would have conceded to ECSC rulings on matters where core concerns of national security would be at stake. Be that as it may, the (admittedly benign) supranational character of the ECSC demonstrated that the national governments were prepared to yield parts of their sovereignty under the conviction that this would be in their national interest.

It is important to note that the European integration efforts were not only supported by West European political leaders, but, in general, also strongly backed by the populace of the member states. Only half a decade after one of the world's most destructive wars had come to an end, the most viable road towards peace and prosperity seemed to be far-going economic and political cooperation. Some of the euphoria and high spirits of the pioneers of European integration can be found in the text of the Preamble to the ECSC Treaty. This may make clear that pooling steel and coal was not merely an effort at short-term economic management. It was declared that the Six,

Considering that world peace may be safeguarded only by creative efforts as great as the dangers menacing it;

Convinced that the contribution which an organized and vital Europe can bring to civilization is indispensable to the maintenance of peaceful relations;

Conscious of the fact that Europe can be built only by concrete actions creating a real solidarity and by the establishment of common bases for economic development;

Desirous of assisting through the expansion of their basic production in raising the standard of living and in furthering the works of peace;

Resolved to substitute for historic rivalries a fusion of their essential interest; to establish, by creating an economic community, the foundation of a broad and independent community among peoples long divided by bloody conflicts; and to lay the bases of institutions capable of giving direction to their future common destiny;

Have decided to create a European coal and steel community.[14]

All this did not apply to the Soviet Union and Eastern Europe. At the height of the Cold War, the six West European governments solemnly declared that their economic cooperation and their community of interests would make 'bloody conflicts' among them impossible. But, at the same time, elaborate military arrangements were made on both sides of the Iron Curtain in order to forestall similar 'bloody conflicts' between East and West.

3.4 The ECSC and foreign policy

Although we will discuss the European Community's *Ostpolitik* in a later chapter, it will be useful to see how the ECSC has dealt with the problems and opportunities in East-West relations. In the period in which the European Coal and Steel Community was the main instrument of West European unity, several dramatic events took place in Eastern Europe, which, of course, evoked a western reaction. From the start it must be acknowledged that in the 1950s there was no sign of a coordinated West European *foreign* policy in any significant way. The ECSC provided coordination of several economic policies, but did not contribute to the coordination of West European foreign policy. The High Authority, the policy-making body of the ECSC, was provided with the task of ensuring 'that the objectives set out in this Treaty are attained in accordance with the provisions thereof' (Article 8 of the Treaty of Paris); the High Authority had a substantial supranational power at its disposal (such as the control of prices, subsidies and aid), but it could not go beyond economics and commerce; politics – let alone *foreign* policy – was out of the ECSC's realm of control.

The ECSC had, however, been set up as an institutional embryo which was expected to develop into a more fully fledged body of West European integration. In this respect the ECSC has more than once been labelled an experiment in 'applied Functionalism'.[15] The Coal and Steel Community had been established according to the thesis that states will only cooperate among each other when cooperation promises to offer them better solutions to their problems in comparison to unilateral actions. But even in that case, traditional problems of collective action might hamper cooperation. The lack of success of the Council of Europe, which sought to establish a European Federation by stressing constitutional and supranational arrangements, had brought home the point that West European integration should start from the 'bottom up', with cooperation on economical and technical matters. However, France especially saw economic integration as a method to control German heavy industry, and therefore as an issue of major political importance. Despite the particular political and security implications of economic integration, it was further assumed that highly politicized questions and concerns of foreign affairs were to be excluded from the ECSC, and had to be left to the national governments of the member states. In the 1950s, problems of foreign policy could therefore not be tackled in a coordinated manner by the Six.

Given the newness of the integration process, it was evident that the High Authority had to be very susceptible to the political views of its members. In most capitals of Western Europe, the readiness to relinquish the prerogative of foreign policy was very limited indeed. The national interests of the Six had certainly not converged to the point where cooperation on foreign policy was deemed possible, or even necessary. During the seven years under discussion here, the national policies of the ECSC member states clearly dominated and no sign of 'European thinking' on foreign policy issues could be observed. Strong political figures, with equally strong views on their countries' role and fate in Europe, overshadowed the West European political scene. In France, General de Gaulle longed to re-establish French *grandeur*, which he interpreted as a continuous increase of French influence in world affairs. His ambitions were to turn his country into a world power, failing to acknowledge the fact that France did not equal the economic and political strengths of the two ascending superpowers: the United States and the Soviet Union. De Gaulle's European objectives were equally demanding. In June 1947, he called for a Europe to be 'organized as a whole, capable of containing any possible ambition of hegemony and of creating between the two rival masses [the United States and the USSR] a factor of equilibrium indispensable for peace'. Thirteen years later, he argued: 'She [France] hopes that ... the future will allow Europe to lead its own life thanks to an equilibrium established between its two parts, which have different regimes'.[16] In the meantime, Western

Europe had to be the mediator between the 'Anglo-Saxon' camp and the Soviet camp. De Gaulle's ambition to preserve the unrestricted independence of the French nation while strengthening the role of Europe had led him to prefer political cooperation over economic integration. However, these political issues were not to be discussed within the ECSC (or the later EC), but in separate intergovernmental platforms.[17]

In West Germany, Chancellor Konrad Adenauer clung to the *Westpolitik* of integrating his country into the structures of West European cooperation, both in the economic, political and military field. The well-known 'policy of strength' *vis-à-vis* the East indicated Adenauer's ideal of achieving German reunification on the basis of close ties with the West and a ban on links with the Soviet bloc (except for the USSR). These aspects of Bonn's security policy constituted the indispensable components of its *Deutschlandpolitik*. Adenauer had declared, in October 1949, that the Federal Republic of Germany was to be considered the sole representative of the German people. This so-called *Alleinvertretungsanspruch* was later supported by the western allies (September 1950).[18] This, in turn, produced the so-called Hallstein doctrine, whereby Bonn's predominant foreign policy became the weakening of the international status of the German Democratic Republic. The adoption of the Hallstein doctrine also limited the Federal Republic's scope of political action *vis-à-vis* the East. This doctrine was first practised in 1957. When Yugoslavia took up diplomatic relations with East Berlin (in October), Bonn immediately rescinded its diplomatic contacts with Belgrade. Although West German inflexibility in its relations with the East were notorious, Adenauer was a champion of West European economic and political integration: 'serious concessions of the Soviet Union are not to be expected as long as the lack of unity gives it the hope to pull a country to its side, thereby disrupting the unity of the West ... Moreover, our long-term relationship with France is only possible on the basis of European integration. Would the integration fail because of our resistance or hesitation, the consequences could not be foreseen.'[19]

When we add to this Great Britain's reluctance to join the Six, it will be clear that these national peculiarities and diverging national interests had made it extremely difficult to come to something resembling a 'West European foreign policy'. Of course, several initiatives towards political union had been taken. We have already referred to the 1953 proposal to set up a European Political Community. Such a Community would have been constructed along federalist lines and would have gone a long way towards forging a common West European foreign policy. It was to incorporate the ECSC and establish a common policy on security issues (the EDC). It would have been known under the general name of 'the European Community'. Among the aims of the EPC was its wish 'to contribute towards the protection of human rights and fundamental freedoms in Member States'; 'to co-operate with the other free nations in ensuring the security of Member States against all aggression'; and 'to ensure the co-ordination of the foreign policy of Member States in questions likely to involve the existence, the security or the prosperity of the Community'.

The EDC was itself a response to the tensions of the Cold War and especially the outbreak of the Korean War. It was above all considered a convenient body to integrate the West German military. It was this latter aspect of the EDC which caused most alarm in Moscow. In March 1952, the Soviet Union started a massive campaign to keep the FRG from joining the European Defence Community. On 10 March, the USSR sent out a note calling for a 'neutral Germany' and the withdrawal of the occupation forces (including those of the Soviet Union itself). The note argued that 'the existence of organizations inimical to democracy and to the maintenance of peace must not be permitted on the territory of Germany'; Germany should also be constrained 'not to enter into any kind of coalition or military alliance directed against any power which took part, with its armed forces, in the war against Germany'.[20] The western response argued closely along the lines of Chancellor Adenauer that free elections should be held in both East and West Germany and that 'the all-German government should be free both before and after the conclusion of a peace treaty to enter into associations compatible with the principles of the United Nations'.[21] Moscow was not willing to accept these western conditions and could not prevent West German officials from signing the EDC Treaty.

With the ratification process over the EDC getting stuck in the French Assembly in August 1954 (with 319 votes against 264, and 43 abstentions), the idea of a European Political Community was of course also aborted. Spaak had severely criticized French Premier Pierre Mendès-France, arguing: 'Had he not struck an all but lethal blow at the cause of European unity?' Ratification, he argued, 'would have been a decisive step towards a united Europe'.[22] It can be questioned whether the French ratification of the EDC would have solved the problems dividing the major West European countries. Because, as Jansen and De Vree have argued correctly: 'it should be recognized that even if both treaties had been ratified, their smooth implementation would have been unlikely. Neither treaty really contributed to solving the basic problems in any major form of international cooperation: the impossibility to form a permanent, sufficiently dominant coalition, able to reach and enforce decisions against the opposition of other states. This problem is not solved by signing a treaty, nor is it likely that either of the treaties could have done much to help it.'[23] Although the lack of agreement of the EDC was indeed a set-back in the process of West European integration, we will later argue that it proved to be not just a temporary one, but that the resulting intermezzo ensued in the *relance européenne* only one year later.

3.5 The ECSC and Eastern Europe

With the death of Stalin, followed by the end of the Korean War a little over four months later, the international climate changed significantly. Most importantly, western fears of Soviet expansionism had slightly abated. What was more, the first signs of cracks in the hitherto solid Soviet bloc seemed to manifest themselves. When Stalin was replaced by a troika of Prime Minister Georgi Malenkov, Foreign Minister Molotov and Lavrentii Beria (as the head of the secret police), Eastern Europe gyrated into a political ferment which threatened to turn into open revolt. With the death of the Soviet dictator, many East Europeans had seized the opportunity to increase their political room for manoeuvre. Moscow's policy *vis-à-vis* Eastern Europe had become more lenient, whereby, for example, further reparations from the GDR were waived. What was more, the USSR advised its satellites to strengthen the role of their Communist Parties by re-establishing the principle of 'socialist legality', which was expected to remove from power the hard-line, Stalinist elements in Eastern Europe. In response to this volte-face in Soviet policy, riots broke out in the streets and factories of Sofia, Prague and East Berlin in May and June 1953. In East Berlin, workers demonstrated against the regime, calling for free and secret elections. This erupted in an anti-Communist protest of some 200,000 people. Martial law was soon proclaimed in most parts of the country. Eventually, Soviet troops and special *Volkspolizei* units quelled the uprising, killing some twenty-two demonstrators and arresting thousands.

This was the first major European crisis in East-West relations since the creation of the ECSC. The United States, which had earlier put forward its policy of liberation of the 'Captive Nations' in the East and the rollback of Communism in the region, reacted surprisingly passively. In spite of the rhetoric of the United States' Soviet policy – and therefore to the astonishment of many – the German rioters were not provided with American arms; Washington restricted its actions to the distribution of food to the Berliners. In December of that year, Washington adopted a policy paper (the NSC [National Security Council Report] 174, called 'United States Policy toward the Soviet Satellites in Eastern Europe') which declared that the USA considered it 'in the national security interests of the United States to pursue a policy of determined resistance to dominant Soviet influence over the satellites in Eastern Europe and to seek the eventual elimination of that influence. Accordingly, feasible political, economic, propaganda and covert measures are required to create and exploit troublesome problems for the USSR, complicate control in the satellites, and retard the growth of the military and economic potential of the Soviet bloc.'[24] These were quite bold and daring statements, which seemed to indicate an American resolve to change the *status quo* in Europe; Washington's actions in Europe were, however, always considerably more restrained than these declarations would lead one to expect.

How did 'Western Europe' react to these events? There was, of course, no united response from all members of the ECSC, since no organizational structure existed for these purposes. One of the first assessments of the ECSC's relationship with the East had been markedly negative. Among the several sub-commissions set up, the Commission on Commercial Politics reported to the ECSC Council of Ministers in November 1952: 'les pays situés derrière le rideau de fer prendront une attitude résolument hostile au Traité instituant une Communauté. Ils ne feront certainement rien pour faciliter l'établissement d'un marché commun. Il semble donc qu'avec ces pays aucune négociation ne peut être envisagée.'[25] But outside the ECSC framework, most West European governments were also cautious, sometimes even extremely cautious. It soon became clear that the East German dissenters could not find any guidance, or even encouragement, in the West. It was acknowledged that the West Europeans had few realistic policy options in response to the East German events. Just to be on the safe side, the Soviet Union had issued a press communiqué which said that 'It should be clear that no "problem of the countries of Eastern Europe" exists. The people of these countries, having overthrown the rule of the exploiters, have established in their countries a people's democratic government and will not allow anyone to interfere with their domestic affairs.'[26] Although the East German repression did provoke criticism in the West, it also seemed to indicate that most West Europeans were too preoccupied with their own economic and political problems to pay much attention to the bitter fate of Eastern Europe.

Since 1955, Nikita S. Khrushchev's star had been rising in the Soviet political firmament. After his famous 'secret speech' in February 1956, the destalinization process began in the Soviet Union, leading to an even further decline of Moscow's direct control over its satellites. The rift between the USSR and Yugoslavia had already indicated that several roads towards socialism were indeed possible, which has had a centrifugal impact upon the political course of many East European countries. This was furthered by Khrushchev's official proclamation of the various national avenues towards socialism (at the 20th Congress of the Soviet Communist Party). In response to Khrushchev's speech, political rioting again erupted in Poznan (Poland) in late June of 1956. Within a few days, the riots were suppressed by the police, leaving more than seventy people killed, some 300 wounded and several hundreds arrested. The Polish Communist leader, Wladislaw Gomulka (who had fallen into disgrace under Stalin, but was now called back), insisted upon his country's 'full independence and sovereignty', but decided to stay within the Soviet camp. In the Autumn of that year, Budapest also made attempts to loosen its ties with Moscow. Rebellion against the Stalinist forces and the USSR went, however, much further than in Poland. Under the leadership of its Premier Imre Nagy, Hungary even experienced a short period of political freedom when the one-party system was temporarily abolished and Hungarian independence from the USSR was declared. This signified a breaking of the Communist ranks which could not be tolerated by Moscow. In late October of 1956, fifteen Soviet divisions with 6,000 tanks made an end of this political experiment; Nagy was subsequently executed.

In the mean time, the major West European countries – Great Britain and France – were fully occupied by their invasion of Egypt (the culmination of the Suez crisis), and were in no position to respond to the Hungarian calls for western assistance in their attempt to throw off the Soviet yoke. United States policy-makers deplored Anglo-French military interference in the Middle East, since this made a firm western answer to the Soviet actions in Eastern Europe impossible. John Foster Dulles, the US Secretary of State, argued: 'what a great tragedy it is just when the whole Soviet policy is collapsing the British and French are doing the same thing in the Arab world'.[27] What is more, the French Foreign Minister, Christian Pineau, had already explicitly warned against all western attempts to 'exploit' the popular uprisings in Poland and Hungary. Pineau had argued that 'men for whom I have the highest esteem, such as President Eisenhower, are right when they indicate that the role of the West is to substitute its own for Russian influence in those countries'. However, he continued, 'It would be dangerous to try to cut the links that countries like Hungary, Poland and Czechoslovakia have with the Soviet Union, This would provide the Soviet Union and some statesmen in those countries with a pretext to go back on de-stalinization.'[28] This French statement implicitly acknowledged Soviet dominance in its own sphere of influence. Despite some rhetoric to the contrary, no French actions could be expected to rebuke Moscow's interventions in its own backyard.

It soon became painfully visible that the Six still lacked both the political will and the incentives to work together in the field of foreign policy, as well as the political instruments to formulate a coherent response to these events in Eastern Europe. In want of a platform for foreign policy coordination, most West European reactions were harmonized within the United Nations. In a special meeting of the UN Security Council, Great Britain, France and the United States accused the USSR of violating the Treaty of Paris (of February 1947, that is), in which the peace between Hungary and the Allied Powers had been established, guaranteeing the 'fundamental freedoms' of Budapest. Only Spain called for a United Nations intervention in the conflict.[29] Acknowledging the central role of the United Nations, Nagy had sent a telegram to its Secretary-General, Dag Hammarskjöld, declaring: 'The Government of the Hungarian People's Republic made the Declaration of Neutrality on 1 November 1956; therefore I request your Excellency to put on the agenda of the forthcoming General Assembly of the United Nations the question of Hungary's neutrality and the defence of this neutrality by the four great powers.'[30] On the same day, Nagy communicated to the Soviet Ambassador, Yuri V. Andropov, that his government would immediately withdraw from the Warsaw Pact, declare Hungary's neutrality and request the help of the four Great Powers.

As said, no West European answer was formulated. It was not only the ECSC which remained passive, the Council of Europe Assembly also displayed its impotence. The Council only urged the European governments to consider approaching the United Nations Security Council about the Hungarian crisis; but no policy suggestions were made by the sixteen-nation Council of Europe Assembly itself.[31] The ECSC could do little more than collect some money under its personnel in an effort to provide the ensuing flood of Hungarian refugees with some preliminary humanitarian support.[32] The Western European Union (with France, Great Britain, Belgium, the Netherlands, Luxembourg, Italy and West Germany as members), established in 1955, was also notable for its lack of decisive action. The WEU had been established in order to coordinate the defence policies of its members and to further cooperation in political, social, legal and cultural matters. However, one of the first serious tests of the WEU's efficacy had exposed the manifest inadequacy of this intergovernmental organization. It was characteristic of the West European *ad hoc* approach that Chancellor Adenauer took this opportunity to stress the fact that recent events in Eastern Europe had proved once again that the security of the FRG could not be adequately safeguarded without its own military forces. Adenauer therefore hoped that the Hungarian onslaught would convince the remaining opponents of German armament of its necessity.[33]

The overall acquiescent stance of the West left both American and West European policy-makers in a crisis of conscience after the military crushing of Hungary. It had become painfully apparent that the nuclear deadlock of the superpowers had seriously limited the room for manoeuvre for the West. As a result, official support for the Hungarian call for national independence and political freedom was tacit; overt encouragement of the uprisings could disturb the delicate East-West equilibrium, risking a major military confrontation. As Michel Tatu correctly argued: 'it was realized or sensed at the time of the Hungarian and Czechoslovak crisis in 1956 and 1968 that a revolution in one of the countries of Eastern Europe was not necessarily to the advantage of Western Governments, even if it reflected the liberal aspirations they share'.[34] This lesson had already been learned during the previous uprisings in the East, in 1953, but the more dramatic and violent Hungarian revolt pressed this point home with unprecedented clarity.

3.6 European integration after Stalin

The failure of the EDC scheme ensued in a search after alternative roads towards European strategic cooperation. This had resulted in the enlargement of the Brussels Treaty Organization into the Western European Union (1955) of which the FRG and Italy had now become members, thus allowing for the rearmament of Western Germany. One of the major initiators of further economic cooperation, which eventually led to the Treaty of Rome, had been the Dutch Foreign Minister J. W. Beyen. In 1952, Beyen had already introduced his plan to establish a West European Common Market.[35] Although his suggestions met with a positive response, these ideas were kept on the backburner for several years. Only after the failure of the EDC were new efforts made to revive that proposal. On 18 May 1955, the Benelux introduced a Joint Memorandum pleading for a customs union amongst the six members of the ECSC and further integration in the fields of, among others, transport, and nuclear and conventional energy. This would require a wider framework of West European integration, with common institutions.

At a conference of the Foreign Ministers in the Sicilian resort of Messina in June 1955, the Benelux plans for the creation of a real Common Market were accepted and the so-called *relance européenne* took off. It was stated that 'it is necessary to work for the establishment of a united Europe by the development of common institutions, the progressive fusion of national economies, the creation of a common market and the progressive harmoniza-tion of ... social policies. Such a policy seems to them indispensable if Europe is to maintain her position in the world, regain her influence and prestige and achieve a continuing increase in the standard of living of her population.'[36] The six Foreign Ministers entrusted Spaak with the task of setting up several study-groups of experts in order to work out plans preparing the way for the Common Market, which he referred to as 'one of the greatest events of European history, of no less importance than the revolution of 1789'.[37] The Spaak Committee submitted its report in early 1956. The report called for the creation of a Common Market without sector integration (atomic energy being the exception), and subsequently to drafting treaties. New institutions had to be set up supervising the integration process and generating common policies. After several intergovernmental meetings of the Six, agreement was reached. In Rome, 25 March 1957, two Treaties were signed: one establishing the European Economic Community (EEC), the other a European Atomic Energy Community (Euratom). This time ratification in the member states' parliaments did not block the Treaties, although the numerical opposition in the French and Italian Chambers of Deputies (342 votes for and 239 against in France; 311 votes for and 144 against in Italy) displayed the opposition of the large Communist parties in these countries.[38] The institutional triad of EEC, Euratom and ECSC later merged into the 'European Community' (EC) proper. (The Merger Treaty was signed in May 1965 and took effect in July 1967.) The Rome Treaty of 1957 set a decisive step towards the construction of West European unity, only a few years after the dramatic accident with the EDC. What had caused this remarkable *relance européenne*?

As G. L. Goodwin has noted correctly: 'a common foreign policy is most likely to evolve in response of the external environment'.[39] During the 1950s, the bipolar structure of the Cold War became institutionalized along strict ideological lines. In response to the WEU and NATO, the Communist countries organized themselves militarily within the Warsaw Pact (set up in 1955). The Warsaw Pact had been one of the major instruments of Moscow to dominate its Communist allies in Eastern Europe. In the mid-1950s, the East-West divide had been ossified as never before, with economic and military alliances limiting the political leeway of all actors on the European stage. Most matters of foreign policy had to be dealt with within this context of bipolarity, which resulted in the unique Manichean world of the Cold War. Stalin's death in 1953, and Khrushchev's 'secret speech' in 1956, had given rise to frantic fermentation in the Communist bloc, which in turn changed the international environment in which the process of West European unification took place. From a strict Neo-realist perspective, Stalin's death would have to be considered as quite irrelevant, not directly touching upon the basic structure of European politics. The process of destalinization, however, resulted in a plethora of centrifugal tendencies within the Soviet bloc which led to a temporary weakening of Moscow's hegemony in the region. The Soviet overlay over Eastern Europe was not so much assured as it had been in the early-1950s, and, as a result, the threat of Soviet expansionism towards Western Europe declined. Khrushchev's ensuing policy of 'peaceful coexistence' continued the Cold War with other means, whereby the threat of a nuclear holocaust and Soviet aggression abated.

Two distinct evaluations of the intricacies of the relationship between East-West friction and West European integration can be distinguished. On the one hand, Derek W. Urwin has remarked: 'As soon as this outside pressure eased ... these [national] differences were forced out into the open; until they were disposed of, integration could not proceed on a satisfactory basis ... The great leap forward of the integrationists after 1954 can be partly attributed to the fact that they were not now motivated primarily on the fears of a Communist takeover, but were willing to operate on the positive and constructive basis of wanting union for its own intrinsic value.'[40] Urwin's analysis boils down to an inverse relationship between West European integration and East-West tension. This would suggest that the easing of international stress directly after Stalin's death induced a more straightforward and sincere drive towards the creation of West European union. Urwin argued that, after the first initial steps towards West European union had been made, further integration had to be based upon innate forces and not so much upon external ones. This would suggest that further European integration would in the future be thriving under conditions of East-West conciliation, or, what was later called *détente*.

Richard Mayne has brought forward a converse argument, when he observed that after the Soviet military invasion of Hungary in 1956, 'this sudden hardening of the "cold war" gave Western Europeans a powerful, if crude, incentive for seeking unity. A more united Western Europe would certainly be stronger, and might well discourage aggression; and even if, in this instance, it could have done little to save Hungary, it was clear that a divided Western Europe could do even less.'[41] This would suggest that traditional rallying round the anti-Communist flag had incited further political and economic cooperation in Western Europe. Particularly in the early post-war years, the looming Soviet threat had indeed brought several West European countries together, temporarily stifling differences among them. This had especially been the case in the construction of the ECSC: Germany's huge economic resources were brought into play, meanwhile containing German power. This was considered essential for constructing a basis for cooperation between Paris and Bonn. Overcoming German-Franco suspicions had been one of the building blocks for further cooperation and integration in Western Europe, finally resulting in the enlarged WEU and the EEC. Part of the explanation can therefore be found in external, systemic factors.

As we have already argued, these early decades of the Cold War were characterized by extreme bipolarity, whereby the two superpowers dominated their respective security alliances. There was, however, one major difference between the two sides: the ECSC and the EEC had to operate *without* close cooperation with their chief military partner, the United States, whereas the CMEA was clearly dominated by the Communist hegemon, the USSR (although because of its strict intergovernmental structure the CMEA was not formally ruled by Moscow). Due to the member states' approximate economic and political equality, the EEC was lacking a natural leader. Bonn's hands were more or less tied because of the 'German problem', whereas France was also unable to take the lead. Moreover, despite Moscow's allegations to the contrary, Washington could only occasionally influence EEC policy. Through membership of NATO, however, the significance of the Soviet threat was clearly translated into the realm of West European economic integration. Bipolarity did, in this circumventing fashion, ensue in both stable economic and security alliances. But now that the West European economies had been re-established and the Communist parties did not threaten domestic stability as before, how did the Kremlin affect the integration process?

In the next chapter we will examine Moscow's direct reaction to the West European drive to unity. Here we will argue that both Urwin's and Mayne's theses only *partly* explain the developments taking place in the 1950s. Combining both arguments brings us close to Carl J. Friedrich's assertion that 'As the [Soviet] threat has faded, or is believed to have done so, this incentive for unification has become weak; yet integration has gone forward ... [I]t has been a recurrent experience in the genesis of federal orders that outside pressures provided the occasion for the start of the process of federalizing rather than the basic cause. The foundation of federal unity lies elsewhere.'[42] Indeed, the argument is compelling that the Soviet threat of the late-1940s and early-1950s had provided the external force setting the flywheel of European integration in motion, but that after the first impetus had been provided, this process had to be geared by internal energy derived from clear-cut economic incentives and the political will of the ECSC (and later EEC) member states to coordinate and integrate policies. Indeed, during the first few years, West European economic union had been characterized by 'negative integration', that is the elimination of discriminatory national rules and legislation in order to permit common rules and legislation. Only in the late-1960s and early-1970s was 'negative integration' complemented with 'positive integration', which marks the adoption of common policies advancing economic welfare and the coordination of foreign policies. This generally requires a consensus on long-range goals and policies, usually combined with the political will to re-allocate resources and to decide upon policies of distribution. The latter also presupposes a more all-embracing and dedicated commitment to economic and political union.[43]

In this chapter we have argued that these external factors have played a crucial role in helping to establish the European Community as a fully fledged regime-cum-institution. The rules, procedures, norms and routines of the ECSC and EEC have provided a new focus on which member states' policies could converge. This has been a very extended and agonizing process. In spite of the efforts of many statesmen to move Western Europe 'beyond the nation-state' by strengthening the structure and authority of the Common Market, it had proved to be very difficult to achieve common ground on political and security-related issues. As Stanley Hoffmann noted in 1966: 'all that is left for unification [in Western Europe] is what one might call "national self-abdication" or self-abnegation, the eventual willingness of nations to try something else; but precisely global involvement hinders rather than helps, and the atrophy of war removes the most pressing incentive. What a nation-state cannot provide alone – in economics, or defense – it can still provide through means far less drastic than hara-kiri.'[44]

4. Moscow's Response to West European Integration, 1947-73

There is a very strong case for saying that the dissolution or at least the undermining of the cohesion of the Community is a maximum objective of the Soviet Union.

Ieuan G. John (ed.), *EEC Policy Towards Eastern Europe* (Westmead: Saxon House, 1975), p.51.

4.1 Introduction

Until 1988, Moscow had balked at recognizing the European Community as an international legal personality, entitled to negotiate in its own right and to represent its members on issues of foreign trade. The CMEA member states also refused to accredit missions to the European Community's headquarters in Brussels, as most other countries in the world have done. On the basis of the Rome Treaty provisions, the EEC had two attributes of legal personality in international relations: both a treaty-making power (*jus tractatus*), and the capacity to engage in diplomacy (*jus missionis*).[1] On this basis, the EEC has conducted a broad range of relations with non-member states. In particular, the development of common policies and the creation of a common external tariff have involved Brussels in an extended network of relations with the outside world. In 1970, the European Community had established diplomatic contacts with 76 states, which had all set up one or more missions at the EC in Brussels. For many years, the European Community itself was represented by a diplomatic delegation in London and by two liaison offices, one in Geneva at the GATT and one in Paris at the OECD. In 1969 the Commission had also opened an official delegation in Washington, DC.

For a very long time, the Communist countries were among the few states that were not represented, some way or other, at the European Community's headquarters in Brussels. This lack of direct and official relations between the EC and the East has strengthened the suspicions between both sides and has increased and perpetuated their antagonism on issues of foreign trade. In this chapter we will examine the Soviet Union's response to West European integration (covering the period until 1973), and we will analyse the oscillations in Moscow's attitude towards the EEC. We will also discuss in what way and to which extent the integration efforts in the West have inspired Communist collaboration, both in the economic and political field.

4.2 Moscow's policy of malign neglect

Moscow's strategy of either open hostility or malign neglect of the institutions of West European integration (be they the ECSC, the EDC/EPC, the WEU, the EEC or Euratom), has formed an integral part of the general Soviet attitude *vis-à-vis* the West. The Kremlin's policy towards the Six has always been embedded in its overall course towards Western Europe, and even towards the West in general. Over the decades, the USSR's attitude towards the Common Market has changed dramatically. In the earlier years of the ECSC's existence, hostility and disregard were the dominant lines of Soviet policy.

There were three sides to this rigid – and at times overtly hostile – Soviet attitude towards the construction of the Common Market. First, there was a plethora of *ideological reasons* for Moscow to renounce the West European drive towards unification and further integration. The Kremlin leaders seemed to cherish the Leninist doctrine which claimed that collaboration among developed capitalist states would be nigh impossible, and that the capitalist world would inevitably become eclipsed in severe internal contradictions. This would, in the end, result in war among them. Closer cooperation among the major West European capitalist countries in the framework of the ECSC, and later also in the European Economic Community, seemed to repudiate this facet of Soviet ideology. In order to prove their point, Soviet spokesmen continued to emphasize the plentiful conflicts among West European states. It was expected that these frictions would intensify the more structural 'capitalist contradictions', whereafter cooperation within the ECSC and the EEC would be undermined. This would eventually result in the collapse of these organizations.

In the mean time, however, the ECSC and the EEC were living proof that West European integration was at least a momentary phenomenon which called for a Soviet policy. These new institutions in Brussels could not be ignored. Luckily, several studies by V. I. Lenin were found in which he had maintained that a 'United States of Europe' was among the possibilities, but only in the form of a union of monopolists attempting to withstand the coming rise of the European working class.[2] As was to be expected, Lenin's opinions were quickly transformed into the new canons of Soviet foreign policy *vis-à-vis* the ECSC and the later EEC.

Moscow's policy-makers could further choose among a wide spectrum of ideological reasons to combat West European union. There were also many ideological answers to the question of why the Six were cooperating in the first place. Among the more popular Soviet explanations for West European economic integration was the argument that western capital was 'outgrowing [its] national boundaries', which had now ensued in a 'division of influence of the monopolies, the tendency to form large economic areas, the development of monopoly capitalism into state-monopoly capitalism and the internationalization of economic life'.[3] When Soviet scholars deliberated upon the process of West European integration, they made a habit of referring to the 'so-called Common Market', or to a 'half Europe', generally putting these phrases in quotation marks, indicating that these institutions were ephemeral in nature and therefore were not to be taken all that seriously.[4]

The USSR also had several distinct *economic reasons* for not being too enthusiastic about the course of integration in Western Europe. The largest western trading partners of the Soviet Union and Eastern Europe were the Federal Republic of Germany, France and Italy. All three of these countries were now working together in the economic field within the setting of the ECSC (and later in the EEC). Although these three countries were not always in agreement on all issues of foreign trade, the Common Market did provide an institutional framework for closer collaboration. This would, for instance, mean that if the Common Market chose to raise its barriers to Eastern exports, this would limit East-West trade and cause a significant reduction of the Soviet and East European hard currency earnings.[5] Marshall Shulman has noted that the Common Market tariffs threaten 'the countries of eastern Europe with diminished trade, with serious shortages, with the loss of an intangible sense of contact with the West, and with enforced increase of dependence on the Soviet Union'.[6]

The development of a West European customs union and further positive integration among the Six (and later Nine), would also result in a marked weakening of the Soviet bargaining position *vis-à-vis* the West. For a long time, the centrally planned character of the Soviet-type economies has also had some beneficial consequences for the East. The State-trading countries were in general able to close their ranks, whereby their foreign trade monopolies could play several West European countries off against each other. This has especially been the case in the field of acquiring advantageous long-term export credits (see on this issue Chapter 5.3). Closer cooperation among the Six in the field of foreign economic policy was expected to nullify a large part of this advantage. The decision to adopt such a so-called 'Common Commercial Policy' for the Six was taken in the early-1960s, whereas such a consolidated approach could only be realized in the mid-1970s. The EC was then expected to conduct the foreign trade relations of its member states in order to prevent disrupting the smooth operation of the EC's Common Commercial Policy. The member states were also expected to harmonize their exports subsidies to non-members 'to the extent necessary to ensure that competition between enterprises within the Community shall not be distorted'.[7] It then became clear for the East European countries that they could no longer conclude trade agreements with individual EC countries; the European Community would (at least theoretically) function as the main negotiating partner on this issue. (See Chapter 5 for a more detailed discussion of the consequences of Brussels' Common Commercial Policy for Eastern Europe.)

Third, there were many *political reasons* for rebuffing the ECSC and the Common Market. Although Soviet spokesmen had more than once acknowledged the economic factors underlying West European integration – 'the objective tendency towards the internationalization of production', as it was called – they considered the EEC as directed against the USSR and the Communist world in general. As K. Petrov argued in 1969: 'This [West European] integration is seen as a means of mobilizing all economic, scientific, technological, military, political and ideological forces of the monopolist bourgeoisie in order to undermine the socialist camp, the labour movement and the struggle for national liberation.'[8] Although the establishment of a European Defence Community, which included close political cooperation, was nipped in the bud, Moscow clearly recognized that economic integration could spill over into closer political cooperation. In this respect, the Marxist-Leninist concept of economics comprising the building blocks for politics, neatly fitted the more Functionalist schemes and expectations of the founding fathers of the ECSC and the EEC.

West European economic cooperation was also considered a countermove to the decolonization process which was taking place almost simultaneously. In May 1956, France had already made its signature under the Treaty of Rome conditional upon the construction of special associative ties with its colonies in Africa (later resulting in the Convention of Yaoundé in 1963, after these territories attained independence). French overseas territories such as Senegal, Sudan, Guinea, Ivory Coast, Dahomey and Upper Volta, could as a result export to France duty-free; Paris was also their sole supplier of development aid. The special relationship of association with the whole EC was expected to maintain western, i.e. French political control in the Third World by other means, despite the strong current of independence in this part of the world. The thought of the construction of a so-called 'l'Eurafique' closely related to the Common Market was particularly disturbing for Moscow, especially since this would imply a considerable extension of western influence over the Third World.[9] It is beyond doubt that Moscow has been fully aware of the attractiveness for third (and especially Third World) countries of a prosperous West European bloc. By its refusal to recognize the Common Market and by downplaying its achievements, the USSR has tried to dissuade candidate members and associates from allying with Brussels.

Taking these three ingredients together, we can conclude that, from Moscow's perspective, close economic cooperation between the Six (or Nine) had to be repudiated for reasons of traditional *realpolitik*. Just as France has favoured the division of the German Empire (and the later German nation) into several independent states, the USSR has based its policy towards Europe on the maxim 'divide and rule'. As Hans J. Morgenthau has maintained: 'the Soviet Union from the twenties to the present has consistently opposed all plans for the unification of Europe, on the assumption that the pooling of the divided strength of the European nations into a "Western bloc" would give the enemies of the Soviet Union such power as to threaten the latter's security'.[10] For the same sort of reasons that western countries have opposed a more coherent Communist trading bloc, the Soviet Union could not be expected to applaud the successes of the ECSC and the EEC. The Treaty of Rome had shifted the balance of power to the advantage of Western Europe now that two traditional adversaries – France and (West) Germany – had agreed to step up their economic and political cooperation. Collaboration among the Six would decrease Moscow's room for manoeuvre. What was more, West European integration was also expected to pose a serious threat to the cohesiveness of the Soviet bloc, since successful economic cooperation would make trade with the EEC more attractive for Eastern Europe. The intensification of economic ties between Eastern and Western Europe would, in turn, weaken Soviet leverage over its satellites.

4.3 Moscow's apprehensions of 'German revanchism' and 'American Monopoly Capitalism'

But on top of the reasons we have just mentioned, there has been one other major political factor which has raised the Kremlin's aloofness *vis-à-vis* West European integration: Germany. It has always been difficult to judge how far Moscow has really been terrified of a resurgent German dominance in Europe. This has been especially difficult since Moscow has often used the spectre of a 'new' German hegemony in Europe as an effective propaganda instrument in order to slow down West European integration. Of course, both elements are not mutually exclusive and most probably both arguments have played a significant role in the Soviet policy towards the West.[11]

  Be that as it may, time and again Soviet commentators have argued that Bonn's *Westpolitik* was prompted by a desire to extend German influence in Europe. Looking at the rationale for constructing the ECSC, the EDC/EPC and even the EEC, it can not be denied that the Soviet apprehensions had some merit. The United States had used its economic leverage of Marshall Plan aid to solve the 'German problem' by integrating German economic and military power in a West European, anti-Communist framework. The efforts of Chancellor Adenauer and most French politicians to 'contain' Germany by anchoring it to West European institutions, had been a two-pronged strategy. Although West European integration would be unthinkable without an active role for West Germany, it should also be clearly acknowledged that German influence in the body of West European politics had increased over the years (and eventually resulted in the economic hegemony of that country within the Community).

Clearly aware of these 'dangers', the ensuing Soviet attacks on the FRG's policies were harsh. It was, for instance, claimed that 'the West German leaders ... need political integration to camouflage their revanchist and militarist plans and to gain automatic support of other West European countries. Loyalty to the supranationality principle is only a smokescreen concealing their nationalism and chauvinism',[12] and 'West Germany is striving more and more openly to control the economy and policies of other Common Market countries in order to adapt that community to the requirements of her *Ostpolitik* and make it to an economic basis of NATO, an appendage of the West German monopolies'.[13] Other efforts to further West European integration were condemned as a thinly veiled German attempt to take over Europe by other means.

A similar analysis was applied to the Atlantic Alliance. In general, West European relations with the United States were regarded as full of conflicts. Soviet analysts argued that Washington had encouraged West European integration after World War II in an effort to create a powerful economic, political and military front directed against Eastern Europe and the USSR. But – and here the 'capitalist contradictions' again came in – the United States soon realized that such a united Western Europe was becoming a severe threat to America's economic interests. Only a few years after the birth of the ECSC, a Soviet commentator labelled this new institution as an element in the 'chain of Europe's economic and political subordination to the aggressive plans of US monopoly capital'.[14] Some ten years later, another Soviet spokesman argued: 'The United States proclaims in words the need to unite Europe, but since such unification has turned against it, it is pursuing a policy of disuniting Europe, fanning contradictions between European states and encouraging the aggressive aspirations of the West German revanchists who threaten all European states without exception'.[15]

These widely diverging appraisals of the nature of the relations between Washington and Western Europe indicate that the Kremlin's perception of the United States' role in West European integration has been rather enigmatic and ambiguous. Was the ECSC (and the later EEC), nothing more than an extension of NATO and American capitalist interests? Or could it be that the process of economic and political integration in Europe was expanding the divisions in the western camp? Relations between the EEC and Great Britain seemed to affirm the latter hypothesis. French President de Gaulle presented himself as a staunch supporter of the EEC, which was one of the reasons why he had demanded a postponement of the British entry into the Common Market in 1967. At times, relations between the EEC and the United States have also been extremely agonizing and bitter. With the steady progress made within the EEC towards a customs union, Washington began to fear that the Common Market would become less accessible to American exports. The so-called 'Chicken War' between the United States and the EEC, in 1963, illustrated the possible detrimental consequences of further West European economic integration to American commercial interests. Washington had requested less Community protectionism on poultry, but the Commission did not budge. Finally, a GATT arbitration panel had to solve these economic quandaries, which had strained relations within the Atlantic Alliance. Soviet analysts could therefore use both arguments at will: when problems arose between the European Community and the United States, Moscow has always been the first to display its *schadenfreude*; when Brussels and Washington showed exceptional understanding, Moscow was there to warn for the inherent aggressive nature of a closed capitalist camp.

Over the decades, Moscow has changed its mind more than once as to the nature and the future of the Common Market experiment. Since the principle of national sovereignty was considered as sacrosanct by the Kremlin, it has had much difficulty coming to grips with the supranational tenet of the ECSC and the EEC. The rationale behind economic integration, with further political cooperation lying ahead, was therefore often not completely grasped by Soviet policy-makers and commentators. In the 1950s and 1960s, the USSR did everything within its means to frustrate the creation of a West European customs union, although the Soviet leaders began to recognize the Common Market as a so-called 'objective economic reality'; as a material economic process of the 'internationalization of industrial production'. However, from Moscow's perspective, the fact that the European Community restricted its membership to capitalist countries indicated that there were 'subjective political factors' in play. Soviet Prime Minister Aleksey N. Kosygin argued in 1967 that 'The very name Common Market is a drawback in that it is not "common" because not all countries are free to join. Markets of this kind should be open to cooperation of all the nations of Europe on an equal footing.'[16]

All in all, Moscow's changing attitude *vis-à-vis* the European Community can best be understood as a function of the West European success in accomplishing economic and political integration. Only when the USSR was confronted with a unitary position of the Six (or the Nine and later Twelve), was it willing to give way. Moscow's policy of 'divide and rule' would only be effective when West European nations failed to act collectively and failed to get their act together. In the period under discussion in this chapter, Moscow had plenty of opportunities to exploit the predicaments of West European integration.

4.4 The Seventeen and Thirty-Two Theses

As said, the Soviet response to West European integration has always been somewhat contradictory, forecasting a sudden collapse of the EEC, meanwhile acknowledging that the Common Market was economically successful.

In the early period of West European integration, several themes in Soviet thinking on the EEC can be identified. Prior to the Treaty of Rome, Moscow argued that the Common Market would be an American plot to dominate Europe; the EEC itself was considered unimportant. Around 1960, Soviet spokesmen began to stress the resurgent German threat, whereas the EEC was taken more seriously. In the early-1960s, the USSR campaigned against the entry of Great Britain into the EEC. And, after the German-French axis had been forged (in 1963), Moscow again began to emphasize the inevitable 'imperialist contradictions' playing havoc with the EEC.

Only a few days before the Six were to place their signatures under the Rome Treaty, Moscow sent several diplomatic notes to the six governments in order to dissuade them from signing the Treaty. The USSR tabled a proposal to create an organization for all-European economic cooperation under the auspices of the United Nations Economic Commission for Europe (ECE). In this proposal, put forward on 16 March 1957, the European Economic Community and Euratom were depicted as serious dangers for world peace and stability.[17] As had been the case with the Marshall Plan, the Brussels Treaty Organization and NATO, the EEC was portrayed as an instrument to split Europe and to complete the encirclement of the Communist bloc. Special reference was made to the 'economic imperialism' of the 'American monopolies', as well as to the 'revanchist tendencies' of German politicians and the dangers of German rearmament. In a statement to the press, on 16 March 1957, the USSR spokesman argued: 'The first thing that strikes the eye is that all those taking part in Euratom and the Common Market are members of the military NATO grouping. It is obvious that the activities of Euratom and the Common Market will be subjugated to NATO aims, the aggressive character of which is widely known. Under the circumstances the creation of Euratom and the Common Market would inevitably lead to the further widening of the rift in Europe, to an aggravation of tension in Europe, would complicate the establishment of economic and political co-operation on a European basis and give rise to fresh difficulties in the solution of the problem of European security'.[18] Soviet specialists also argued that Euratom was likely to be an American-controlled organization, since Washington would pay most of Euratom's expenses and would furnish the enriched uranium (Uran-235), the raw material necessary for generating atomic energy.

After the 20th CPSU Congress, a document was published by a newly-established foreign policy think-tank, the Institute of World Economy and International Relations (IMEMO), in which the formation of the EEC was clearly condemned. In these so-called 'Seventeen Theses Regarding the Common Market', it was, among others, argued that:

– the EEC was the economic foundation for NATO;
– the EEC was set up in order to exploit the working classes;
– the EEC was a veiled organization for German revanchism and militarism;

– the EEC was in fact a form of neo-colonialism; and
– the fact that Great Britain had refused to join the EEC had once again
  brought to the light the 'capitalist contradictions'.

The quite customary and very orthodox tenet of these theses indicated that the
USSR still had to come to grips with the continuing process of West European
economic integration. The ideological automatic pilot of Marxism-Leninism
was again activated in an effort to formulate an official response; but this was
not taken seriously in the West. Although Moscow vehemently opposed the
EEC, it was still convinced that it was of no great political importance, since,
as was argued, it was not 'a reality in an historical sense'. It must be noted that
Moscow's scepticism towards the EEC was not very surprising, taking into
account that the USSR had just successfully launched the *Sputnik*, the world's
first earth satellite. These dramatic Soviet achievements in space – topped off
with Yuri Gagarin's space flight on 18 April 1961 – seemed to prove the
superiority of the planned economies over capitalist chaos and strife.
Moreover, the Soviet growth rate was staggering and the western colonies
were gaining independence on a massive scale, which opened up opportunities
for Soviet activities in the Third World. The construction of the Common
Market, it was expected, could not alter the facts that 'history' was working
against it.
    In 1959, the IMEMO even 'honoured' the EEC by organizing a conference
on the economic and political developments taking place in Western
Europe.[19] Although limiting their analytical tools to those provided by the
well-known Marxist-Leninist paradigms, Soviet academics freely debated the
origins and future of the EEC experiment in the West. Two basic approaches
could be discerned: either the EEC phenomenon was best explained as the
basis of an imperialist struggle against socialism, whereby the EEC was
mainly considered a political pact; or the Common Market could be best
interpreted as an expression of monopolist capitalism on a world scale. In
both cases, of course, the integration efforts of the Six were castigated and
were viewed as a useless excursion into a dead-end street.
    Despite these Soviet apprehensions, several East European countries had
already adopted a much more realistic policy *vis-à-vis* the EEC. The Treaty of
Rome was signed in a period in which the Soviet bloc was in turmoil. The new
Soviet leader, Nikita Khrushchev, had attacked the personality cult of
Stalinism during his well-known 'secret speech' in 1956. The ensuing turmoil
in Eastern Europe, most notably in Poland and Hungary (see the previous
chapter), resulted in a temporary lack of Communist unity *vis-à-vis* the EEC.
This was especially visible in the Polish approach to the EEC. After the
attempts of Wladislaw Gomulka to forge a Polish road towards socialism,
Warsaw was too occupied with bringing its own house in order to spend much
time formulating a sharp rebuke against Brussels. Moreover, censorship was
still lax, and – perhaps most important – the Polish government was genuinely

interested in acquiring long-term credits from the West. As a result, West European integration was looked upon dispassionately and with relative lack of bias. It was a year later before the Soviet view began to predominate in Warsaw and the Polish media started to observe Moscow's line.

Although the Bulgarian Communist Party Secretary, Todor Zhivkov, maintained that the Common Market was a western instrument in the 'struggle against the socialist world-system',[20] other East European reactions to the EEC were at times surprisingly neutral. Romania had decided to step up its economic contacts with the EEC in an effort to resist the creeping integrative tendencies of the CMEA,[21] whereas the German Democratic Republic sought to establish trade relations with the West in order to obtain official recognition (thereby repudiating the West German Hallstein doctrine). Despite these efforts to use trade links with the EEC for particular national objectives, East European freedom in the field of foreign policy was limited. This East European *rapprochement* has nevertheless been interpreted as their *de facto* recognition of the EEC. During that period, a number of long-term trade agreements with several EEC member states were concluded in an effort to step up East-West trade. This was certainly successful, since trade between the Common Market and Eastern Europe almost tripled in the period from 1958 to 1967 (see Table 4.1).

After the Common Market had been in existence for a few years and had stimulated economic growth among its member states, Soviet reactions became even more ambivalent: acknowledging the EEC's initial successes, meanwhile also claiming its inferiority *vis-à-vis* the CMEA. The Soviet propaganda machine was therefore working at full speed in order to convince West European citizens that the Common Market was detrimental to their interests. The Communist World Federation of Trade Unions made several agitated attempts to launch a wave of labour strikes in Western Europe directed against the EEC; but to no avail. Most West European workers seemed all too pleased with their rising wages and the new jobs resulting from the Common Market arrangements. Soviet diplomacy was especially working overtime within several international organizations, especially the ECE (see also Chapter 7.2), where numerous, sometimes rather fantastic, plans were brought forward in an effort to hamper and slow down the West European integration process.

Since the USSR had to acknowledge that its alternatives to the EEC did not take root, Moscow now sought to limit the scope of the EEC to its current Six. Keeping Great Britain, Austria, Sweden, Norway, Denmark and the newly independent countries of Africa out of the EEC-realm – which had opened up the opportunity of so-called association agreements (Article 238 of the Treaty of Rome)[22] – stood at the basis of Soviet diplomatic activities in the early-1960s. The association agreements with several former colonies had made Moscow wary of an even further extension of the scope of the Community's economic power. It was argued that such agreements only

Table 4.1 Total EC trade with Eastern Europe (million ECU)

	1958	1960	1965	1970	1975
USSR					
Exports	386	604	563	1,415	5,064
Imports	477	706	1,066	1,554	4,064
GDR*					
Exports	57	95	177	219	494
Imports	61	91	166	230	519
Poland					
Exports	197	209	315	604	2,745
Imports	229	278	438	689	1,733
Czechoslovakia					
Exports	136	178	283	565	1,068
Imports	143	184	281	478	874
Hungary					
Exports	72	134	195	416	980
Imports	70	103	198	372	713
Romania					
Exports	56	105	256	500	1,105
Imports	72	111	224	462	989
Bulgaria					
Exports	30	63	152	231	689
Imports	33	50	127	191	222
Total smaller CMEA*					
Exports	550	788	1,387	2,550	7,118
Imports	609	818	1,436	2,430	5,076

*Excluding internal German trade.

Source: Eurostat

reaffirmed 'the associated countries as raw material suppliers to the E.E.C. countries and opened the African markets for the latter's manufactures. The policy of the Common Market is a factor tending towards preservation of the colonial economic structure for other developing countries as well.'[23] In order to pre-empt these developments, the Soviet Union proposed, in 1962, to set up a world-wide trading organization without any discriminatory groupings. Such an organization would be open to all developing countries and was thereby expected to water down the EEC's influence in Africa. Similar pressures from the South for changes in the structure and operation of the system of international trade eventually resulted in the United Nations Conference on Trade and Development (UNCTAD), which convened for the first time in 1964. Although the UNCTAD did indeed prompt closer cooperation among many former colonies, it has never been a powerful force in the Third World's call to put trade relations with the EEC member states on an equal footing.

'It is difficult to describe the wave of confidence felt in most Western capitals about the progress of integration during the latter half of 1962. The Russians were also aware of it and the full significance of the trend it forbode.'[24] In response to these developments, the USSR Academy of Sciences published another set of theses – thirty-two, this time – under the title 'Concerning Imperialist "Integration" in Western Europe ("The Common Market")'. This paper, disclosed on 26 August 1962, primarily dwelled upon the malevolent nature of the EEC. The further drive towards economic integration in the West was this time also interpreted as the response of the capitalist monopolies to the increased strength of world socialism. Only one day later, Khrushchev published an article in the most important official theoretical journal of the Communist Party, *Kommunist*, calling for structural reforms of the CMEA. The article maintained that

> The world socialist system, it should be said, can forge ahead only through the all-round co-operation of the countries belonging to it, through their co-ordinated effort, bearing in mind the interest of each country and the socialist community as a whole. There is no other way ... After the Second World War the trend towards integrating the foreign policy and the economies of the capitalist countries became more pronounced. We saw the rise of international organizations such as the European Coal and Steel Community, the Common Market, the Organization for Economic Co-operation and others. The rulers of the western world, notwithstanding all their antagonisms, have partly succeeded in forming inter-state alliances.

In response to these developments in the West, Khrushchev argued in favour of stepping up socialist integration: 'Co-ordinating the national-economic plans together with co-ordinated and specialized production will help to bring the economies of the socialist countries closer together and will add to our common economic potential'.[25]

Despite all negative remarks about cooperation within the Common Market, Khrushchev acknowledged the considerable benefits of further *Communist* economic and political integration. This change in the Soviet attitude towards the basic principles upon which the EEC was based can be traced back to several motives. From Moscow's perspective, West European integration had proven surprisingly successful. The earliest phase of the transition towards a free internal market had been reached one year ahead of schedule (1 January 1962). Moreover, the process of association with several African states went according to plan, whereby a specially established European Development Fund administered West European aid to these former colonies. In July 1963, the Yaoundé Convention (dealing with trade, technical and financial cooperation, service and capital movement) formalized these ties. As a result, the international standing of the EEC had increased notably. In Eastern Europe the recognition of the EEC's accomplishments followed similar lines. As the Czechoslovak Professor Vladislav Pavidt acknowledged: 'Most economists were not interested in the phenomenon of [West European] integration, because they considered it political in nature, and no economic problem ... [But] in 1962, a research centre for integration problems was set up at the Economics Department in Prague ... At the Institute for International Politics and Economy in Prague, the first academic conference on the problems of West European integration was held.'[26] West European economic integration was now a subject of serious study.

4.5 Late *rapprochement*

This realistic assessment of the new status of the European Economic Community also had its consequences for the political organization of the Communist world. As David Forte had remarked in 1968: 'Practically speaking, this meant a policy of uniting the Eastern bloc countries to prevent any further attraction the Common Market had upon them, and it also meant that the USSR was ready to recognize the relative permanency of the Common Market'.[27] Peter Marsh has also argued that 'the new approach to the EEC was designed more for fulfilling Soviet purposes in the CMEA and persuading the Eastern European states of the benefits of closer integration'.[28]

Of course, the East and West European brands of integration were markedly different. Socialist cooperation (*sotrudnichestvo*) was clearly distinct from western 'integration' (*integratsiya*). The former was to be based on the coordination of economic plans and collaboration within an intergovernmental framework, whereas the latter had to rely upon the fluctuating and 'anarchic' market forces. Nevertheless, a first basis of implicit recognition of the EEC had been laid. The belief that the capitalist contradictions were insurmountable was discarded. As a result, the Communist trade unions in the West were now called upon to work *with*, instead of *against* the EEC.[29] Some observers have argued that this Soviet change of heart was, at least partly, prompted by political pressures from the Italian Communist Party (PCI). The PCI, as well as several other West European Communist Parties, had acknowledged that the Common Market had yielded beneficial results for their national economies;[30] it was difficult for Moscow to ignore these facts.

Khrushchev's 'new look' towards the EEC provided extended East European leeway to develop ties with the Common Market. Without delay, both Poland and Hungary took the initiative of sending economic attachés to Brussels in order to start semi-secret negotiations with Community officials. Since November 1964, Poland had maintained 'unofficial contacts' with the EEC through high-level officials at the Brussels' embassy. Warsaw's interest in closer economic contact with the West was already exemplified by its application for GATT-membership, in 1959. Several meetings of economic experts took place, where most time was devoted to arguments over the Community's quota system for specific goods, its customs and its barriers for agricultural products. These negotiations eventually resulted in several agreements (the so-called 'agricultural arrangements') between the European Commission and a specific East European State-trading agency. The EEC generally agreed not to apply supplementary levies on the imports of a range of products, while an East European country guaranteed not to export at prices below the Community sluice-gate price.[31] These arrangements started with the exemption of Polish eggs, poultry and pig-meat from EEC levies (which were over time 'ratified' by an exchange of letters), but later covered a wider range of products in similar arrangements between the EEC and Bulgaria, Czechoslovakia, Hungary and Romania.

Prague and Budapest established 'unofficial contacts' with the Commission in 1968. Their positive attitude towards the EEC was witnessed by the objective fashion in which the Czechoslovak and Hungarian press usually reported about Common Market issues. The EEC was depicted less as an imperialist plot than as an economic reality to be dealt with on an unbiased, day-to-day basis. Even orthodox Bulgaria later followed the new course of *rapprochement* triggered by its Communist neighbours. Only Romania was a case apart. As Charles Ransom has argued: 'The Rumanian attitude is more complex in that the EEC is held to embody the principle of supranationalism which Rumania utterly rejects as a model for Eastern Europe.'[32] Acknowledging the success of the West European integration efforts would weaken their stance against similar integrationist forces within the CMEA. This did not, however, prevent Bucharest from conducting similar 'unofficial negotiations' with Brussels.

As a result of this increase in contacts, East European charges against the Common Market shifted from ideological criticism to down-to-earth complaints about economic discrimination. These grievances were entirely understandable and even to a large extent justifiable. The EEC tariffs for agricultural products and several industrial products were high. Especially the so-called Common Agricultural Policy (CAP) of the EEC put a brake on the further development of East-West commercial relations. The EEC internal customs reductions of 1962 first brought home the point that successful West European economic integration could be detrimental to East European commercial interests. A Hungarian economic journal had figured that 'The customs discrimination means a loss of 80 million forints in foreign exchanges'.[33] These developments have played an instrumental part in the Communist attitude towards the EEC. Ignoring Brussels was no longer a viable option.

But Soviet recognition of the Common Market was clearly not yet on the cards. In September 1963, Brussels had offered the Soviets several tariff concessions (among others on vodka, caviar and crab-meat, which explains

why they were sometimes informally referred to as the '*dolce vita* concessions'). Quite remarkably, this offer has never been answered by the Soviet
Union.[34] We have already seen that from the very start, not granting official
recognition of the ECSC and the EEC has been one of the Soviet tactics to
thwart West European integration. Moscow's policy was, however, in most
cases counter-productive. Since most East European countries increasingly
favoured a more 'objective attitude towards the EEC' – which implied *de jure*
recognition of Brussels' authority – Moscow's obstinacy in neglecting
Brussels increased the political tensions within the Soviet bloc. This had
everything to do with the fact that East European economic interests in trade
with the EEC, in comparison to the USSR, were considerable. Moreover, for
Moscow the *economic* necessity of recognizing the EEC was lacking since
most Soviet exports to the West were not subject to tariffs or quotas.

But there were also *political* obstacles on the *western* side which hampered
East-West economic *rapprochement*. In the Spring of 1965, Yugoslavia and
the EEC began negotiations over an economic and trade agreement. This was
considered a quite remarkable event, since up to then Belgrade had always
followed Moscow's line and rejected the Common Market as an economic
'bloc' which was maintaining the East-West divide. However, as an 'independent' country, not belonging to either the CMEA (Belgrade only had observer
status) or the EEC, Yugoslavia found itself unluckily exposed to trade
discrimination from both the East *and* the West. This unfortunate and
unfavourable economic position provided the economic rationale for a
rapprochement to Brussels, as well as the political leeway to do so. Besides the
obvious commercial reasons, Belgrade also had political reasons to come to
terms with the EEC. The Yaoundé Convention of 1963 had extended
Brussels' influence in Africa, which was expected to jeopardize the formal
neutrality of several non-aligned countries. Tito's hopes of organizing these
non-aligned countries into a powerful force in world politics – with, of
course, Belgrade at the helm – made him suspicious of the EEC's actions in
this region of the world.[35] Be that as it may, Community policy-makers
recognized the political importance of Belgrade's willingness to negotiate
with the EEC. Tito's acquiescent approach towards Brussels was expected to
set an important precedent for Eastern Europe at large. However, this time
the political and ideological obstacles proved to be on the side of the West,
since West German officials were still prone to apply the Hallstein doctrine.
Belgrade had recognized the German Democratic Republic and thereby fell
under Hallstein's spell.[36] Bonn therefore insisted that the EEC Commission
would only negotiate with Yugoslavia on a 'technical' level and not on the
usual diplomatic level.[37] Partly because of the short-sighted West German
attitude towards Belgrade, negotiations on a trade agreement lasted several
years and were only concluded towards the end of the 1960s.[38]

With the introduction of a new and more flexible *Ostpolitik* by Bonn's new
Grand Coalition Government – which took up office in late 1966 – the EEC's

hands in its policy towards the East were untied. In 1967, negotiations were again resumed, and in February 1968 Yugoslavia was the first Communist country to recognize the Common Market and to apply for a diplomatic mission with the European Community. Belgrade had stressed the fact that the rationale for its ties with Brussels was to evade the EEC's network of tariffs and quotas. It is likely that the Yugoslav example has cleared the way for other East European countries to develop their relations with the Community. It could hardly be a coincidence that from 1968 onwards, Eastern Europe has actively sought closer contact with Brussels. Another part of the explanation of the Communist *rapprochement* was, perhaps somewhat paradoxically, that Moscow still regarded the EEC as a rather insignificant and at least not yet mature actor on the West European political stage. Indeed, in the second half of the 1960s, Common Market politics had been pestered with one crisis after the other. After the initial failure of the EDC/EPC Treaty in the 1950s and the demise of the ambitious Fouchet Plan in the early-1960s, major problems arose in 1965 over the establishment of a Community regime regulating agriculture (the CAP). Among the central issues were the financing of the CAP and the institutional arrangements (especially the commitment for progressively more majority voting in the EEC Council). De Gaulle rejected the strengthening of the EEC institutions proposed by the European Commission, and refused to participate in the EEC Council. For several months, the French seat in the Council remained empty. In January 1966, the so-called 'Luxembourg compromise' was reached, which in reality was an 'agreement to disagree'. The French maintained that in very important questions ('vital matters'), the provisions of the Treaty on qualified majority voting should not be applied in practice. This led to rigid intergovernmental-ism and put a significant brake on the dynamics of the Community spirit.

These major conflicts within the EEC were accompanied by a crisis within the NATO Alliance, when General de Gaulle decided to withdraw from NATO's integrated command structure in an effort to maintain full control over the French military. In the light of these 'capitalist contradictions', Soviet leaders apparently assumed that somewhat closer relations between Brussels and Eastern Europe could do little harm to Communist bloc unity. The 'rotten' state of affairs inside the Common Market was clarified in the colourful picture of Community matters by a commentator of *Pravda*, early in 1968: 'Some people in the West today regard Brussels as the capital of half-Europe. The pseudo-government set up there in July, 1967, is modestly called the "Commission of European Communities" ... On the top of a building on Joyous Entrance (Joyeuse Entreé) Street 14 commissars are meeting, on the instructions of their governments, in an attempt to analyze the not so joyous state of affairs they inherited from the three separate leviathans of half-Europe; the 'rotten' dossier of Euratom ...; the depressing matter of the declining six-member European Coal and Steel Community; and finally, the not very inspiring dealings of the "Common Market" of those same six countries, which are riddled with discord, jealousy and suspicions.'[39] To deal with such an awkward, seemingly uncoordinated organization in order to gain some commercial advantages could hardly be considered as politically or ideologically risky.

4.6 Keep Britain out!

Keeping Great Britain out of the Common Market has been one of the key goals of Moscow's policy *vis-à-vis* Western Europe. London's isolation from the EEC formed the basis for the Soviet policy of 'divide and rule'. The United Kingdom had set up the ·European Free Trade Association (EFTA) in November 1959, comprising Austria, Denmark, Great Britain, Norway, Portugal, Sweden and Switzerland (Iceland joined in 1970, and Finland later became 'associated member'). The EFTAns were reluctant to go beyond economic cooperation in a free-trade zone; economic integration, let alone political integration, were forbidden ground for 'the Seven'.

Moscow recognized that the accession of Britain to the EEC would undoubtedly imply the entry of other EFTAns, but also other countries with a distinct Atlantic disposition, like Denmark and Ireland. What was more, the existence of two West European regional economic organizations – the EEC, or 'Little Europe' on the one hand, and EFTA on the other – conveniently fitted into Moscow's world-view of 'imperialist contradictions'. In the Summer of 1961, however, the British Government announced that it was keen to start negotiations on entry to the EEC.[40] Successful negotiations of Britain's admittance (which started in the Autumn of 1962), would have confronted the USSR with a centre of power economically far superior to the CMEA.

In response, Moscow opened a virulent diplomatic and media propaganda spectacle against London's entry. Britain was depicted as the 'Trojan horse of American imperialism', implying that London's EEC membership would strengthen Washington's political influence and would facilitate American commercial access to the Community market. The 1962 IMEMO report (containing the 32 theses) should also be seen in the light of the more assertive external role which the EEC was beginning to play in the early-1960s. The Yaoundé Convention was in the making and the EEC's first reductions of internal customs had provided Brussels with a greater lever in its external commercial affairs. The IMEMO report argued that: 'In Great Britain the making ready for entry into the EEC signalled the strengthening of the policy of freezing wages, raising indirect taxes on mass-consumed goods and cutting down on social service spending'.[41] The same report also maintained that 'Britain is economically strong enough to keep up the struggle and remain outside the "Common Market". However, the line taken by the ruling circles in this question is first and foremost determined by political motives, that is fear about the weakening of NATO.'[42] In short, London was strongly advised not to enter this 'anti-socialist coalition', which would make Moscow's heralded 'Pan-European' cooperation schemes less feasible.

Moscow's apprehensions about the United Kingdom's strong Atlantic ties were shared by de Gaulle, who feared that Britain's entry would diminish Western Europe's political 'independence' by tying it closer to Washington. De Gaulle maintained that 'England is, in effect, insular, maritime, linked through trade, markets and food supply to very diverse and often very distant countries ... This is obviously incompatible with the system the Six have quite naturally set up for themselves.' The extension of the EEC to Britain would also result in an '11-member, then 13-member and then perhaps 18-member Common Market that would be built which would, without any doubt, hardly resemble the one the Six have built. Moreover, this Community, growing in that way, would be confronted with all the problems of its economic relations with a crowd of other States, and first of all with the United States.'[43]

For the USSR, President de Gaulle's veto of the British application to the Common Market, on 14 January 1963, was a gift right out of heaven. Although Soviet propaganda had hardly influenced de Gaulle's decision, Moscow could nevertheless boast a significant success in its *Westpolitik*. The friction within the EEC and NATO which was still to follow, only reinforced the Soviet conviction that capitalist cooperation was beginning to crumble. This, in turn, influenced Moscow's subsequent attitude *vis-à-vis* the Community. The more realistic assessment of the nature and the accomplishments of the EEC which were stated in Khrushchev's article in *Kommunist* only one year earlier, were again abandoned. The Anglo-French controversy seemed to prove the weakness of the EEC-framework, and, as one Soviet commentator remarked: 'The fiasco in Brussels cannot remain without its consequences for the various blocs that connect the Western powers. The complete knot of contradictions – the hegemonic role of the USA and the role of its partners in NATO, the pandemonium over nuclear weapons – will be tied even further.'[44] The impending frictions within the EEC and NATO seemed to prove their point.

The Soviet Union's efforts to intimidate potential new EEC member states has never ceased. Moscow became especially strident after the Labour Government of Harold Wilson put forward Great Britain's renewed application to the EEC in July 1967.[45] The crisis of 1965 had moderated the Common Market's supranational aspirations, which made entry even more appealing from London's perspective. In November 1967, de Gaulle issued his second veto, but this time further negotiations were not halted. Soviet commentators aired their usual explanations for Britain's interests in 'bridging the channel': 'to make it easier for British monopolies to penetrate the market of the "Six", with its 190,000,000 consumers, and to broaden the sphere of financial operations of the City of London'.[46] The Soviet media frequently published all sorts of negative accounts of the possible effects of London's accession to the EC, which would limit its political sovereignty and be counter-productive to the welfare of Great Britain's working class.

In 1969, prospects for West European union brightened up after a change of office in both France and West Germany. Georges Pompidou was less suspicious of Great Britain's foreign policies which facilitated negotiations over London's entry into the Common Market. During the The Hague Meeting of the six Heads of Government, in December 1969, a decision in principle on the necessity of enlargement was achieved. In The Hague, plans were made for the further development of an Economic and Monetary Union (EMU), as well as closer political cooperation. Remaining obstacles concerning agriculture and the British Commonwealth were eventually resolved. In 1971, publications in serious Soviet academic journals again argued against Britain's entry in the EEC. N. Yuryev clarified that London's membership of the Community would 'lead to a drop in the country's living standards by 3.5 per cent. Britain's adoption of the common agricultural policy would result in additional costs of 400 million pounds a year ... An enlargement of the Common Market would harm the neutrality of Sweden, Switzerland and Finland, and would also complicate commercial relations between Britain and the socialist countries.'[47] Moscow's theoreticians stressed the fact that Britain's entry would hot up the atmosphere within the enlarged Common Market. This, one would expect, should have made Moscow rejoice; but on the contrary, it did not. In 1973 not only the United Kingdom, but also Ireland and Denmark joined the Common Market, despite Soviet apprehensions. All in all, Moscow's voice in this first enlargement debate had been unimportant.

A wide range of arguments was aired in order to discourage other possible EEC members. In March 1971, *Izvestia* argued that 'If Austria joined the "Common Market", the F.R.G. – economically the most powerful country in the European Economic Community – would undoubtedly penetrate the Austrian economy still more deeply and take over the more important positions there ... It would be called a new *Anschluß* – a term universally understood.'[48] The interest of several Scandinavian countries for the EEC was considered as an endeavour of NATO to strengthen its northern flank, which would threaten the neutrality of Sweden and Finland. For Austria and Finland, Moscow's apprehensions have been central to their decision not to enter into negotiations aiming at full membership of the Community. For other West European countries on which the USSR could not wield any leverage, Moscow's role has been negligible.

4.7 The EEC and East European integration

In the previous chapter we have already referred to Shulman's concept of 'integration by induction', which implied that West European integration efforts could have encouraged similar processes in the East. In this respect, Peter Marsh has argued: 'it was in response to the disunity within its regional system demonstrated by the Czechoslovakian crisis, that the Soviet Union renewed its interest in the revival of Comecon as an effective means of alliance management'.[49] Indeed, in response to the successes of West European economic integration, both the Soviet Union and several East European countries have pressed for further economic cooperation within CMEA.[50] Communist Party officials have repeatedly proclaimed the superiority of 'socialist' over 'capitalist integration'. Although there was little reason to be optimistic about cooperation between the Soviet-type economies, it was nevertheless argued that only centrally planned economies would be able to construct wise and well-balanced blueprints. As Hannes Adomeit has noted, socialist integration was expected to emphasize 'the potentially bright *future* as against the sorry present state of affairs and, for the rest, makes the most of the *moral* argument ("their" integration at the moment may work better, but "ours" is more legitimate and just)'.[51]

This 'integration by induction'-mechanism, if it can be called that way, was not new. In the early-1960s, Khrushchev had already argued that the CMEA should respond to West European integration efforts with developing a more comprehensive institutional structure, which should result in joint planning among the member states.[52] It is, however, important to note that the arguments of the proponents of Communist integration have differed considerably. The Kremlin first of all backed CMEA integration in order to strengthen its hold over its satellites. Moscow simultaneously worked for *détente* between East and West in an effort to gain access to western high-technology and export credits. Increasing socialist integration was expected to go a long way in achieving both goals: a stronger CMEA was supposed to boost Moscow's bargaining position *vis-à-vis* the EEC, meanwhile controlling the political risks involved with the ensuing closer contacts between Eastern Europe and the West.

Poland and Hungary also drew important lessons from the successful experiences of the EEC. As a result, they became more favourably disposed towards CMEA integration which partly served as a kind of alibi for closer cooperation with the EEC. Early in 1968, the Hungarian Prime Minister, Jenö Fock, argued that 'The Common Market is a fact and we, who are always realists, have to acknowledge its existence ... If our trade relations required us to call on some of the Brussels offices of the Common Market, we would not consider this step as a renunciation of our principles. It is quite obvious that we should take advantage of this possibility, too, if this proves to benefit our country.'[53] In order to encourage Communist economic integration, the USSR called a meeting of the CMEA Executive Committee in January 1969. The Soviet leaders went so far as to introduce plans for creating supranational planning organs. The Polish leader, Wladislaw Gomulka, favoured the construction of a genuine Communist 'common market', which should also include political integration.[54] Other East Europeans, however, ardently refused to participate in a framework in which Soviet influence was expected to increase.[55] The Soviet plans were therefore shelved.

In July 1971, the so-called 'Comprehensive Programme' of the CMEA was agreed upon by the member states.[56] Bucharest was among the most fervent opponents of Moscow's attempts to achieve integration by supranational or joint planning. The Romanian Communist Party leader Nicolae Ceauşescu, had declared that he did 'not favor integration and had no wish to take part in supranational bodies'.[57] As a result, the principles of the CMEA Charter of 1960 were again repeated, maintaining that the CMEA was 'primarily an inter-governmental system of co-operation between sovereign states, that national planning is the responsibility of the national state and that supranational institutions are unacceptable'.[58] However, Moscow had achieved its main aims: bloc unity was preserved and the USSR could claim the legitimacy of bargaining on behalf of all the Communist countries. Although this latter claim lacked a formal and legal basis, it was of special importance since the Soviet Union was poised to counteract the EEC's so-called Common Commercial Policy *vis-à-vis* the State-trading countries (see Chapter 5). After the end of the transition period in 1970, Brussels had the exclusive right to negotiate trade agreements in the place of its member states, a development which spurred the 'integration by induction' process in the East. However, East European reluctance to accept the principle of supranationality within the CMEA, made Moscow's efforts less fruitful.

Since the late-1960s, Soviet policy-makers and commentators underscored the protectionist nature of the Common Market. In particular, the CAP was considered detrimental to the development of East-West trade. In order to dissolve the bloc-structure of European politics and economics, Moscow put a number of far-reaching plans on the table for what it labelled 'Pan-European economic cooperation'. These schemes would – almost by definition – include all European countries (including the USSR), but they would keep the United States and Canada out. In 1970, Yuri Shukov argued that only such a Pan-European solution would increase East-West trade and foster *détente*. The basic tenet of these Soviet proposals date back to the 1950s, when the USSR argued for 'non-discriminatory' trade agreements. West European political observers acknowledged that these new Soviet proposals had the very same objective: hampering integration within the European Community. In March 1972, Soviet leader Leonid Brezhnev repeated the argument that Soviet 'proposals for a Conference and our overall European policy aim to undermine the European Community', were 'silly ... The Soviet Union by no means ignores the existing situation in Western Europe, including the existence of an economic grouping of capitalist countries such as the "Common Market". We are carefully observing the activity of the "Common Market" and its evolutions. Our relations with the participants of this grouping will, needless to say, depend on the extent to which they recognize the interests of the members states for the Council for Mutual Economic Assistance.'[59] Moscow's proposals for economic cooperation eventually culminated in the CSCE Accords which were signed in Helsinki, in 1975. This initiative to frustrate West European integration had thereby clearly failed. (For a further discussion of the issue of the EC and the CSCE, see Chapter 6.4.)

This brings us to one final relationship between the EEC and East European integration. One of the major consequences of West European integration has been the resurgence of West German economic and political power. This boost of German power in the West has been one of the reasons for the Communist countries to get their act together. Until 1969-70, Moscow frequently beat the 'German revanchist' drum, whereby it was time and again argued that Bonn's *Ostpolitik* was a thinly disguised *Drang nach Osten*. Every move of the European Community in a similar direction was interpreted in the same light. After the Soviet-German Treaty of Non-Aggression was signed in Moscow on 12 August 1970 (which declared that 'The Federal Republic of Germany and the Union of Soviet Socialist Republics consider it an important objective of their policies to maintain international peace and achieve détente' [Article 1]), Soviet criticism of West European economic integration changed in tone and content. With the conclusion of the so-called *Grundvertrag* between the FRG and the GDR, the post-war *status quo* was at last officially recognized and the allegations of the 'Fascist tendencies' in German foreign policy were somewhat played down within the Soviet press.

In conclusion we can say that the European Community has influenced development within the CMEA in two different, be it closely related, ways. First, West European integration has been an *example* of how economic growth could be achieved through economic cooperation. It showed that autarky and economic nationalism were inferior to the coordination of national policies in a market environment. The decline in economic growth in the Communist countries brought home this point quite convincingly, although it would take more than one decade for the Soviet leadership to act upon these 'objective facts'. Second, the European Community has functioned as an *economic magnet*. The Common Market constituted an attractive trading partner, although the Common Commercial Policy (laid down in Article 113 of the Treaty of Rome) has confronted the East European with one 'economic bloc'. The change of the Soviet attitude towards the Community (which occurred in 1973; see the next chapter), was the result of the Kremlin's designs to increase the flows of East-West trade and technology transfer. Moscow could not apply its policy of 'divide and rule' as before, now that Brussels had initiated its Common Commercial Policy and several other major West European economies had decided to join the Common Market.

5. The EC's Common Commercial Policy

Economic relations with Eastern Europe have been one issue on which the co-ordination of policy within the EEC has proven to be unusually difficult, but the difficulties have arisen more from problems of internal co-ordination than from Soviet policies.

Charles Ransom, in Peter Stingelin (ed.), *The European Community and the Outsiders* (Don Mills, Ontario: Longman Canada Ltd., 1973), p.146.

5.1 Introduction

Starting with the integration of the coal and steel markets of the Six, the ECSC and the EEC have constructed laws, rules and procedures which have provided the basis on which a collective commercial policy *vis-à-vis* the outside world could be forged. Articles 110 to 116 of the Treaty of Rome set out the final goal of a common trade policy of the Community's member states conducted by Brussels. The Treaty also envisaged an initial transitional period of some twelve years in which, from phase to phase, the tasks of the Community would expand, and qualified majority voting in the Council of Ministers on proposals by the European Commission would become the regular decision-making procedure.

From the very beginning, it was clearly acknowledged that harmony on trade issues could not be achieved within a few years time. Although the original Spaak Report had called for the automatic advance from one stage to the other, France had immediately persisted in a more gradual and more cautious course in which the member states would still be able to postpone the first phase in the integration process. In order to allow the member states sufficient time to adapt themselves to these new circumstances and their new obligations, a general transitional period was proclaimed which was supposed to end on 31 December 1969. During these years, it was assumed that the EEC members would iron out the differences in their foreign trade policies towards third countries. This would imply that – in parallel with the establishment of the common external tariffs – many aspects of external policy (such as the negotiation of trade agreements, export promotion measures, the management of quantitative import controls as well as export credit policy), would fall within the sole competence of the Community. However, several member states were not ready to shift these foreign economic policy-making powers to Brussels at that specific time. As a result some characteristics of the transitory period were extended for another three years (until 1973), but under central Community supervision and only in the relations with the State-trading countries.

Since trade policy constitutes an important aspect of overall foreign policy, most member states have been reluctant to hand over this particular element of their national sovereignty to Brussels. This has been an issue of special relevance in the case of the European Community's relations with the Communist countries of Europe. Since East-West commerce has for long been one of the few channels of direct bilateral negotiations between East and West, it has always been used in order to further the specific national interests of the member states.[1] The Six have never cherished parallel political objectives in their policies towards the State-trading countries and in many instances the EEC member states' economic interests in the East have widely diverged and sometimes even openly collided (see Chapter 6.3). As was to be expected, the transfer of this particular niche of foreign policy to the competence of the European Community has been an excruciating task for most member states, especially for those with specific goals in the East, be they political or economic.

In this chapter we will present an analytical overview of the commercial relations between the EEC and the CMEA and their member states, covering the period of 1957 to the late-1970s. The EEC's external trade regime has been based upon two principles: the Common Customs Tariff (CCT) and the Common Commercial Policy (CCP). The CCT is a code of law which was adopted in 1960 (based upon Articles 18-29 of the Treaty of Rome); the CCP (together with the Balance of Payments provisions and the Conjunctural Policy) forms part of the Community Economic Policy.[2] Here we will especially consider the European Community's Common Commercial Policy and the ensuing 'autonomous trade policy' towards the East. We will see that despite the final goal of a common foreign trade policy of the EEC, as laid down in the Treaty of Rome, the member states have successfully retained control over large parts of their commercial ties with the East. The ways in which they have circumvented the EEC's efforts to forge a consolidated trade approach among the Six (and later Nine/Twelve) once again indicates their initial opposition to supranational policy-making in realms where basic national interest are at stake. Nevertheless, during the 1970s, major inroads have been made in strengthening Brussels' hand in the coordination of the member states' foreign trade policies.

5.2 A major step towards positive integration?

We have already referred to the basic differences between policies of negative and policies of positive integration. Negative integration is mainly concerned with issues like liberalization of the internal market, competition policy or legal harmonization, whereas positive integration deals with the adoption of common policies which generally require basic agreement on political goals. The latter form of integration is usually more precarious since it also has to deal with politically sensitive issues of resource reallocation and distribution among the EEC member states. Since the costs and benefits of the many common policies devised by Brussels are unevenly divided among the member states, the process of positive integration has to overcome huge political dilemmas and conflicts. This has also been the case with the forging of the EEC's Common Commercial Policy. Although the policy lines set forth by the European Commission have in most cases been satisfactory for the major member states (e.g. on GATT issues and Lomé), policy *vis-à-vis* Eastern Europe proved to be markedly more difficult, and many a member state either ignored or circumvented Brussels' decisions.

Nevertheless, the fact that the EEC had been able to initiate its Common Commercial Policy in the first place has been seen as a major step forward in the process of positive integration within the Common Market, and an indispensable undertaking to enter a qualitatively higher stage of economic union. According to the expectations of several ardent EEC-watchers, positive integration in the field of commercial policy would also spill over into the field of foreign policy. Ernst Haas, for instance, has argued that this might even result in a European *political* community as early as the mid-1970s.[3] Haas has characterized this spill-over from positive economic integration as a spontaneous process in which some level of supranationality in one particular policy sector would infect other sectors. Haas took up the Functionalist tenet that under the present international circumstances, governments have no other choice but to work together. Under the pressure of previous decisions new sectors have to be included into the EEC's integration process: 'Lack of agreement among governments can give rise to increased delegated powers on the part of these [supranational] institutions. Dissatisfaction with the results of the partial economic steps may lead labor and industry to demand new central action. Supranational institutions and national groups may create situations which can be dealt with only through central action, unless the nations are willing to suffer deprivations in welfare ... No statesman, even if he deeply dislikes the process, can permanently isolate his nation from a commitment to unity which is only partially implemented, unless he is willing to pay the price in diminished welfare',[4] Haas argued. In short, the political and economic expectations of many observers were set high. We will see that these hopes were rather inflated.

During the debate on the Spaak Report, in the mid-1950s, it had been decided by the Six that the construction of a modest free trade association would not be sufficient; a fully fledged customs union was preferred. A free trade zone would still require extensive internal border controls without providing a common trade policy *vis-à-vis* the outside world. For political reasons such a scheme was considered too loosely structured: it would probably be insufficient both to contain German economic and military power and insufficient to counterbalance the Soviet threat. In other words, negative integration was deemed inadequate for both economic *and* political reasons. A customs union, on the other hand, would not only eliminate tariffs among its members, it would also require the application of a common external tariff on trade and distributing the customs revenue according to an agreed upon formula.[5] All in all, such a customs union was expected to provide the economic basis for a unitary foreign trade approach of the Six. The Common Customs Tariff was to form the external customs barrier for the EEC members, the Common Commercial Policy should integrate the member states' trade policies with the outside world into a single Community framework, a prerequisite for a truly free internal market.[6]

However, from the start, it was made abundantly clear that such a Common Commercial Policy would not lead up to one, harmonious and homogeneous trade policy of the EEC. Although Brussels was more than willing to strengthen its role, it was evident that during the first phase such a common trade policy would 'only' be based upon a set of agreed upon abstract principles.[7] Article 113 of the Treaty of Rome mentioned that the Common Commercial Policy 'shall be based on uniform principles, particularly in regard to tariff modifications, the conclusion of tariff and trade agreements, the establishment of uniformity as regards measures of liberalization, export policy and protective commercial measures to be taken in cases of dumping or subsidies'. During the transition period, the member states were expected to 'consult with each other with a view to concerting their action and, as far as possible, adopting a uniform attitude'; whereas in the end the Six would 'only proceed by way of common action'. Measures of this kind were considered especially urgent since export restrictions among the Six had largely disappeared by the end of 1961. Without the construction of such a Common Commercial Policy, trade deflection would loom around the corner. This would give rise to a multitude of commercial conflicts among the Six and hamper further economic unification. In order to forestall these kind of problems, the individual member states would have to transfer their right to sign bilateral trade agreements to the EEC. In this area, Brussels would replace the traditional role of the nation-state and become the sole actor for the Six in the field of foreign trade.

During the 1960s, the European Commission had been actively involved within several multilateral fora, negotiating tariff issues with the participants of the GATT. In a number of so-called 'rounds', the GATT members agreed on substantial tariff reductions, and devised commonly agreed rules pertaining to their commercial relations. However, since most State-trading countries did not actively participate within GATT, trade with the East was practically excluded from these GATT-regulations. This had some inconvenient consequences for the coordination of East-West trade. As Gordon Weil has noted: 'the existence of special forms such as association or the multilateral GATT framework has limited the focus of a potential common commercial policy to the Eastern European countries and Japan. Thus the Community's common policy is to be used for those same few countries where members might still find the conclusion of trade agreements of some marginal use.'[8] Consequently, Brussels' Common Commercial Policy has encountered most difficulties in the field of East-West trade.

Due to the fact that East-West trade has attracted most attention and has created most controversy, the Soviet Union has argued that the EEC's Common Commercial Policy has been especially designed to challenge the CMEA and its member states. Brussels' attempt to coordinate foreign trade among the Six was considered as an imperialist strategy of *divide et impera*, trying to form a single front *vis-à-vis* the East. This, however, has certainly not been the case. For Brussels the coordination of external trade relations with the East was quintessential for economic *and* political reasons. As we already mentioned, the fact that the State-trading countries did not actively participate within GATT has led to distinct commercial problems. Although countries like Poland and Romania were (latent) members of GATT, the basic principles of reciprocity and most-favoured nation status had no edge in relation to them. The exceptional economic structure of the centrally planned economies made the provisions of the GATT, which were devised to regulate commerce among decentralized market economies, inoperative in their case. The Communist foreign trade monopolies, the lack of rational pricing mechanisms and the subsequent non-convertibility of East European currencies, had set the State-trading countries apart from the rest of the world. 'Tariffs' and 'dumping' were useless concepts in a non-market environment. West European governments therefore installed a wide range of protective measures in order to prevent economic dislocations due to the exports of East European products. It was these import quotas, among others, which had to be harmonized under the EEC's Common Commercial Policy.

In July 1959, the Economic and Social Committee of the EEC had already argued that the coordination of foreign trade practices among the Six was especially necessary in the case of East-West commerce, since the artificial East European prices could disturb free trade within the EEC.[9] The first concrete step was taken on 20 July 1960, when the Council of Ministers of the EEC issued a resolution which called upon all member states to include a so-called 'EEC Clause' into their bilateral trade agreements with non-members. The clause was to read: 'When obligations resulting from the Treaty instituting the EEC and relative to the progressive creation of a common commercial policy shall make it necessary, negotiations will be begun in the shortest time possible in order to make any necessary changes in this agreement'. Existing bilateral treaties had to be altered (or even annulled), when the EEC's Common Commercial Policy would eventually come into force. In order to minimize the anticipated difficulties, the Council of Ministers (on 9 October 1961) called for the 'uniformization' of the length of the trade agreements to be signed by its members; the validity of new bilateral treaties should *not* exceed the duration of the transitional period (which was to say, not beyond 1972). Moreover, the EEC Commission would have the opportunity to examine all trade agreements of the Six, starting from January 1966.[10] Member states were expected to announce their plans for new trade agreements and enter into prior consultation with the Commission on all aspects of the proposed agreement.

In September 1962, the EEC Council stepped up its efforts and initiated a so-called 'Action Program'. This new programme spelled out several concrete measures for adopting a Common Commercial Policy such as the unification of the import systems, export rules, trade expansion and agricultural trade. Uniform rules had to be established covering anti-dumping measures and countervailing measures; state-subsidized exports and export rules had to be harmonized. The Commission also called for the replacement of all national quotas in East-West commerce with a list either unilaterally decided by Brussels, or agreed upon in negotiations with the State-trading countries. Due to the fact that the Action Program had put forward far-going proposals, it was soon approved by the member states. The reasons for this 'success' have been provided by Weil, who noted: 'This action program went well beyond the Rome Treaty in specifics concerning the common commercial policy. One reason for this relative ease of its adoption, however, was the fact that it was essentially a statement of intentions, a road-map, rather than a series of binding obligations. The members continued to be bound only by the Treaty provisions calling for a common commercial policy by the end of the transition period.'[11] The combination of high aspirations and a very modest legal status proved to be one of the shortest roads towards disappointment, since the Action Program did not result in concrete actions by the Community.

Brussels' laxity had already led to a number of complications, especially in the field of economic relations with the CMEA countries. The Community still lacked effective and efficient levers to bring its member states to rescind their individual foreign economic policies. The governments of the Six did not adopt the EEC Clause in their bilateral agreements, partly because the CMEA countries had refused to sign an agreement which would include such a clause. In some instances (such as the Italian-Polish Agreement), the EEC member state would add a unilateral declaration repeating the proviso of the clause; but it was evident that such a statement would not make it binding.[12] In a memorandum, dated 26 February 1963, the Commission therefore underscored the need for a unified commercial approach towards the State-trading countries. In particular, Article 115 of the Rome Treaty was beginning to cause severe problems. This article enabled a member state to take protective measures at the internal Community borders against imports of goods from countries outside the EEC, which had first been imported by another member state.[13] Several EEC members had issued complaints about the imports of cheap products from the East which were allegedly being 'dumped' on their market by a detour. In 1954, Bonn complained that the agreement between the USSR and the Netherlands and Belgium concerning the exports of Soviet steel had resulted in a considerable disruption of the West German steel market. Bonn argued that the Benelux countries had in turn exported cheap Soviet steel to the FRG, to the detriment of the Ruhr-based steel factories.[14] Similar conflicts arose among the other member states dealing with a wide range of products emanating from the CMEA-area. More than once, the Commission aired its worries that the uncoordinated character of East-West trade would eventually result in the disruption of the Community market and that Article 115 would become a widely used method to hamper free trade among the member states. Despite all regular efforts, Commission proposals to the Council to strengthen common action towards the State-trading countries did not even result in a Council decision.[15] It was evident that the European Community's institutions lacked legal muscle and that the member states lacked both the political will and the economic incentives to cooperate actively in the field of foreign trade. As Weil has argued: 'In plain words, the Community failed to offer any real appeal for common action, because much profit could be made from bilateral action'.[16] For these reasons, the preparation of the Common Commercial Policy was in the doldrums during much of the 1960s.

5.3 Credit

One of the major bones of contention in the European Community's efforts to come to a Common Commercial Policy has been the issue of state-backed export credit insurance and (state-guaranteed) export credits to the East. It was generally acknowledged that without abundant and soft exports credits, it would be nigh impossible to stimulate East-West commerce. For this purpose, most West European countries have established special programmes which worked through the existing government-backed agencies for export credit insurances.[17] The planned economies lacked sufficient hard currency and could therefore only import to the amount that they had earned foreign currency with their exports to the West. No mechanism existed whereby additional financial resources could be generated domestically to boost imports. This had not been a problem in the 1950s, since the USSR and Eastern Europe were then still in the phase of basic industrialization for which they could acquire equipment and credit within the CMEA. For ideological reasons, most Communist countries were then also reluctant to get into large debts with the West. However, with the onset of the Communist economic reform programmes in the early-1960s, large imports of western equipment and high-technology were needed.[18] In order to expand the level of East-West trade, the State-trading countries either had to augment their hard currency exports, or to attract export credits from the West. In many cases the former method turned out to be much more difficult than the latter. In the light of these circumstances, the need for western finance had risen sharply in the mid-1960s.

Efforts to coordinate the practice of export credits go back to 1934, when the Berne Union of Credit Insurers (officially: the Union d'Assureurs des Crédits Internationaux) was founded. The Berne Union is principally a gentlemen's agreement without binding legal force. Until 1958, the consensus among the eighteen members of the Union had been that commercial credits to Eastern Europe should be limited to a five-year period and subject to a cash down payment of at least 20 per cent of the purchase price. It is beyond doubt that these credit limitations were based upon political and security considerations; as Angela Stent has argued: 'the Berne Union has not been the main policy-making body to decide on credit restriction against communist nations, but was rather used as an instrument for a policy that was decided by NATO. Certainly, the Soviets claimed that it was NATO, led by the United States, that set the credit limits.'[19]

However, since export credits had played a major role in determining the competitiveness of foreign trade, they were *expected* to fall under the EEC's Common Commercial Policy. Due to the intermingling of political, security and commercial motives to restrict credits to the East, this intricate problem could not be resolved and debate continued until the 1980s as to the exact competence of the Community on export credit issues. In a Council decision of May 1962, the EEC had decided that all export credits exceeding the five-year limit set by the Berne Union, would be subject to prior Community consultation. Brussels was wary of the Six entering into an export credit competition which would result in granting the State-trading countries extremely long credit periods on relatively favourable terms. By a Council decision of 27 September 1960, a Policy Coordination Group for Credit Insurance, Credit Guarantees and Financial Credits had already been established. This group was particularly responsible for arranging the consultation procedures among the EEC and its members on export credit subsidies. In 1962, another committee was set up (of the Permanent Representatives of the member states at the EEC), in order to monitor the harmonization of credit practices among the Six. This committee would gather in order to examine member states' transgressions of the five-year limit.[20]

Not very surprisingly, most credit rules were frequently ignored. Non-member states, like Great Britain and Japan, had started to provide elaborate long-term credits to the USSR in order to boost their exports to the East. In

September 1964, the British Government had provided a twelve to fifteen year export credit (with a ceiling of 100 million pounds sterling) to the Soviet Union, in order to finance Moscow's purchase of a British polyester fibre plant; Japan provided equally soft credits to the USSR, with a term of eight years. As a result, many a West European country – but especially France and Italy – felt pressed to provide the East with similar long-term export credits in order to keep up with the Joneses. Several EEC countries which had initially been willing to restrict their export credit policies *vis-à-vis* the East (like Belgium) now declared that they would follow the British and Japanese example. It became painfully clear that the EEC was unable to curb the centrifugal tendencies in its members' credit policies. Although several efforts were made to forge one EEC-line, it was evident that the national interests of the member states were too prominent and too widely diverging. Within the Economic Committee of NATO, the FRG and the United States had called for restraint, but London argued that export credits to the USSR would buy jobs for British workers; moreover, the Communist reputation for the punctual repayment of credits was well known. This was certainly true since the State-trading countries could exercise strict control over their price levels and showed a high degree of financial restraint, both in external and domestic policies. Particularly in France and Italy, several branches of heavy industry were in desperate need of extra business and the often big-scale assignments in the East were expected to fill this gap. In 1966, Rome guaranteed a US$ 367 million credit for the construction of a huge Fiat-plant in Togliattigrad, with a fourteen-year maturation. The temptation for West European governments to use the instrument of export credit subsidies to favour their own business communities was too overwhelming. As a result a fully-fledged credit race towards the East started off in 1966.

This came as no big surprise to Community officials. As early as 1960, the EEC had acknowledged that the credit policies of its member states had to be coordinated in order to avoid a competitive bidding up of terms. Without coordination, the Community's Common Commercial Policy towards Eastern Europe would remain a dead letter. But it was not only concern for the watering down of the process of West European integration which had motivated the requests for a unified EEC credit policy; several member states had their own particular reasons. Bonn, for instance, was especially concerned that East Germany would be able to benefit from favourable credit conditions once a western credit race began. This was especially worrying since such a credit competition would limit the Federal Republic's economic influence over what it still labelled: 'the Soviet occupied zone', or 'the so-called GDR'. The Erhard Government did not give in to the pressure from German industrialists to permit more lenient export credits under the principle that Bonn would not make economic concessions until the Soviet Union had changed its attitude towards the German question. France occupied the other extreme position on the issue of EEC export credit coordination, arguing for maximum freedom of all member states. Paris wanted to retain total liberty in its economic policies *vis-à-vis* the East, mainly in order to demonstrate French independence from the United States. Consulting within the EEC's coordinating framework was also expected to restrict the French latitude to compete economically with Great Britain, which was, of course, not participating in this platform.

Fuelled by the French quest for autonomy, the issue of export credits was cause for great concern by most western countries. It was clearly acknowledged that the issue of export credit subsidies was of strategic importance and that a credit race would inhibit western security. The credit race therefore became a subject of intense discussion within NATO, where several rounds of negotiations were held in an effort to arrive at some measure of coordination in this field; but to no avail. The US and West German efforts were defeated by the French, Italian and British case for more East-West trade. Early in 1966, the French argued that the granting of export credit had to be considered an issue of national foreign policy and did therefore fall outside the competence of the European Community according to Article 113 (which is concerned with 'export policy' to third countries.)[21] Paris argued that it would have to be proven that its credit subsidies were distorting competition among the Six. In response, the EEC Council declared (May 1966), that it would investigate its members' credit policies; but no common code of conduct was forged as a result.

Some progress was made in 1970, when the Council of Ministers adopted two directives which provided common standards on credit insurance for the medium term and the long term. These standards were, however, not applied to the practice of East-West trade. A European Community information document, issued in June 1971, argued that 'For the purpose of an active commercial policy, a financial establishment is needed comparable to the Export-Import Bank in the United States. This role could perhaps be entrusted to the European Investment Bank, on which it would fall to seek or develop the most appropriate means for co-operation between private firms in the Community in their quest for new markets abroad: and those of Eastern Europe in particular.'[22] However, during the period of East-West *détente*, in the first half of the 1970s, the demand for export credits rose to an all-time high. The FRG had embraced its new *Ostpolitik*, and Japanese, American and West European countries all tried to secure their slice of the potentially huge Communist market. Providing lavish and lax export credits was made especially tempting due to the fact that the oil crisis had provided the West European commercial banks with abundant 'petrodollars'.[23] These 'petrodollars' could now be used to finance East-West commerce. The terms of western credit to the East were therefore also very favourable. Whereas domestic borrowers were sometimes charged up to fourteen per cent interest, credits to the CMEA countries carried only 2-7 per cent for loans for up to twenty years. These cheap credits totalled to a huge donation to the East, amounting to DM 200-500 million annually in the early-1970s.[24] As one observer has argued: 'The profitability of the credits, the scope for portfolio diversification, confidence in the clout of the centralized economies in the event of an economic crisis and belief in the umbrella theory (whereby the Soviet Union would use its surplus resources to support the other Comecon countries with financial problems) led to more credit being granted between 1970 and 1975.'[25] This mixture of economic and political incentives clearly favoured bilateral action, easily offsetting the European Community's distant call for export credit cooperation.

That the European Community had failed to coordinate the credit policies of the Six in the early-1970s, was clearly indicated by one member of the European Parliament who, in 1973, complained that 'The situation should not arise where a German delegation arrives in Moscow and is told "What do you mean by credit? We have 6 per cent from the French and you want 9 per cent, there is no point in any further discussion". This is what happened to us a few weeks ago with a delegation from Parliament.'[26] The political commitment to reach consensus on this issue was altogether lacking during the 1960s and early-1970s. Some further progress was made with the beginning of the multilateral preparatory talks in the framework of the European Security Conference, which would eventually result in the Helsinki Accords of 1975 (see Chapter 6.4). The EC member states began to coordinate their separate economic and political approaches towards the East in several subcommittees in an effort to close their ranks during the Helsinki talks. It turned out that these efforts were rather successful and since then regular consultations have taken place. In the mean time, the European Commission had brought the question of Community competence in this thorny field to the European Court of Justice. In November 1975, the European Court decided that export credit subsidies were to be considered an instrument of commercial policy and did therefore fall within the competence of the EEC under Article 113 of the Treaty of Rome.[27] This strengthened the hand of the Community, although member states still cherished the flexibility of a bilateral policy towards the East, especially since non-EC members continued to provide long-term export credits on soft terms.

In 1976, the first so-called 'OECD consensus' was reached on loan conditions and interest rates. The OECD was an important forum since it included all major industrialized states. Further, and more détailed, guidelines were developed in 1978. Limits were imposed upon government-backed export credits of a period of more than two years. Dissimilar guidelines applied to export credits for different categories of countries according to their GNP per capita, whereby the lowest income countries were granted the most favourable conditions. Until the early-1980s, most CMEA countries remained in the middle grouping.[28] After 1975, western governments began to realize that the CMEA countries were now heavily indebted. Between 1974 and 1981, their gross external debt quadrupled from US$ 20.1 billion to US$

87 billion.[29] After the international debt crisis set in in 1982, credit facilities for the State-trading countries were reduced abruptly.

The West European credit race in East-West trade has been a clear example of the problems of collective action. Although *all* member states could have been better off if they had coordinated their export credit policies within a multilateral framework, the lack of forceful sanctions against defectors has made cooperation difficult.[30] Moreover, in foreign trade, relative gain is often considered more important than absolute gain, which makes it even more difficult to collaborate among nations. Robert O. Keohane has maintained that Joseph Grieco's statement that 'the fundamental goal of states in any relationship is to prevent others from achieving advances in their relative capabilities',[31] does not apply to the relationships among members of the European Community. Keohane argued that the Neo-realist assumptions 'are theoretically implausible when applied to situations in which substantial mutual gains can be realized through cooperation and in which governments do not expect others to threaten them with force'.[32] Although the EC was certainly successful in several other fields, the credit issue illustrates that Neo-realist concepts certainly can be applied to intra-EC relations and that the weak structure of the EC has for a long time been unable to limit the still basically 'anarchic' character of the relations among the EC members. Taking all things together, we can say that the weakness of the European Community organization and the subsequent lack of power in Brussels, has for a long time blocked collective action on the issue of export credits to the East. In this respect, it is quite remarkable that export credits *still* remains an issue of dispute within the EC.

5.4 EC protectionism in East-West trade

Since World War II, the level of trade between Eastern and Western Europe has remained relatively low (see Table 4.1). This is especially remarkable when one takes into consideration the fact that the economic structures of the USSR and the EC have been complementary. Soviet exports have focused mainly upon energy-related products and raw materials, which have always been much needed within the EC. Poland (apart from its export of coal), Hungary and Czechoslovakia, on the other hand, have mainly exported foodstuffs, semi-finished products and low-quality manufactures, which have encountered significant obstacles against entry into the Community market.

In the previous chapters we have seen that this low level of interbloc commerce can largely be explained by political and historical factors. The specifics of the Cold War, the division of Germany and Europe, the military confrontation between East and West as well as the western restriction of the transfer of high-technology through CoCom, have all been factors inhibiting the development of commercial links between West and East. During much of the 1950s, East-West trade was considered 'trading with the enemy': the West fearing Communist economic warfare, the East hostile to capitalist trading practices. However, on top of these well-known 'political' factors, the EC member states now also had their own elaborate protectionist network shielding the Common Market from a wide range of East European products. The reasons for such a network were both economic and political. Since State-trading countries did not actively participate within GATT and market forces were not allowed to play any role whatsoever in the pricing of their goods, East European agricultural products, steel and coal, as well as textiles and shoes, were likely to be 'dumped'. West European governments and firms had therefore maintained that safeguarding against 'dumping' of East European products was indispensable in order to protect the Community market against serious commercial disruption.

This ensemble of protective instruments of the European Community – ranging from agricultural levies and quotas on imports of manufactures, to selective safeguards and sectoral agreements – has struck a noticeable blow to the export capacity of most State-trading countries. Brussels' rationale for protectionism against East European products was mainly based upon the centrally planned nature of the Communist economies: since it has been impossible to determine whether the East Europeans have had a comparative advantage in trade with countries of the European Community due to the irrational price-setting structure of their economies, commercial relations between the two blocs could hardly come off the ground. Since the opportunities for East-West trade improved markedly in the mid-1960s, the CMEA countries have accused the European Community and its member states of protectionism. In particular, the East European countries have issued complaints, since their exports could hardly surmount the EC's high protectionist barriers. Under the regulations of the GATT, however, Brussels was warranted the right to restrict the (too) low-priced exports from non-market economies. The level of EC protectionism has been the highest in sectors such as agriculture, coal and steel, and textiles. The composition of East-West trade has therefore been crucial for the level of EC protectionism. We have already referred to the fact that the composition of EC trade with the USSR and Eastern Europe has been very different. EC-Soviet trade has generally been an exchange between crude materials and mineral fuels, and manufactured goods and machinery and transport equipment. Since the EC's Common External Tariff for raw materials was low (or even zero), and the importation of raw materials was almost free of quotas, Soviet exports have hardly been hindered by protectionist measures from the Community. As John Pinder has argued, 'although the Soviet Union has a substantial interest in trade and economic cooperation with the Community countries, the commercial policy for which the Community itself carries responsibility on behalf of the member states is limited to matters (tariffs, quotas, import levies) which are of little interest to the Soviet Union, in view of the predominance of raw materials in Soviet exports to the Community'[33] (see Table 5.1). The composition of the East European exports to the Common Market, on the other hand, has been more evenly spread, ranging from food, fuel, minerals, chemicals and manufactures. Most of their exports have been directly confronted with protectionist measures. East European products such as ceramics, shoes, textiles, glass, and in most cases also machinery and equipment, have been subjected to both the normal tariffs and non-tariff barriers (levies, quotas and so-called 'voluntary export restraints') by the EC.

Table 5.1 The composition of EC-Soviet trade (per cent)

	Exports		Imports	
	1979	1987	1979	1987
SITC 0	6	9	1	1
SITC 1	1	0	0	0
SITC 2	2	2	10	10
SITC 3	1	1	61	70
SITC 4	0	1	0	0
SITC 5	14	17	9	5
SITC 6	37	33	12	8
SITC 7	35	29	3	3
SITC 8	4	6	0	1
SITC 9	1	3	3	1
Total 0-9	100	100	100	100

Key:
SITC 0: Food
SITC 1: Beverages and tobacco
SITC 2: Crude materials, inedible, except fuels
SITC 3: Mineral fuels, lubricants and related materials
SITC 4: Animal and vegetable oils, fats and waxes
SITC 5: Chemicals
SITC 6: Manufactured goods classified chiefly by material
SITC 7: Machinery and transport equipment
SITC 8: Miscellaneous manufactured articles
SITC 9: Commodities and transactions not classified according to kind
Source: Eurostat

A number of bilateral trade agreements have been in force to regulate East-West trade since the early-1960s. These accords reached between the East European countries and the EEC member states usually took the form of basic framework agreements, wherein lists of quotas were annexed which marked the maximum quantity of goods to be traded in a given year. A price clause was also attached, which provided that East European export prices should be in accordance with the world market. They were accompanied by agreements on payments, since the CMEA countries did not have convertible currencies. Although the mere existence of these bilateral trade agreements was of political importance, signalling the willingness on both sides to increase East-West trade, their importance should also not be overestimated. In most cases the maximum quantities of the quotas were not reached due to the intricacies of interbloc commerce. Moreover, for most commodities West European importers had to obtain import licenses, arrange export credits, or enter into barter arrangements.

Community protectionism has been most ardent in the sectors of coal and steel, and agriculture. The ECSC regulated the trade flows of coal and steel products within the Common Market and powerful lobbies have guarded their sectoral interests with care. These sectoral interests have gained a powerful voice in EC policy-making, and partly due to their entrenched positions Brussels commercial policy towards the East has been a rigid one. In January 1962, the EEC's Common Agricultural Policy (CAP) was established, which, in 1980, covered most agricultural products. It would go too far to go into the specifics of the CAP, which constitutes an extremely complicated regime of subsidies, intervention purchases and external policies. For the purpose of the analysis in this chapter, it will suffice to say that the CAP has been based upon two principles: internal price support and external protection. In the first case, so-called 'target prices' were set, at which intervention agencies were obliged to buy products that could not be sold elsewhere against a higher price. These target prices were set by the Commission in order to guarantee EC farmers a stable income, to create a stable market and to set reasonable consumer prices.[34] External protection was achieved by imposing levies to bring agricultural imports up to the target price.[35] Although this has meant that imports were initially free from quantitative restrictions, both approaches have been detrimental to the East European export capabilities.

Similar mechanisms for controlling and checking the imports of iron, iron-ore and steel, had been established by the ECSC, in mid-1963. The ECSC had made it mandatory for its member states to publicize all price changes which were made in response to low prices in third countries. Particularly, in 1962-3, steel prices had come under pressure from cheap imports from the East. In response, the member states agreed that all imports of steel and iron-ore from the State-trading countries would be monitored by the ECSC High Authority. The High Authority would now also be consulted when these issues were being discussed during bilateral trade negotiations.[36] Similar provisions could, however, not be achieved in the field of coal imports from the East, where the individual interests of the member states were probably too diffuse to close the ranks. In the sector of steel and iron-ore, one of the reasons for the Community to regulate trading has been to prevent dangerous dependence upon East European supplies. This political factor has, of course, also played a role in the case of energy trade with the USSR. Within the EEC, an energy working group dealt with these issues, although no common policy towards the East had been established in the 1960s and 1970s.

Mainly in response to several of these restrictive Community measures, Poland decided to approach Brussels directly. It had become evident that the bilateral agreements with the EEC member states were insufficient, since protectionist measures in the crucial sectors of steel and agriculture were now decided within the Community framework. During 1964-5, Warsaw and the EEC conducted preliminary, unofficial negotiations on the possibility of liberalizing Polish agricultural exports to the Common Market. Several years later, in 1969, similar talks were also taken up between the Commission and Bulgarian, Hungarian and Romanian government officials. During these negotiations, concrete arrangements were made which improved East European access to the Common Market area in exchange for price discipline. The process of liberalizing quotas was clearly reinforced by the improvement of the political atmosphere in East-West relations during the mid-1960s. Several hundreds of quotas were officially abolished during the period 1966-70. Due to the ratchet-mechanism of Community law, it has been very difficult to reinstate these quotas once they had been removed from the list. Even after the political weather in East-West relations had deteriorated a few years later, these quotas were therefore not reinstalled.

Brussels' commercial relations with the GDR have been the exception to its protectionist rule. The Treaty of Rome had already acknowledged that intra-German trade would not be subject to the Common Commercial Policy of the EEC, for the obvious reason that commercial relations between the FRG and the GDR were not considered 'foreign trade'. In practice, this meant that East Berlin's exports were not subject to the Community's Common External Tariff. Bonn was, however, obliged to impose several quantitative measures on intra-German trade, of which it was required to inform other EEC members. Bonn had also been instrumental in creating the so-called 'swing' credit arrangement for the GDR, which had eased its monetary problems during the 1970s and 1980s.[37] For these reasons the GDR has sometimes been called 'the silent member' of the Common Market.

The long record of Community protectionism against East European imports, which has been in place during periods of economic crisis and economic prosperity as well as during Cold War and *détente*, indicates that protectionism has largely been based upon domestic, autonomous factors. One could argue that Brussels' Common Commercial Policy, the Common External Tariff, as well as the CAP, have been signs of the enhanced role of the European Community. Stephen George has maintained that the CAP has been an 'example of a positive common policy, that is interventionist, rather than merely negative and simply concerned with the removal of barriers to the working of a free market. It was the success of agriculture which sustained the hopes of the advocates of integration during the 1960s, when it was seen as the start of a process which would lead to other common policies.'[38]

5.5 Circumvention by the member states

In the preceding chapters we have already paid attention to the strong incentives for the EEC member states to embark upon independent commercial escapades towards the State-trading countries. The issue of so-called 'defection' or 'free-riding', has always been central to the problems involved with collective action among nations. As long as the EC was lacking the legal and political clout to make unilateral actions of the member states less desirable than multilateral action within the EC framework, these difficulties would remain. It is beyond doubt that this would require a high degree of supranational decision-making power of the Commission and the Council. But even if Brussels were successful in constructing and maintaining such an unprecedented strong regime, unilateral action could hardly be prevented in all circumstances, since it is difficult to imagine core national interests of major member states being overruled by Community decisions.

Be that as it may, in the period under discussion here it has been evident that the European Community was only laying the foundations of such a sturdy regime. During the 1960s, the national interests of major West European states had been dominating the economic and political arena, whereby Brussels could only operate within the margins left by Italy, France, Germany and (indirectly) Great Britain. Paris considered 'the promotion of trade with the East [as] an integral element in [its] Gaullist foreign policy aimed at recapturing complete freedom of action by dissolving the Cold War blocs and resisting any supranational EEC disposing of the means of conducting a common commercial policy'.[39] In turn, Italy had very different reasons, being extraordinarily interested in oil imports from the East. By establishing large-scale Fiat automobile industries in both the USSR and Eastern Europe, Rome also managed to maintain the independence of the Italian car industry against economic threats from Japan and the United States. London, both before and after it had entered the European Community, made every effort to maintain full independence on issues of foreign policy, and vehemently resisted federalist tendencies. The Federal Republic, in turn, was in the first stage of formulating a more conciliatory *Ostpolitik*. This panoply of fragmented goals and aspirations has made it difficult for the European Community to implement its Common Commercial Policy. This was especially arduous since Brussels lacked the financial resources to implement certain decisions. In these cases, Brussels has been fully dependent upon the participation and cooperation of the member states.

Anticipating the hostility of many member states towards the Community's CCP, the Council of Ministers had decided, in late-1969, that a unified trade policy was especially essential in the case of the State-trading countries.[40] This decision emphasized the necessity of coordinating the bilateral commercial relations between the Six and the East. It was acknowledged that the member states would still be obliged to respect existing bilateral trade treaties, but they were also summoned to take every opportunity – for instance when trade agreements were being revised or renewed – to eliminate incompatibilities with Article 234 of the EC Treaty and replace their national bilateral trade agreements by Community agreements. In order to achieve this progressive standardization of the trade agreements, a scheme of special procedures was established. According to this procedure, all bilateral trade negotiations with the East would become subject to a double consultation with the Commission. Prior to the bilateral talks, the Council of Ministers would decide upon the margins of negotiations with the State-trading countries and afterwards give (or deny) its approval of the eventual proposal. These were rather direct measures. A special provisional regime was set up allowing all member states to continue their current practice of negotiating bilateral trade agreements with the East until 31 December 1972, with the sole stipulation that no bilateral agreement should be in force at the end of 1974. This also proved, however, problematic since several member states had already signed trade agreements reaching well beyond the end of the proposed extra transitional period. Italy had negotiated several agreements expiring in 1974 and 1975; France had even signed a trade agreement with Moscow running until 1981.

But there were other factors impeding the construction of a genuine CCP. One of the most influential aspects has been the fact that most member states had entered into numerous so-called 'economic cooperation agreements'. Due to the simple fact that these accords did not directly touch upon the issue of trade, they automatically fell outside the legal jurisdiction of the European Community. Since the member states were still free to sign these kind of accords, important commercial collaboration began to shift from the traditional trade agreement to the 'new' economic cooperation agreements. Most long-term agreements provided for 'Mixed Commissions', which (generally on a yearly basis) brought together the commercial representatives of both countries. This gradual shift in emphasis from trade agreements to economic cooperation agreements was not merely a smart legal method to circumvent the authority of the EC. Since the development of East-West trade had become increasingly contingent upon the availability of western export credits and the Communist states began to favour the import of western high-technology and know-how, economic cooperation agreements began to overshadow the classical trade agreements in practical importance. Although economic cooperation agreements could, at least officially, not deal with *trade* issues, credit arrangements, political support for joint ventures and so forth, could well be dealt with.

In response, the European Community made several efforts to bring the fields covered by these economic cooperation agreements under its authority.[41] It was clear that the Commission's main problem was that the Treaty of Rome did not refer to these economic cooperation agreements in any way, and Brussels therefore had no official say in them. As we have seen in the previous section, Community action to coordinate credit policies among its members had been without much success. Without a legal basis and without political consensus, Brussels was powerless. This was again the case here. In July 1974, the Commission had established a special Committee for scrutinizing these economic cooperation agreements on their compatibility with the provisions and the general idea of the Community's Commercial Policy.[42] In several cases, this Committee had commented upon the content of its member states' cooperation agreements, especially when they did indeed cover points which would normally be covered by trade agreements. France was found to be especially prone to including explicit trade issues (for instance dealing with the exports of agricultural products) in its economic cooperation agreements with the State-trading countries. The effects of Brussels' efforts were, however, very modest.

It soon became evident that the Community's aspirations of becoming the main West European actor in the field of economic relations with the East had to be moderated, and that the transitory period had to be extended. Since Brussels lacked the power to get influential member states into line, the deadline of 1973 was extended for another three years. France, for example, had already refused to abide by the December 1969 Council decision. Other major member states were also reluctant to give up the prerogative of their direct negotiations with the East. This transitional commercial policy towards the East was therefore a realistic compromise intended to persuade recalcitrant member states to adapt to one, unified European Community line.

5.6 The EC's autonomous trade policy

For the East European countries and the Soviet Union, the circumvention by the EC members of the CCP was widely acclaimed. The structure of numerous bilateral economic cooperation agreements was preferred over an EC monopoly on trade issues, since the latter would end the Soviet policy of playing West European governments and firms off against each other. A successful CCP would eventually also include stronger coordination in the field of export credits, which was expected to result in less favourable terms for Communist trading agencies.

In the previous chapter we have discussed Moscow's negative response to the process of West European economic integration. In this light it is not very surprising that the CMEA members have been loath to sign trade agreements with Brussels. Acknowledging the right of the European Community to coordinate foreign trade issues would go against Moscow's policy of ignoring the EC as far as possible. Although most East European countries have been eager to enter into backroom negotiations with the Commission in efforts to iron out several commercial problems, Moscow has blocked official *rapprochement*. On the other hand, the EC's protectionist trading practices could hardly be ignored by the East Europeans, who therefore decided to enter into a number of unofficial bilateral settlements with the EC, generally by means of a simple exchange of letters. Negotiations on these accords (which in most cases dealt with agricultural trade), have been conducted between the European Commission and the relevant Ministry and export organization of a particular State-trading country. In general, the Communist trading organization promised not to export their goods below a certain price, whereas the European Community agreed not to apply supplementary levies on its imports of specific products. These agreements followed the structure of the conditions determined by the GATT for commerce with State-trading countries. In the early-1980s, a number of so-called 'voluntary restraint agreements' were concluded with several CMEA member states, specifying annual EC import quota and bilateral consultation mechanisms. Although the large number of agreements did not add up to any formalization of the trade ties between Brussels and the East, they undoubtedly created a kind of half-way house between the official recognition of the European Community by the Communist countries and the orthodox official Moscow line of unrestricted disregard.

In May 1974, the Council – reminding the CMEA members that the power of the EC member states to negotiate trade agreements was coming to an end – announced its readiness to negotiate fully fledged trade agreements with the Communist countries. Several months later, the Commission sent a first draft of such a proposed trade agreement to all State-trading countries, as the starting-point for further bilateral negotiations. It was characteristic of Moscow's reluctance to bargain openly with the European Community that Brussels' letters were either ignored, or were sent back. (See Chapter 7.3 for a further discussion on this issue.) This model for trade agreements, generally referred to as 'the memorandum', contained five basic points:

1. Brussels was willing to conclude a long-term non-preferential trade agreement, aimed at guaranteeing a harmonious development of reciprocal trade with the East;
2. The reciprocal application of the MFN-clause;
3. The reduction of quotas (not applicable to the CAP);
4. Several *ad hoc* provisions for payments and trade financing; and
5. Arrangements for Mixed Commissions to supervise the application of the agreements.[43]

The Commission sent drafts of these agreements to the governments of all State-trading countries, but to no avail. Of all Communist countries addressed by the Community, only the People's Republic of China reacted positively, by inviting the Commission's Vice-President to pay an official visit to Bejing. This initiation of commercial contacts led to the formal recognition of the EC by the Chinese, and eventually resulted in the first trade agreement between China and the EC (signed in 1978). A Chinese diplomatic mission was already opened in Brussels in 1975.

How was the EC to respond to the silence in the East? With much difficulty the Commission had managed to gain a monopoly on signing foreign trade agreements for the Community, but now the group of countries for which the coordination of trade mattered most had refused to deal with the Community in public. Since no channels of direct communication could be opened between the EC and the East, the Council decided to formulate a so-called 'autonomous trade policy' *vis-à-vis* the CMEA and its member states. In practice, this has meant the Council (unilaterally) decided upon the list and scope of the Community's quotas, the granting of such commercial favours as the Generalized Scheme of Preferences (GSP); the actions taken under the Community's anti-dumping legislation had of course always been 'autonomous'. This autonomous trade policy has confronted the State-trading countries with numerous *faits accomplis*, and in the mean time ascertained the European Community's responsibility on foreign trade issues. In December 1974, the Council decided that the national quota lists which applied to trade with the East had to be incorporated into one list coordinated by the Community. Only in the exceptional case where Communist countries had already signed trade agreements with the EC (such as Romania and China), were Mixed Committees able to negotiate (annually) on the nitty-gritty of the quota arrangements. In any other case, the EC decided upon the exact conditions within the framework of its autonomous trade policy. This unilateral framework has led to regular requests by member states to alter some specifics of the quotas, sometimes for political reasons, sometimes on clear economic grounds. In order to meet the demands by its member states, Brussels decided to establish a so-called 'Consultative Committee' (which met every week), which had to settle the appeals for changing the State-trading quotas. However, since the annually revised Community list had left a margin of some 20 per cent (each way) within which every member state was free to adjust its quotas, the Consultative Committee has had to take relatively few difficult decisions.

The application of anti-dumping rules and countervailing measures has been the other major element in the EC's autonomous trade policy. Anti-dumping rules apply to goods originating from third countries when the export price of a product is less than its 'normal value' or that of a like product.[44] According to GATT, anti-dumping measures may be imposed if the dumping practice causes (or threatens to cause) material injury to an established Community industry, or materially hampers the establishment of a planned Community industry.[45] These measures mainly encompass provisional or definitive customs duties. Countervailing measures are directed against subsidized exports and follow a similar course to the anti-dumping measures. These EC rules – which have been based upon the GATT code – have been of special importance in the context of East-West trade. This is because it has always been difficult to determine whether goods produced within a non-market environment have been dumped or have received undue state subsidies. Since the Communist planning agency has arbitrarily decided upon the (export) price of a product – which does not bear any direct relation to the production costs involved – anti-dumping rules have been difficult to apply to East-West trade. What is more, although Article 113(1) of the EEC Treaty has given Brussels the exclusive competence to issue 'measures to protect trade such as those to be taken in case of dumping or subsidies', it was not until 1968 that the member states also actually accepted the consequences of this Community prerogative. In several cases, foreign trade organizations of State-trading countries have been before the European Court in which they were charged for dumping and undue state subsidization. In the 1980s, approximately half of the anti-dumping procedures initiated by the EC have involved the non-market economy countries.[46]

The EC has adopted the regulation that 'A product shall be considered to have been dumped if its export price to the Community is less than the normal value of the product'. Crucial here is, of course, what is to be considered as 'normal value'? Article 2(3) of the Council Regulation (EEC) no.2176/84 (23 July 1984) has defined it as 'the comparable price actually paid or payable in the ordinary course of trade for the like product intended for consumption in the exporting country or country of origin'. In order to make comparison somewhat easier, the Community has decided to apply the system of so-called 'reference countries' (also called 'analogue countries'), whereby the imports from the CMEA members are related to the imports from market economies (often developing countries). Similar systems of third-country prices have already been adopted by the GATT in its reports on the effects and preconditions of the accession of Poland, Romania and Hungary to this basically market-oriented organization. The choice of the reference country has been an important and, for a long time, unresolved question. Some countries, such as the United States, have compared State-trading countries with market economies of a comparable level of economic development. The EC has generally used other criteria, such as the similarity of the scale and techniques of production, or the similarity in the access of raw materials. In many cases brought before the European Court, the choice of the reference country has played a crucial role in determining whether dumping had actually occurred or not.[47]

Although the definition of 'normal value' has been determined by the EC, this too has become the subject of much debate. State-trading countries have argued that their planned economies could profit from considerable econo-mies of scale and other advantages not open to market economies. CMEA members have also argued that their low export prices are due to low labour costs. The Commission has always refused to acknowledge the merit of such arguments and has argued that 'the comparative advantages [of the State-trading countries] are not known with certainty and they may be more than offset by other comparative advantages enjoyed by the market economy producer. An advantage resulting from access to cheaper raw materials, for example, might be out-weighed by advantages resulting from economies of scale or better production techniques in the market economy country ... But the main objection to making any allowance for differences in comparative advantage lies in the fact that this would involve the need to rely on the methods and the costs of production in the State-trading country, an exercise which the use of a third market economy analogue is designed to avoid.'[48] This policy of the European Community has made every complaint of the State-trading countries very difficult to substantiate, since, as Susan Senior Nello has argued: 'EC anti-dumping legislation is based on the concept of an analogue country because it is believed that the non-market country cannot show effectively that it can produce the goods cheaper than can the analogue country; if such proof were possible, the analogue-country rule would be superfluous.'[49]

5.6 Trade policy is foreign policy

We have already referred to the Neo-functionalist strategy which sought to advance the process of West European integration via incremental problem-solving. The basic ideas of this strategy have been three: welfare-maximization offers a major incentive for further integration; institution-building is a vital element in creating and maintaining consensus; and increasing economic interdependence undermines the logic of national frontiers and autonomous national policies.[50] The related concept of spill-over has stressed the importance of *economic* integration which was expected to trigger off collaboration and policy-making integration in the field of 'high politics', like foreign policy and defence. Scholars like Joseph Nye and Robert Keohane have argued that the intensification of transnational and transgovernmental relations have reduced the nation states' autonomy, most importantly the states' ability to forge an independent foreign trade policy. These transnational and transgovernmental links include relations across state borders that are not controlled by the central executive of foreign policy organs or national governments.[51]

These arguments have been widely criticized. Neo-functionalists have argued that the character of the state as the central unit of foreign policy has changed beyond recognition. This has proved to be a premature conclusion.[52] Thomas Schelling, for instance, has correctly maintained that 'Aside from war and preparations for war ... trade is the most important relationship that most countries have with each other. Broadly defined to include investment, shipping, tourism, and the management of enterprises, trade is what most of international relations are about. For that reason trade policy is national security policy.'[53] Indeed, the distinction between 'low politics' versus 'high politics', which has often been made, is hardly tenable. The obstacles and predicaments encountered during the decades in which Brussels has tried to implement its Common Commercial Policy are a clear indication that the formulation of trade policy constitutes an essential element of each country's foreign policy. We have already indicated that this statement has been especially applicable to West European policy towards the State-trading countries. The specific political or commercial objectives in the East have generally been stronger than the political commitment and economic necessity to transfer the national prerogative of foreign trade policy to the European Community. The circumvention of the CCP through economic cooperation agreements has been one of the clearest illustrations of the 'obstinacy' of the West European state to maintain national control over important aspects of external commercial policy. It has thereby simultaneously demonstrated the weakness of the position of the EC Commission as well as the shortage of political commitment to integration by the member states.

It would, on the other hand, also be incorrect to disregard the arguments of Neo-functionalism altogether. The three incentives for economic and political integration, which we mentioned at the beginning of this section, have achieved some marked changes in the body of West European politics. It would go too far to analyse these changes here, but we will later argue that the impetus of economies of scale and the permanence of a strong EC regime, have eventually resulted in a meaningful modification of the economic and political relations among the Twelve.

6. The Lack of an EC *Ostpolitik*, 1957-1985

The existing instruments [of the European Community] have already acted quite powerfully on the East Europeans, what has been lacking is a policy for their use.

> John Pinder, in Kenneth J. Twitchett (ed.), *Europe and the World. The External Relations of the Common Market* (London: Europa Publications, 1976), p.59.

6.1 Introduction

Political cooperation among the member states of the European Community has always been an arduous matter and has proven to be exceptionally difficult to accomplish. We have already seen that the ECSC and the EEC had been established not only for the obvious economic reasons, but that these organizations have also had an implicit political rationality. It has always been clear that whereas the immediate aims of the European Community were economic, the long-term goals have been political. Several efforts have been made to institutionalize political cooperation among the Six and to incorporate political cooperation within the structure of the EC. In the 1950s we witnessed the plans for a European Defence Community and a European Political Community, which were followed up with the so-called 'Fouchet Plan' in the 1960s. Both schemes were unsuccessful. In this chapter we will discuss the failures and successes of the European Community's efforts to coordinate the foreign policies of its member states towards the East. Special attention will be paid to the specific national interests which have been at stake in the making of Brussels' *Ostpolitik*.

6.2 Lack of consensus, lack of power

After de Gaulle's plans to set up a western triumvirate of the United States, Great Britain and France had failed, the French President became an ardent supporter of West European political cooperation.[1] In the early-1960s, de

Gaulle's plans captured the headlines and eventually a Committee was established, under the leadership of the French diplomat Christian Fouchet, to work out more concrete proposals for EEC political cooperation. The Committee suggested that 'the Six should compare their foreign policies and harmonize them as far as possible'.[2] Fouchet's plan would have provided for consultation among the Six without establishing any supranational decision-making institutions. However, negotiations on the Fouchet Plan soon broke down due to the irreconcilable positions of the member states, whereby the Dutch veto of the plan proved decisive. Without participation of Great Britain, the smaller countries feared the hegemony of France and the FRG within such a structure of close political cooperation.

Major steps were taken during the Summit Conference of the EC leaders in The Hague, in December 1969, where the new French President, Georges Pompidou, relaunched the process of West European political cooperation. During that meeting, a Political Committee was established (initially under the chairmanship of the Belgian diplomat Vicomte Davignon), which was to meet twice a year in order to prepare meetings of the EC's Ministers of Foreign Affairs. A number of other working groups emerged from this 'Davignon machinery', in which the member states consulted each other on the most important issues of foreign policy.[3] The direct objective of this teamwork was to accomplish a better mutual understanding on the major problems of international politics and to strengthen the sense of a common purpose by the harmonization of ideas, positions and, where it appeared possible or desirable, policies. Although there were no Treaty provisions for foreign policy cooperation, the EC member states had created this brand new European Political Cooperation (EPC) machinery alongside the formal EC framework during the early-1970s. During these EPC meetings, East-West relations, the European security conference and the problems of the Middle East were among the most important topics of discussion. As Neill Nugent has argued perceptively: 'EPC points to the fact that the really crucial influence on policy development has not been so much the Treaties as the perception of the states of what is desirable, allied with their individual and collective capacities for translating these perceptions into practice'.[4]

Although the EPC provided the basic framework for consultation, consensus on foreign policy issues remained difficult to achieve. The EPC had indicated that many member states were only prepared to cooperate within a strictly intergovernmental framework, only willing to consult but not to coordinate or to integrate their foreign policies. For these reasons, Brussels has been unable to forge something even remotely resembling a Community foreign policy, let alone a fully fledged *Ostpolitik*. As Michel Tatu had maintained in 1973: 'Although a generation has elapsed since World War II the European Community has still not worked out a common response to the challenges it faces in the division of Europe'.[5] Such a coherent strategy *vis-à-vis* the Soviet Union and Eastern Europe would require a community of interests among the EC member states and the compatibility of their policy goals towards the East; elements which have been lacking until this present day.

It is beyond doubt that economic relations have constituted the most important element of the EC's involvement with the East; we have discussed these issues extensively in the previous chapters. But how far have *political* objectives been pursued and accomplished? During the period under discussion in this chapter, the European Community has developed from a relatively passive bystander into a major force in world affairs, without, however, developing a clear-cut foreign strategy. In particular, the lack of an EC *Ostpolitik* has often been criticized. John Pinder had, for instance, remarked in 1974: 'Since it is in economics that the West Europeans are relatively strong, and the Economic Community is their strongest collective instrument, one might reasonably expect that they would use it, as some political compensation for their military inferiority. Yet they have failed to do so.'[6] The Treaty of Rome has not instituted a framework for political cooperation and the EC has therefore also lacked an 'official' political doctrine, to which all member states have had to subscribe. In marked contrast to the ambiguous nature of the EEC's foreign policy objectives, the CMEA Programme had stated that the Communist countries would aim at 'the growth of the economic power of the world socialist system, strengthen the economies of the individual countries and constitute an important factor in the consolidation of the socialist system's unity and its supremacy over capitalism in all spheres of public life and in ensuring victory in the contest between socialism and capitalism'. The Rome Treaty had of course not spelled out policy goals *vis-à-vis* the socialist world, although the Preamble to the EEC Treaty expressed the determination to 'lay the foundation of an ever closer union among the peoples of Europe'.

However, there have been several touchstones for the West European policy-makers dealing with external affairs. It has been possible to identify a number of basic, strategic objectives on which most foreign policies of the EC members have been based. First of all, there has been tacit consensus on the need to overcome the division of the European continent, and *ipso facto*, the need to forge German unity. Although this has been an almost dogmatic principle of foreign policy during the period of the Cold War, there has never been unanimity about the most appropriate way to achieve this goal. In this respect, the lofty objective of 'European unity' has been unable to provide a unifying force in the member states' policies towards the East. The same can be said of the other principle on which there has been some tacit understanding, namely the idea of 'Atlantic unity' shaped within the framework of NATO. For instance, the dual-track policy derived from NATO's Harmel Report of 1967 – deterrence coupled with *détente* and a strong Western defence coupled with a policy of political negotiations with the East – has set some basic standards for the member states' policies towards the East. But here too there have been a number of important caveats. Ireland – an EC member state but no NATO partner – has consistently pursued a neutral foreign policy. The same can be said of the French approach to world politics. In 1966, de Gaulle decided that France would withdraw from the integrated command structure of NATO, without, however, leaving the Alliance altogether. Cherishing its own nuclear arsenal, France has done almost everything in its power to prevent the continuation of what it considered as harmful 'bloc politics'.

One other, again only implicitly, agreed upon axiom has been that the member states' policies towards the East should not hamper the process of integration within the Common Market. This has been an exceptionally flexible postulate, since the member states' attitudes towards the EC have always differed significantly. In the previous chapters we have seen that the independent and unconstrained national economic policies of several member states towards the East have thwarted the increase of the EC's influence and prestige. It has proved to be relatively easy to adhere to the abstract principles of closer relations between the member states and closer union among the European peoples (as laid down in Article 2 of the Treaty), as long as the national *carte blanche* to implement them has not been withdrawn. It should therefore be noted that most of these axioms have only provided the flexible margins wherein the foreign policies of the European Community and its member states have been framed. In this respect, Brussels' policy towards the East has remained utterly dominated by the political courses set out by the major member states, which have rarely adopted matching policies towards the East. Due to its lack of authority, the EC has not been able to arrest these differences. As a result, the EPC has long remained a forum for discussion and consultation only, without the political and legal clout to forge a common line on matters of foreign policy. Only since the Single European Act was brought into effect on 1 July 1987, has the EPC been officially incorporated within the EC framework. Article 30(1) now calls for the member states 'to endeavour jointly to formulate and implement a European foreign policy'. The Maastricht Treaty, initialled in December 1991, has spelled out that the European Union will 'implement a common foreign and security policy including the eventual framing of a common defence policy, which might in time lead to a common defence'.

In order to clarify the underlying reasons for the rudimentary nature of the European Community's *Ostpolitik* during the period 1957-85, we will briefly touch upon the political and economic idiosyncrasies of the main West European actors: France, Great Britain and the FRG. In order to complete the picture we will also shortly touch upon the attributes of the foreign policies of Italy and the Benelux countries. In the latter half of this chapter we will analyse the role of the European Community during the negotiations prior to the Helsinki Accords and examine Brussels' role during the so-called 'Second Cold War', which started off in the early-1980s.

6.3 France, West Germany and Great Britain: three distinct views

In Chapter 3 we have already briefly touched upon the foreign policy conceptions of the French President de Gaulle and his German counterpart, Chancellor Adenauer. Both statesmen have cherished quite distinct objectives in their policies towards the East. Historical links with the Eastern *Hinterland* aside, the German efforts at formulating an *Ostpolitik* have converged around one, very concrete cause: the unification of the German nation. It is important to stress that all other West European countries have lacked such a distinct objective in their policies towards Eastern Europe. Neither France, nor Great Britain, nor Italy, have ever had such explicit and well-defined goals. This contrast has been theoretically classified by Arnold Wolfers as the difference between so-called 'possession goals' and 'milieu goals'. Possession goals are specific, concrete and direct, whereas milieu goals are general, abstract and indirect in nature. 'Because of the possessive nature of these [former] goals, they are apt to be praised by some for being truly in the national interest, while condemned by others as indicating a reprehensible spirit of national selfishness or acquisitiveness. Milieu goals are of a different character. Nations pursuing them are out not to defend or increase possessions they hold to the exclusion of others, but aim instead at shaping conditions beyond their national boundaries.' Wolfers' distinction is a crucial one and goes a long way in explaining both the manner and the intensity with which the EC member states have formulated and pursued their policy towards the Communist countries.

The French have always regarded their economic relations with the USSR and Eastern Europe as *haute politique*.[8] In order to maintain the national prerogative of foreign policy, Paris has vehemently opposed any EC activity in East-West affairs which would go beyond the rather narrow propositions of the Common Commercial Policy as laid down in the Rome Treaty. French history lacks a tradition of political and economic relations with Russia and Central Europe. Of course, several Napoleons have made desperate military efforts at gaining control over Russia and Poland, and both France and (Soviet) Russia have fought on the same side in more than one war. This could, however, not compensate for the fact that Paris lacks concrete 'possession goals' in the East, which is especially due to the absence of borders between France and Eastern Europe. Nevertheless, after 1945, French politicians have habitually stressed the need to formulate a distinctive French policy *vis-à-vis* the East. This French *Ostpolitik* has manifested itself most profoundly in the diplomatic field where the French have often taken the lead, opening up unknown and innovative paths in East-West relations. As Pierre Hassner has argued: 'From de Gaulle to François Mitterrand, French leaders were cast more than ever as specialists in vision rather than policy, in words rather than deeds'.[9]

There have been a number of compelling explanations for the specific French approach to *Ostpolitik*, none of them being directly related to the

Communist countries themselves. First, Paris has sought to increase its contacts with Moscow and the other members of the Soviet bloc in an effort to contain German foreign policy.[10] Consciously or unconsciously, policy-makers at the Elysée have sought to counterbalance Germany's involvement in its traditional backyard of *Mitteleuropa*. This strategy of *alliance de revers* – alliances with the neighbours and potential adversaries of one's potential enemy – has been a classical device during the centuries of French foreign policy.[11] In this case, however, Paris has been faced with an unsolvable problem: its political ambitions and its economic capabilities were clearly out of sync. Close commercial and economic ties with the East would require more financial resources than the French economy was able to provide. Since German productive power has always been significantly higher than the French, Paris has had to choose between two options. First, it could make active use of its diplomatic and bureaucratic edge over other European powers by allying with them and then trying to become their most articulate spokesman. Clear examples of this course can be found in the French efforts to establish a politically and economically unified European Community in which Paris was playing an active and prominent role. The second course of action would be to do just the opposite: *avoid* close alliances and encourage French independence in an effort at increasing its political flexibility in East-West affairs.

France has tried both options after World War II. During the periods in which Charles de Gaulle dominated French politics Paris adopted an independent course, making all possible efforts at establishing itself as the major independent power of Western Europe in both the Kremlin and the White House. France has more than once used its commercial relations with Moscow in order to raise its status as a world power. Time and again, de Gaulle has made independent policy strides towards the East trying to offset American and Soviet influence in both West and East. As we have already mentioned above, Paris was prepared to provide the CMEA countries with elaborate export credit guarantees in order to establish French firms in the USSR and Eastern Europe.[12] It is not surprising that Moscow has always applauded France's independent political course, but only as long as its autonomy turned itself against the United States, West Germany, NATO or the European Community. De Gaulle's favourite concept of a 'Europe from the Atlantic to the Urals', on the other hand, has been considered revanchist and utterly aggressive. This French milieu goal, so typical for de Gaulle, challenged the legitimacy of the superpower overlay in Europe and called for a more powerful and independent 'Europe' whose boundaries, structure and political make-up were still very ambiguous. In 1963, for example, de Gaulle maintained that the day would come when 'a complete change in the relations between East and West in Europe' would become feasible, and that 'when this day comes ... France expects to make constructive proposals concerning the peace, equilibrium, and destiny of Europe'; this would – most likely – come to mean the absorption of Eastern Europe and Russia into a larger European Community.[13]

Since Georges Pompidou took over office in the late-1960s, this course of action has been exchanged for a policy in which French political influence was channelled in different ways, employing several multilateral fora (such as the CSCE-process and the European Community) as the primary vehicles for defending French national interests.[14] Through its active involvement in shaping the EC's policy towards the East, Paris has tried to satisfy its deeply rooted need for international recognition as a power to be reckoned with in international affairs. This craving after international status as well as the fervid use of French diplomatic skills, can be explained as a method to compensate for France's limited geographical and economical importance. France's loss of political weight and international status became even more evident during the period of decolonization in the 1960s. It must be acknowledged that France has made active use of its exquisite diplomatic skills, acting energetically in the preparatory phase of the CSCE negotiations and making successful efforts at forging unity among the Nine in their economic and political stance *vis-à-vis* the USSR and its allies. The manner in which Paris has influenced EC policy-making through diplomacy may serve as an example of Hans Morgenthau's assertion that 'Of all the factors that make for the powers of a nation, the most important, however unstable, is the quality of diplomacy ... Diplomacy, one might say, is the brains of national power, as national morale is its soul. If its vision is blurred, its judgement defective, and its determination feeble, all the advantages of geographical location, of self-sufficiency in food, raw materials, and industrial production, of military preparedness, of size and quality of population will in the long run avail a nation little.'[15] In this respect, it has often been argued that France has needed the East-West problem as an issue on which it could focus its strategy, its vision and its self-image as a world power. As Robert Keohane has argued: 'Governments may desire "positional goals", such as high status, and may therefore resist even mutually beneficial cooperation if it helps others more than themselves'.[16] This has certainly applied to France.

Of course, things have been markedly different for the Federal Republic of Germany. Quite in contrast to France, the FRG has lacked the political freedom of manoeuvre in its *Ostpolitik*, but has had abundant economic prowess to turn itself into an attractive commercial partner for the East. But, as any Sumo wrestler can tell, weight is not everything, it has to be used with skill, boldness and persistence. This has also applied to German economic strength. Although the possession goal of German reunification has dominated Bonn's foreign policy agenda, the FRG has been very careful in formulating an independent *Ostpolitik*. Germany's historical heritage – most notably its backroom deals with Soviet Russia (first in Rapallo, later with the Molotov-Ribbentrop Pact) – has made independent conciliatory steps towards the East politically suspect. This was witnessed by Chancellor

Adenauer's persistent *Westpolitik*, as well as the rigid implementation of the Hallstein doctrine. Both have been the result of the FRG's unique geographical and political position during the Cold War. Bonn's need to cast strong anchors in NATO and the European Community was a result of its exceptional international position and status. Only after the *Grundvertrag* was signed in 1969 and most of the post-war borders had been implicitly accepted through a number of quasi-Peace Treaties (between the FRG and the USSR, and the FRG and Poland, in 1970), and the Helsinki Accords of 1975, had West Germany accomplished significantly more political leeway in its dealings with the East.

Due to these peculiar circumstances, the Federal Republic has made more than average use of Western multilateral organizations to achieve its foreign policy goals. One could perhaps even go as far as to speak of a 'communalization' of Bonn's foreign policy. Without doubt, trying to achieve its foreign policy aspirations through the framework of the European Community has had several advantages for the FRG. First, it silenced criticism – both from the West *and* the East – of a German *Drang nach Osten*. When Bonn was firmly rooted within the Common Market, reproaches of German revanchism could be effectively neutralized. Soviet allegations of German aggression in Community disguise have been oft repeated, but they have never been able to put a brake on Community efforts to formulate a policy towards the East since they were wholly incredible. Although less audacious, similar suspicions were shared by several West European policy-makers. France and the Benelux countries, on the other hand, have considered Bonn's close ties with the Community as a guarantee against a resurgent German *Alleingang* eastward.

Since Bonn has recognized that its possession goals could only be achieved in very close cooperation with other Western countries, the communalization of German *Ostpolitik* was a quite logical step. This has been the second advantage for Bonn to work within the framework of the European Community. Chancellor Willy Brandt's *Ostpolitik* has been based upon the contention that German unity could only be realized within the context of a more general settlement of Europe's political division. In line with the *Politik der Bewegung* (the policy of movement) of his predecessor Gerhard Schröder, Brandt has been careful to steer a middle course between the policies of *détente* (based upon cooperation with Moscow), and polycentrism (based upon the encouragement of centrifugal tendencies within the East European bloc). Commercial links between West German industry and Eastern Europe and the USSR were encouraged and supported. Both commercial and political interests have constituted the building blocks for such a policy. First of all, commerce with the State-trading countries was expected to provide West German heavy industry with quintessential raw materials (most notably energy), meanwhile forming a stable element in Bonn's foreign trade structure. The powerful *Ostausschuß der Deutschen Wirtschaft* (Eastern

Committee of the German Economy) has persistently lobbied for greater involvement of German commerce in the State-trading countries. On the political front *Osthandel* was seen as a puissant instrument in Bonn's overall *Ostpolitik*. As a result of these economic and political pressures, Bonn has been a fervent proponent of increasing East-West trade and technology transfer, both within the European Community, NATO and CoCom. At times, this has resulted in political problems with the United States, for instance over the West Siberian (Urengoi) pipeline deal, in 1982 (see section 6.5).

Much to French displeasure, the strength of the West German economy – in combination with the attraction of German capital, high-technology and industrial cooperation – has provided Bonn with a prominent position in East-West affairs. Since the early-1970s, West German relations with the Kremlin leadership have improved markedly, challenging the French pivotal position in East-West diplomacy. Quite perceptively, West German policy-makers have recognized the fact that they need French cooperation – both bilaterally and within the context of the European Community – in order to achieve basic German policy goals. As a result, West German policy-makers have been careful to relate German *Ostpolitik* to the political ideas of the Quai d'Orsay, knowing that opposition from Paris would be counter-productive to the realization of their own plans. Close bilateral political cooperation dates back to January 1963, when de Gaulle and Adenauer signed a Franco-German Treaty which provided for consultations 'prior to any decision, on all important questions of foreign policy and in the first place on questions of common interests, with a view to reaching, as far as possible, an analogous position'.[17] This Treaty has developed into the famous Bonn-Paris axis which has played a central role in the process of West European integration and has often set out the course of the EC's approach towards the East.[18]

The very existence of the Paris-Bonn axis could, however, never disguise the diverging German and French conceptions of 'Europe'.[19] German *Ostpolitik* has been based upon a somewhat romantic conception of 'Europe' and the future political architecture of this continent. In Bonn's view, European unity could be achieved through international *détente*, increased East-West economic collaboration and a reduction of the political relevance of the nation-state. In Bonn's understanding, the state and its national borders were among the major barriers to European unity. Due to its federal structure, 'federalism' has never been considered a dirty word in West Germany, as it has been, for instance, in Great Britain. On the contrary, federalism was considered a viable solution to Europe's economic and political problems. All in all, the German concept of the 'new, post-war Europe' – comprising both East and West (but with or without the Soviet Union?) – has been an ambiguous one. Not very surprisingly, Paris has not looked forward to such a vague and nebulous version of the 'new Europe', since this would imply that France would play second (or even third) fiddle to Germany. In order to get some clarity in this fuzzy picture, France has defined the concept of 'Europe' first and foremost as *Western* Europe, and more concrete, as the European Community. Paris has found it very hard to imagine how a European order could be achieved without maintaining the clear-cut units of the nation-state and the traditional political rules which tend to accompany them. France has considered the political cooperation within the EC as one of the most important mechanisms to prevent a German *Alleingang* towards the East.

This brings us to the other major West European political power: Great Britain. Although London has considered itself as a 'European' power, it has also carefully cherished its so-called 'special relationship' with the United States, which was ostensibly based upon a shared Anglo-Saxon political culture and the same language. Britain's leading role within the Commonwealth has also provided it with a broader view on East-West affairs than most other West European actors. London's refusal, and later hesitation, to enter the ECSC and EEC, have been characteristic of its concern of losing its political and economic independence within supranational and federalist Community structures. In the 1950s and 1960s, London therefore argued that its independence on issues of foreign affairs was essential in order to play a mediating role in East-West relations. Great Britain's self-image as a fully fledged Great Power can best be explained as the painful heritage of Winston Churchill's leading role in the politics of World War II. Churchill's dealings with the leaders of both superpowers – Roosevelt and Stalin – were considered as an example of Britain's appropriate post-war international role. This, however, did not take into account Britain's plunging political weight and status due to the 'loss' of its colonies. As a result, most British Prime Ministers, from Harold Macmillan and Anthony Eden, to Harold Wilson, have considered London's *Ostpolitik* as an important element of Cold War politics.[20] British independence has manifested itself in proposals and acts which, at times, have highly surprised and annoyed other West European countries. Eden's independent initiatives for arms control in the mid-1950s, Macmillan's quest for a compromise over Berlin during the period 1959-62, as well as his efforts at 'building economic bridges' towards the East, have been considered obnoxious by other West Europeans.[21] Wilson's declaration in 1964, that Great Britain was prepared to recognize the Oder-Neiße border between the GDR and Poland – something which was highly disputed in West Germany – once more indicated that London was regularly out of touch with the delicacies of Western Europe's relationship with the East.

Like France, Great Britain has lacked possession goals in the East. Edwina Moreton has argued that London's policy towards Eastern Europe has 'been predicated on two often contradictory desires: for stability and security in all of Europe and for whatever political change for the better was possible in Eastern Europe. In practice, for at least two decades after the war, the desire for security overrode the desire for change. Britain's concern with the Soviet threat and its close relationship with the other superpower, the United States, even at times to the exclusion of its West European allies, left little room for active diplomacy in Eastern Europe.'[22] London has therefore not played a significant role in the formulation or the coordination of West European policy towards the East. Since London needed West German approval for its application for entry into the Common Market in the early-1970s, Britain's policy towards the East was kept more in line with Bonn's newly formulated *Ostpolitik*. Somewhat paradoxically, London's urge to become more involved in the process of West European integration was also driven by the necessity to maintain the balance of power within Europe, which was jeopardized by the West German *rapprochement* to the USSR. Although London continued to lean heavily upon the United States, a more coherent West European unit was nevertheless considered advantageous, whereby 'Britain's most promising avenue to a European construction [has been] through collaboration with Germany'.[23]

Less prominent actors in East-West affairs, such as Italy and the countries of the Benelux, have generally adopted policies of benign neglect *vis-à-vis* the CMEA and its member states. Like Great Britain and France, they have lacked clearly defined possession goals and have espoused milieu objectives like strengthening *détente* and developing East-West economic relations. As a medium power in the European Community, Italy has played a modest role in the formulation of West European *Ostpolitik*. Commercial relations with the East have assumed a significant component in Rome's foreign policy.[24] Italian firms like ENI, Fiat and Olivetti have negotiated important large-scale economic transactions with the State-trading countries. Rome's backing through state-guaranteed export credits has been a crucial factor in realizing these projects. Although East-West trade was therefore considered worthwhile on commercial ground, more aspiring political goals were also pursued. The view of Giovanni Agnelli, the Chairman of the Board of Fiat, that interbloc trade would bring East and West closer together, is well known. In 1980 Agnelli argued: 'I believe that, on the whole and within certain limits, trade does indeed encourage the growth inside Soviet society, of forces and views naturally oriented toward the pursuit of more peaceful relations with the rest of the world ... Any time I go to Moscow and see cars in the street – not just official cars, but private cars in increasing numbers – I can't help seeing an evident relation between freedom of moving around and political freedom, or, at least, a growing desire for it.'[25]

A similar analysis also applies to the *Ostpolitik* of the countries of the Benelux. It has been argued that 'The Dutch role of faithful NATO ally made the Government a follower rather than a pioneer in detente with the Soviet Union'.[26] The Hague has waited until 1964 to pay its first official visit to the Soviet Union. Although the Netherlands has always been interested in developing its commercial relations with the East, it has never given much thought about formulating an independent policy towards this region. Only in the early-1970s, the position of the Netherlands changed somewhat with the start of the Helsinki negotiations. Dutch diplomats have played an active role in the preparations for the CSCE negotiations with the East, putting forward a number of draft proposals which have made it into the final text of the agreement. The Hague has especially put emphasis on the aspects of humanitarian contacts among the European countries. Holland was at first considered the odd man out in this field and has been ignored by the USSR and the Western nations alike. West Europeans have often questioned the likelihood that the principled Dutch objectives could be realized, whereas Soviet leader Brezhnev referred to the 'Dutch cabaret' within the CSCE.[27] The issue of human rights has remained a central aspect of the Dutch policy *vis-à-vis* the East and the Netherlands has given this point much attention, both in its bilateral relations with the Communist countries and during the Follow-up Meetings within the CSCE process.[28] Although Belgium has conducted a considerably more active *Ostpolitik*,[29] with energetic politicians like Paul-Henri Spaak and Pierre Harmel, the role of the Benelux countries has been marginal.

6.4 The Conference on Security and Co-operation in Europe (CSCE)

The preparations for the Conference on Security and Co-operation in Europe in the early-1970s overlapped with the creation of a structure of political cooperation among the EC member states. From 1970 to 1973, the basic rules and procedures of the EPC were formulated. Whereas the first meeting of the EC Foreign Ministers, in November 1970, had mainly dwelt on the situation in the Middle East, the following EPC summits generally focused upon 'matters connected with the possible holding of a conference on European security'. The European Community has revealed itself as an active player during the talks prior to the Helsinki Final Act of 1975. But before examining the EC's role in East-West relations during this period, we will first sketch the historical background of the CSCE.

Soviet proposals for a Pan-European agreement on 'collective security' were first submitted by Soviet Foreign Minister Molotov to the Four Power Conference of Foreign Ministers in Berlin, on 10 February 1954.[30] In November of that year, Moscow dispatched an official paper to all European governments in which the Soviet plans were spelled out. Another two years later, during a session of the European Commission for Europe (ECE), similar suggestions were aired. On that occasion, Moscow submitted a draft proposal calling for the development of an elaborate network of bilateral and/ or multilateral trade agreements, covering both Eastern and Western Europe. This network would include a set of multilateral payments agreements, agreements on Pan-European transport as well as the utilization of the continent's natural resources. During following sessions of the ECE (1957-9), Moscow made similar proposals and brought forward even more vague and ambiguous plans. The Seventeen Theses of 1957 were also accompanied by suggestions for such an economic conference. All these efforts were not very surprising, since Moscow had made no secret of its view that such a European security conference should be seen as a viable alternative to West European integration. Soviet commentators have always maintained that the EEC was an impediment to the creation of a 'new' Pan-European economic system, whereas the CMEA was considered as fully compatible with such a scheme. This would mean that in the event such a Pan-European agreement would see the light, the Community would have to be dissolved, whereas the CMEA could continue its present work.

In July 1966, the Political Consultative Committee of the Warsaw Treaty Organization (WTO), launched a similar idea (the so-called 'Declaration of Bucharest'). This was the beginning of a 'communiqué dialogue' between the Warsaw Pact and NATO. After the invasion of Czechoslovakia led by the Red Army, in 1968, the stream of Soviet proposals was arrested for a while. But when Finland invited all European countries to participate in a 'Pan-European' gathering (May 1969), such a conference again came in sight. It took the West European countries some three years to change the nature of the conference from a fully fledged 'security conference', devised by Moscow to sanction the post-war *status quo*, into a more all-embracing meeting, in which a wide range of political, humanitarian and cultural issues would also be among the topics for discussion. After the conclusion of the first Strategic Arms Limitation Talks (SALT) between the United States and the USSR, in May 1972, and Moscow's acceptance of the USA and Canada as full members of a European security conference, the so-called 'Multilateral Preparatory Talks' (MPT) for the CSCE could start on 22 November 1972.[31] As Alfred E. Pijpers has argued: 'The MPT were ... legally not a real conference or pre-conference, but just an informal diplomatic *salon-de-thé*. Officially the representatives of the 35 countries were not even allowed to call themselves "delegations".'[32] For the European Community, this European security conference came during a hectic period in which it had to incorporate a number of new member states. The international status of the EC was on the increase both due to the inclusion of Great Britain, Denmark and Ireland, and the EC's newly acquired monopoly of external commercial policy.[33] The Six had become Nine, who – at least now – also seemed able to present themselves as one club, with one spokesman.

Since important economic issues would be discussed, the EC had decided that the European Commission should be a partner during the negotiations for what was now officially called the Conference on Security and Co-operation in Europe. At a gathering of the EC Heads of State, prior to the first preparatory meetings, a communiqué was issued which declared: 'In order to encourage *détente* in Europe, the Community confirms its intention to pursue a common commercial policy *vis-à-vis* the countries of the East, after January 1, 1973 ... This policy of cooperation is in its current stage closely linked with the preparations and the results of the Conference for Security and Co-operation in Europe, in which the Community and its member states are expected to contribute in a coordinated and constructive manner.'[34] It was clear that the CSCE was to be not only the first important challenge for the Community's proclaimed Common Commercial Policy, but also a test case for Brussels' intentions to forge greater solidarity among its member states' foreign policies towards the East.[35] Not many were optimistic about the chances that the Community would be strong and persistent enough to meet this challenge, since Brussels had until then achieved little in this field. Since the intergovernmentalist attitude dominated among the member states – despite a number of lofty declarations to the contrary – it was expected that the CSCE process would once more be used for narrow national purposes, where Bonn would pursue its own *Deutschlandpolitik* and *Ostpolitik*, the French would look after their particular national and regional interests (such as the Mediterranean area), and (after their accession in January 1973) the Danes would be especially interested in Scandinavian issues.

From the beginning it was expected that NATO would become the most effective and opportune framework for the West in order to prepare for such a 'security' conference. However, it soon turned out that most discussions were held among the West Europeans within the EC and the EPC. During the preparatory phase of the Conference – most notably during the meetings in Geneva where representatives of the Six coordinated their policy stances – important steps were taken in the direction of a common Community *Ostpolitik*. A so-called 'Groupe *ad hoc* CSCE' had been set up in February 1971, consisting of delegations from the EC member states and the Commission, preparing the way for common ground on economic issues. This group was especially set up in order to bring the Commission into the consultation process. A similar group, called 'Sous-Comité CSCE', was set up within the EPC in order to tackle the political issues. As a matter of course, the Commission was *not* represented in the latter group, since politics was still considered forbidden ground for the European Community. Talks continued almost as long as was necessary for achieving one, unified position on all important points. If consensus could not be achieved on this level the particular argument was generally solved during meetings of the Political Directors of the Foreign Ministries of the member states. As a result, the main platform for coordination shifted from NATO to the European Community. This can partly be explained by the fact that the United States remained rather aloof from these negotiations, thereby giving more diplomatic leeway to its West European partners.[36] The Community's efforts to meet its challenge far exceeded the stamina and unity of other 'blocs' participating in the Conference, such as the neutrals and the Communist countries. EC preparation on all points far excelled that of others, giving it an advantage over the other participants. The expertise of the European Community was acknowledged by many neutral countries, such as Sweden, Switzerland and

Austria, which had many political and economic interests in common. These countries therefore generally followed the course set out by the Community during the MPT.

For the USSR, the active role of the EC was cause for alarm. They had initiated the negotiation process in an effort to weaken the economic and political influence of the EC in Western Europe, but now the exact opposite was imminent. In order to inhibit the EC's commitment, the USSR began to question the Commission's mandate. At first, Soviet delegates issued official complaints as to the legality of the Commission's involvement in the preparations for the CSCE. They argued that the Conference was a meeting among *nations*; organizations could therefore not play a role and a 'bloc-to-bloc' approach was to be avoided. From the start, Commission officials were apprehensive that the Soviet Union would react to the presence of the EC by claiming a similar status for the CMEA. However, it soon turned out that the Soviet leaders wisely refrained from such a counteract, since this was expected to complicate the process considerably. In order to circumvent upcoming Soviet criticism, the European Community formulated a compromise: the Chairman of the EC Council would represent the Community only on trade issues and would have a Commission official in his delegation, who would take the floor on matters of Community competence. On political and security issues, the Chairman would officially only speak for his own country. This canny cosmetic concession of the Community was apparently adequate to appease the USSR, since the complaints from Communist delegates gradually came to a halt.

Although the CSCE comprised some thirty-five participants, most important negotiations were conducted between only two actors: the European Community and the USSR. This can be explained by the fact that the Soviet Union and Eastern Europe have been primarily interested in economic and technological cooperation with the West. The so-called 'Second Basket' (CSCE-speak for cooperation in the field of economics, science, technology and the environment), was precisely the area where the Community had just acquired a negotiating monopoly. Since the United States was far from cooperative on East-West trade, the European Community soon turned into the principal discussion partner for the USSR. Although this dialogue did not touch upon the nuts and bolts of East-West trade, it has set several steps to remove political obstacles for increased interbloc commerce. The final resolution for the Second Basket was almost entirely based upon draft proposals which had originated from the drawing boards of the European Commission.

But in the other two Baskets as well (European security and cooperation in humanitarian and other fields), cooperation among the Nine was intensive and, all in all, very successful. Between September 1973 and July 1975, the Sous-Comité CSCE of the EPC-mechanism produced some ten bulky reports, examining and explaining the developments of the negotiations and suggesting useful approaches for further discussions. These reports have become the main beacons for the Nine in steering a steady course during these early years of the Helsinki process.[37] Cooperation among the Nine reached its apex in the system of 'chefs-de-file', whereby the main responsibility for a certain subject area of the Conference was trusted to a delegation of one of the nine EC member states. Each delegation had to take care of the internal reporting about its specific subject, had to formulate suggestions for common positions and had to maintain the contacts with the East Europeans, the USSR and the neutral countries.[38] This division of labour among the Nine made efficient use of specific expertise within each member state, which also made it possible for the smaller EC members to advance their opinions and to boost their role before the media.

The USSR was so eager to make the Helsinki negotiations successful, that it did not even protest against the Italian Prime Minister, Aldo Moro (then Chairman of the EC Council), signing the Treaty on 1 August 1975, both in the name of his country *and* for the European Community. Neither did the Soviet Union respond to the official communiqué of Moro after the final ceremony. This final declaration, after the Helsinki Final Act had been signed, has frequently been labelled as the most important document on EC policy towards the CSCE. The European Council declared, on 17 July 1975: 'The Conference was characterized by a concentrated contribution of the Community, acknowledging the expectations of the negotiations of Helsinki, made in Paris by the Heads of State and Government, October 22, 1972. The negotiations of Helsinki and Geneva have provided the opportunity to the Nine to come to a common policy, which is exemplary for constructive co-operation; it has also showed that the process of unity, in which the countries of the Community will live up to their historical responsibilities, has entered its ripening phase.'[39] It was noteworthy that, on the part of the Communist countries, no mention was even made as to the role of the CMEA in the Helsinki process.

The political tools developed for that purpose were maintained, which led to a common Community stance at the CSCE Follow-up Meetings in Belgrade (October 1977 – March 1978) and Madrid (November 1980 – September 1983). This was partly the result of the very regular meetings of the Working Group of CSCE-experts of the EC member states, something which was decided during the Helsinki negotiations. This Working Group has been very active in drafting the mandates for the Follow-Up Meetings and most western proposals come out of the EPC-hat. The Ten Heads of Mission met a number of times a week with the President of the EC delegation, and EC specialist meetings took place on a daily basis.[40] The Soviet opposition to the Community's position within the CSCE framework obviously wore down. Whereas either the USSR or one of its allies generally used to raise points of order whenever somebody spoke on behalf of the EC, this no longer occurred at the Madrid Meetings.[41] By the end of the 1970s, the role of the European

Community in the CSCE process had become less pronounced. This had everything to do with the demise of the period of *détente* and the subsequent return of the Second Cold War. The United States became more involved in the CSCE process since it had come to realize that the Third Basket provided a useful mechanism for criticizing the Communist record on human rights. Moreover, since the Madrid Meeting, the issue of so-called 'Confidence Building Measures' had gained more emphasis, which was more a subject for NATO than for the EPC or the European Community. As Alfred Pijpers has argued: 'In such circumstances there is presumably less room for a "civilian power" like the EC'.[42]

Michel Tatu has correctly argued that 'In the East, the aim of [the Soviet proposals for a CSCE] is to consolidate the *status quo*, to strengthen the cohesion and integration of the members of the system, and to limit its penetration by Western influence. In the West, on the other hand, the aim is to loosen the bonds among the members of the EEC and between them and the United States, to hinder further integration, and to facilitate the penetration of Soviet influence.'[43] One can certainly say that the effect of the CSCE process has been exactly the opposite of Moscow's intentions. It is somewhat ironic that the CSCE, devised by Moscow as a Pan-European *alternative* for the European Community, has been one of the catalysts for closer cooperation and consultation on foreign policy issues among the EC member states. The CSCE process has helped along Community unity on foreign affairs issues, meanwhile promoting centrifugal tendencies within the East European countries. As William Wallace has argued: 'The CSCE presented the most immediate issue for consultation, and arguably the most incentives for cooperation ... the division of the agenda of the conference into separate "baskets" of issues neatly fitted the distinction between Community competence and political questions ... the CSCE had made a decisive contribution to the development and the tone of political cooperation.'[44]

However, although the CSCE negotiations have provided the EC with a habit of consultation and a set of common stances on foreign policy issues, no political cooperation machinery on East-West affairs had come into existence. The EPC had only provided a framework for coordination and loose harmonization of the member states' foreign policies. Whenever the member states did not agree with the EPC compromise, they were free simply to link up with others. This has occurred frequently, whereby Denmark, for instance, tended to join the Scandinavian countries, and Italy other Mediterranean countries. Although strict intergovernmentalism still ruled the EPC, it cannot be denied that the experiences of the CSCE consultations, as well as the structures of cooperation which were set up in that context, have established an important network of rules, procedures and expectations for cooperation among the EC members. In this respect, the CSCE process has been the motor of the EPC regime which has later been incorporated within the overall EC framework.

6.5 Afghanistan, Poland and the Urengoi pipeline row

Another test for the EC and the EPC presented itself in the late-1970s and early-1980s. First of all, there was the Soviet invasion of Afghanistan in December 1979. This event considerably changed the political atmosphere of East-West relations leading up to a replay of the Cold War. Although Moscow maintained that the Red Army had received an invitation from the political leaders in Kabul to lend assistance, it was clear to the outside world that the USSR was in an expansionist mood. However, due to the delicate nuclear stalemate between East and West, western military actions were not seriously considered; instead economic instruments of statecraft were used. Klaus Knorr was certainly right when he maintained that the 'coercive employment of economic leverage is an option most likely to appeal to conflicting governments in issue areas in which military threats are inapplicable because their use would be regarded as illegitimate or otherwise disproportionally costly ... Recourse to economic coercion is then seen not as a substitute for resorting to military force but as an instrument for protecting national interests not vital enough to bring military options into play, yet too valuable to be easily abandoned.'[45] After the Soviet invasion the United States considered that economic and political sanctions were in order to air their indignation; Western Europe followed the American course with more modest sanctions.

But the early-1980s had much more in store. When the Polish Communist regime declared martial law, on 13 December 1981, in order to quell the ascent of the Solidarity trade movement, the US Reagan Administration imposed further economic sanctions against the Soviet Union, which was considered responsible for the incidents in Poland. The reactions of the EC member states were mixed. Whereas London approved the US sanctions, both Paris and Bonn were reluctant to follow Washington's lead. In early January, the European Community issued a statement that it would not compromise the American sanctions and later imposed rather mild economic sanctions on the Soviet Union. On 15 March 1982, Brussels announced that it would cut down some imports from the USSR (on, among others, caviar, diamonds and electromotors), by approximately 25-50 per cent.[46] The economic reprisals of the EC were only meant to signal disapproval, since it was clearly acknowledged that it would be nigh impossible to alter Soviet foreign policy through economic linkage. In many respects, the difference in response to the Soviet invasion was based upon a fundamental divergence between the United States and in particular the FRG and France as to the effectiveness and appropriateness of economic sanctions as a tool of foreign policy. The lack of a firm and coordinated West European response to the Afghan crisis also illustrated the confusing state of affairs within the EC. Neither the EC nor the EPC were authorized more than in a formal way to deal with these security issues,[47] which remained the prerogative of the national governments and

NATO. Moreover, the Soviet invasion occurred during an impasse in the EC's management: 'during the Christmas holiday, with the Irish Presidency in the process of transferring the responsibilities to the Italian Government, and with the German Chancellor on holiday in Spain'.[48]

In the early-1980s, the issue of East-West trade and economic sanctions was developing into a major crisis within the Atlantic Alliance. The intra-western debate focused upon four closely related issues: the US grain embargo, technology transfer, export credits and energy security. In particular, the American grain embargo against the USSR from January to April 1980 caused friction between Washington and the European Community. The United States started to accuse the EC and its member states of accepting the grain orders which would normally go to American suppliers, thereby undercutting the American embargo. This would have been contrary to the EC Council's decision of January 1980, which had declared that 'The Community fixed the principle that Community deliveries should not replace directly or indirectly United States' deliveries to the Soviet market'. The Council therefore 'invited the Commission to take measures necessary in respect of cereals and products derived from cereals and to propose possible other measures for other products, while respecting the traditional volume of trade'.[49] These measures to restrict grain sales to the East were mainly issued in political solidarity with Washington.

The controversy on East-West trade between Western Europe and the United States became harsher when Washington had decided to step up its vigilance on the export of high-technology to the Communist countries. The United States argued that CoCom should be refurbished, much to the dismay of Western Europe. This issue was closely linked to the American objections to West European export credit subsidies. The Siberian export pipeline, linking the Western Siberian Urengoi gasfield to Western Europe, became the core of this dispute. Only one week after the Soviet invasion of Afghanistan, the West German firm Ruhrgas had announced that it was going to start up a long-term project with the Soviet gas trading agency Soyuzgazexport, which would result in the export of more than 30 BCM per year to Western Europe. In 1982, the USSR gained export credits from Western Europe and Japan for an amount of more than US\$ 14 billion, on favourable terms. American policy-makers aired their indignation over these decisions, arguing that Western Europe would endanger Atlantic security by sharing high-technology with the Soviets; it would also risk political Finlandization by becoming overly dependent on Soviet energy. Opponents to the pipeline in the US Department of Energy went as far as to argue that 'It is in the national security interest of the United States and the West to constrain Soviet energy development in the coming decade'.[50]

In June 1982, Washington claimed extraterritorial jurisdiction for the US sanctions over West European and Japanese subsidiaries of American companies. The West European firms which were producing under licence of

US firms, as well as firms using American-made parts, were effectively prohibited from exporting to the USSR and Eastern Europe. Not very surprisingly, West European governments and firms reacted with indignation, and London and Paris issued special legislation ordering their firms to honour their contracts with the East.[51] During the pipeline row, the European Community acted both as a spokesman for its member states, as well as a mediator between the conflicting parties.[52] The EC Council had questioned the legality of the American sanctions against West European firms, and the EC delivered a formal protest to Washington on 14 July 1982. One month later, the Commission again protested in Washington, this time delivering a memorandum in which the American complaints were disproved.[53] Several studies of the Commission's Directorate-General for Energy (DG XVII) had provided the technical arguments necessary to refute the American charges. The Community also actively participated in invited meetings of the International Energy Agency, which was asked to investigate Washington's criticism of West European energy dependency. The EC's legal services also played an important role in questioning the legality of the American regulations.[54]

Most West European countries have clearly favoured the construction of the pipeline. They failed to see the security threats of energy cooperation with the USSR, more particularly since the Helsinki Final Act had called for exactly these long-term energy projects. Moreover, the other suppliers of oil and gas, such as Iran, Iraq and Libya, could hardly boast a better record of conduct in world politics than the USSR.[55] When Gaz de France and its Soviet counterpart signed a long-term gas import contract, on 22 January 1982, Pierre Mauroy, the French Prime Minister, declared: 'Let us not, on top of the suffering of the Polish people, add the suffering of the French people who would be deprived of heating this winter.'[56] Once the American sanctions had been lifted in November 1982, the West European firms were free to fulfil their export obligations. However, the pipeline row had caused serious frictions between the United States and the European Community. What began as an East-West conflict developed into a major West-West confrontation. This intra-Alliance crisis was eventually solved by a solemn declaration during the Summit of the G-7 in Paris, in 1983. During the whole quandary, the European Community presented itself as a useful framework of foreign policy cooperation among the member states which was able to formulate the closest thing to a 'West European' position on issues of East-West trade and technology transfer.

The lack of EC foreign policy coordination during the Afghan and Polish crises has furthermore launched renewed efforts to improve the mechanisms and procedures within the EPC. In November 1980, the German Foreign Minister, Hans-Dietrich Genscher, called for EC coordination in the field of security policy, which resulted in the so-called Genscher-Colombo proposals on this issue. In October 1981, the Foreign Ministers of the Ten adopted several measures which were devised to streamline the European Community's response to international emergencies. The now well-known 'troika' principle – whereby the Council President is assisted by the preceding and succeeding Presidents – was adopted. But more importantly, ministerial meetings could now be summoned within forty-eight hours in case of international crisis situations. But besides these new procedures the EC had emerged from the intra-Alliance dispute with renewed vigour and confidence. The conflict with the United States had brought home the point that the European Community was in many respects well placed to defend the economic, political *and* security interests of many member states.[57] As Julie Katzman has argued:

> A classic example of an external threat promoting internal solidarity, the pipeline row served, in the final analysis, to strengthen the Community and to increase the credibility of the Commission. What started as a multilateral intergovernmental controversy – a matter for bilateral negotiations – came to be co-ordinated, at many levels, in Brussels, and widely regarded as a Community affair ... During the latter months of the pipeline row with the US, the Ten did project a European identity, and with each new transatlantic crisis their sense of identity increased. The European Community, when and wherever allowed, has assumed new responsibilities as the champion and vehicle of that identity.[58]

6.6 Europe's changing role

This concise analysis of the different approaches towards the East of the EC's member states may have raised some understanding as to Brussels' difficulties in formulating a coordinated and effective *Ostpolitik*. The divergence of national foreign policy goals has significantly hampered the European Community's ability to speak with one voice. The lack of cooperation among the member states can be brought back to three reasons: (1) historical animosity; (2) misunderstanding and misperception; and (3) basic differences in national interests. All three factors have been closely connected, sometimes neutralizing each other but in most cases generating even more barriers to collective action. Knowing – with the luxury of hindsight – that the EC member states have nevertheless successfully transferred a considerable portion of national sovereignty to Brussels (both in the field of economic, monetary and foreign policy), it will be interesting to examine how the member states have overcome their apprehensions of a coordinated *Ostpolitik*.

In earlier chapters we have seen that external pressures and the post-war structure of bipolarity have been forces encouraging West European economic integration. Among the external pressures the towering Soviet threat during the Cold War has been the most manifest. During the period of regime formation on political cooperation within the EC, the role of the Soviet Union has been less portentous, although the systemic factors have been consequential. As Alfred Pijpers has argued: 'the EPC performance in the period 1973-1975 probably was also stimulated by external factors like the above mentioned aloofness of the United States, and more generally by some favorable conditions for *détente*, which caused a relaxing of bipolarity between East and West, and created more room for manoeuvre for the non-military powers and blocs'.[59] This looks like a plausible explanation for the earlier period of political cooperation. After the demise of *détente*, however, the external situation had altered markedly. In this context, two explanations of West European economic and political integration stand out.[60] First, a number of systemic factors have to be taken into account. With the deterioration and looming breakdown of the multilateral structure of the international economy (a process which has its origins in the fading away of American hegemony caused by a relative decline of American power), the impetus for the West European countries to unite has increased considerably. It was recognized that the United States could no longer wield its economic power to manage the liberal international order in the way it had done during the first postwar decades (see Chapter 8.2). Western Europe, and the European Community in particular, had to anticipate these long-term developments and get its act together.[61] With the demise of Communism in the late-1980s, the external pressures for the EC to step up the process of economic, political and military integration have escalated.

The second explanation stresses the activities of international and transnational actors. Two major 'pressure groups' have been identified: (1) the Commission of the European Community; and (2) transnational business groups. The Commission has frequently been considered as a powerful motor, setting the EC's agenda and generating new policy initiatives. The rejuvenating work by the Commission President Jacques Delors, for example, has been held partly responsible for the success of the 1992 initiative. Another factor has been the large number of West European firms who have actively lobbied for a free internal market for goods, capital and services within the EC. The so-called 'White Paper' for the construction of this free internal market – as presented by Lord Cockfield in the Summer of 1985 – has been heavily influenced by the ideas and vision of a small group of West European captains of industry (under the leadership of Wisse Dekker, the Chairman of the Board of Philips, the Dutch multinational).[62] State borders and economic nationalism were considered incompatible with the requirements of the increasing globalization of the world economy.

Both explanations present powerful insights into the background of the development of integration within the EC. Both hypotheses pay little attention to the part played by the East, and it will be clear that Moscow has indeed hardly had a role in this process. When we examine the development of the European Community's foreign policy towards the East, it is, however, important to be aware of these structural changes in the world economy and to recognize their impact upon the process of West European unification, both in the economic and political field. These changes in the structure of world politics have led to a significant transformation of the political commitment of West European leaders. A large number of interstate bargains among the EC member states – which have reflected their national interests and their relative power – have shaped a strong and sturdy regime of economic and political cooperation. Although we are now getting somewhat ahead on our analysis of the nature of the regime formation within the EC, this chapter has once again pointed out the central importance of external factors for moulding a strong framework of integration. In no case, however, has the European Community been able to go beyond the limits set by the national interests of the major member states; intergovernmentalism, lowest common denominator bargaining and modest transfers of sovereignty have all characterized the formation of a regime for the EC's foreign policy towards the East.

7. The EC and the CMEA: Deaf-Mutes Communicate

Der 'Dialog der Taubstummen' zwischen EG und RGW schleppt sich nunmehr seit 1973 hin und macht bei jedem Treffen von Delegationen weniger Schlagzeilen.

Axel Lebahn, 'Alternativen in den EG-RGW Beziehungen', *Aussenpolitik*, vol.31, no.2 (1980), p.147.

7.1 Introduction

In the previous chapters we have more than once touched upon the complicated relationship between the European Community and the CMEA (which has sometimes been mistakenly called 'the EC of the East'). It is little wonder that since the Soviet Union and Eastern Europe have refused to recognize Brussels' legal right to bear responsibility for the external trade relations of the Community, they have also refrained from establishing official ties between the economic organizations of both blocs. In this chapter we will analyse the links between the CMEA and the European Community, a relationship which has been aptly characterized as a case study in 'a dialogue between deaf-mutes', that is to say, contact between both blocs has been possible, but troublesome and at most times arduous and frustrating. Three stages can be identified in the CMEA-EC relationship.[1] First, a decade of mutual neglect, covering 1957-69. Second, a period in which both economic organizations initiated negotiations without a realistic possibility of a breakthrough (1970-84). Third, a phase in which negotiations entered the *perestroika* maelstrom, finally resulting in a Joint Declaration in which mutual recognition was acknowledged (in 1988).

7.2 A period of mutual neglect

During the 1960s, Moscow had continued in its exceptionally hostile attitude towards the Common Market. Although the East European countries did enter into unofficial contacts with Brussels, the Soviet leaders had never allowed these ties to hamper Communist unity. Moscow's satellites were permitted to conduct relations with Brussels on a minimal basis, barely sufficient to regulate a basic level of commercial relations between both blocs. The Vice-President of the USSR Academy of Sciences, Alexei Rumyantsev, argued in 1969 that the mutual ties between the CMEA members 'are a direct stimulus to their ever-closer economic consolidation and *ultimately* to the union of their economies in a single whole ... [and] in developing relations with the capitalist countries each socialist country bases itself on its fraternal links with the whole socialist community'.[2] In Chapter 4 we have examined Moscow's economic, political and ideological reasons for keeping the European Community at arm's length. This triad of reasons can also be applied to the CMEA's approach to the EC. Although closer ties between East and West had been ideologically sanctified under the more lenient conditions of 'peaceful coexistence', direct and official communication between the CMEA and the Community was non-existent.

It is, however, important to stress the fact that this lack of official relations between the European Community and the CMEA and its members certainly did *not* imply that contacts had been reduced to zero. On the contrary, there have always been a number of ways to settle the multitude of commercial problems which sprang up during the day-to-day practice of East-West economic relations. Firstly, there was the network of economic cooperation agreements between the EC member states and a large number of CMEA countries. These bilateral agreements usually installed a practical infrastructure for monitoring the flows of East-West trade. For example, the Franco-Soviet cooperation agreement had established no less than three different commissions: a 'Grande Commission' bringing together high-level governmental officials, a technical (so-called 'Petite') commission, and a Franco-Soviet Chamber of Commerce which was actively promoting and assisting commercial relations between both countries. Most EC member states had established similar networks of commissions which met regularly to discuss aspects of economic cooperation. Due to the fact that these commissions have created an infrastructure for regular bilateral consultations between West and East Europeans, they have certainly been useful. Over the years, however, these annual meetings acquired a rather procedural and predictable character. Commercial problems of any importance were usually not tackled and resolved at these meetings, where East European delegates limited themselves to reading prepared statements which hardly changed in contents over the years. These bilateral commissions could therefore most certainly not compensate for the lack of direct links with Brussels.

An important role was also played by the multilateral platforms and international organizations in which the EC Commission could negotiate both with several East European countries and with the USSR. This so-called 'second front' of EC contacts with the State-trading countries must not be overlooked. Organizations like the United Nations and its specialized branches (for instance the Economic Commission for Europe and the UNCTAD), but also negotiations within the framework of GATT and the meetings in the CSCE process, have been useful channels of communication on economic and commercial issues.[3] Since 1974, both the European Community and the CMEA have acquired observer status within the UN organizations. Brussels has tried to use its position within the UN to foster a more coherent position on East-West trade issues among its member states; the policy stances of the East European countries were already quite homogeneous, mainly due to Soviet dominance within the CMEA. Moscow has been remarkably active within the UN Economic Commission for Europe.[4] The so-called 'Brezhnev Proposal' within the ECE of 1976, was a case in point. This Brezhnev Proposal called for more elaborate and constructive East-West commercial cooperation by arranging for 'Pan-European economic congresses' where all issues and problems of East-West trade could be discussed. Like most of these Soviet grand schemes, this offer underwent a quiet death. Although the ECE has been a useful platform for economic consultation between the two economic blocs, in which both the European Community and the CMEA were able to maintain contact even during the darkest years of the Cold War, it has never been able to provide a genuine alternative for direct and official cooperation based upon mutual recognition.

As of May 1964, the EEC as such, represented by the Commission, had been taking part in negotiations within the GATT. Several State-trading countries had also been accepted within this organization. Czechoslovakia, for instance, had been among the founding members of GATT – in 1947 – although Prague had not actively participated within the GATT since the Communist coup of February 1948. Among the other East European GATT-members were Poland (since 1967), Romania (1971) and Hungary (1973); Bulgaria acquired observer status within the GATT in 1967. Although every member of GATT has been *de jure* entitled to trade concessions on the basis of the most-favoured nation (MFN) principle, the State-trading countries have always been an exception. Since the GATT system had been set up for market-oriented economies, nations with a so-called 'non-market status' have had to sign separate protocols of accession to GATT, comprising a commitment to increase (or 'develop and diversify') their imports from other GATT members at a specific annual rate. Although the market economies extended MFN-tariff treatment to them, they maintained import quotas against them for certain sensitive products. This has set them apart from the other participants within the organization. The European Community has refused to extend the MFN-concession to the CMEA members in a blanket fashion, but the MFN status for tariffs has in practice been granted to each of the State-trading countries individually, even before they became members of GATT. As Susan Senior Nello has argued: 'For non-Gatt members such as the Soviet Union and Bulgaria MFN status was given *de facto* but not *de jure*, which was largely a question of negotiating tactics since if the status were granted *de jure*, it would no longer be a concession'.[5] Within the multilateral forum of the GATT, the East Europeans have accepted the EC Commission as a worthy negotiating partner and have managed to iron out many of their commercial problems.[6] The USSR has never been admitted within the important international economic organizations. For a long time, Moscow had simply discarded GATT as a 'club of the rich', as the pinnacle of western capitalism with which it did not want to deal with in any way. In a similar fashion, the USSR has disregarded the IMF, the World Bank and the OECD. Only in 1986 did the Soviet Union air its first approving statements on both GATT and the Bretton Woods institutions; in August of that year Moscow declared that it wanted to become a fully fledged member of GATT.[7] Contacts between the EC and the East at this 'second front' have, however, also never fully compensated the lack of official relations.

In the 1960s, a few tentative and very cautious moves were made on both sides to examine how and what sort of ties could be established between the EEC and the CMEA. The first Soviet 'reconnaissance' visit to the European Community's institutions was paid by two Russian journalists, in 1962. One year later, in October 1963, Soviet officials agreed to accept a European Community paper on tariff concessions dealing with the export of vodka and caviar; but only under the strict condition that the acceptation of this document would not be considered as an indication that the USSR was ready to recognize the Community.[8] The EEC's offer itself was, however, never honoured with a Soviet answer (see Chapter 4.5). Several months later, Jean Rey, then in charge of external relations in the Commission, invited the Soviet Government to send a delegation to Brussels in case it was interested in increasing its trade with the Six. The Soviet response was characteristic: in October 1964, the Soviet Vice-Premier argued in response that he would most certainly *not* establish contacts with the Commission for the simple reason that he did not know of its existence. With this display of a lack of interest in (and perhaps even the lack of knowledge of) the European Economic Community, Moscow wanted to prove the marginal importance of the process of West European economic integration, denying the EEC's status as a prominent actor in its own right.

Such political 'ignorance' was at that time also widely spread among the other Communist states. However, in the ensuing years, several CMEA member states nevertheless decided to send informal representatives of trading agencies to the Community, whereby most East European countries established contacts with Brussels (on 'technical issues') during the period 1964-8. It took Moscow until late 1968 to follow the example of its CMEA partners, when the First Secretary of the Soviet Embassy in Brussels, Yourii Buzykin, visited the Commission's Headquarters. Soviet spokesmen stressed that the meeting between Buzykin and Jean-François Deniau, the Commissioner for External Trade (on 13 December), had 'no official character', but that it was to be considered a routine visit in order to obtain 'further information'. The Kremlin's laconic statement did not, however, explain the timing of this Soviet advance to the European Community. Only a few months earlier, the EC Council of Ministers had announced its decision that it would begin to distinguish among market and non-market economies in its external trade practices. This would require that the European Community would apply a different set of commercial rules and procedures to trade with Communist countries as compared with trade with the rest of the world. The Soviet visit to the EC Commission was perhaps intended to modify Brussels' new approach to the East, but nothing of substance was proposed during that meeting. This first EC-USSR meeting took place in top secret and it was more than a month later that the western press first made mention of it, labelling it an initial step along the road of Moscow's recognition of the European Community. Although it was indeed one of Moscow's first steps, the road towards full recognition proved to be much longer than most observers had envisaged in the late-1960s.

7.3 *Détente*: let's get together

A significant shift in the Soviet attitude towards the European Community occurred in the early-1970s. Again, this was hardly a spontaneous change of heart, since the Kremlin's new approach to Brussels followed on the one hand the successful enlargement of the EC with the United Kingdom and Denmark, and on the other hand had everything to do with the dawn of *détente* (or 'peaceful coexistence' as the Soviet leaders preferred to call it) between East and West. During this relatively short period, the Manichean world of the Cold War was temporarily exchanged for a more cooperative attitude on both sides of the Iron Curtain. The negotiations in preparation for the Helsinki Accords had unquestionably played a role in overcoming some of the ideological and political barriers which had been constructed during the decades of Cold War (see Chapter 6.4). Much has been written on the origins of this half-decade of East-West conciliation. Although this is hardly the place to discuss the roots of *détente*, it is nevertheless important to point out one of the most important factors explaining Moscow's policy shift towards trade with the West and subsequently its attitude towards the European Community.

One of the crucial factors explaining Soviet *rapprochement* has been the continuing slow-down of economic growth within the USSR and the State-trading countries at large. Communist leaders have acknowledged the fact that the autarkic course of their economies – as well as the closed nature of their societies – has excluded them from the so-called 'technotronic revolutions' which had been taking place in the capitalist world. Together with most countries of the capitalist West, the members of the European Community had experienced a period of rapid economic growth and conspicuous prosperity. It was evident that the USSR had to change either its domestic policy or its foreign policy in order to adjust to these structural drawbacks. For this reason, the Communist leaders found themselves on the horns of a dilemma: they had to choose between structural domestic reform on the one hand, and international *rapprochement* on the other. It was clearly realized that a *perestroika avant la lettre* would have unknown and probably undesirable political side effects, eroding the Communist powerbase. Stepping up East-West interaction and cooperation, on the other hand, could also result in the undesired exposure of Communist society to western values. It was expected that opening the window to the West would let in an undesired draught of economic political liberalism. However, the latter option was still deemed less hazardous, and reviving East-West trade and technology transfer became one of the important objectives of Soviet and East European foreign policy. Soviet leaders declared during the 25th CPSU Congress of 1976: 'We, like other states, wish to use the advantages conferred by international economic relationships as an additional means of solving economic problems and gaining time, of raising productivity and improving technological progress'.[9] As one Moscow major policy-maker added: 'The purpose of *détente* was to make the process of international change as painless as possible' for the USSR.[10] Changing the Communist attitude towards trade with the West in general went hand in hand with a more conciliatory policy towards the European Community.

The East European impetus to overcome its political and ideological objections to a more official arrangement with the EC was also economic in nature. Most of the East European countries had been confronted with the Common Market's protectionist policies springing from the CAP. Since the CAP had effectively limited most East European exports to the EC, pressure built up in the East to discard its current policy of ignoring Brussels and instead conclude an official trade arrangement with the Community in which its commercial interests could be much better represented. Many East European countries had also complained that the enlargement of the European Community with Great Britain, Ireland and Denmark, in 1973, had had adverse implications for their export capabilities to the Common Market, especially in sectors such as steel, textiles and agriculture. As Moscow's first attempt to get into contact with Brussels (in late 1968) had been made in response to the European Community's unitary stance towards the East, the subsequent Soviet and East European attitude towards the EC was also largely determined by Brussels' success in implementing its Common Commercial Policy. The more forcefully and the more unitedly the European Community began to conduct its external trade policy, the more Moscow seemed ready to accept Brussels as a powerful political entity. Whereas the EC had been enlarged and had acquired more authority in foreign trade matters, the economic prospects for the centrally planned economies looked increasingly dim. All this implied that Moscow's bargaining position *vis-à-vis* the West had been weakened and that the CMEA members now had to come to terms with the idea that the European Community had become an economic and political organization which could no longer be ignored with impunity.

In March 1972, Soviet leader Leonid Brezhnev had already – albeit implicitly – referred to some kind of trade-off between East and West: Moscow had indicated that it was willing to recognize the Common Market on the condition that Brussels would reciprocate and would agree to recognize the CMEA as the trade representative of the East. A similar proposal was again brought forward during the preparatory negotiations for the CSCE in Helsinki, which had started in December of that year. Not very surprisingly, Brussels turned this offer down, arguing that the European Community and the CMEA were organizations of a totally different legal standing and that it could therefore not take up relations on the basis of equality. This line of argument has formed the basis of the European Community's general approach *vis-à-vis* the CMEA; we shall discuss this issue more elaborately later in this chapter.

Further *rapprochement* seemed to lie ahead in January 1973, when Brezhnev suggested to his French counterpart, Georges Pompidou, that they should explore the possibilities of closer cooperation between the European Community and the CMEA.[11] The successful start of the negotiations in Helsinki had markedly improved the political atmosphere between East and West, something which made an agreement between the EC and the CMEA less unlikely. It was the USSR which took the initiative of placing EC-CMEA talks on the East-West agenda. On 3 July 1973, Soviet Foreign Minister Andrey Gromyko informally communicated the CMEA's intention to enter into negotiations with the Community. Gromyko's overture towards the EC was quite appropriately made during the first CSCE meeting, where he made his suggestion to the Danish Minister of Foreign Affairs, K. B. Andersen (then EC Council President). When the French and Luxembourg Ministers of Foreign Affairs (M. Jobert and G. Thorn) paid a visit to Moscow later that month, Soviet officials again came forward with proposals to place official EC-CMEA cooperation high on their respective political agendas. On 27 August 1973, the first (but still unofficial) contacts were established when the CMEA's Secretary-General, Nicolai W. Faddeyev, visited Copenhagen (ostensibly while he was 'on holiday'), and discussed the issue with the Danish Minister of Foreign Trade, Ivar Norgaard (then EC Council President). With exceptional caution and diplomatic cumbersomeness, Faddeyev proposed a meeting between delegations from the CMEA and the European Community where 'the possibilities of cooperation could be discussed'.

After a lukewarm response from the European Community (which stressed that the EC Commission should be approached, not the individual Ministers or the Council), Moscow did not press this point any further. Brussels was not interested in dealing with the CMEA on the basis of equality and the Kremlin refused to budge immediately. It has also been argued that the USSR lost interest in an EC-CMEA arrangement because it 'came to realize that the EEC's introduction of a common trade policy would have little effect on Soviet foreign trade'.[12] Indeed, it had soon become clear that simultaneously with the construction of Brussels' Common Commercial Policy, the actual significance of the traditional trade agreements and tariffs for trading with the East had declined. First of all, the range of commodities subject to these Community quotas had been reduced notably over the previous few years. The fact that the member states began to circumvent the CCP with their own network of bilateral cooperation agreements with the State-trading countries (see Chapter 5.5) had also been important. These agreements covered the domain of industrial, scientific and cultural cooperation, which had become more important due to the East European need for western know-how, high-technology and export credits. Within the framework of these bilateral cooperation agreements a network of Mixed Commissions had been established which was expected to deal with the plethora of commercial problems. Since the EC could do little to harmonize these bilateral agreements, much of the Common Commercial Policy's clout was lost, which, from the Soviet perspective, diminished the urgency of an EC-CMEA agreement.

In May 1974, the Community took a further step on the road toward a fully fledged EC commercial policy after the expiration of the last series of individual trade agreements of its member states, and put forward a set of proposals to the individual countries of the CMEA for negotiating new trade agreements which should replace those expiring bilateral trade agreements of the EC member states (see Chapter 5). In November of that year, the Council also issued a statement emphasizing the fact that these EC agreements would also include the status of most-favoured nation in tariff matters. The Commission sent outlines of such agreements to all State-trading countries, but to no avail. Only the People's Republic of China responded positively to the Community proposal and in 1975 a Chinese mission was opened in Brussels. The (unofficial) East European answer was classical; Radio Budapest maintained that 'The socialist countries do not want to give up their bilateral ties with the individual EC countries for contacts with the Community as a whole, since they are fundamentally opposed to closed blocs and the division of Europe, obstructing the international division of labour'.[13]

At the same time, a letter from the EC Commission was handed to Faddeyev (on 15 May 1974), which announced that Brussels was now ready to accept the much repeated request for negotiations aired by the CMEA. This was an obvious diplomatic manoeuvre by the Commission to confront Moscow with the dilemma of either accepting the EC offer, thereby recognizing the Commission's 'supranational' authority within the European Community, or refusing the offer, which would reduce the prospect of increasing beneficial trade ties. Illustrative of the Soviet Union's reluctance to recognize the authority of the Community was the fact that the CMEA persisted in addressing the *Presidency* of the EC Council; in all cases the Commission of the EC was meticulously ignored. This attitude seemed to change on 12 September 1974, when CMEA Secretary Faddeyev responded to the EC's offer by inviting the President of the Commission, François Xavier Ortoli, to come to Moscow. Although Brussels did not reject this invitation, the visit never took place, mainly due to the European Community's reluctance to commence high-level talks from scratch. Instead, Ortoli proposed organizing a series of preliminary meetings at a diplomatic level. These meetings did indeed take place (at the level of Directors of the Departments of External Relations of both the EC Commission and the CMEA Secretariat), in early February 1975. The Community delegation – headed by Director-General Edmund Wellenstein – paid a visit to the CMEA's Secretariat in Moscow. Although the European Community had sent a heavyweight delegation composed of several experts, it did not find a similar group of high-level CMEA interlocutors to negotiate with.[14] It was therefore little wonder that this first visit remained without success. Despite this initial unsatisfactory meeting, the Commission invited the CMEA to Brussels to give it another try. The European Community was ready to engage in negotiations with the CMEA in the fields of transport, statistics, medium and long-term economic forecasting, technical standards and the environment. These technical issues had to be addressed in order to continue mutually advantageous trade relations. For some reason or other, the Commission's suggestion to meet in Brussels was not heeded by the CMEA Secretariat. Although EC-CMEA relations seemed to have returned to square one, this interlude probably made it easier for some East European countries to negotiate and sign a number of bilateral sectoral agreements with Brussels, covering trade in textiles and steel.[15]

On 16 February 1976, the Chairman of the CMEA's Executive Committee (H. Weiss) presented the EC Council President (G. Thorn) a draft EC-CMEA agreement covering the basic elements of interbloc relations.[16] Here problems arose over the European Community's insistence that it was only prepared to discuss the details of foreign trade with the *individual* East European countries, but *not* with the CMEA (neither with the Secretariat nor with the Executive Committee). In its 15-article draft,[17] the CMEA proposed to set up a network of bilateral and multilateral contacts, 'conventions and agreements between the member countries of Comecon and the bodies of the EEC, between the member states of the EEC and the bodies of Comecon, and between their economic and competent organizations'.[18] Article 1 of the CMEA draft formulated the 'official relations between the Council of Mutual Economic Assistance and the European Economic Community'. Apart from a number of quite modest suggestions for the organization of joint conferences and symposia, the proposal also included the suggestion to eliminate the Common Market's discriminatory quantitative restrictions in agriculture and trade, which would imply the abolition of the Community's Common Agricultural Policy. Such an infringement of Brussels' *acquis communautaire* was, of course, judged unacceptable. It would not only imply the official recognition of the CMEA as an organization on an equal footing with the Community,[19] but would also imply the abrogation of the process of further economic integration among the Nine.

After several meetings and the continuous sending back and forth of new drafts, the bargaining positions got stuck, in late 1976. Both sides did not budge from their positions. But although the Community's first response to the CMEA proposal had been an unenthusiastic one, Brussels had not officially rejected it. After more than six months, the Community nevertheless officially renounced Moscow's proposal but promptly promulgated its own draft for an EC-CMEA arrangement (on 17 November 1976). This EC draft was rather meagre, to say the least; Brussels suggested quite minor forms of cooperation between both organizations but did not come up with proposals on important issues such as quotas, non-tariff barriers or the formation of Mixed Commissions, since it wanted to settle those matters with the individual CMEA member states.

From an economic perspective the lack of official ties between the European Community and the CMEA was perhaps anomalous at first sight, but irrelevant in practice: it was not the CMEA which conducted trade policy for its members, but the individual countries themselves. However, from the beginning of *détente* in 1972, until the mid-1970s, trade between the CMEA members and the EC more than tripled (see Table 4.1). The surge in East-West trade exceeded the expansion of world trade in general. However, despite the boom of East-West trade during *détente*, the share of the State-trading countries in EC foreign trade remained exceptionally modest. In 1975, only 2.0 per cent of EC(12) exports went to the USSR, and 1.6 per cent of EC(12) exports went to Eastern Europe. Conversely, the EC share in the exports of the CMEA countries was markedly higher: from 11.5 per cent for the USSR to as high as 22.5 for Hungary (in 1986) (see Tables 7.1 and 7.2). These statistics also indicate that EC-CMEA trade has been asymmetrical. It is very likely that this asymmetry has influenced the attitudes of the European Community and the CMEA member states towards further *rapprochement*. Studies on the nature of economic power have generally stressed the fact that a relationship of economic dependence can be used for political reasons.[20] In this context, the dependence of the CMEA countries on West European manufactured goods and machinery and transport equipment, partly explains their determination to conclude deals with the EC. A similar impetus has been lacking for the EC and its member states.

Table 7.1 The share of East European countries in EC trade (per cent)

	EC(12) exports			EC(12) total imports			Extra-EC imports		
	1958	1975	1988	1958	1975	1988	1958	1975	1988
USSR	1.1	2.0	1.1	1.3	1.5	1.4	2.0	3.1	3.4
GDR	0.2	0.2	0.1	0.2	0.2	0.2	0.3	0.4	0.4
Poland	0.6	0.1	0.3	0.6	0.7	0.4	1.0	1.3	0.9
Czechoslovakia	0.4	0.4	0.2	0.4	0.3	0.2	0.6	0.7	0.6
Hungary	0.2	0.4	0.3	0.2	0.3	0.2	0.3	0.5	0.6
Romania	0.4	0.2	0.1	0.2	0.4	0.2	0.3	0.7	0.6
Bulgaria	0.1	0.3	0.2	0.1	0.1	0.1	0.1	0.2	0.1

Source: Eurostat

Table 7.2 The EC share in trade of the East European countries (per cent based on $ values)

	Imports			Exports		
	1985	1986	1987	1985	1986	1987
USSR	12.2	11.5	14.4	18.1	13.2	11.4
GDR	20.2	15.9	15.5	19.6	18.2	15.8
Poland	18.5	17.0	18.1	22.6	23.6	23.4
Czechoslovakia	9.5	9.7	10.6	9.0	9.6	9.5
Hungary	21.6	22.5	24.3	16.0	17.3	19.7
Romania	10.1	11.6	10.2	24.6	26.1	24.1
Bulgaria	8.4	9.4	9.5	6.4	6.4	4.9

Source: Eurostat

7.4 Deadlock, but no break

These economic considerations have, however, never been compelling enough to overcome the prominent political hurdles obstructing the establishment of official relations. Since 1976, negotiations have been in the doldrums and with the demise of the cooperative 'spirit of Helsinki',there was no reason to expect that the EC-CMEA deadlock could be broken in the near future.

In the mid-1970s, further negotiations on this issue were made especially arduous by a political conflict over the question of Soviet and East European access to the European Community's fishing zone. The EC member states had already transferred their competence on these issues to the European Community, which in 1977 resulted in the introduction of the EC's Common Fisheries Policy (CFP).[21] In two EC Council Regulations, Brussels had proclaimed a new zone of 200 nautical miles (on 1 January 1977) which would accord Community fishermen equal access to the 'Community pond'.[22] The

Council also issued an ultimatum to the CMEA members to the effect that they either had to inform the European Community of the size of their fishing fleet and start negotiations on their fishing quotas, or they would be expelled from the new EC-zone.[23] This attitude of the Community confronted several Communist states with a dilemma. It was clear that Brussels' hand in East-West economic relations had been strengthened by the introduction of the Common Fisheries Policy, whereby the EC's member states were united in their positions. After 1976, the Commission was authorized to negotiate fishery agreements with third countries and Moscow had little chance to break the ranks of the western parties concerned. In an effort to gain admission to the EC's newly imposed fishing zone, Moscow decided to enter into negotiations with the Commission in Brussels (16 February), and sent a Minister to do the job. Poland and the German Democratic Republic immediately followed Moscow to the Brussels negotiating table, where a debate on a framework agreement on reciprocal fishing rights was opened on 10 March.

In response to Moscow's new approach, the question immediately arose whether this implied that the USSR was now *de facto* recognizing the European Community's authority to handle foreign trade issues on behalf of its member states. It was beyond doubt that – for the first time ever – the Soviet Union had acted upon the assumption that the EC was indeed legally qualified to represent its member states' commercial interests. The CFP had confronted several CMEA members with a *fait accompli*, and the EC Commission President, Roy Jenkins, was understandably enthusiastic about this Soviet compromise, characterizing the talks as a 'great achievement'. The Soviet Minister of Fisheries had, however, indicated that he had merely received a mandate to sign an agreement with the EC *member states*, and not with the European Community as such. Soviet officials also continued to argue that these issues should be dealt with in separate negotiations between the CMEA and the EC.[24] The Brussels talks were abruptly abrogated in May 1977 and when Soviet ships left EC waters the incident was soon closed.[25] Nothing had actually changed, but the CFP episode had once again illustrated that the USSR and the CMEA would only comply with the EC's demands when Brussels was able to negotiate from a position of strength and when the EC's ranks were closed.

This did not mean that the EC-CMEA negotiations were also completely cancelled; on the contrary. In September 1977 a novelty in EC-CMEA relations occurred when the Chairman of the CMEA's Executive Committee (M. Marinescu) met an EC delegation in Brussels headed by the Council President (H. Simonet). The details of this meeting have been veiled in secrecy, but the final press communiqué noticed how Simonet had 'introduced' Mr Marinescu to W. Haferkamp, the Vice-President of the EC Commission and the person responsible for external affairs.[26] This method of bringing the EC Commission around the negotiating table with the CMEA was among one of Brussels' smartest diplomatic manoeuvres. At the same time, the digressive and cumbersome manner of bringing both parties together was a clear indication of the immature and perhaps even childish nature which has characterized the relationship between the European Community and the CMEA. This whole affair also clearly indicated that the political will on both sides was sufficiently persistent to come to a better working relationship between both organizations and that the CMEA was now even prepared to establish a line of direct contact with the Commission, be it with a considerable detour. In his opening address, Haferkamp had once again stressed the abnormality of the lack of official ties between the European Community and the *member states* of the CMEA, especially in the light of the fact that more than a hundred states had already established normal relations with Brussels.[27]

Several expert meetings took place in the following months, which were followed up by high-level talks between Faddeyev and Haferkamp (first in Moscow, from 29 May to 30 May 1978, later in Brussels, 22-25 November 1978). Despite these regular meetings no breakthrough eventuated. Both sides continually tried to put the blame for the lack of progress upon the other side. The CMEA argued that the European Community was unwilling to enter into negotiations on an equal footing, whereas Brussels maintained that the CMEA demanded unreasonable quid pro quos, such as the abolition of the CAP. Although the negotiations did not end up with concrete results, the importance of these preliminary contacts should not be underestimated since these months of discussions clearly brought to the light the differences of opinion on both sides. Identifying the main topics of contention – such as the authority of the EC and the CMEA *vis-à-vis* their member states, the role of a possible Joint Commission, the granting of MFN status, as well as the status of Berlin – have undoubtedly helped to focus the formerly fuzzy discussions and negotiations.

A breakthrough in EC-CMEA relations seemed in the offing when Faddeyev informed Haferkamp that a forthcoming CMEA proposal would accept the (now five-year old) offer of the European Community to conclude bilateral agreements with the CMEA member states. Moscow's compromise came entirely out of the blue. When another round of EC-CMEA meetings was held in October and November 1979 (in Moscow), both Eastern Europe and Brussels were hoping for Moscow's green light finally to break the spell of mutual neglect and to establish fully fledged trade agreements. For the EC this would have signified a boost of its international prestige; for the East Europeans it would have meant the possibility of obtaining better access to the Common Market and of diminishing their trade dependence upon the Soviet Union and each other. All in all, Faddeyev's proposition considerably raised the expectations that a more significant accord was now finally becoming a realistic possibility.

Both the EC and the USSR were particularly eager to display their good intentions of arriving at an agreement since the issue of economic cooperation would again be among the topics of discussion during the CSCE Follow-Up Meeting in Madrid (starting in September 1980). In order to show its goodwill Brussels also concocted a new proposal, which was published in late October of 1979. In all draft articles, the Community carefully avoided mentioning trade issues of any kind, but instead suggested cooperation in the field of long-term economic forecasting on industrial and agricultural production as well as consumption, trade and economic statistics, the environment and standardization. It was little wonder that Moscow considered such a loosely structured EC-CMEA agreement unsatisfactory, and since both sides failed to come one inch closer the negotiations were again put on ice. After the Soviet invasion of Afghanistan, in late December of 1979, and the Polish crisis of the early-1980s, East-West relations turned sour. Faddeyev's off-hand proposal for bilateral agreements between the EC and Eastern Europe had now also gone up in thin air. The likelihood of an EC-CMEA agreement was reduced even further; the scheduled April 1980 meeting had been cancelled and no date for a new gathering was announced. What was left of the 'spirit of *détente*' was now completely overtaken by renewed political, economic and ideological conflict between East and West (see also Chapter 7.6).

7.5 Dilemmas of the EC's *realpolitik*

The dialogue of deaf-mutes between the European Community and the CMEA has illustrated the ossified negotiating positions on both sides of the Iron Curtain. Although regular talks had taken place since the mid-1970s, compromises were hardly to be expected. The mere fact that East-West trade had been far more important for the CMEA countries than for the EC members, had provided Brussels with potential economic leverage over the CMEA and the Soviet Union in particular. However, this economic leverage could not be used bluntly. Only a balanced agreement between the EC and the CMEA would be acceptable for Moscow since overt economic pressure from the West would imply a severe loss of its international prestige. It has been argued that Soviet policy could not be influenced by external factors when these would try to challenge fundamentally core values such as Soviet sovereignty, security or systemic continuity (the so-called unacceptable S's).[28] In this case, EC trade agreements with the individual East European countries were considered a serious challenge to Soviet hegemony in this region. Such trade agreements would increase East-West trade and would augment West European economic influence in the Soviet Union's backyard.

The European Community's approach to the CMEA has been a widely debated issue. Over the years, the discussion as to whether the CMEA should be accorded the status of a negotiating partner equal to the Community itself has crystallized into two sets of arguments. First, there has been the hard-line view which has suggested that the Community should refrain from official contacts with the CMEA *without* parallel direct relations with the CMEA members. This line of argument has maintained that Brussels' policy-makers should not even consider taking up relations with the CMEA, since direct EC-CMEA negotiations would strengthen Soviet control over Eastern Europe. Second, there have been the advocates of a much more lenient policy *vis-à-vis* the CMEA, who have based their argument on the contention that official relations between the EC and CMEA would go a long way in stimulating mutually beneficial trade and a wide range of technological and cultural exchanges, thereby strengthening *détente*.

All in all, the hard-line approach towards the CMEA has been dominant within the Community's policy-making circles. One of the main reasons why the EC was wary of adopting relations with the CMEA on the Soviet terms (i.e. without direct ties with the individual CMEA members) was related to the latter organization's internal balance of power. Whereas the European Community did not have one, clearly dominant member, the geographic, economic and military hegemony of the Soviet Union over Eastern Europe could not be denied. Accepting the CMEA as a trading partner, instead of its members, would most probably further Communist centralization, which would augment Moscow's predominance in the region.[29] What was more, the CMEA had three non-European members: Cuba, Mongolia and Vietnam, which could hardly be treated on an equal basis in a 'bloc-to-bloc' agreement between the CMEA and the EC. Community officials also argued that bilateral links with the CMEA members were to be preferred in order to take into account the diverging economic circumstances in each country. Some East European states were members of GATT, but not all; the structure of foreign trade of the CMEA members was dissimilar, and some State-trading countries had to cope with huge debts.[30]

The CMEA Charter also explicitly mentioned the organization's *inter*-governmental character,[31] in contrast to the EC's (admittedly modest) supranational features. In essence, the CMEA could better be defined as an organization coordinating its member states' economic policies than as a body with an independent legal personality under international law.[32] In this respect, the CMEA bore more resemblance to, for instance, the OECD, than to the European Community. Several reports issued by the European Parliament have clearly recognized the fact that the CMEA was 'only empowered to issue recommendations and these only assume legal force when adopted by the member countries'; the CMEA 'has no legal powers whatsoever to impose the implementation of such an agreement on its members'.[33] The European Parliament had more than once summoned the EC Commission *not* to enter into agreements with the CMEA of a nature which would 'encourage ... even stronger bonds between the smaller East

European state-trading countries and the Soviet Union, whose power is already overwhelming'.[34] Opponents of mutual recognition were also concerned that an EC-CMEA accord would water down the West European drive towards a free internal market, meanwhile fostering Soviet influence over its satellites. As a result, it became Community policy to avoid actions which might possibly further Soviet pre-eminence in the East.

In the 1970s and early-1980s, there were not many western supporters of an EC-CMEA relationship on the Soviet terms. The few proponents of such an agreement argued that formal ties would overcome many of the economic and financial barriers which were now hampering the flow of East-West trade. It was expected that increased commercial contacts between the blocs would also resolve many of the political and ideological conflicts and misunderstandings between East and West and would build an economic basis for a more stable and peaceful Europe. Proponents further argued that an EC-CMEA deal would enhance the status of the Community in world politics. It was also maintained that with the adoption of the new CMEA Statutes, in July 1974 (where, for the first time, a certain CMEA role in external relations was laid down), no legal obstacles stood in the way of Community recognition.[35] The 1974 amendment of the CMEA's Charter had stipulated that 'international agreements may be concluded with the member countries of the council, third countries, and international organizations'. The CMEA had already signed several trade and cooperation agreements with third countries, among others with Yugoslavia (1964), Finland (1973), Iraq (1975), Mexico (1975) and Nicaragua (1982). However, these agreements were actually empty shells, doing little to regulate trade relations (which remained within the competence of the individual CMEA member states). Although agreements signed by the CMEA were *not* automatically binding for the member states, the argument in favour of a balanced EC-CMEA accord gained some strength in the mid-1980s. Robert Cutler, for instance, made a case for such a deal arguing that 'so long as the principle of unanimity continues to hold sway in CMEA councils, a real basis will be hard to find for the fear that Soviet economic influence may limit the sovereignty of the East European countries. It is questionable, therefore, whether any agreement between the CMEA and the EEC could make such limitation possible.'[36] From this perspective, the CMEA's intergovernmental credentials were considered an antidote against the risk of Soviet dominance within the organization. The arguments pro and con mutual recognition proved difficult to reconcile, since the CMEA's intergovernmental character might diminish the risk of Soviet hegemony within the region, but it also prevented an agreement with the European Community on the basis of equality.

The East European members of the CMEA were confronted with a similar dilemma in their relations with Brussels. As we have already noted above, export-oriented East European countries like Poland, Hungary and Czechoslovakia had encountered serious problems in their efforts to sell their products in the Common Market. EC quotas have effectively curbed the imports of East European foodstuffs and manufactures. Since bilateral trade agreements with the EC would provide a framework in which these commercial difficulties could be tackled, the East Europeans pressed for *direct* negotiations with Brussels. However, they also believed that without at least a basic level of East European economic integration, their small and vulnerable economies would not be viable in the long run. Within the structure of bilateral trade ties and the CMEA, they would be able to profit from economies of scale and specialization. For the East European countries the energy crisis of 1973 had again brought home the point that these ties were vital, guaranteeing access to inexpensive Soviet oil and many other raw materials. Until 1975, trade was conducted with fixed prices for a period of five consecutive years on the basis of average world prices (a mechanism generally known as the 'Bucharest Formula'). From 1975 (in response to the oil crisis), a new system of pricing was adopted under which prices were adjusted on an annual basis (the so-called 'Moscow Formula'). These changes did, however, leave unchanged the fact that intra-CMEA trade was conducted with the so-called 'transferable rouble' (which was a non-convertible currency), which stood in sharp contrast to the oscillating prices on the world market payable in unstable American dollars. Until Soviet energy prices came to reflect realistic market prices, the terms of trade had favoured the East Europeans. According to some economists, this CMEA pricing system has constituted a *de facto* Soviet subsidy to the East European members. The adoption of world prices to be paid in hard currency (a system which had been put into force in January 1991), would have had detrimental effects for most CMEA members.

It was therefore not saying too much that trade with the USSR constituted an economic lifeline for most East Europeans; an economic umbilical cord, however, which has also certainly increased their political dependence on Moscow. These two elements, economic and political dependence on Moscow, were two sides of the same coin. East European countries who refused to participate actively within the CMEA, like Romania,[37] could afford a more independent foreign policy but also had to do without the economic benefits of favourable terms of trade with the USSR. But, as John Pinder has remarked: 'if [the East European countries] negotiate independently with the Community, their relative strength is small and their bargaining position weak; whereas if CMEA negotiates for them as a group, their interests may be subsumed in defining the CMEA policy, where the Soviet interests would necessarily dominate ... to the extent that the Community restricts its imports from Eastern Europe, the East Europeans are forced into heavier reliance on the Soviet economic link.' In conclusion: 'If there is a loser from the absence of trade negotiations, it is likely to be the Eastern partner.'[38]

It is rather complicated to assess the expediency of Brussels' policy in this particular case. As to the political reasons for the European Community to give the CMEA a cold shoulder, Sheila A. Chapman has argued that Brussels' argument 'appears rather weak, given that it is precisely the Commission's refusal to negotiate with the CMEA which could force the latter to act, in order to obtain the powers similar to those of the European Community. This would inevitably lead to the strengthening of the Soviet position within the Eastern bloc, which is exactly what the Commission claims not to want.'[39] Although the rigid intergovernmental character of the CMEA has prevented this from happening, Chapman's critique points to the ambiguity in the EC's attitude. In the past, Moscow has indeed argued in favour of closer economic cooperation among the CMEA members in response to progress made within the EC. Axel Lebahn has therefore pointed to the resemblance between the attitude of the EC towards the CMEA and the West German Hallstein doctrine: in both cases a mixture of political, ideological and legal arguments has determined the course of western policy and in both cases this policy has resulted in a very peculiar regime of unwritten codes of behaviour pertaining to this specific relationship.[40]

From the East European side criticism on the EC's approach towards the CMEA has been harsh. The Polish Communist scholar Wojciech Morawiecki, for instance, has argued that the 'fundamentalist position' taken by the EC in its bargaining with the CMEA appears 'quite strange and inconsistent when compared with its policies adopted at the same time with regard to other regional organisations and groups of countries. In fact, the EEC did not raise the problems of their contractual capacity and did not hesitate to conclude agreements ... with organisations and groups of countries much less cohesive and integrated than the CMEA.'[41] In order to prove his point, Morawiecki referred to the economic agreements which have been concluded by the European Community and the Gulf states (signed in 1980), and the cooperation agreement with the Cartagena Treaty Group, signed in 1983. At first sight it might indeed seem somewhat strange that Brussels has been willing to maintain relations with the League of Arab Nations (since 1974), that it has signed the Lomé Convention (the first in 1975, the fourth in 1989) and that it has been prepared to conclude agreements with the now 66 'developing' African, Caribbean and Pacific Ocean (ACP) countries, as well as with the Association of South-East Asian Nations (ASEAN), without, however, taking up official contacts with the economic organization of its Communist neighbours. The EC has, however, always been prepared to enter into formal relations with the CMEA on the condition that this would not foreclose direct ties with the CMEA member states. This had also been the case with Brussels' relations with the ACP and ASEAN countries, which were all having a seat around the negotiating table when they were dealing with their trade ties with the Community.

All in all, it can also be argued that Brussels' hard-nosed policy *vis-à-vis* the CMEA has proved successful. During several decades, Brussels has used its economic statecraft and commercial prowess in an effort to determine the terms of cooperation between the two economic blocs. Later in this chapter we will see that the European Community's objectives *vis-à-vis* the USSR and Eastern Europe have almost all been reached. With the demise of the CMEA in 1990, and in the light of the new central role Brussels is currently playing in the construction of post-Cold War Europe, the historic dispute between the European Community and the CMEA has had only one, final winner.

7.6 The Cold War revisited, *perestroika* and Berlin

In the previous chapter we have already discussed the role of the European Community in the early-1980s, a period of rising East-West tensions. Despite pressures from Washington the EC refused to adopt a policy of economic sanctions *vis-à-vis* the USSR and Poland. But although Western Europe did not react with the Reagan Administration's anti-Communist fervour, it was nevertheless quite evident that the prospects for a EC-CMEA deal had diminished considerably. This is, however, not to say that Cold War II had completely lamed the negotiations between the Community and the CMEA; during this period, EC-CMEA negotiations had not been abrogated at *all* levels. Behind the scenes three technical meetings took place in Geneva where representatives from the EC Commission, the CMEA Secretariat and the CMEA member states gathered in order to discuss further cooperation.

In April 1980, Commissioner Haferkamp had officially cancelled the scheduled talks between the EC and the CMEA arguing that the negotiations had entered a cul-de-sac; a large number of high-level diplomatic visits over a period of many years had failed to accomplish a framework agreement. However, as early as October 1980, the Chairman of the CMEA's Executive Committee, A. Lukanov, sent a letter to the EC Council's President, G. Thorn, in which the CMEA expressed its renewed interest in negotiations with the EC. On 20 March 1981, Haferkamp (and *not* the President of the Council) responded with the requisite suggestions for 'resuming the dialogue'. But Moscow was apparently not in a hurry since several *years* elapsed before the Commission's (new) President, Jacques Delors, received a reply in the form of an invitation to visit the CMEA's Moscow Headquarters.[42]

During the first half of the 1980s, the Soviet perspective on Western Europe went through a metamorphosis. This was, for example, witnessed by the fact that the Soviet Union brought the EC before the European Court on accusations of unjustified anti-dumping measures in the Summer of 1983, thereby indirectly acknowledging the Community's competence on issues of foreign trade. During the June 1984 meeting of the CMEA, it had been announced once more that the CMEA would develop trade 'with all countries of the world'; in particular, the commercial ties with capitalist countries were to be improved. In the early-1980s, East-West trade had slowed down and the economic recession in the West had given rise to even stricter protectionist policies which dampened the already low level of East European exports to the Common Market. In the East, several Communist countries had to face the problems caused by economic mismanagement and the considerable foreign debts which had been built up in the 1970s. The lack of hard currency put a serious brake on the improvement of East-West commerce. What was more, the European Community's enlargement with Greece (January 1981)[43] and the preferential treatment of trade with the EFTA-countries were all to the detriment of the export capabilities of the CMEA countries.

Past experience had demonstrated that the Communist economies could hardly function without a considerable input of advanced western technology and know-how. The exact impact of western high-tech on the performance of the centrally planned economies has always been a matter of dispute. Particularly within CoCom, discussions have at times erupted concerning the Soviet benefits of East-West trade. Be that as it may, in the early-1980s the condition of the Soviet economy had become so deplorable that even the export of the USSR's main commodity, energy, was nigh impossible without the use of high-level western technology. One of the giant CMEA-projects, the *Soyuz* gas pipeline, had to import some 80 per cent of the utilized materials from the West. The slow-down of economic growth in the Soviet-type societies had once more brought home the point that the CMEA countries were isolated from the mainstream of the world economy. Since they did not participate in the world's monetary and economic institutions, Communist countries had no say whatsoever in the important matters which were being decided within the IMF, GATT or the G-7. In an effort to institutionalize East-West trade relations the dialogue between both 'deaf-mutes' was again revived, this time on the initiative of the Bulgarian Foreign Minister (Ch. Christov), who visited the EC Commission in late 1984. With the change of guard in the USSR, in the Spring of 1985, relations between the European Community and the CMEA entered the maelstrom of *perestroika*.

In May 1985, the EC Commission received a proposal from the new Secretary-General of the CMEA, V. Sytchov, requesting the establishment of official ties. Moscow was now prepared to lift several of the traditional objections which had previously blocked EC-CMEA relations. Most importantly, Moscow seemed also willing to allow fully fledged bilateral trade agreements between the CMEA member states and the European Community, although it still remained rather ambiguous on this specific subject. After a silence of some five years, the Soviet leaders were keen on finally concluding a trade agreement with the Community, be it on the condition that the EC and the CMEA would first establish official contacts and proclaim their mutual political recognition. Moscow argued that an EC-CMEA agreement would not have to encroach upon possible bilateral trade agreements between Brussels and the CMEA member states. However, Willy De Clercq, the EC Commissioner for External Affairs, decidedly rejected Moscow's suggestion of establishing relations with the CMEA, arguing: 'We want to continue discussions on a partner-to-partner basis, rather than on a bloc-to-bloc basis. We do not want bloc-to-bloc discussions because this would imply condoning the separation of Europe.'[44] In September, Sytchov suggested that an EC-CMEA agreement would establish relations between both organizations 'within their respective fields of competence', which implied that the Community did not have to recognize the CMEA as an equal partner. This remarkable volte-face broke the deadlock and opened the way to further *rapprochement*.

As of February 1986, the EC entered in the process of negotiations with both the CMEA *and* with the individual East European countries. Letters were sent to the seven East European capitals calling for the 'normalization of relations' with the European Community. Quite understandably, the CMEA member states were keen on establishing official relations with Brussels, having a plethora of commercial problems to settle. The negotiations between the EC and the CMEA took place in Geneva, from September 1986. These discussions would *not* cover trade issues, since, as De Clercq argued: 'Comecon is dominated by the Soviet Union, which is doing its best to strengthen internal ties. This worries us.'[45] After more than a year of consultations, agreement was eventually reached on the content of a Joint Declaration (in March 1988). One controversial point did, however, remain: the so-called 'EEC territorial clause' dealing with the legal status of Berlin. The status of this German city had for decades been one of the major bones of contention in the already conflict-ridden relationship between the EC and the CMEA.[46] In a number of official documents signed after the defeat of Nazi Germany, Berlin was provided with the status of occupied territory governed by the Allied Council comprising the Four Powers: the United States, Great Britain, France and the Soviet Union. After the Berlin crisis of 1948, Moscow decided to leave this Allied Council whereby Berlin was split into two: an eastern part supervised by the USSR and a western part governed by the three remaining Council members. In the Treaty of Rome, the status of West Berlin had been officially acknowledged, thereby becoming a part of the territory covered by Community law. In 1957, the FRG had taken that occasion to declare that the EEC Treaties would equally apply to the *Land* Berlin; as a result Berlin has been systematically included in every treaty between the Community and third countries.

Bonn had already signed economic cooperation agreements with a large number of East European countries (except the GDR), which had all included a special clause stipulating that the agreement would also be 'valid for the area of the D-mark West'; this, of course, also included West Berlin. In the early-1970s, the issue of West Berlin had become a matter of special attention during the negotiations between the FRG and the USSR over a bilateral trade agreement. The Brandt Government had stipulated that no treaty could be signed without a Berlin agreement. Moscow's desire to improve trade with the FRG clearly took precedence over its political objectives in the Berlin question since it was willing to accept Bonn's right to act for West Berlin in trade matters. The separate Berlin Treaty – which was initialled by West Germany and the USSR in September 1973 – had stipulated that although the city was no constituent part of the FRG, West Berlin could nevertheless maintain and develop its special ties with the Federal Republic. This had been considered a remarkable breakthrough in the Kremlin's attitude, especially when one took into account Moscow's sometimes very aggressive attempts to make Berliner life as difficult as possible, be it by blockades or otherwise. However, for Moscow the Berlin Treaty did not signify the official recognition of West Berlin as a section of the FRG. It was time and again argued that since the city was not under the jurisdiction of Bonn (but according to international law was still under *occupatio bellica*), West Berlin could not be a part of the European Community either.[47] Little wonder then that an agreement between the EC and the CMEA had to come to terms with Berlin's status.

After a short period of debate, the Berlin issue was resolved in the Spring of 1988. Moscow had to give in to the Community's – or, more specifically, Bonn's – demands since it was desperate to establish the much-wanted trade ties. Gorbachev's policy of *perestroika* and *glasnost* had set in motion a dramatic change in the USSR's policy to the West which now became both cooperative and pragmatic. The Soviet Union had agreed to accept the so-called 'Hungarian Formula' which (indirectly) confirmed West Berlin's status as a constituent part of the Community.[48] It could hardly be a coincidence that this breakthrough occurred during a period in which the economic relationship between the Federal Republic and the USSR had become very cordial. In early May, Bonn had earmarked DM 3.5 billion for export credits for Moscow, especially aimed at the dire modernization of the Soviet consumer goods industry. During a meeting with the West German Economics Minister, Martin Bangemann, the Soviet Prime Minister, Nikolai Ryzhkov, had stressed that the USSR would 'do everything to get this [EC-CMEA] agreement ready for signing before the end of June'.[49]

These Soviet efforts proved successful, since on 25 June 1988 the EC and the CMEA issued their 'Joint Declaration on the Establishment of Official Relations Between the European Economic Community and the Council for Mutual Economic Assistance'.[50] In this official declaration it was notified that 'As regards the application of this Declaration to the Community, it shall apply to the territories in which the Treaty establishing the European Economic Community is applied and under the conditions laid down in that Treaty'. Although still somewhat tongue-in-cheek, this passage implied that West Berlin was a constituent part of the EC-area. The Declaration as such was rather meagre, not mentioning a single concrete aspect of mutual cooperation. Its political consequences were nevertheless beyond doubt and the way was now fully open for closer relations between the European Community and the CMEA member states. The EC Commission later argued that 'The establishment of diplomatic relations implies recognition by the East European countries of the EC as such, which is more than the sum of its twelve Member States. It marks the formal reversal of East European policy towards the EC and is an important step in the normalization of relations.'[51]

Not much time elapsed before the first bilateral trade and economic cooperation agreements were signed between the European Community and Hungary (1988), Poland and the Soviet Union (in 1989), and Czechoslovakia, Bulgaria and the GDR (in 1990). Moscow's radical change in attitude towards the EC now leaned over to a rather optimistic reading of the future of West European integration. Vitaly Zhurkin, the head of the European Institute of the Soviet Academy of Sciences, argued in November 1988 that 'We are practically sure that the internal market [of the EC] will be established by 1992. Maybe not in all its complexity ... but fundamentally economic problems of a common domestic market will be settled. For the Soviet Union and COMECON, it creates a multi-dimensional challenge: areas both of concern and opportunity.'[52] This unequivocally indicated that the USSR had come full circle. However, Moscow's attitude was not a static one. It was, for instance, clear to the Kremlin that the European Community was slowly developing from an economic organization into an institution with distinct political and even military ambitions. This accurate judgement stood at the basis of President Gorbachev's remark: 'We are not watching integration in Western Europe in a purely critical way, we see it in all its aspects. Our fears are tied only to the attempts to militarise this process.'[53]

8. 1989 and 1992, Two Revolutions?

The example of Western cooperation through the European Community has already had a dramatic effect on Eastern attitudes towards economic liberty. The success of this great European experiment, perhaps more than any other factor, has caused Eastern Europeans to recognize that people as well as nations cooperate more productively when they are free to choose. The ballot box and the free market are the fundamental instruments of choice.

> James A. Baker (US Secretary of State) to the Berlin Press Club at the Steigenberger Hotel in Berlin, 12 December 1989.

8.1 Introduction

Since the chain is generally as strong as the weakest link, the Soviet Union's external empire broke down after Hungarian border guards cut a tiny opening in the Iron Curtain in the Spring of 1989.[1] Being the first East European country to have acceded to the UN Convention on Refugees in March 1989, Hungary began to tear down its fences along the borders with Austria. This opening window on Western Europe let in enough fresh air to inspire East German youths and families to making an escape effort, most often successfully. Hundreds, and thereafter thousands, of citizens from the GDR crossed the Hungarian-Austrian border where they were welcomed in Vienna before travelling to West Germany. This shattering of borders would neither have been possible, nor would it have had such cascading effects in Eastern Europe, without the political backing provided by the policy of *perestroika* and *glasnost* initiated by Soviet leader Gorbachev. The economic and political reforms in the USSR provided more leeway for the regimes in Eastern Europe to experiment and to explore the limits of Soviet hegemony. The Brezhnev doctrine had been revoked and it all seemed as if the lid was now removed from the Communist box of Pandora, with, undoubtedly, many surprises lying in store for Europe at large.

In this chapter we will examine the East European revolutions of 1989-90 in relation to the 1992 initiative of the EC. We will argue that both the reform plans in Eastern Europe and the reformist zeal in Western Europe have been initiated in response to corresponding endogenous pressures generated by the structural changes taking place in world politics at large.

8.2 Two parallel revolutions?

The process of change in the East started with President Mikhail Gorbachev entering the political stage in Moscow in March 1985. Approximately at the same time, the momentum of West European integration was increased from the lethargic Europessimism of the late-1970s and early-1980s into the Europhoria of the 1992 initiative. It is beyond doubt that one should always be particularly cautious to assume a causal relationship between social events which are happening simultaneously. This is also the case when we want to place the *perestroika* and the 1992 initiatives into proper perspective.

At the same time, it remains tempting to suppose something beyond sheer coincidence in the fact that the publication of the so-called 'White Paper' (June 1985) practically coincided with the genesis of Soviet *perestroika*. We will argue that the causes of both initiatives can be brought back to similar motivations and that both *perestroika* and the 1992 programme have served comparable purposes. The White Paper – prepared by Lord Arthur Cockfield (the EC's Internal Market Commissioner) – presented a reform package containing some 279 proposals to create 'an area without internal frontiers in which the free movement of goods, persons, services, and capital is ensured'.[2] The leaders of the EC states committed themselves to gather several times a year in order to realize the liberalization of trade in services and the removal of internal non-tariff barriers. The aspired free internal European market was to be a modern, more advanced version of the customs union which had already been accomplished a few decades earlier. One of the important elements of this comprehensive programme has been that it has set an explicit deadline for reaching these goals: 31 December 1992. It has also identified some three hundred problems to be solved in order to reach this ultimate target. The 1992 deadline and the catalogue of problems have symbolized the urgency and the challenge of EC reform. It has also established a clear-cut scenario which was expected to rejuvenate the West European economies along the same lines as the Baron Münchhausen accomplished when pulling himself out of the morass by his own hairs. The EC member states approved the 1992 initiative by signing the Single European Act in 1986, and introduced the institutional changes (notably increased voting by qualified majority in the Council) to implement it.

Gorbachev's *perestroika* of the Soviet economy and the democratization of Communist political rule constituted a perhaps even more ambitious project of social engineering. In an effort to spur economic growth in the USSR a large number of existing economic and political barriers of Communist-style planning had to be removed. *Perestroika* has addressed a large number of long-cherished Communist dogmas, challenging the role of the Communist Party in Soviet society and calling upon Soviet citizens to develop their own initiatives for private enterprise. Transforming the Soviet economy and Communist society was considered one of the main goals, although both Gorbachev and many of his advisors had only a vague notion of what would have to replace the traditional system of state planning. In the mid-1980s, the new EC Commission President, Jacques Delors, seized the idea of creating a 'new Europe' and provided European integration with a remarkable new thrust. Soviet leader Gorbachev's reformist plans tried to achieve a similar goal in the East. However, whereas Delors' plans eventually resulted in the further *integration* of economic and foreign policy in Western Europe, Gorbachev's plans finally brought about the *decomposition* of the Soviet sphere of influence and the cessation of the traditional East-West controversy. In trying to explain *why* these changes have taken place, many have first asked the question: why *then*? Why was it in the mid-1980s that the USSR started to withdraw its hegemonic overlay over Eastern Europe? And why did the European Community embark upon a renewed and ambitious effort to establish a free internal market at almost the same time?

These kind of questions did not seem all that difficult to answer for the Soviet case. With idiosyncratic factors playing such a prominent role in Soviet politics it was as if Gorbachev's rise to the position of Secretary General of the CPSU explained almost everything. After several decades of Stalinist totalitarianism, Khrushchevian recklessness and Brezhnevian lethargy, the USSR seemed to have entered the era of Gorbachevian reform. The strength of this explanation has been reinforced by the extraordinary attention which the Soviet leader has received in the West, both in the media and from academics and policy-makers. Sceptics usually referred to the western (and especially West European) 'Gorby-mania' or to the 'Gorbasm' of western applause each time the Soviet leader aired new proposals for the creation of a comprehensive system of international security, chemical-free zones or another unilateral moratorium on nuclear tests. However, it soon became quite evident that personalized explanations had all been far too simple. After the sad but short Chernenko intermezzo, the Soviet Politburo had opted for a reformer. A majority of the top-level Soviet Communist leaders had come to realize the dire need for structural reform – and not just superficial change. The Soviet quest for reform proved to be a question of survival; without structural change the USSR's demise would have been as inevitable as the extinction of the Dinosaur after the Ice Age.

Both Soviet and western statistics showed the dramatic decline of the Soviet economy. Since the American Reagan Administration had shifted the superpower competition into such areas as microelectronics and other sophisticated technologies, Soviet leaders feared a serious assault on their position as a military power. The American Strategic Defence Initiative (SDI) had been established in order to invigorate the United States' military programme and to outspend and outperform the Soviet Union in the economic and technological field. Although the USSR barely managed to apply high-technology in a few secluded areas to which the central plan had given extra attention for political and security reasons – such as space technology and the military – the technological sophistication of the Soviet work-force and the Soviet economy at large lagged several decades behind the West. The majority of the Soviet *nomenklatura* undoubtedly realized these facts when it decided to opt for the reformist Mikhail Gorbachev as its new Secretary General. A few more decades of traditional central planning and extreme economic dirigism would have resulted in the crumbling of the Soviet empire due to a lack of economic prowess. The choice for structural reform had been taken in an effort at boosting Soviet strength as a rational response to the USSR's diluted power position within the international system. *Perestroika* clearly illustrated the 'shaping and shoving' of states to adjust to the changing circumstances in order to maintain or improve their position within the international political environment.

To a certain extent, similar reasons have been behind the European Community's new policies. The 1992-programme and the SEA have reinforced several aspects of the Rome Treaty. The SEA stressed the goal of a 'single internal market' and extended majority voting in the Council on issues dealing with the realization of the goals of '1992'; the Maastricht Treaty on European Union, initialled in December 1991, has made efforts to set further steps in the direction of economic and political integration. In explaining this prolonged integrationist process, two factors have been identified.[3] To begin with, there were the structural causes to which we referred in Chapter 1. The relative decline of the United States, and the ascent of the countries of the Pacific and most notably Japan, have entailed a major shift in the distribution of economic power resources within the international system. America was no longer the undisputed economic hegemon within the West, which obliged West European countries to rethink their traditional transatlantic links. Since World War II, Western Europe has heavily leaned upon the United States for its economic and military security. Washington had been able and willing to provide the rules of the game of the liberal world economy and had been prepared to maintain a nuclear umbrella over Western Europe. Under the American aegis of economic and military security, West European countries had established the EC-regime. With the relative decline of American power – be it through 'military overstretch' or other mechanisms[4] – Washington had become less willing to enforce the regime of global free trade and introduced a number of protectionist measures of its own. It has been argued that the United States has also had to pass the torch of significant technological development to Japan, which has become the new vanguard nation in the production of the sophisticated semiconductors and integrated circuits which are used in computers. This process has been accompanied by the eroding predominance of Wall Street in the global monetary system; Frankfurt, London and Tokyo have now emerged as competing financial centres of the capitalist world.

These structural developments have posed significant new problems for the West European countries. How were they to react to them? The conflict over the Urengoi gas pipeline in the early-1980s, and especially the extraterritorial sanctions imposed by the United States on West European exports to the East (see Chapter 6.5), had clearly brought home the point that Western Europe should try to get its act together and diminish its reliance on America in the crucial field of high technology. One of the most attractive options for the West European states has been to rally round the now well-known flag of the EC, to stimulate West European-based research programmes (such as ESPRIT, RACE and BRITE)[5] and to act more coherently in world affairs.

The introduction of the European Monetary System (EMS) in December 1978 can be considered as one of the first successful answers of the European Community to compensate for the breakdown of the Bretton Woods system, a system that had been dominated by the United States between 1945 and the early-1970s. The Rome Treaty had little to say concerning monetary matters, mainly because 'the Bretton Woods system was thought to provide the appropriate framework for monetary cooperation. The dominant position of the United States, exemplified by the role of the US dollar in the post-war system ... made any attempt to establish an independent monetary system in the context of the European Community completely unthinkable.'[6] (And, one might add, superfluous.) These endogenous circumstances were now changed due to the gradual weakening of the dollar. At the The Hague Summit of the EC Heads of State in December 1969, the new French and German leaders – Georges Pompidou and Willy Brandt – had launched their initiative for an Economic and Monetary Union (EMU),[7] which has been adopted by the Council of Ministers in February 1971. After several major international crises (most notably the two oil shocks of the 1970s and President Nixon's decision to float the dollar in August 1971), the European Community decided to set up a so-called 'zone of monetary stability in Europe', which was expected to compensate for the extreme uncertainty resulting from the United States' new monetary policies. The ensuing 'snake-in-the-tunnel' established a system of exchange rates among Community members, holding their value jointly *vis-à-vis* the US dollar. Several of these 'snake'-systems had been implemented during the 1970s, with a highly volatile membership of West European states. In March 1979, the 'snake' was followed by the much more structured European Monetary System and the European Currency Unit (ECU).[8] The ECU had been especially devised to peg the currencies of the EC member states to one another. The ECU-system, in turn, generated increased pressure on the EC governments to coordinate their national economic and monetary policies. Over the years, the German Mark – without doubt the strongest West European currency – became the (informal) reference currency for the EMS. These earliest conceptions for an EMU, the construction of the 'snake' and the EMS, have been the first steps towards the more comprehensive plans for an Economic and Monetary Union as they have been formulated in the Delors Report of 1989.[9] In this respect, both the EMS and the EMU can be considered as the European Community's adjustment to the structural changes taking place within the world economy. What had been 'completely unthinkable' for Brussels in the 1950s, had become imperative in the 1980s. The EC has therefore had to 'shape and shove' in similar ways as the USSR in an effort to come to terms with the changes taking place in international politics and the world economy.

These explanations for the changes in Soviet and EC policy follow the lines of Neo-realist argument. Opening the 'black box' of the state, that is to say, examining the domestic sources of change within the USSR and the European Community, is, however, also called for. When we restrict ourselves to the EC a number of important 'internal' forces calling for new policies can be identified. Most attention has to be paid to the important element of the institutionalization of the EC by Community law. It is important to acknowledge that during the 1950s and early-1960s, no powerful European institutions actively promoted the cause of economic cooperation among the West European countries. With the strengthened role of the EC Commission and the increased authority of EC law, these circumstances have changed. The Commission, for instance, is now considered 'an entrenched, self-interested advocate of further integration'.[10] The European Commission has played an important role within the GATT negotiations and with the crumbling of the system of free world trade the European Community has turned into a powerful institution in defence of West European economic interests. The political vision and statesmanship of the Commission's President, Jacques Delors, must also not be underestimated. As Peter Ludlow has argued: 'most people would regard [the "Delors effect"] as the most obvious cause of change in the mid-1980s'.[11] Several other organizations working within the EC have also been important. For instance, the SEA has provided for a stronger EC Secretariat in order to assist the Presidency of the European Council (in which all member states take turns each half year), and which works closely together with the EC's bureaucracy in the preparation of the meetings of EC ministers. The Secretariat also plays an important role in monitoring the implementation of the ministers' decisions. It soon turned out that on important issues this Secretariat could provide a basis for continuity which was able to compensate for the revolving-door system of the half-year Presidency. Due to the Secretariat's expertise, this small organization has transformed itself into a force in the EC's drive towards a fully fledged European Union.[12] One could therefore argue that two factors have been important. First, the changes within the international system have given the European Community the *opportunity* to enhance its role and authority; second, the EC organization has *seized this opportunity* by actively stimulating the process of West European integration by means of new policy initiatives.

All in all, two 'revolutions' can be identified. One in the East prepared by Gorbachev's *perestroika* and *glasnost*, which – at least for the time being – has reached its apex in the unification of Germany (1990), the regained autonomy of the Central European countries and the demise of the USSR as a unitary nation-state (1991). And one in the West: the 1992 initiative which has resulted in a remarkable reconstruction of the 'European idea' as well as a reorientation of Europe's role in the world at large. The causes of both upheavals can for an important part be found in the structural changes in the international system. In this respect one can say that *perestroika* and the 1992 initiative have been responses to similar external factors and that both revolutions have influenced each other to a certain extent. Domestic factors can largely explain the ways in which these responses have been formulated. How and to what extent the '1989' and '1992' revolutions have motivated and inspired each other, is among the questions which will be tackled in the subsequent chapters.

8.3 *Perestroika*, Central Europe and the West

In the previous chapter we have examined the ties between the European Community and the CMEA. After more than two decades of malign neglect and some fifteen years of burdensome negotiations, both organizations had established official relations in June 1988. This was one of the most tangible outcomes of the increased flexibility in Moscow's approach to the West and to the European Community in particular.

The USSR had already been forthcoming in negotiations on arms controls and disarmament, which were expected to provide the Soviet economy some highly needed breathing space in the field of civilian production. It was of course also a clear sign of the Soviet Union's desire to buttress its economic links with the capitalist West. Simultaneous overtures to organizations like the GATT, the IMF and the World Bank, had indicated that Moscow was seriously striving after integration into the world economy. In August 1986, Moscow aired its aspirations of becoming a full member of GATT and officially applied to participate in the GATT talks. A Soviet official argued that 'The system of foreign economic links of the Soviet Union does not in any way contradict the principles, rules and practices of GATT. Its present restructuring will facilitate a greater integration of the USSR in the multilateral trade system.'[13] Although Moscow was still critical towards the IMF, IMF membership was expected to improve the USSR's credit standing with western commercial banks. Soviet officials also expected to benefit from the expertise and detailed economic analyses of the Fund.[14] These organizations were, however, rather reluctant to open their doors for a giant Soviet economy which was still based upon the orthodox principles of central planning and State-trading monopolies. The mere size of the Soviet economy made the prospect of Moscow's membership of these organizations extremely unlikely. Moreover, Soviet membership of GATT was expected to complicate the already complex and strenuous Uruguay Round which had started off in the mid-1980s.

The depth of the economic crises has differed considerably among the East European countries.[15] This has made it especially interesting to examine to what extent the specific domestic circumstances and predicaments of the individual CMEA members have fashioned their response to the Soviet policy of *perestroika* and *glasnost*. From 1985 onwards, several East European countries have followed Moscow's line on economic and political reform very closely, apprehensively observing the Soviet scene for new signs of reformist zeal. Poland and Hungary went furthest in their plans and policies to restructure their Soviet-styled system. Of all the Communist countries, Poland was in exceptionally bad shape.[16] Since 1981, the Polish economy had been under continuous scaffolding but the economic restructuring had only been concerned with the edifice. Inflation was rampant, whereby many basic consumer goods became ten times as expensive over a period of five years (1981-6). In 1986, Poland had defaulted on its debt payments to western governments, and in July 1987 a debt restructuring agreement was reached with western commercial banks. In December of that year, Poland also reached agreement with the 'Paris Club' of western creditor governments to reschedule its debt (over ten years, with a five-year grace period). Warsaw had joined the IMF and the World Bank in June 1986, but this had not yet resulted in IMF credits and World Bank investment loans.

Hungarian reformers, in turn, were not so much concerned with purely *economic* restructuring, but more with developing *political* pluralism. Gorbachev's policies were nevertheless welcomed, although the Soviet plans were a station long passed by both Warsaw and Budapest on their lengthy road towards a more viable economy. In May 1988, Janos Kádár, the Hungarian Communist leader since 1956, was relieved from his post and replaced by the reformist Karoly Grosz. A series of so-called 'Round Table Talks' started early-February 1989 in Poland, which eventually led to the non-Communist Polish Government led by Prime Minister Tadeusz Mazowiecki, on 12 September of that year. The GDR, Romania and Bulgaria, on the other hand, kept themselves afar from the new reformist Soviet course. East Berlin became an ever fiercer proponent of the notion of 'a national road towards socialism', the classical ideological rationale for ignoring Soviet policy as much as possible. Czechoslovakia was taking a similar conservative position, censoring the Soviet leaders' speeches for inflammatory words. All in all, Prague acted more as a passive bystander than as an interested party.

East European latitude to go their own way was, however, still restricted. In 1987, Gorbachev continued to follow the standard line, arguing that 'It goes without saying that no socialist country can successfully move forward in a healthy rhythm without understanding, solidarity and mutually beneficial cooperation with the other fraternal nations, or at times even without their help.'[17] This indicated that the Soviet leader favoured a balanced and coordinated process of reform in all CMEA countries whereby Moscow would, of course, set the pace and lead the way. In December 1985, at the 41st CMEA Session, Gorbachev had launched his so-called 'Comprehensive Program for the Scientific and Technological Progress of the CMEA Member Countries up to the Year 2000', which was designed to invigorate and strengthen relations among the CMEA members in the sphere of high-technology. It soon became clear that Moscow lacked the economic clout to manage the CMEA as well as the political stamina to do so. With the USSR now almost completely absorbed with its domestic reform issues, East European leaders took their chance to radicalize their agendas for change.

In July 1989, Gorbachev told the French President, François Mitterrand, that both Poland and Hungary were now free to decide on their own political future. What this would mean in practice was still left ambiguous, especially since the Soviet leader still argued that every Communist country should choose 'a new quality of life *within the socialist system*'.[18] Did this imply that the Warsaw Pact would become obsolete, or did he refer to nothing more than a looser security structure? Were Warsaw and Budapest now free to join western economic and security organizations, such as the European Community and NATO? Could they become market-oriented economies with democratic political institutions? For several months these issues were left unclarified. But soon most doubt was eliminated; during the meeting of Foreign Ministers of the Warsaw Pact (26-27 October 1989, in Warsaw), it was officially confirmed that the so-called 'Brezhnev doctrine' had been renounced. For the first time, the countries of Eastern Europe did not feel the direct weight of Soviet hegemony. With the breakdown of the post-war structure of bipolarity these countries were now free to 'join Europe'.

8.4 Brussels' initial response

These challenges in the East prompted action from the European Community, especially since the new drive towards the positive integration of the Community – which had been initiated by the SEA – had called for a more outspoken and coordinated approach of the Twelve's foreign policies. Much had changed since the late-1970s, when the European Community had reacted so slowly and confusedly to the Soviet invasion of Afghanistan. Now, more potent arrangements for consultation and cooperation on issues of foreign policy had been set up, whereby the process of European Political Cooperation (EPC) had become embedded in the Community's structure. The European Council Meeting ('Summit') had become a Treaty-based EC institution, bringing together the Heads of State (and Government) as well as the President of the EC Commission. It was decided that the European Council would meet at least twice a year and would 'play a strategic role and give direction and political impetus [to] the Community'.[19] Since 1987, the EC member states had been obliged to 'endeavour jointly to formulate and implement a European foreign policy', whereby a process of mutual information and consultation would maximize the impact of their combined influence on foreign affairs through coordination, convergence, joint action and the development of common principles and objectives.[20] Quite a number of these lofty objectives could be put to the test almost immediately due to the rapid changes in European politics.

During the EC's European Council Meeting in Hannover, 27-28 June 1988, the West European leaders had already expressed their determination to 'continue to play an active role' in East-West relations, meanwhile welcoming 'the more outward-looking attitude now being shown by Eastern European countries in their economic contacts with the West'.[21] Several months later, in the Autumn of 1988, the EC Foreign Ministers gathered in the northern Greek town of Ioannina for an informal meeting in the EPC framework. On that occasion three documents on East-West relations were prepared: one for the EC Rhodes Summit of December, one for the CSCE meeting in Vienna and another draft on economic relations between the European Community and the CMEA. Fundamental differences in approach among the Twelve in their foreign policies towards the East became prominent. One line of argument – most forcefully represented by Great Britain and Portugal – favoured a rather *passive* Community policy *vis-à-vis* the East. These policy suggestions were mainly based upon the assumption that the reforms in the Soviet Union were still highly unpredictable and, most importantly, not yet irreversible. Britain's Prime Minister, Margaret Thatcher, was adamantly opposed to western projects which she expected to 'fund the incompetence of the Soviet system'.[22] This line of policy also had many supporters in the United States and was most cogently captured by Henry Kissinger, who argued in early-1988: 'I am annoyed when people say that we must help Gorbachev. He must help himself'.[23] (See also Chapter 10 on these issues.)

The other circle within the EC, mainly represented by the Federal Republic of Germany, called for an *activist* strategy. It was maintained that *perestroika* deserved immediate western support and that a 'wait-and-see' approach of the EC would only hamper the Soviet and East European reform efforts. Bonn was fearful that without outside support and without a positive western attitude, the Soviet momentum of reform could be lost. This approach was in large part based upon the Federal Republic's *Ostpolitik* of the 1970s and 1980s, which had combined a policy of commercial cooperation with efforts to achieve political goals through tacit economic linkage.[24] Over the years, Bonn had become used to an *Ostpolitik* made up predominantly of economic carrots (like export credits, loans and trade), without wielding the economic stick of sanctions and embargoes. What was more, for many Germans the long-cherished goal of national unification was becoming less utopian with every move made towards genuine East-West conciliation. In order to reinforce and speed up this process the FRG took the initiative to strengthen East-West trade and to reinforce West German economic leverage *vis-à-vis* Moscow by offering export credits and by supporting German-Soviet joint ventures and other forms of commercial cooperation.

This German policy was illustrated by the heavy delegation of more than sixty captains of West German industry which accompanied Chancellor Kohl during his visit to Moscow, in late-October 1988. One of the aims of this meeting had been to establish preliminary contacts with Soviet trade organizations. These economic contacts were expected to strengthen Gorbachev's position and to legitimate his reform program *vis-à-vis* Communist hard-liners. For a number of reasons this German-Soviet commercial *rapprochement* provoked a critical response from several western allies, especially from the side of the United States, Great Britain and France. Firstly, old fears of a German *Alleingang* towards the East invoked the shadow of Rapallo (1922) and the Nazi-Soviet Pact (1939). Although these apprehensions were clearly exaggerated, they nevertheless constituted the emotional backcloth against which German policy towards the East was often evaluated. Secondly, Bonn's western allies grumbled over the manner in which the FRG was setting the pace of East-West conciliation by confronting them with several unpleasant *faits accomplis*. One example could be found in the issue of East-West trade and technology transfer. The transfer of strategic high-technology was, of course, still restricted under the CoCom rules. Most West German political leaders, however, considered the long list of embargoed technology as an outdated instrument of the Cold War. Wolfgang Roth, the economic spokesman of the West German SPD, argued that 'if we want to overcome the technological and economic division of Europe and build a new security relationship, every technology embargoed (except the small sector of weapons), is a relic of an aged conception of security. It is a leftover of the Cold War.'[25] Roth's argument formulated the new idea that the technological divide between East and West should be crossed, instead of maintained. In 1989, the West German Foreign Minister Hans-Dietrich Genscher, therefore argued: 'The main question for the West is: Is Gorbachev's success in the Western interest? I say: Yes. His success is not only better for the peoples of the Soviet Union, but also better for East-West relations. We must therefore try to make the reform process and the achievements in East-West relations irreversible. We must therefore not adopt a static approach but must act energetically and constructively.'[26] Italy's Prime Minister, Giulio Andreotti, had formulated this position as follows: 'The Twelve can't wait for the Soviets to become Victorians before reacting'.[27]

London and Washington in particular had occupied a much more cautious position on these issues, which had resulted in political tensions within the

Atlantic Alliance. This controversy was fuelled by Gorbachev's severe criticism of the western technology embargo, arguing that CoCom was hampering the construction of East-West joint ventures.[28] However, in 1989, the Bush Administration was still of the opinion that it was too soon to be certain about Mikhail Gorbachev's honourable intentions and the success of *perestroika*. Several US policy-makers, ranging from Deputy National Security Advisor Robert Gates, to Secretary of Defense Richard Cheney, predicted that President Gorbachev would be overthrown by the Soviet military and hard-line Communist factions and that the West should therefore not lower its guard. This guarded approach of the United States met with abundant criticism. Jerry Hough, for example, had argued (in May 1989) that America's Soviet policy was 'conservative in the sense of being content with the status quo. It is hard to imagine that [it has] any desire for the sheer unpredictability of revolution in the other nuclear Superpower at a time when the Soviet Union is posing no particular short-term or medium-term threat.'[29] Although basic differences still remained, both lines of argument slowly began to merge during the revolutionary year of 1989, when it became increasingly clear that Gorbachev's reforms had far-ranging political consequences and when *perestroika* seemed irreversible.

This change of heart was also reflected in the European Community's policy towards the East. Already during the EC Council Meeting in Rhodes (2-3 December 1988), the Community had aired its willingness to advance the economic ties with the reformist CMEA members. In its final declaration, the Council proclaimed its insistence on strengthening the role of the EC as an actor on the international stage, which was, among others, based upon the understanding that the 1992 programme would augment the Community's political and economic position in world affairs. It was also argued that the division of Europe could be overcome by promoting economic reform as well as 'western values'. These elements were reflected in the conditions set by the Commission in its negotiations with the CMEA members on trade and cooperation accords (see below). Similar priorities *vis-à-vis* the East were set during the Madrid Summit in June 1989. Only one month later, during the Summit of the Group of Seven major industrialized countries (the G-7) in Paris, the European Community's Commission accepted the request to coordinate the assistance towards the East of the Group of 24 OECD countries (the G-24). We will discuss the EC's role in the aid efforts to the East in the next chapter.

8.5 Gorbachev's 'Common European Home'

With the abandonment of the Brezhnev doctrine, which had for decades settled the USSR's dominance in Eastern Europe, an end had been made to the post-war structure of confronting blocs. Not surprisingly, it took some time for both West European and American policy-makers to realize that European politics was on the threshold of a new era; during the 1990s, new security and economic structures had to be set up and existing organizations had to be reshaped or even replaced by brand new ones. Structural rethinking of economic, political and security issues was now called for. Since 'security' was increasingly defined in terms of economic (and environmental) terms,[30] the EC emerged as the framework in which a wide range of important matters were expected to be solved. In response to these exceptional challenges, several proposals and concepts were formulated which had been allowed to drift around in Europe's geopolitical stratosphere for a considerable time. In this section we will discuss Gorbachev's notion of a 'Common European Home' and we will examine how this concept has related to the developments taking place within the European Community.

In search of a 'new European architecture', Soviet President Gorbachev launched his notion of a 'Common European Home' in which both the EC, Eastern Europe and the Soviet Union would have their own rooms. The building blocks of this 'European Home' would be constructed of the alleged common western values; the roof would be fabricated by common institutions on economic and political cooperation. During his visit to Yugoslavia in March 1988, Gorbachev argued: 'We are against the further cleavage of the European continent. We strive after the building of a European Home which is really comfortable for the people who live in it.'[31] One year later in his speech to the Council of Europe in Strasbourg (July 1989), Gorbachev spoke of a new, united Europe stretching from the Atlantic to the Urals.[32] The perhaps intentional vagueness of this new notion raised several important questions: did Gorbachev consider the EC only as some sort of free trade area, disregarding the fact that the Community had quite distinct political aspirations, the so-called *finalité politique*? And what was more, did the Soviet leader seriously suggest that the Asian part of Russia should be left outside the 'Home'? Moreover, did his 'Common European Home' imply that the United States and Canada would find themselves shut outside?

Time and again Gorbachev's ideas were presented by Soviet officials, presumably in an effort to influence the West European discussion on the future structure of the European Community. It has also been suggested that Gorbachev's concept of a 'European Home' was just one more try to disengage Western Europe from the United States by offering an 'All-European', or 'Pan-European', alternative to the previous structure of East-West separation and confrontation. Although both the United States and Canada were participating within the context of the CSCE process, there was no obvious role for them to play within the 'Common Home', thereby also leaving unclarified what the future position and function of NATO would be and what kind of security arrangement would eventually replace the Atlantic Alliance. As Neil Malcolm has argued perceptively: 'In 1985 the Common European Home was above all a slogan: a weapon in the East-West diplomatic game at a time when Moscow felt the need to focus attention on conflicts of interest within NATO ... From 1987 onwards, however, the Common Home idea began to acquire more substance. It embodied a genuine offer of greater consultation and rapprochement with the West European powers, and a promise to the Central European states on both sides of the East-West divide that ways would be sought to overcome their unnatural separation.'[33] Indeed, in the late-1980s, Soviet policy-makers began to realize that they had to come to grips with a revitalized drive towards economic and political cooperation in Western Europe. The integrationist momentum generated by the SEA and the 1992 initiative had minimized Soviet opportunities to thwart the further development of the EC. Whereas previously the USSR had tried to discourage these tendencies in the West, it was now confronted with several unmistaken *faits accomplis*. In response, quite remarkable shifts in the Soviet attitude could be noticed. The 'Common European Home' concept was now used in order to link up with the EC's new dynamic. For instance, Moscow now even asserted that a more independent role of Western Europe within NATO could be beneficial to the USSR and that a free internal market in Western Europe could bear some fruit for the East.

Aleksandr N. Yakovlev, Secretary of the CPSU Central Committee and close ally of Gorbachev, set the new tone of the Soviet Union's new policy towards the European Community. In a speech to the Italian Communist Party Congress (March 1989), he argued that Russia (*sic*) should be included in the process of European integration: 'In itself, the idea of a European Community is not new ... it has been put forward by many generations of our predecessors. Its roots go back to the Middle Ages, to antiquity ... Throughout the centuries, a united Europe was not imagined without Russia. The cultural, political and economic ties of Russia with Western Europe go back to the times of Kievan Rus, if not earlier.'[34] This remarkable volte-face in Soviet policy towards the EC was followed up by President Gorbachev, who in his speech to the Council of Europe quoted the French novelist Victor Hugo to the effect that 'The day will come when you, France, you, Russia, you, Italy, you, Britain, you, Germany, all of you, all of the nations of the continent, without losing your distinctive features and your splendid originality, will all indissolubly merge into a kind of higher society and will form a European fraternity. The day will come when the only field of battle will be markets open for trade and minds open to ideas.'[35] In that same speech, Gorbachev also argued that 'The USSR and the USA are a natural part of the European international political structure'. The Soviet leader obviously feared that Moscow would be left aside, becoming isolated from the seemingly successful process of economic integration in the western rim of Europe. He therefore maintained that 'The model of economic drawing closer together between Eastern and Western Europe will be determined, not in the last instance, by the relationship between the western regional associations of the EEC and EFTA and the CMEA. Each of them has its own dynamics of development and its problems. We have no doubt that the integrational processes in Western Europe are acquiring a new quality. We are not inclined to underestimate the emergence in the next few years of a single European market.'[36]

What kind of relationship should be developed between the EC, EFTA and the CMEA was left unclarified. In December 1989, on the occasion of signing the EC-Soviet 10-year trade and cooperation agreement, Soviet Foreign Minister Eduard Shevardnadze had called for a continent-wide 'European Economic Space' (EES) and the formation of a 'Trilateral Commission' which would have to encompass the European Community, EFTA as well as the CMEA. However, due to the rapid demise of the CMEA, nothing could come from such a trilateral framework of cooperation. It was in response to Gorbachev's lack of conceptual clarity that the former French President Valery Giscard d'Estaing brought to attention the option of a better-defined form of cooperation between the European Community and the East: 'association'.[37] Giscard maintained that the Soviet plans for East-West cooperation were far too ambiguous. In order to achieve some conceptual clarity, he argued, one could better speak of a 'European village' comprising a number of 'homes': the EC Twelve, the EFTAns, the East European members of the Warsaw Pact, independent countries like Yugoslavia, Albania and Malta, and the European part of the USSR. In his speech, Giscard stressed the crucial importance of the different levels of political and economic development of the European countries. The relations between the EC and the East European 'homes' would therefore be contingent upon the latter's achievements in economic and political reform.[38]

In her annual speech in the Guildhall, on 13 November 1989, the British Prime Minister, Margaret Thatcher, took up this idea and enthusiastically supported the option of new forms of cooperation between the EC and reformist Central European countries, most notably through the conclusion of association agreements along the lines of the EC's agreement with Turkey. (For a more elaborate discussion of the issue of association agreements with the East, see Chapter 10.4.) These association agreements were expected to establish solid economic and political links between these countries and the EC. The reformist Communist countries would receive economic and financial assistance and obtain a number of essential trade advantages such as increased market access. Mrs Thatcher's proposal for an associate membership of Hungary met with a very positive response in Budapest. In December 1990, negotiations between the EC and three Central European countries could start. After a year of strenuous bargaining, the EC concluded association agreements with Poland, Hungary and Czechoslovakia mid-December 1991. But before these issues could be settled, Brussels first of all had to deal with the even more delicate question of German reunification.

8.6 The new German Question

The fall of the Berlin Wall (November 1989) and the incorporation of the GDR in the Federal Republic of Germany (October 1990) have been the most dramatic direct result of the successful 1989 revolutions in the East. Without the collapse of the Soviet overlay in Central Europe, German unity would have remained a day-dream. At the same time, the unification of Germany has raised a number of arduous questions as to the new role of the FRG within the EC and Europe at large. In this respect, the 1989 and the 1992 revolutions have been closely linked. Among the major questions are whether a unified Germany will become (too) dominant or whether it will, on the other hand, lose its interest in West European integration and pursue its own goals unilaterally? The EC Commission's Vice-President, Frans Andriessen, expected (April 1990) that the process of European integration would be accelerated by German unity, both where the EMU and the institutional development of the EC were concerned.[39] We will deal with these questions more elaborately in Chapter 10. Here we will examine the ways in which the EC and its member states have responded to the opportunities provided by the changes in Eastern Europe in 1989 and pay special attention to the new 'German Question' prompted by the unification of Germany in the Autumn of 1990.

Bonn's ultimate foreign policy goal has been German unification. Since the late-1960s, West German 'new' *Ostpolitik* has tried to bridge the Cold War divisions in Europe, realizing that German unity could only be achieved when the traditional East-West conflict was overcome. As Josef Joffe has formulated it: 'It is the bipolar system that limits the FRG's aspirations; to realize [unification], the West Germans must change [bipolarity]. To reassociate the two Germanys requires reassociating the two halves of Europe by breaking down the barriers of bipolarity and weakening its hold over the Continent.'[40] During the several decades of extreme rigidity in East-West relations, only ardent optimists had cherished the hope that such a dramatic systemic change could come about in the short term. Most scenarios and contingency plans have been based upon the expectation that Soviet-style Communism and Soviet hegemony in Eastern Europe were here to stay. The political developments taking place in the late-1980s have dramatically altered the likelihood of all the available scenarios for Europe's future. All of a sudden the prospects for German unification improved.

For decades, the European Community, the EC's member states and most other western countries had said that they approved and even supported Bonn's aspirations of national reunification. The mantra of 'German reunification' was often repeated during high-level political meetings and added to many communiqués. Even the French President de Gaulle loyally declared (March 1959): 'The reunification of the separated parts into a united Germany that would be entirely free seems to us to be the normal future of the

German peoples, provided that the present borders in the West, East, North and South are not again called into question and Germany tries one day to fit contractually into a pan-European organization for cooperation, freedom and peace.'[41] The special relationship between the two Germanys was exemplified by the special German provisions of the Treaty of Rome, which had spelled out that intra-German trade was not to be seen as foreign trade and was therefore not subject to the EC customs regulations which applied to imports from third countries. For these reasons the GDR has sometimes been called the *de facto* 'silent' or 'thirteenth' member state of the EC. But despite the declarations of the ultimate aim of German unity, several West European policy-makers have once in a while abandoned this line of argument. Among the most famous disloyalties has been François Mauriac's statement: 'I love Germany so much that I am happy there are two of them.' On another occasion, the Italian Foreign Minister Giulio Andreotti criticized the notion of German reunification when he visited East Berlin in 1984.[42] These were, however, exceptions to the general rule that German reunification was endorsed.

This West European attitude towards German unity has always been rather gratuitous, since (apart from the FRG itself), no West European country has actually envisaged this happening shortly. As Stanley Hoffmann had maintained in 1985: 'Paris assured the West Germans that it stood up for its ideal of reunification ... At the same time, France indicated to the other western powers that she had everything under control; no reunification could take place.'[43] To the despair of many, it soon became clear that with the demise of the Communist regimes in Hungary and Poland, the continuity of the GDR was also in doubt. When Poland would adopt a liberal, market-oriented economic and political system and the USSR would follow suit, the endurance of the GDR was very unlikely indeed. This implied that the traditional 'German Question' of the post-war era had to be fundamentally redefined. The West German President Richard von Weizsäcker, acknowledged the ambiguity of both Eastern and Western Europe *vis-à-vis* German reunification when he argued: 'Most Europeans dislike the wall about as much as they do the idea of a large German state in central Europe'.[44] Whereas a number of EC officials had immediately argued that the prospect of German unity would spur the momentum of West European integration, it was not at all clear whether Bonn would be able to pay sufficient attention to its national unification *and* the challenges which were lying ahead in the Intergovernmental Conferences on the establishment of a European Union.

Chancellor Konrad Adenauer had tried to accomplish German unity by a policy of strength and by associating the FRG closely to the western security organizations. Integration into the West was for Adenauer also a strategy to prevent Germany from drifting to neutrality; he had considered neutrality a too exorbitant price for unity. We have already argued that the FRG had also cast its anchor in the EC's institutions in order to reassure western neighbours that its aim of national unity would not develop into an *Alleingang* towards the Communist East.[45] In turn, Bonn's close cooperation within the EC also provided the West Europeans with a number of tangible checks upon the Federal Republic's *Ostpolitik*. Moreover, the Four Powers' responsibilities for all questions relating to 'Germany as a whole', and their recent special arrangement on Berlin, gave both the United States, Great Britain and France a direct say in these delicate issues. The USSR also used this to limit the margins of Bonn's foreign policy. For both the USSR and most western nations this arrangement had been acceptable and perhaps even quite comfortable. However, now that the Soviet bloc was gradually coming apart, the prospect of German reunification had to be faced. The tried Soviet concept of 'You take care of your [West] Germans, and we will take care of our [East] Germans', was now out of date, but no new strategy could instantly succeed it. It soon turned out that the rapidity of the developments left many West European countries temporarily without a clear policy towards the new 'German Question'.

France in particular was in a temporary state of limbo. For decades Paris had made use of its 'special relationship' with West Germany in order to balance the USSR and vice versa. (See our examination in Chapter 6.3.) In de Gaulle's judgement 'the collapse of Germany, the tearing apart of Europe, and Russo-American antagonism offer[ed] France, saved by a miracle, exceptional opportunities for action'.[46] Roger Morgan has argued that France has always had three basic options in its policy towards Germany. First, it could form an alliance with Germany's eastern neighbours (Poland or Russia/USSR); second, it could seek an alliance with the 'oceanic powers': Great Britain and the United States; and third, it could draw Germany into an alliance with France itself.[47] Over the past decades, particularly the last option had been tried. The framework of the EC was used to contain Bonn's economic power and to monitor the West German efforts to achieve its possession goals in the East. With the construction of the Bonn-Paris axis in the early-1960s, the French status within West European politics had been enhanced. It was therefore expected that France's influence in Europe would decline markedly due to German unity. This would result in 'an economically superpowerful Germany, politically dominant in central Europe, and a France reduced to a secondary role; an end to Gaullist dreams of a Europe directed politically by a nuclear France'.[48] Before reunification, France and West Germany were roughly equal. France maintained a nuclear arsenal as well as a special relationship with francophone Africa, whereas West Germany had a larger population and a larger GNP. When German unity was realized, this balance would change since one German nation would be more powerful both geographically and economically. Moreover, with the millstone of national division thrown off, Germany was also expected to regain its political reassurance and pride.[49] No European nation could be confident that Germany would use its regained political and economic muscle in a respectable manner. All in all, the prospect of German unification spelled ill for the French position in Europe. Within a short time, the German Question had been transformed from achieving security *for* Germany into being secure *from* Germany.

In 1989 it was still unclear whether the Soviet Union would endorse its East German ally to link up with the FRG. Moscow considered the GDR as one of the main corner-stones of both the Warsaw Pact and the CMEA. In this respect the national interests of Paris and Moscow coincided; both France and the USSR had much to lose when Germany would reunite. It nevertheless took many by surprise when the French and Soviet Presidents aired their worries about a possible German reunification during their meeting in the Ukrainian capital Kiev on 6 December 1989. Both statesmen argued that a German *Wiedervereinigung* constituted a potential threat to peace and stability in Europe, especially since it would imply the changing of borders which were – at least implicitly – confirmed by the Helsinki Accords of 1975. Soviet Foreign Minister Shevardnadze had unreservedly shared President Mitterrand's view that 'not a single European country can act without taking into account the interests of others, or without taking into account the current historical situation that has taken shape as a result of the Second World War'.[50] A few days after the Kiev meeting, Gorbachev maintained in his speech at the Plenum of the CPSU Central Committee, that Moscow would stick with its strategic ally the GDR and that Soviet policy should proceed from the post-war 'reality' of the existence of two separate and sovereign German states. Any departure from these 'political facts' would result in destabilization at the very heart of Europe, in particular since it would signify a profound change in the alliance structures of both NATO and the Warsaw Pact. With a unified and saturated Germany in the heart of *Mitteleuropa*, both France and the USSR would see their political influence dwindled.

It has generally been considered a tactical mistake that France had first tried the policy option of balancing German power by allying with the USSR. France had definitely misjudged the effects of its reserved stance towards German unity. It soon became evident that reunification could not be blocked by a Franco-Soviet alliance since the USSR was mainly dependent upon trade with West German industry. Moreover, Bonn's economic and financial assistance to the USSR were considered quintessential to the successful implementation of its domestic reform plans. Without the support of Bonn, Gorbachev would lose a powerful and rich western ally. After Mitterrand's escapades in Kiev had met with a negative response in Germany and the rest of Western Europe, Paris returned to the tried strategy of the 'Paris-Bonn axis' within the EC. Only a few days after the Kiev meeting, the European Council met in Strasbourg where the European leaders 'reaffirmed their commitment to German unification through free self-determination in a peaceful and democratic process, in full respect of the relevant agreements and treaties and of all the principles defined by the Helsinki Final Act, within a context of dialogue and East-West cooperation'.[51] During the following Summit in April in Dublin, the Commission had prepared a report which provided an integration scenario for both Germanys, arguing that the integration of the GDR into a unified Germany (and hence in the EC) constitutes a special case. Article 237 of the Rome Treaty – which relates to the accession of other states – did therefore not apply.

Repenting its Kievian sin, France sought to consolidate its direct ties with Bonn. As a result, France quickly became the most zealous proponent for a 'European Union'. The commitment of the French policy-making elite to further West European integration in the EC framework was considerably fortified by these experiences. Paris realized that in order to maintain French influence, the EC structure would have to be strengthened and the process of European unity would have to be vitalized. Mitterrand argued that the prospect of German reunification called for 'strengthening the structures of the Community. It is particularly necessary that the European alliance should have genuine content imparted to it.'[52] As Dominique Moïsi has argued: 'Either we'll get a strong Germany within a divided Europe, or a strong Europe and within it a powerful Germany'.[53]

In an effort to assuage these fears, Chancellor Kohl has time and again repeated that the FRG would remain a fierce proponent of EC unity since West European cohesion had always been a *precondition*, and no *substitute* to German unity. This, he argued, has given Bonn an additional stake in EC integration in comparison to other member states. It is exactly this issue which stands at the core of the current German Question: whether 'Germany's economic power remains harnessed to the promotion of integration in the EC and cooperation in the wider international economy, rather than that of containing the expansionist pressures of a restless Reich, whether the Second or the Third'.[54]

All in all, the internal balance of power within the EC has been significantly altered by German reunification. Over the decades, the Bonn-Paris axis has provided much of the internal drive for West European integration. The traditional apprehensions between these two states had been temporarily set aside during the Cold War division of Europe. Bonn needed the support of Paris in its efforts to achieve its possession goals in the East, whereas Paris tried to enhance its international prestige by associating with the FRG. With the 'old' German Question being solved, the spectre of a strong Germany throwing its political and economic weight around in an instable Europe again looms large. Now that the bipolar structure of world politics has been replaced by a less clear multipolar one, the internal dynamic of the EC has come under renewed stress. The EC now lacks a clear-cut external threat and US economic and military hegemony has become a thing of the past. In short, the 1989 and 1992 revolutions have significantly altered the outlook of European politics. In the remainder of this book we will deal with the new questions and problems which Brussels will face in the years ahead.

9. Brussels' Lighthouse: Coordinating Western Economic Assistance to the East

President Gorbachev will need courage and luck, but the governments of the West can offer little more than moral support.

Editorial, *The Financial Times*, 12 March 1990.

9.1 Introduction

During the four decades of Cold War the possibilities of the West for encouraging economic and political reform in Eastern Europe have been marginal. With the exception of the FRG and the United States, most western governments have been sceptical about the prospects of persuading the Communist states to adopt the principles of market economics and political pluralism. In particular, Bonn has persistently tried to encourage reform in the East by proffering attractive economic 'carrots' before the hungry eyes of East European policy-makers. US policy-makers have been more inclined to wield the economic stick in an effort to achieve similar political goals. With the quick demise of Soviet hegemony over Central Europe, the prospects for western economic statecraft *vis-à-vis* the East have improved markedly.

During the late-1980s, western policy-makers on both sides of the Atlantic had to decide whether they would remain passive bystanders and simply watch how the East European revolutions were unfolding, or whether they would aspire to play a more active part, for instance by providing economic assistance to the eastern iconoclasts. During the initial phase of the East European reform process, most western governments had remained acquiescent under the assumption that the Communist revolutions were basically a domestic affair and that the West could only provide some of the marginal preconditions for reform. Moreover, during the late-1980s, it was still far from clear whether overt western support to the reformists in the East would be tolerated by Moscow. Although the reform process of *perestroika* was more radical and far-ranging than previous efforts to change Soviet society, western policy-makers were well aware of the fact that the Brezhnev doctrine still applied to Eastern Europe. However, after the changes in Poland, Hungary and Czechoslovakia seemed irreversible, calls for a more active western approach gained force, which eventually culminated in several plans for assisting Central Europe.

. In this chapter we will examine the role played by the European Community in assisting Central European countries to transform their socio-economic systems and to adopt the western-style principles of market and democracy. The EC has been the international organization which has played a pivotal role in coordinating western assistance to the East. We will argue that the EC's active stance has boosted its political prestige and has strengthened its grip on the design of post-Cold War Europe. This has been one of the remarkable results of the weakened structure of bipolarity of world politics in the 1990s. The EC as a 'civilian' – that is mainly economic – power, will be able to play a more independent part on the European stage now that the United States and the former Soviet Union lack the economic clout to determine the East-West dialogue. As Flora Lewis has maintained: 'The new power balance is expressed through economic might'.[1] President Bush's remark – in early-June 1989 – was to the same effect: 'the role of NATO shifts, our own role shifts, from the main emphasis on deterrence to an emphasis on the economic side of things'.[2] Since economic power is expected to play an important role in the 1990s, the position of the EC seems especially robust. Whether the Twelve will be able to live up to the expectations and get their act together, still remains uncertain.

This chapter will mainly examine the setting and the experiences of the EC with coordinating western aid. It will also discuss the role of several newly established international organizations for providing assistance to the East (most notably the European Bank for Reconstruction and Development – EBRD), and evaluate the efficacy of western aid in the Central European reform process. It has been argued that western assistance to the East is part of a so-called 'Triple R Agenda', which is composed of reform, reintegration and regional security.[3] In this context, western aid has been used to facilitate the reforms in the East, to reintegrate their economies and societies into the world economy and political international organizations. The final goal of this agenda would be to construct a new post-Cold War order which will provide a system wherein the political and security interests of all major world powers will be guaranteed. These are ambitious aspirations. Here we will examine how the EC has handled the issue of Communist reform and what strategies it has adopted in order to achieve some of the goals of this Triple R Agenda.

9.2 The G-7 Paris meeting and PHARE

In Chapter 8 we examined Brussels' initial response to the upheavals in the East. In 1989, the end of the Cold War was celebrated as a victory of the West and, due to the lack of bloody conflicts which normally accompany radical revolutions, a feeling of euphoria was widespread. With the breakdown of the East-West political and ideological divide, Europe was expected to be united at last.

For these reasons the momentous changes in the East during 1989 (and 1990) have provided an enormous challenge for the European Community to live up to its aspirations of turning itself into a major international political actor. During a meeting in Moscow in mid-June 1989, Vice President of the EC Commission, Frans Andriessen, argued that 'the bold initiatives in political reform and economic liberalisation under way in east Europe ... have our full support as moves to ensure the effective exercise of human rights, to guarantee genuine economic freedoms and to overcome the division of Europe. The Community', he maintained, 'is determined to mobilise the considerable policy instruments at its disposal in pursuit of these objectives.' On that occasion, Andriessen also explicitly pointed out that the 'Single European Act, which brings together in one document provisions governing political cooperation and economic integration, has enabled us to promote East-West cooperation in a coherent and dynamic way'. This indicated that the EC Commission considered itself particularly well placed to help overcome the division of Europe and to end the Cold War 'by developing a network of East-West cooperation to replace the rivalries of past decades'.[4] In the end, the EC might realize the aspirations of the Preamble to the Rome Treaty: to 'lay the foundation of an ever closer union among the peoples of Europe'.

While the revolutions in Eastern Europe were gaining force, consensus built up in the West to provide a helping hand. During the climax of the bicentennial celebrations of the French revolution – on 14 July 1989 – the G-7 met in Paris where East-West relations appeared on top of the agenda. Whereas the utility of aid to the East had been a topic of dispute in 1987-8, agreement could now be reached on a strategy of western economic and financial support for the East European revolt against Communism. Over the past few months it had also become clear that in order to attain their economic and political objectives, the western countries should collaborate in their aid programmes to the East. West European aid efforts *vis-à-vis* Hungary and Poland – the two most reformist Communist countries – were already on the cards. In 1989, the Hungarian Government of Prime Minister Miklós Németh had achieved a remarkable record of political and economic reforms; constitutional changes for multi-party democracy and western-type market economy had been made. In Poland elections had been held in June 1989, showing the lack of support for the Polish Communist Party (PUWP), which was soon to be replaced by a non-Communist government led by Mr Tadeusz Mazowiecki (in September 1989). Now that the Iron Curtain was ascending and the prospects for further reforms were considered good, the G-7 decided during the Paris meeting to jointly expand western aid to Warsaw and Budapest. For that reason, the G-7 presented the EC with the accolade of coordinating western assistance *vis-à-vis* Hungary and Poland. At the splendid Arche de la Défense, the EC Commission was invited to organize a conference where plans for the coordination of western (G-24) aid would be presented.

In many respects, these new political responsibilities for the European Community were a gift right out of heaven. Coordinating western assistance to the East was a prestigious assignment which corresponded with Brussels' ambitions to assume greater responsibility in the field of foreign policy. For most members of the G-7, the EC had been the obvious organization for taking up this new task. Appointing Brussels as the new coordination centre suited specific interests of several major EC member states, as well as those of the United States. First of all, funnelling western aid through the multilateral channels of the EC was expected to serve as a mechanism to limit Germany's potential economic influence in the East. The FRG was without doubt the strongest economic power in Western Europe and its traditional interests in the East had only been intensified by the prospect of a non-Communist Central Europe. By coordinating large parts of German economic assistance within a multilateral framework, Bonn's influence was expected to be kept in check. This method of balancing German influence by strengthening the EC was particularly endorsed by G-7 members like Italy and France. Only Great Britain was reluctant, since it had realized that this plan would once again strengthen the authority and power of Brussels in Western Europe's *Ostpolitik*.

The United States, on the other hand, had also backed the EC's new central role. For political reasons, Washington had argued that the West European countries should assume prime responsibility for aiding the reformist governments in the East. At the same time, the United States lacked the financial leeway to play a more active part since its foreign aid funds were severely limited by budgetary problems. It was rumoured that during his earlier trip to Poland, President Bush had been overwhelmed by the enormous demand for economic aid in the former Communist countries; it was very unlikely indeed that the United States would be able to shoulder much of that financial burden. For the United States this had been a unique occasion since it was the first time that such an important foreign policy issue had been left to the European Community. Apart from these motives of political expediency, the organizational structure of the EC also seemed especially qualified for this new and grand assignment. Several obvious geographical advantages aside, Brussels already had many years of experience with the arrangement of regional economic programmes (such as the

European Regional Development Fund which had been set up in 1975) and in coordinating aid to the Third World.[5] It was therefore expected that the EC's bureaucracy could best handle this new task. The EC Foreign Ministers had already decided in April 1989 (during the Luxembourg Summit), that the Twelve would coordinate their policies towards the East within the Community framework. All these developments seemed once more to indicate that the superpower overlay of the European continent was becoming a thing of the past and that the EC's foreign policy role would be enhanced.

Immediate action was taken when the EC Agricultural Ministers approved ECU 110 million emergency food programme for Poland, on 24 July. One week later, senior officials of the twenty-four OECD members were invited to meet in Brussels in order to discuss the coordination of western aid efforts.[6] These first G-24 meetings were little more than an initial stocktaking of the bilateral projects which were already under way. In the mean time, Commission officials were gathering information about the economic needs of the two Central European recipient countries and were starting to coordinate national aid commitments. One of the EC Commission's main tasks has been to provide both guidance and transparency in the continuously expanding bilateral and multilateral undertakings. The Commission therefore set up a special Task Force to oversee G-24 and EC aid. This so-called G-24 Coordination Unit has functioned as a 'scorekeeper' in order to 'provide information on G-24 programs to Commission services, donors and beneficiary countries; to strengthen complementarity and coherence of G-24 assistance; and to promote joint actions and new initiatives'.[7] The G-24 Coordination Unit was to function in an unrestricted manner, whereby the EC Commission would oversee and coordinate bilateral assistance but the governments of the G-24 countries would still remain free to enrol or to eschew a particular aid programme.

Coordinating aid was considered especially necessary since experiences with western aid to the Third World had learned that good intentions and money were no water-tight recipe for success.[8] There were four compelling reasons for coordinating western aid: (1) coordination would result in the optimal use of assistance; (2) it was expected to bring other non-G-24 countries into the scheme (for instance the OPEC and South-East Asian countries); (3) it would result in closer cooperation with the IMF, the World Bank and the OECD; and (4) it would allow the recipient Central European countries to negotiate with the entire 'donor community' to adopt the most coherent and effective aid programmes adjusted to their reform requirements. During the first meetings, the main priority areas for western aid were identified and a rudimentary western assistance plan was formulated. At the same occasion the so-called 'Operation PHARE'[9] (Poland and Hungary: Assistance for Restructuring Economies) was launched, which was going to provide elaborate western economic aid to Poland and Hungary. The EC and its member states have been the largest contributors to the PHARE programme, joined by the United States and Japan. A number of multilateral organizations were later brought in as observers, such as the OECD, the IMF, the World Bank, the European Investment Bank (EIB) and the Paris Club of creditor nations. In 1991, the Bank for International Settlements (BIS) and the International Energy Agency (IEA) were also included in the coordination framework.

The PHARE programme was based upon five major elements, all aimed at helping the recipient countries to carry out their reforms: (1) supplying immediate food aid; (2) facilitating Central European access to the EC market; (3) giving Poland and Hungary admittance to the EIB and the other financial institutions of the EC; (4) providing special training in order to transfer know-how concerning market-oriented management; and (5) providing special assistance for protecting the environment.[10] On all these five points Brussels has undertaken immediate action. Foodstuffs were provided to Poland where the sale of supplies went towards the creation of so-called Counterpart Funds (which were designed to finance Polish agricultural cooperatives). The EC could fall back on its experience during the period of 1981-3, when it had also supplied food and medicine to Poland. Several trade restrictions for Polish and Hungarian goods were eased, most participating states granted formal MFN status and the GSP was extended. Programmes for financial assistance and vocational training (especially in financial services and banking), were set up and almost US$ 50 million were earmarked for some twenty-five environmental projects in Hungary and Poland.[11] In late-September 1989, the Commission advanced its new aid package for the two reformist countries amounting to ECU 300 million (one-third for Hungary, two-thirds for Poland). Both countries would now also become eligible for soft-loans from the EIB. Another ECU 200 million was added to the EC budget for the other Central European countries which were stepping up their reforms. In 1991, the European Community committed itself to an amount of ECU 850 million, which has been increased to ECU 1 billion over 1992.

The course of Central European reform has differed per country, whereby Poland has chosen for a 'big bang' shock therapy and Hungary and Czechoslovakia for a gradualist approach. For all these countries, however, it soon became evident that the Soviet-led CMEA structure was to be dissolved in order to integrate fully with Western Europe. Central European reform had resulted in an unprecedented fall in the volume of trade among the CMEA countries (an estimated 14-16 per cent in 1990).[12] Trade between the USSR and Central Europe fell almost as steeply. The traditional trade and payments system of the CMEA had been criticized during the 45th CMEA Session in Sofia, 9-10 January 1990. With the *de facto* economic decentralization of the USSR, traditional Central European exports declined and Soviet exports of energy had also become less assured. In previous chapters we have examined the East European efforts to balance Soviet dominance by strengthening the economic ties with Western Europe. In the late-1980s, this was even more essential since trade dependence upon the USSR would make the Central European reform process contingent upon the success of Gorbachev's *perestroika*. In order to strengthen the economic reforms and to hasten reintegration within the world economy, Brussels had already signed several bilateral trade and cooperation agreements with a number of Central European countries, generally on trade in industrial products. In July 1988, the EC and Hungary had concluded a comprehensive trade and cooperation agreement whereby some 2,000 quantitative EC restrictions were to be scrapped (in three phases by the end of 1995). After more than five years of negotiations the accord was signed just one week after the EC and the CMEA had taken up official relations. It was generally expected that this would be the most far-ranging agreement which the EC was likely to sign with any of the six Central European countries since Hungary had implemented the most radical economic reforms programme of the Communist East. Brussels had indicated that it was only prepared to lower its protectionist guard to CMEA members which had already introduced significant market-oriented reforms. European Community officials mainly stressed the economic rationale of this policy, arguing that orthodox centrally planned economies would, *nolens volens*, practice dumping.

Since Czechoslovakia had not yet adopted far-ranging reform measures, a much more limited trade agreement was signed with Prague on 19 December 1989. Following the path of the other CMEA members, East Berlin and Brussels also started exploratory talks on a possible trade agreement in June 1988. Negotiations on a new and more detailed trade and cooperation agreement with Romania (replacing the old one of 1980), had already commenced in April 1987. In April 1989, however, the EC Foreign Ministers had suspended these talks because of Romania's horrendous human rights record. In September 1988, the EC had already aired its concern about the planned destruction of some 7,000 villages in that country. During the CSCE negotiations in Vienna, Ceaușescu's policy was denounced as catastrophic for Romanian cultural heritage and human rights. Bucharest had obviously fallen from the top to the bottom of Brussels' list of priority countries in little less than a decade. In 1980, Romania had been the first East European country to sign a trade agreement with the Community, but now it had to bear the scorn of Brussels for its failure to meet its human rights commitments. In December 1989 – a few days before the fall of the Ceaușescu regime – the Committee of Permanent Representatives of the EC member states (Coreper) recommended suspending Bucharest's GSP as well as the 1980 trade agreement. After the violent breakdown of Communist rule, negotiations with Bucharest were resumed in May 1990 and a new accord was eventually signed on 8 June. In a similar vein, the EC had also suspended its negotiations with Bulgaria from May 1989 till March 1990, because of Sofia's violations of the rights of the Turkish minority.

In late-November 1989, the European Community and the USSR also completed their talks on an agreement envisaging the granting of formal MFN status, cooperation between customs services, arbitration and assistance to businessmen and companies as well as (among others) statistics, industry, banking, tourism and management. Such an EC-USSR trade and cooperation agreement was signed three weeks later. Soviet policy-makers welcomed this agreement as the beginning of a new era and a step towards the acclaimed 'Common European Home'. Speaking on that occasion, Soviet Foreign Minister Shevardnadze argued that

> The agreement between the Soviet Union and the EC is not an ordinary document; it is innovative by even the strictest of current standards. In terms of its nature it reflects the tumultuous dynamics of the renewal process in Europe. In terms of its content it brings one step nearer the practical laying of economic foundations for the Common European Home ... Overcoming the blinkered approaches of the past, we arrived at the conclusion that integration in Western Europe is not only a reality but also a major European factor, not just an economic but also a foreign policy factor. Our co-operation with the EC is a promising channel for mutual adaptation to one another, for overcoming the division of the continent – with, of course, the involvement of our CMEA partners in this process, which can only be welcomed ... We perceive the scale and depth of integration co-operation within the EC and the radical *perestroika* of the Soviet economy with its active involvement in world economic ties as a realistic base for collaboration between 'The Twelve' and the Soviet Union, for bringing their economic complexes even closer together, for making their economies supplement each other still further ... The agreement between the Soviet Union and the EC carries a considerable political and, I would say, conceptual charge for a large-scale European plan for the future. It offers food for collective thought and practical considerations as regards the gradual shaping of an integrated economic complex in the continent.[13]

Although it is of course not unusual for politicians to sketch rosy scenarios on these occasions, Shevardnadze's remarks have shed an interesting light upon the USSR's economic and political intentions of its policies towards the European Community. *Perestroika* and the 1992 initiative were considered parallel processes which would over time result in an 'integrated economic complex in the continent'. Soviet policy-makers showed increasing interest in the EC phenomenon since it was acknowledged that integration among the Twelve could possibly prove a good example to overcome the dissolution of the USSR's internal empire. The Baltic republics were already keen to leave the Union and other Soviet republics were expected to follow suit. The EC had shown that economic and political cooperation among countries with widely diverging interests could be possible and fruitful. One week after the failed August 1991 coup in the USSR, the Soviet Ambassador to the EC argued that the European Community is 'a very relevant example for the USSR', whereby 'the future of the peoples of the Soviet Union depends to a great extent on the policy of the European Community'.[14] In this respect, the

EC constituted an example for the USSR to emulate. As Michel Tatu argued: 'There are not so many things the West can do to help, except to remain what it has been for so many years: an example of success'.[15]

In late-1989 and early-1990, the EC's policy *vis-à-vis* the East changed rapidly. Both the EC and the G-24 countries had to widen their scope of assistance since now all Central European countries (with the exception of Albania) had adopted reformist policies. On 6 November 1989, the EC Council first of all decided to scrap all quantitative restrictions on Hungarian and Polish industrial exports from 1 January 1990 (rather than phasing them out over a period of five years as was originally planned), and extended the GSP to both Budapest and Warsaw. In February 1990, the Commission considered the requests for aid from the GDR, Czechoslovakia, Romania, Bulgaria and Yugoslavia. At the July Summit of the G-24 Foreign Ministers the PHARE programmes were extended to these five newcomers. Despite these concessions and extended aid programmes, many Central European reformers had been disappointed. Both Warsaw and Budapest aired their discontent over the fact that the GSP would only cover a narrow range of products and would, for instance, not apply to meat and textiles. The Hungarian Ministry of Trade also pointed out that the range of products affected by this EC measure (such as shoes, gloves, toys and pottery), represented only a few per cent of Hungary's overall exports, affecting an aggregate of a mere US$ 30 to 40 million.[16] Central European criticism has pointed to the reality that EC protectionism was not reversed under influence of the changes in the East. This was also witnessed by the fact that in all trade and cooperation accords which had been signed with the Central European countries, sectoral agreements had been attached: the textile agreements were modelled on the GATT Multifibre Arrangement (MFA), and self-restraint arrangements for steel and agricultural products had been included. Brussels' commitment to remove its quantitative restriction for Central European imports were also accompanied by so-called 'safeguard clauses' which would be applied in case of 'injury' to EC producers. From the earliest discussions between EC Commission officials and representatives from Central Europe, the issue of access to the Community market has been a critical point. In September 1989, a top official of the Hungarian Chamber of Commerce argued: 'Quantitative restrictions are not the biggest existing problem against our export. Tariffs are much more significant.'[17] In the next chapters we will again examine EC protectionist tendencies which flared up during the negotiations over the association agreements with Central Europe.

Of all PHARE funds actually allocated, Poland and Hungary have received the lion's share (34 and 26 per cent respectively). Czechoslovakia (8 per cent), Romania (5 per cent) and Bulgaria (5 per cent) had to adopt further reform measures before they were to benefit from western aid. This was partly the result of the western policy of conditionality, since assistance would only be forthcoming provided that the East European governments would carry out specific political and economic reforms. (Humanitarian aid has been the exception to this rule of thumb. See Chapter 9.3.) Without doubt, however, this focus of G-24 aid has also mirrored western security priorities. As Jeanne Kirk Laux has argued: 'A striking disparity will likely remain between Europe's northern and southern tiers as most western officials simply dismiss the possibility for Bulgaria and especially Rumania to make a fully democratic transition. This attitude raises the worrisome question of history repeating itself. The cultural/religious affinity and geopolitical self-interest which bonds Western Europe to the three northernmost countries could, if aid disparities persist, make stagnation and alienation in the Balkans a self-fulfilling prophecy.'[18]

9.3 No money for nothing

One of the more important consequences of the East European revolutions has been that the issue areas of East-West relations have been thrown in the melting-pot. It soon became increasingly difficult for the European Community to separate problems of trade and cooperation agreements from political and human rights issues. In the early-1980s, it was still possible to treat Romania with preference and to bargain with the CMEA as if political, economic and security matters could be dealt with separately.[19] In 1989 this was no longer the case. As Jacques Delors has argued: 'There is a grave risk that these [East European] countries will become bankrupt and the democratic reforms will be stifled.'[20] In this respect, western aid to the East was a matter of self-interest based upon a wider definition of western security. At the same time, the West European opportunities for economic leverage had increased. The political changes in the East had made Communist leaders more susceptible to western demands and their desire to open up their economies to the West had placed an important and powerful political instrument in the hands of western policy-makers. Now Brussels was able to link the level of financial assistance to the degree of economic and political reform and the human rights record of the recipient countries. Previously this would have been denounced as a blunt interference in internal Communist affairs. Since 1989, however, western conditionality concerning aid has hardly been a matter of dispute since the East European governments have themselves subscribed to the principles of market economics and democracy. The precise *application* of these principles has, however, been a topic of debate (see Chapter 9.4).

Only a few days after the fall of the Berlin wall and the opening of East Germany's borders, a special informal meeting of the twelve EC Heads of State was called (18-19 November 1989). During this rendezvous at the Elysée Palace an effort was made to work out a collective and comprehensive European Community approach towards the East. A common EC stance on the revolutionary changes in the East was especially called for since US President Bush and Soviet leader Gorbachev were to meet in Malta in early December. And, as Giscard d'Estaing had argued: 'It would not be acceptable that the analysis of the situation in Europe be made by the Americans and the Soviets and not by the Europeans themselves.'[21] This was of course especially true since the EC had become the main coordinator of western assistance to the East.

After the meeting, President Mitterrand had formulated the consensus of the Twelve by maintaining: 'We are ready to co-operate by all available means in creating healthier economies in exchange for a proven return to democracy, respect for human rights and the organisation everywhere of free elections.'[22] This had been a remarkable outcome of the informal summit, since the Community had hitherto refrained from formulating specific conditions for aid and had only stressed the necessity of an East European *commitment* to reform. These agreed-upon criteria were mainly political in nature, leaving it to international organizations such as the IMF to establish the economic requirements for receiving economic and financial aid. Representatives of the IMF, the World Bank, the OECD and the Paris Club now frequently visited the high-level meetings on aid to the East which were organized by the Commission. Although the nature of the Paris meeting had been informal and was not assumed to result in concrete policy decisions, the Twelve had agreed that Brussels would pressure the IMF to conclude agreements with Poland and Hungary before the end of the year, opening the way for loans from EC members. The IMF – which had made financial assistance conditional upon the implementation of comprehensive plans of economic austerity measures – came to an agreement with Poland in mid-December. Poland and Hungary had first to come to an agreement with the IMF for adopting economic austerity programmes before they became eligible for a US$ 1 billion stabilization fund (for Poland) and ECU 870 million structural adjustment loan (for Hungary). This also made available the substantial bridging loans from the BIS and the United States.[23]

Whereas Poland and Hungary now shared the principles of market economics and liberal democracy, the Soviet Union still restricted itself to the more limited programme of *perestroika*. Western economic leverage could therefore not be as easily applied to the USSR. Although Leonid Abalkin, the Soviet Deputy Premier, had called for 'mutually beneficial, unrestrained co-operation' with the Community in November 1989, he had also made it clear that the Soviet people were more prepared to suffer continuing economic austerity than to request the West for aid.[24] The USSR had not been included into the PHARE programme since Moscow had not made an official request to that effect. Moreover, western conditionality for aid would most probably have been rejected by the Soviet superpower-in-retreat. It was also acknowledged that during this period of systemic change, special attention should be given to Moscow's security requirements. Although the West was happy to rock the boat, EC leaders were careful to avoid policies which might have given the USSR the impression that the West was encroaching upon its sphere of influence. Although that was of course obviously the case, no triumphant statements of the European Community to that effect were made, mainly in an effort to save the Kremlin's face. Nevertheless, the new ties between the EC and Central Europe could be considered as some sort of 'Finlandization in reverse', whereby several former Soviet satellites would gradually come under the influence of western-style capitalism and liberal, democratic values.

It was now clear that western economic assistance – either to the USSR or to the countries of Central Europe – would not be free; a number of specific conditions had been set. The EC had provided five basic requirements; each recipient country had to (1) establish the rule of law; (2) respect basic human rights; (3) create a multi-party system; (4) organize free and secret elections before the end of 1990; and (5) implement a policy for introducing a market economy. These conditions summoned both economic and political reforms. As John Pinder has argued: 'The more powerful [economic] instruments that were brought into play from the beginning of 1990 in response to democratic and market reforms were clearly, and usually explicitly, intended to support the prospects for the success of the reforms, and discriminated in favour of the countries that were judged to have the most credible reform programs'.[25]

Western conditions for aid were based upon the assumption that economic reform could only be successfully pursued within a democratic environment, whereas democracy could only succeed in a capitalist system of free enterprise. This tacit consensus has followed the logic of Fukuyama's analysis which we have discussed in Chapter 1. A similar strategy had not yet been applied to, for instance, development assistance to the Third World. It was beyond doubt that the establishment of the rule of law would require a substantial transformation of the legal systems in the East, which would not only substantially bolster the democratic process in these countries but was also generally considered imperative for the generation of healthy commercial relations. These five conditions could also be seen as a major lever for political and economic change in parts of Central Europe where the transformations were taking place only haphazardly. In particular, the precarious develop- ments in the Balkan countries were reasons for concern since numerous previously dormant nationality problems were now threatening to erupt. Western conditionality was expected to provide incentives for these countries to adopt reform policies along the lines of Warsaw and Budapest.

The French President also used the informal dinner meeting to stress the necessity of dealing with internal Community issues, such as the nature and pace of the future European monetary union. It was clear that Paris would make every possible attempt to maintain the momentum of Community integration, especially now that the EC's new foreign tasks could possibly shift attention from the 1992 initiative to the new challenges in the East. The French fears of a return to pre-1914 Europe, with its nationalistic clashes, were forcefully voiced by Mitterrand. His recipe was also clear: 'If we want to transcend these traditional national rivalries, then only one great thought, one great constructive endeavour, can take the place of all this. That could be a great mission for the European Community.'[26] A few weeks earlier – in a speech to the European Parliament – Mitterrand had already declared that the developments in the East should spur the West European drive towards political and economic union. He argued that the construction of a 'political Europe' was the only conceivable answer to the eastern revolutions. Monetary union would be the best instrument for managing the economic transitions towards market and democracy in the East and a new European order in general.[27] 'The only response to the challenge being presented to us by the East is to reinforce and accelerate the union and cohesion of the European Community', he added.[28]

Not very surprisingly, Great Britain has responded completely differently to these new developments in the East. Prime Minister Thatcher argued that 'it is ironic, at a time when Eastern Europe is moving towards greater democracy, that some in the Community want to take economic and monetary policies away from our national parliaments and hand them over to a body which is not democratically accountable'. Just to make sure that she was not misunderstood, Mrs Thatcher added that the EC was 'only *one* manifestation of Europe's identity'.[29] It again became clear that the 1989 revolution was going to be extremely consequential for the further development of the European Community. Providing aid to the East in support for reform was only a short- and medium-term endeavour. But when East European reform was successful, the other two R's – reintegration and regional security – would still remain unresolved. What was more, it was doubtful whether reform could be effective when the prospect for East European reintegration and regional security remained ambiguous. As David Buchan argued in January 1990: 'Just as the Twelve were about to sit down to a rich diet of economic and monetary union, gate-crashers from the East start knocking on the door, threatening to gain admission to the club and to spoil the Community feast'.[30] We will examine the EC's policies on these questions in the next chapter.

9.4 The debate about aid

Although the strategy of the European Community in handling the issue of economic assistance to the East has not come under serious criticism during the initial phase of commitments, the calls for a more *massive* aid plan – preferably along the lines of the Marshall Plan – have never really died down. Western aid was often considered overly cautious and often overdue. In many respects the different approaches towards the East which we have identified in Chapter 8.4 again came to the fore. Debate also focused upon the speed of the

East European transformations and the sequencing of the reform measures. Clarity on these issues proved difficult to attain.[31] Although a number of countries had earlier tried to make the leap from authoritarianism to democracy and capitalism (e.g. Greece, Spain and Portugal), it was acknowledged that the transition from a central plan to a market-oriented economy would be unique. Consequently, no clear-cut reform scenarios were readily at hand. Both the pace and the direction of East European reform have therefore been questioned. Two major problems were frequently addressed: (1) Should *more* aid be channelled to the East?; and (2) Were present economic and political conditions for aid *too stringent*?

Several arguments could be discerned in this debate. First, it was held that the lessons of the 1970s, when lavish western credits to Poland had resulted in a mounting debt crisis, should be kept in mind; it was little use to throw good money after bad money. The West should therefore restrict its aid policy and only help those who were willing to help themselves. As *The Economist* has formulated it: 'It is beginning to be understood in Eastern Europe that the mistake of the 1970s is not going to be repeated. In 1989 no salvation lies in vast new loans from the West, because Eastern Europe's economies are still organised in a way that would send most money down the drain. Foreign exchange is needed, but only in conjunction with policy reforms that would make good use of the stuff.'[32] In this context it has been argued that western assistance might even hamper the reform process since this could interfere with the advancement of market forces. For instance, giving food aid could keep domestic agricultural prices artificially low which would diminish the commercial incentives for farmers. It was also often argued that making western economic assistance conditional upon far-ranging changes could considerably help Central European reformers to push through unpopular reform programmes. To some extent, western conditionality could even be fruitful in the case of the Soviet Union. According to some Soviet economists: 'attaching economic conditions to [western] aid could just be the lever needed to get things moving'.[33] Moreover, since financial resources were limited and Third World countries were competing for western aid, G-24 assistance should remain limited. Was it, for instance, ethical that in 1989-90, Poland was the largest recipient of EC cereals Food Aid with 1.4 million tonnes, whereas Ethiopia was the second largest recipient with a mere 300,000 tonnes?[34]

The problems of the aid debate were most forcefully captured by Lawrence Eagleburger, the American Deputy Secretary of State (and coordinator of US financial aid to Central Europe), who has argued: 'The issue isn't just what they need. The issue is also how they can use what they're given. The analogy with the Marshall Plan is fundamentally flawed ... in Eastern Europe, which is emerging from a 45-year time capsule, our primary goal must be to provide the democratic institution-building skills and entrepreneurial know-how without which privatization will not succeed. We must aim to create the infra-structure of a market economy.'[35] United States President George Bush also maintained: 'Why put X billions of dollars of money into the Soviet economy when it's not reformed, when they're spending 18 per cent on the military, and when they're spending an estimated $ 5 billion in Cuba?'[36] The initial approach of the United States to the developments in the East has therefore been very cautious. Similar comments on the utility of aid from the West could be heard from British and Dutch policy-makers. With this cautious approach of the United States, Great Britain and the Netherlands – in combination with Japan's reluctance to provide aid to the USSR due to a decade-long imbroglio with the Kremlin over the Kurill Islands – no comprehensive 'Marshall Plan for the East' could seriously be envisaged.

The FRG, in contrast, was a more 'generous' Maecenas. German policy-makers generally argued that the West – and especially the European Community – should display its willingness to overcome the East-West divide by staging a massive, Marshall Plan-like, aid operation. Only a large-scale financial, economic, technological and managerial injection could ensure the smooth transformation 'from Marx to market'. Bonn has maintained that West European security was in need of a new definition, since military security should be considered insufficient under the present circumstances. More than once, western aid was regarded as a new form of defence spending (see on this issue also Chapter 10). As Poland's President Lech Walesa, has argued: 'The Iron Curtain has been destroyed; we do not want it to be replaced by a "Silver Curtain" dividing Europe'.[37] Herr Genscher has also argued against the construction of a new economic wall dividing East and West: 'That can not be our goal. We want one Europe. The West bears a great responsibility, and by economic assistance, and co-operation by know-how transfer and technology transfer, it can contribute to the success of the reform policies. These are no gifts to the East, but they are investments in a common European future, since stability in Europe will in the future no longer be defined in military terms. Stability means: economic stability, social stability, ecological stability. These are the future tasks of the Europeans in Europe ... A house will not remain peaceful when the one hungers, and the others have plenty.'[38] Both views on aid to the East have testified to two distinct views concerning the purpose, the efficacy as well as the scale of western aid. It has also clearly demonstrated a different notion of the western role during the process of Communist reform. In the next chapter we will examine how these two positions have led to equally different views on the EC's long-term policy towards the East.

Nevertheless, the comparisons with the Marshall Plan were frequently made in order to draw useful 'lessons of history'. In the light of this debate, William Pfaff has also referred to some valuable experiences of the post-war Marshall Plan for the problems which Central Europe would face during the 1990s. Pfaff argued that the American aid programme in the late-1940s was a *qualified* offer of help, on the condition that the Europeans would collectively define their economic needs and would provide Washington with a plan for using the aid they were to be given:

> This is the approach needed today. If the Soviet government wants assistance, Moscow should provide the United States and the West European governments with a coherent program explaining what it intends to do with that aid so as to make a fundamental change in the Soviet situation. Similarly, if the governments of Hungary, Czechoslovakia and Poland, or the three of them in common with the two ex-Communist Balkan states, would define their common problems of structural reform, and develop a program of cooperation to solve those problems ... they would get a far more positive response from the United States, and even from the European Community, than now is the case.[39]

Following a similar line of argument, Zbigniew Brzezinski has argued that western aid should perhaps be made contingent to some degree 'on the recipients' willingness to engage in multilateral cooperation'.[40] However, cooperation within the CMEA-framework was considered ill-fated by the new non-Communist governments. Several proposals for a free trade area between Hungary, Czechoslovakia and Poland have been aired, but none of them have proven a fruitful basis for cooperation.[41] New trading organizations to replace the CMEA were, however, considered inopportune since this was expected to slow down efforts of Central European reintegration in the world economy.

9.5 Promises, reimbursement and efficacy

In his speech to the European Parliament in October 1989, President Mitterrand raised the idea of establishing an independent financial institution principally concerned with assisting the transformations in the East. This idea was earlier advanced by Alfred Herrhausen, the former President of the Deutsche Bank. This initiative has illustrated that western help was expected to be a long-term endeavour and that the newly-established Central European governments needed immense financial resources in order to modernize their economies. Although Central Europe could apply for macro-economic stabilization programmes of the IMF and micro-economic restructuring projects of the EC and the World Bank, this would not actually reintegrate these countries in the world's financial institutions. The European Bank for Reconstruction and Development (EBRD) would, on the other hand, accept the USSR and the Central European countries as full members with voting rights.

After the Strasbourg Summit of the European Council, 8-9 December 1989, the West European Heads of State declared in their joint statement that 'At this time of profound and rapid change, the Community is and must remain a point of reference and influence. It remains the corner-stone of a new

European architecture and, in its will to openness, a mooring for a future European equilibrium.'[42] The Summit also expressed support for German unification and agreed upon the establishment of the EBRD, which had to be set up 'as soon as possible'. It was stated that the EBRD's 'aim will be to promote, in consultation with the IMF and the World Bank, productive and competitive investment in the states of Central and Eastern Europe, to reduce, where appropriate, any risks related to the financing of their economies, to assist the transition towards a more market-oriented economy and to speed up the necessary structural adjustments. The states of Central and Eastern Europe concerned will be able to participate in the capital and management of this bank, in which the [EC] member states, the Community and the European Investment Bank will have a majority holding.'[43] The Articles of Agreement of the EBRD were signed in Paris in May 1990. The EBRD started with a membership roll of forty countries, and with a capital stock of ECU 10 billion, which could be offered in direct loans, used for policy advice and technical assistance, equity investment and for underwriting securities offerings in the Central European capital markets. Article 1 has clearly pointed out that: 'The purpose of the Bank shall be to foster the transition towards open-market economies and to promote private and entrepreneurial initiative in the Central and Eastern European countries committed to and applying the principles of multiparty democracy, pluralism and market economics.' The EBRD has thereby adopted both a policy of economic and political conditionality. Articles 2 and 35 have also explicitly advanced environmental safeguards as prerequisites for financial assistance.[44]

From the beginning, the EBRD has been dominated by the EC and its member states. Taken together, the Twelve, the EC Commission and the EIB put up more than fifty-one per cent of the EBRD's capital.[45] London was chosen as the Bank's seat and the ECU its currency unit. During the period of negotiations on the Bank, Washington has complained about the EC's influence but has not been able to make the EBRD a more 'Atlantic' organization.[46]

After the initial euphoria of the western victory of the Cold War had died down, it became disturbingly clear that the East European transformations were going to be extremely costly. Officials from both the EBRD and the G-24 Coordination Unit within the EC Commission have therefore frequently stressed the dangers of so-called financing fatigue in the West. Other international crises and domestic concerns have sometimes overshadowed the predicaments in the East. Apart from the negative impact of the demise of the CMEA-regime, the Gulf crisis of 1990 had seriously disrupted the oil deliveries from Iraq and had resulted in a loss of several Middle East markets.[47] It has been estimated that the total of G-24 aid has hardly compensated for Central European economic costs of complying with the United Nations' embargo of Iraq. Little wonder therefore, that in Central Europe the 'return to Europe' has resulted in disappointment. Whereas most western countries had been willing to commit themselves to provide assistance to the East, it proved much more difficult actually to reimburse these financial resources for the realization of reforms. Perhaps not very surprisingly, national governments have started to complain that the G-24 Coordination Unit has been exaggerating the Central European financial requirements, that it has not at all been evident that aid to the East would actually serve the purposes which had been agreed upon and that the European Commission was acting more and more in its own interest. It was now also argued that the EC was not well equipped for this important assignment. One journal has noticed that 'The EC's aid efforts for eastern Europe was slow to get off the ground largely because there was neither a team of specialists nor an infrastructure in place to deal with the problem. The Phare department in the EC did not answer its telephones for the first few weeks of its existence, while it recruited a 30-strong team to handle an aid scheme that promises to run into billions.'[48] All in all, when rhetoric had to be followed by sustained action, a number of traditional collective action problems arose which have been difficult for the EC Commission to resolve.

Two problems can be identified. First of all, it was clear that not all donors were willing to provide sufficient information concerning their bilateral aid programmes. This has had much to do with the wide range of donors within most EC member states. Moreover, the G-24 Coordination Unit has asked the *national* governments for information, although the national governments have not always been kept well informed about the activities of their regional governments, let alone the activities of firms and non-profit organizations. In Germany, for instance, the *Länder* (provinces) have pursued active aid policies towards the Central European countries, which have not always been sufficiently monitored by the national authorities. Similar mechanisms have been at work within the national governments themselves, since Ministries and Departments at the governmental level have also provided aid without mutual consultations. This has made it very difficult for the G-24 Coordination Unit to incorporate these aid efforts within one, coherent programme. Another, closely related, problem has concerned the bureaucratic structure of the EC Commission organization itself. Several Directorates now oversee the implementation of the aid programme. The DG I (External Relations) has taken the principal responsibility, but the DG II (Economic and Financial Affairs) and several sectoral DGs have also dealt with these issues. Moreover, the European Parliament has also been active in the field of initiating aid programmes. It will go too far to say that these DGs and the European Parliament have failed to coordinate their activities. However, there have certainly been instances in which approved projects have not got off the ground where the reason can be found in bureaucratic struggles over competence.

Another problem has concerned the *quality* of western aid. Countries which have taken a guarded approach in the debate about aid have generally also adopted less favourable forms of assistance. Japan, for example, has mainly provided export credits and loans rather than fully fledged grants and technical assistance projects. In particular, Central European officials have criticized the nature of western assistance. Bronislav Geremek, Solidarity's Floor Leader in the Polish Parliament, has argued that 'we expect a strategy from the West, but so far nothing has been presented ... What the East has received until now has been emotions and words, but very little action'.[49] Moreover, loan guarantees, interest-bearing loans and marketing and investment incentives to western firms, have often been placed on the G-24 scoreboard as aid proper. Since credits provided on a commercial basis are debt-creating, western assistance may not always be as respectable as might be assumed on the basis of the rhetoric and statistics of western government officials. Moreover, although most project lending will take place on a multi-year basis, Brussels has more than once registered the full amount of the project in the first year, rather then when the project actually transpires. Several aid programmes have also been criticized for a lack of focus (like the TEMPUS programme for educational exchange with Central Europe).[50] Illustrative of both problems has been the factor that the EC Commission has not been able to overcome the practices of several G-24 countries to utilize aid to the East for narrow national purposes. Many western countries have provided tied aid in an effort to boost their own economies. On other occasions, western countries have used aid for specific political reasons which have fallen outside the accepted strategic scope of the G-24.

9.6 The new Europe: primed for peace?

Stephen van Evera has argued that 'the West should use its economic leverage to encourage Eastern European states to adopt democracy, protect human rights of national minorities, accept current borders, and eschew the propagation of hyper-nationalism'.[51] The EC and the G-24 countries have adopted exactly such a strategy in order to facilitate the East European reform process and to build a peaceful and stable Europe. In many respects, western aid has been a matter of enlightened self-interest. West European policy-makers now seem to have adopted wider definitions of security which also take into account the prospects of mass-migration from the East to the West and environmental issues. However, the predicaments which have arisen during the implementation of western aid programmes to the East – most notably the deficient disbursement of aid – have indicated that traditional collective action problems again present themselves. Notwithstanding the growing cohesion within the EC, the West European political arena remains characterized by a complex pattern of cooperation and discord. West European debate on the 'Triple R Agenda' for Central Europe and the former USSR is likely to continue whereby conflicts on the most appropriate EC strategy on reintegration and regional security may prove even more substantial than the debate on western aid. Barry Buzan *et al.* have argued: 'In the run up to 1992 there seem to be two main conflict lines in the community: French versus British approaches to integration/free trade, and French versus German visions for Europe.'[52] These issues will be examined further in Chapter 10.

Several less optimistic scenarios have been developed in which a united Germany will again seek European hegemony and where the East will be ruled by praetorian governments rather than liberal democratic ones.[53] Channelling western aid through the EC has, among others, been used as a means of limiting German influence in the East. This has only been partially successful. Despite the economic costs of national unification, Germany's economic power has been felt in Central Europe. The amount of German aid, both bilateral and multilateral, has strengthened Bonn's say in the western strategy *vis-à-vis* Central Europe and the former USSR. Whether the G-24 mechanism will be able to contain a possible German *Alleingang* eastward remains very unclear indeed. As to the prospects of weak states in Central Europe, a differentiation should be made between Poland, Hungary and Czechoslovakia on the one hand, and the Balkan countries on the other hand. As Jeanne Kirk Laux correctly emphasized, western assistance has been concentrated on Warsaw and Budapest, whereas the Balkans have long been excluded from massive aid. This also applies to the successor states of the USSR. Countries like Kazakhstan, Uzbekistan, Turkmenia, Tajikistan, Kirgizia, Azerbaijan, Armenia and Georgia in particular might be prone to praetorian polities whereby hypernationalism might quell the quest for democracy. The importance of western economic leverage for guiding the countries of the former Soviet republics towards the market and democracy should, however, certainly not be overestimated, especially since these countries will never be able to become members of the Community. After the demise of the USSR and the creation of the Commonwealth of Independent States, in late-1991, the Twelve have tried to provide some guidelines for the recognition of the emerging states in the former-Soviet Union. During the Maastricht Summit of 9 and 10 December 1991, five criteria for recognition were advanced:

1. respect for the provisions of the Charter of the United Nations and the commitments subscribed to in the Final Act of Helsinki and in the Charter of Paris, especially with regard to the rule of law, democracy and human rights;
2. guarantees for the rights of ethnic and national groups and minorities in accordance with the commitments subscribed to in the framework of the CSCE;
3. respect for the inviolability of all frontiers which can only be changed by peaceful means and by common agreement;

4. acceptance of all relevant commitments with regard to disarmament and nuclear non-proliferation as well as to security and regional stability; and
5. commitment to settle by agreement, including where appropriate by recourse to arbitration, all questions concerning State succession and regional disputes.[54]

These are, of course, very ambitious and lofty principles. Although major conflicts have not erupted in the former USSR (at least not until late-1992), it can be seriously doubted that the disintegration of Moscow's internal empire will go without severe problems. It is to be foreseen that the EC's role in these future conflicts in the East will be limited.

10. Wider or Deeper?
The EC's Economic
Security Dilemma

Having looked around we found the EC as the most impressive, successful, advanced and comprehensive integrational process in Europe. A sort of 'high tech' in integration. Thus, the EC is the best choice for Hungary through which she can best realize her reintegrational aims.

> László Demus (16 February 1990). Quoted in M. Skak, 'East Europe, the Soviet Union and Europeanization: A Challenge for the European Community', Paper presented at the 87th Annual Meeting of the American Political Science Association (1991), p.18.

10.1 Introduction

Although providing humanitarian relief and various forms of aid to the reforming Communist countries – ranging from emergency aid to balance of payments assistance – has been the short- and medium-term western response to the cascading developments in the East, it soon became clear that more structural arrangements had to be made in order to fill the economic, political and security vacuum created by the retrenchment of the USSR. During the Cold War, bipolarity had given rise to a number of organizations in both East and West whose membership has been divided along ideological, political and economic lines. As we have discussed in Chapter 7, the EC and the CMEA were the most apparent examples where the market-oriented West European countries stood *vis-à-vis* the Communist East, with NATO and the Warsaw Pact as the military embodiment of this confrontation. After the fall of the Berlin Wall in November 1989, this clear-cut dichotomy between East and West disappeared almost overnight. Military cooperation within the Warsaw Pact became a dead letter and economic and technological collaboration within the CMEA was rejected by the new non-Communist governments in Central Europe since this was expected to prolong their economic dependence upon the USSR. During the early euphoric months of the liberation from

Communism few observers worried much about the institutional homelessness of Central Europe. This had everything to do with the unprecedented speed with which major and breathtaking developments were unfolding in the East. Most concerns were focused upon successfully pursuing these revolutions in the first place. However, it soon became quite evident that with the demise of the WTO and the CMEA, the Central European countries lacked institutional frameworks wherein their reforms efforts could be coordinated and managed. Since most Central European policy-makers considered the European Community as the 'high-tech' of economic cooperation, most attention was given to reinforcing their ties with Brussels. The new roles of the EC, NATO, the CSCE and the WEU have concentrated on what was soon labelled 'Europe's new architecture'.

This chapter will examine the major plans for this new European architecture. Special attention will be paid to the drafts in which the European Community is expected to play a central role. We will discuss the proposals for association agreements with Poland, Hungary and Czechoslovakia and examine the debate on whether the EC would do best to widen its scope towards the East, or to deepen the integration process of the Twelve before incorporating the former Communist countries. Before we examine Brussels' predicaments, we will argue that the European Community is faced with what we will call an 'economic security dilemma'. In the final chapter of this book we will go further into the question as to whether the West European integration process will be able to maintain its momentum now that the international political atmosphere and systemic surroundings have changed so dramatically. There we will examine the theoretical debate on these issues and evaluate the EC's relations with the East from both a Neo-realist and a Neo-liberal institutionalist perspective.

10.2 The EC's security dilemma

In Chapter 8 we argued that the 1989 and the 1992 revolutions were closely linked. The European Community has taken up the responsibility of assisting the reform process in the East not only to spread western values of economic freedom and political liberalism, but also for more egotistic reasons of building a secure Europe. Many policy-makers and academics have argued that the concept of 'security' is in need of revision in the 1990s.[1] Military instruments of statecraft and military security will, for example, neither be sufficient to protect Western Europe against another Chernobyl, nor the onslaught of acid rain and mass emigration from the East. During the Cold War era, the Iron Curtain focused most attention on military matters. But now that the East-West controversy has been settled, economic and environmental issues have gained in importance. In the post-Cold War era, nuclear arsenals and the prospect of mutual assured destruction still play a central role in the security debate. The military aspects of western security have therefore not become less serious, it is only that several other facets of security have become more prominent on the political agenda of West European policy-makers. This has been of special importance since these non-military security aspects have fallen under the EC's competence and have thereby increased Brussels' role.

Despite these changes in the essence of security, some established security concepts still go a long way in clarifying the current relationship between the EC and the East. In the late-1970s, the American scholar Robert Jervis argued that East and West were confronted with what he called a 'security dilemma'. Jervis maintained that the West would be unable to create a higher level of security for itself without endangering the East. But, paradoxically, western security has partly been based upon the Kremlin feeling secure and saturated. In short, the security dilemma indicates the fact that 'under many circumstances an increase in one state's security will automatically and inadvertently decrease that of others'.[2] This concept of security starts from the premiss that security – like power – is basically of a zero-sum nature. The problem then arises from the fact that the security aspirations of the EC and the countries of Central Europe may be very difficult to reconcile. Further economic, monetary, political and even military cooperation and integration among the current twelve EC members will raise the threshold for third countries to enter the Community. New EC members will have to adopt the *acquis communautaire*, which will certainly become more difficult when the process towards the European Union is keeping pace. What might provide 'security' for the current EC members, might therefore increase the lack of security for those outside the EC, especially for the Central European countries. Although we will argue below that the zero-sum nature of the relations between the EC and the East are not always as rigid as we have assumed here for the sake of argument, we will nevertheless assert that during much of the 1990s, the European Community will be confronted with a clear-cut (economic and political) security dilemma.

The day after the informal EC Paris meeting of November 1989, *The Financial Times* noted in an editorial: 'With the summit meeting of the Twelve on Saturday evening, the European Community has taken on a new political stature as an actor on the world stage.'[3] Indeed, with the end of the traditional military and ideological East-West conflict in which the two superpowers and their security alliances have dominated European politics, the EC quite naturally emerged as the heart of the new Europe. However, it is questionable whether the EC will prove economically strong and politically cohesive enough to take on the internal challenges of further economic, monetary and political integration as well as the new external challenges posed by Central European reform. Both challenges are closely intertwined; although they are altogether distinct processes they are destined to influence each other. It is, for instance, common opinion that the 1992 initiative of the Twelve can only be successfully implemented within the context of a stable and peaceful European continent. Civil war in multi-ethnic states like former Yugoslavia and the former Soviet Union, border conflicts between Hungary and Romania or an authoritarian backlash in the former Communist states certainly do not provide the optimal environment for West European integration. As is being said so often nowadays, the spectre roaming the European continent is not labelled 'Communism' any more, but 'instability'.[4] Famine or civil war in Russia or the Ukraine would, without doubt, spill over into the border regions and play havoc with the Central European reform process. This points out that the EC cannot guard itself from potential chaos and civil war in the East, but that it must develop active policies in order to make the reforms in the East successful. Brussels is now aware that new investment needs to be geared to those specific projects which will contribute to employment generation and migration stabilization. EC policy must, however, go far beyond *ad hoc* aid. Regimes of cooperation must be developed in order to bolster reform, democracy and East-West cooperation institutionally.

But that is not all. On top of economic and financial aid, EC ecological assistance to the East by modernizing smoke-stack industries can be considered crucial for diminishing environmental decay in all of Europe. In particular, Scandinavian countries, Germany and the Netherlands have suffered from acid rain caused by sulphur emissions from Central European power stations. Another distinct environmental hazard is caused by the nuclear power stations of the Chernobyl-type. These are horrifyingly unsafe, but as long as countries like Bulgaria and Czechoslovakia remain to a considerable extent dependent upon their menacing nuclear energy installations, no other option will be open. In all these respects, the EC has a major task to assure that the Central European reform process will meet with success so that these ecological problems too can be solved. Both the example of the threat of mass migration from East to West and the threat of environmental disaster, point to the fact that West European security is closely linked to Central European security. In some cases the security requirements for East and West clearly overlap and do not conflict with each other. However, especially when we examine the institutional requirements of Central European security (i.e. membership of the EC), Brussels' security dilemma comes into effect.

Meanwhile the Twelve are occupied with their own revolution. After the approval of the Single European Act in 1987, a series of so-called Intergovernmental Conferences (IGC) have been devoted to making the EC a more forceful actor on the world stage by introducing further constitutional and institutional changes. The Maastricht Summit of December 1991 has mapped out the road towards an economic and monetary union and has opened up the possibility of a defence role for the EC.[5] However, the ratification process of the Maastricht Treaty by the member states has not been without major problems. In early June of 1992, the Danish electorate rejected the Treaty in a referendum, which started a wide debate on the prospects of further economic and political integration in Western Europe. In this period of uncertainty, even the backing from several fervid EC-supporters seemed far less assured than in previous years; the Irish 'Yes' vote in mid-June was unable to change that. Even the French, always ardent supporters of the idea of European economic and political union, only endorsed the Maastricht Treaty in a referendum (20 September) with a minimal majority of 51 per cent. Bonn, for example, had become wary of giving its strong and reliable German Mark up in exchange for the more volatile ECU. Other aspects of the Maastricht Treaty have also aroused much criticism after the dust of the December 1991 Summit had settled. In late July, for example, the results of an IMF study were disclosed suggesting that economic growth rates in Western Europe would be retarded by between 0.4 and 0.8 per cent annually from 1993 through 1996 due to efforts of the EC to achieve further economic integration.[6]

Despite these doubts, the consensus remains that the Twelve have much to gain from the successful implementation of the free internal market scheme and further union on monetary and security issues. But in order to succeed Brussels still has to overcome a plethora of obstacles. The Maastricht Treaty has decided how, and in what tempo, the EMU will be effected, but it still remains an open question which countries will be allowed to participate within the first tier of this EMU after 1998. Although there are several reasons to be optimistic, it may also be clear that the success of the 1992 initiative is still not fully assured. The integration process is also not exempt from conflicts concerning its financial costs and the geographical reorientation of economic activities. The budgetary proposals of Commission President Delors ('Delors II') on the new and expanded EC budget have met with disapproval by most richer EC members. Moreover, there is concern that further unification might obliterate the cultural identity of smaller countries, which was probably one of the major reasons for a majority of the Danes to reject the Maastricht Treaty in its initial form. In short, there is every reason to believe that if the political relations among the Twelve deteriorate, '1992' might be postponed forever. (Or, as Ralph Dahrendorf has said, '1992 will surely come, but when?') In this light, it does not come as a surprise that the EC is currently not anxious to take on all the further troubles which will accompany the membership of countries like Poland, Czechoslovakia and Hungary.[7]

Nevertheless, political leaders of these three countries have time and again aired their wish to join the Community within a few years. The Czechoslovak Prime Minister, Marian Calfa, has argued that his country aspires to join the Common Market before the year 2000. 'We are prepared to do everything in order to reach that goal,' he said.[8] His Hungarian colleague, Jozsef Antall, has also aired the hope that his country could enter the EC in 1995.[9] ('To us the European Community is the most important target. We would like to join as soon as possible.')[10] The Polish President Lech Walesa has argued in an address to the European Commission, in early April 1991: 'Neither today nor tomorrow will there be a more important issue for Poland than her membership of the EC.'[11] All three maintain that Central European membership of the Community is required in order to stabilize their fragile markets and their still shaky democracies. They argue that without close cooperation with the EC the infamous Iron Curtain would be replaced with an economic and financial one; Europe would then not be divided by ideologies and armies but by a welfare gap separating rich and poor nations.[12] This line of argument is certainly not new to Community policy-makers; only a few years ago the same logic was applied in order to justify the swift entry in the EC of former authoritarian countries like Greece, Spain and Portugal.

In this respect, the 1989 and 1992 revolutions will be very difficult to reconcile. The European Community therefore faces a dilemma: in the short term, the EC's interests lie in a swift and smooth realization of the EMU and political integration without being bothered by the quandaries and obstacles of closer ties with the former Communist countries in the East. In the long term, however, political stability on the continent should take precedence over the immediate economic concerns. Here the question arises as to how the integration process in the EC can be continued without slamming the door of the Berlaymont in the faces of potential Central European members? In Brussels' Eurospeak, this problem is known as that of 'widening versus deepening'.[13] After East European reform, Western Europe has to come to terms with the other two Rs of the Triple R Agenda: reintegration and regional security, which may not at all be uncomplicated.

Most Community officials and West European policy-makers, however, fail to face the difficulty of reconciling the EC's integration and its eventual enlargement.[14] What is more, it is even generally argued that both developments are mutually reinforcing. Both political and economic arguments for a simultaneous deepening and widening have been brought forward. As a group major West European industrialists argued in a report: 'Enlargement must not dilute what has been achieved, indeed the reverse is true. The Community will need to be stronger and more coherent in order to take the strain of enlargement.'[15] It is sometimes also maintained that the Central European revolutions have only speeded up the process of EC integration since Brussels is aware that it can only cope with the challenge of playing a serious role in the construction of a new European architecture when it has its own house completely in order.[16] Tibor Palankai, an Hungarian economist, argued that 'The process of European unification will not be weakened, as is sometimes supposed, but strengthened by [Central European entry to the EC] ... Central and East European changes will not hinder the process of West European integration, but instead will give new impetus for accelerating the implementation of plans for monetary union and the political integration of the EC.'[17]

Besides the more political arguments for widening and deepening at the same time, there have been the economic reasons for adopting such an ambitious strategy. The logic of the economic argument has been spelled out by Italy's Foreign Minister, Gianni de Michelis, who has argued that 'Over the medium term the EC economies may grow by 4.5-7 per cent through the various effects of achieving a single market ... This growth should create opportunities for the EC's trading partners, including those in the East.'[18] These are, however, rosy scenarios which disregard the political, economic and institutional tensions which a wider and deeper European Community will generate.

10.3 A wider Europe? National views and different scenarios

The sentiments and speculations on the future architecture of Europe and the role of the European Community differ significantly from nation to nation. We have already examined the differences of milieu and possession goals of the major EC member states in earlier chapters. With the advent of the new German question, these differences have only become more prominent. Great Britain, for instance – and most notably former Prime Minister Margaret Thatcher – has been a proponent of the inclusion of the Central European countries in the EC.[19] In late 1990, Mrs Thatcher argued that 'the Community should be open to the countries of Eastern Europe, and indeed other West European countries if they want to join, once they are ready. It would be contrary to all we are trying to do politically to support democracy and help those countries who have only recently emerged from 40 years of totalitarian system, if the Community was to make itself an exclusive club which kept them outside. These are the standards – freedom and openness – against which I judge proposals put forward in the Community and why I am not convinced that the full Delors plan for Economic and Monetary Union is either feasible or desirable.'[20] The last reference, in particular, to the further economic and monetary union of the EC, makes clear that Mrs Thatcher sees widening of the Community as a major opportunity to put a welcome brake on the further drive towards deepening. In Aspen, Colorado, she had earlier that year already said that 'The Community should declare unequivocally that it is ready to accept all the countries of Eastern Europe as members if they want to join, provided that democracy has taken root and that their economies are capable of sustaining membership.' Britain's new Prime Minister, John Major, has followed a similar line.[21] One of Britain's other reasons for early entry of Central Europe is that an expansion of the EC will make it less likely that one country – and Germany in particular – is going to dominate.

Most other member states of the EC are still pondering over the question as to what might be the optimal answer.[22] However, like Great Britain, Germany is clearly favouring EC membership for the Central Europeans. As early as August 1989, German Chancellor Kohl maintained that Hungary could be a member of the Community by the year 2000.[23] For Germany, the dream of *Mitteleuropa* is being revived, with abundant economic and political opportunities and benefits lying ahead. The shift of Germany's governmental centre from Bonn to Berlin symbolizes these expectations.

France, on the other hand, is not too anxious to let Central Europe join the Community family. In mid-June 1991, François Mitterrand argued that it could take 'dozens and dozens of years' before the Central European countries will be admitted to the EC.[24] In contrast to London's view, Paris has acknowledged that with an eastern enlargement of the Community, German power will be increased. Most French policy-makers have therefore stressed the necessity of strengthening the EC's structures under the presumption that Paris can thereby contain Germany, using the Community as a vehicle to serve French interests. France fears that a largely expanded European Community will result in a Europe of the lowest common denominator, especially in the field of security. This will make the containment of Germany more difficult and will diminish French influence in the EC. Mitterrand's plans for constructing a loosely-structured 'European Confederation', in which the the Central European countries would have their place, must be seen in this light. Such a confederation would lengthen the Central European stay in the antechamber for EC membership. It was therefore little surprise that the conference held in Prague, in mid-June 1991, chaired by Mitterrand and Havel, did not set any steps in the direction to such a European Confederation; the idea has thereafter known a quiet death.

On 19 September 1991, Mitterrand chose Berlin as the location to issue an emotional appeal to Germany to remain closely anchored to the EC; Bonn should 'reinforce the Community – through economic and political union – before seeking to enlarge it'.[25] Along similar lines, Hubert Vedrine (Mitterrand's security adviser), has argued that the EC Commission's task 'is made much more important because of the German question. We French want to de-dramatize this. There's no reason to get hysterical, and it serves no purpose to make people afraid. The unity of Germany is a legitimate aspiration, although it does pose problems. But the German problem is only serious if a strong Germany sits next to a weak Europe.'[26] Thierry de Montbrial, Director of the French Institute for International Relations in Paris, has noted that 'there is nonetheless a risk of profound change in the heart of the European Community from a Germany that is too strong, even if democratic'.[27] The French perspective on the future of Europe therefore clashes both with the British and the German view. This is mainly because 'The French Europe is necessarily *Western* Europe. Only Western Europe can ... become coherent enough to act decisively.'[28]

There is, however, more on the European menu than the mere 'widening' or 'deepening' of the EC; several alternatives to all-out membership have been brought up. First, it was argued that the Central European countries could set up their own organization which might, after à certain period, associate with the European Free Trade Association (EFTA). This would create a nice and cosy antechamber to the EC. Delors has argued that Central Europe could thereby enter the outside of a set of three concentric circles. After association with EFTA, Central Europe could slowly move – via membership of EFTA – to the sacrosanct EC itself.[29] This could be seen as an acceptable settlement to sooth the urge for Central European integration in the West European economy, meanwhile impeding their immediate entry into the EC. At first, the EFTA countries showed little enthusiasm for this scheme, not willing to hamper the already difficult negotiations with Brussels on the so-called European Economic Area (EEA), which was planned for 1993. Since September 1991, however, negotiations between EFTA and the three Central European countries have been under way to come to a free trade agreement.[30]

One other possibility would be to set up a Central European Free Trade Association (CEFTA), along the lines of the current EFTA. In most cases, this proposal has been accompanied by the suggestion to construct a 'Central European Payments Union', which would enable firms in these countries to 'exploit comparative advantages for their own benefit, but within the parameters set by overarching commercial and foreign exchange policies'.[31] In February 1991, Hungary, Poland and Czechoslovakia had already issued a declaration in which they announced closer economic cooperation. The first trilateral meeting to coordinate Central European *Westpolitik* took place in Bratislava, on 9 April 1990, and was followed by a meeting in Visegrad on 15 February 1991. The so-called Declaration of Visegrad had been the first sign of closer regional collaboration among the Central European countries, intended to strengthen their hand in negotiations with Brussels over future EC membership and possible means of economic cooperation.[32] A follow-up meeting of these three countries was held in Cracow on 6 October 1991.[33] During the Cracow Meeting, the Three had declared that they would make efforts 'to associate themselves with the European community'; the Czechoslovak President Vaclav Havel maintained that cooperation among the Central European countries would be 'a stabilizing factor and a good example of a regional contribution to the building of a new democratic order in Central and Eastern Europe'.[34] Although regular consultations have thereafter taken place, it remains unlikely that this will in the short term develop into more institutionalized forms of economic and/or political cooperation. Other subregional platforms of cooperation, like the Pentagonale (Austria, Czechoslovakia, Hungary, Italy and former Yugoslavia), and the Baltic Council (Lithuania, Latvia, Estonia, Denmark, Germany, Sweden, Norway, Finland, Russia and Poland) also seem too weak and too diverse to play a significant role.

For the time being, these plans remain on Europe's drawing-boards and do not provide an answer to the question as to how the EC's architectural dilemma can be resolved. From December 1990, the European Commission negotiated with the Central Europeans on the exact content of the association agreements. French Prime Minister Michel Rocard, argued that with association agreements the Central European countries could already feel themselves 'moral members of the European family'.[35] Along similar lines, the Vice-President of the EC Commission, Frans Andriessen, introduced the term 'Europe accords' for these agreements, thereby implying that they could somehow cross the politico-economic divide between the two parts of the continent. Not surprisingly, these agreements form some sort of half-way house between short-term membership and a policy of malign neglect. In this respect, they could be a viable solution to Brussels' economic security dilemma. The association agreements could tie Central Europe to the EC, both economically and politically, prepare them for future membership by slowly adopting the EC's *acquis communautaire* and make the EC ready for widening. Since speedy entry in the EC remains a chimera, Central European officials have for almost a year bargained with Commission representatives over the proper size of their slice of the pie in the sky.

10.4 Association agreements and the Iberian example

From the outset, the European Community has signed numerous association agreements with third countries, among others with Greece (1961) and Turkey (1963), but also with the ACP countries.[36] Article 238 of the Treaty of Rome stipulates that the Community 'may conclude with a third country, a union of States, or an international organization agreements creating an association embodying reciprocal rights and obligations, joint actions and special procedures'. Association agreements may be explicitly designed to result in full membership or it may leave this matter open. The Turkish case may illustrate that association does not automatically or necessarily have to lead to accession. The object of association in the case of Greece and Turkey (but not in the other cases) was 'to create a customs union between the Community and the associated country and to enable the latter to adjust its economy and so to prepare itself for the assumption of duties consequent upon accession'.[37] The procedure of concluding these sort of agreements is equal in all cases: the EC Council must conclude the agreement unanimously after receiving the assent of the European Parliament; the negotiations are conducted by the EC Commission under the Council's directions and mandates.

   In the past, 'association' has served a wide spectrum of political and economic purposes for the Community. In 1957, France – followed by Italy and Belgium – had demanded special treatment for its (former) colonies, which finally led to the above-mentioned Convention of Yaoundé. The long-range goal of the association agreements with Greece and Turkey was to 'promote a continuous and balanced strengthening of the commercial and economic relations between the contracting parties with full consideration of the need to ensure the accelerated development of the economy of Greece (Turkey) as well as the elevation of the level of employment and the living standards of the Greek (Turkish) people' (Article 2 (1) of both the Greek and Turkish association agreements). In each case, Councils of Association have been set up which were authorized to make recommendations for the proper operation of the association, meanwhile also functioning as the central organs for mutual consultation and the exchange of information.

The Central European countries have considered these agreements as a stepping-stone for membership. They have often referred to the Greek association agreement which envisaged a 22-year transition period, an estimate coming quite close to Athens' eventual full membership of the EC in 1981. In 1962, the Community had earmarked US$ 125 million for the economic development of Greece, but the financial clauses of the association were suspended during the reign of the military junta (1967-74). In 1975, Greece applied for EC membership. The Commission reacted cautiously to this request; the structure of Greek agriculture and its weak industrial base were expected to lead to significant problems during the process of integration within the Community. Nevertheless, for political reasons Greece was accepted as a member, mainly in order to strengthen Athens' parliamentary democracy. Portugal and Spain have followed similar scenarios. After the demise of the Salazar and Franco regimes, both countries had applied for membership (in 1977), and entered the Community in 1986.[38] In all three cases, the new democracies were embraced within the EC as a solid framework of economic and political stability. In particular, the Spanish and Portuguese precedents have been major trump cards which could be played by the Central Europeans. For instance, during a conference in Rotterdam, 9 November 1990, the Hungarian Minister of Foreign Affairs, G. Kodolanyi, argued that the entry of Spain and Portugal to the EC had been the result of a political settlement.[39] Kodolanyi maintained that the Community would do the right thing now to take a similar decision, for similar reasons.[40] Western politicians have often challenged this contention, arguing that negotiations with Madrid and Lisbon over their entry have taken over seven years. What is more, Greece, Spain and Portugal have had totally different political and economic problems to deal with. Restructuring a planned economy will probably be more difficult than bringing an already basically capitalist system into the mainstream of the world economy. Lack of experience with the intricacies of the modern-day financial markets make such a transition even more problematic.

There are, on the other hand, also some arguments for expecting that Central Europe will manage to close the economic and technological gap with the EC rather swiftly. As a recent study on the historical precedents of the economic transitions in Central Europe has concluded: 'backward countries possess an enormous opportunity for accelerated growth once they are able to start closing the gap between the level of productivity which they have actually achieved, and the potential level represented by the performance of the more advanced countries. Put simply, it is easier for followers to move rapidly towards an already established frontier of best-practiced performance, than it is for pioneers to shift that frontier further forward by various forms of innovation.'[41] It would, however, be unduly optimistic to assume that the economic and technological gap between East and West can be closed in less than one decade.[42] To a certain extent, the Iberian example has captured the EC's dilemma: a further enlargement would most probably bring Central Europe in the world economy, but could also seriously hamper the current momentum of Community integration. The less developed regions of the southern flank of the EC have received financial support from the richer EC members; the Central Europeans would need even more support when they entered the EC which could overload the EC's budgetary limits. (For a further discussion of this issue, see Chapter 10.6.)

Anticipating these difficulties, the association agreements with Central Europe could serve a wide range of goals.[43] Negotiations on the association agreements have comprised the following aspects: trade, economic, commercial, and cultural cooperation, technical and financial assistance of the EC and a political dialogue.[44] The Commission has argued that these 'Europe accords' would serve several purposes: (1) creating a climate of trust and stability in which political and economic reform could be successful; (2) encouraging trade and investment, especially in the private sector; (3) improving management for the transition from a planned to a market economy; and (4) making EC financial aid more coherent and transparent. Association would eventually bring the Central Europeans in the 21-nation zone of free movement of goods, services and capital. All four objectives are crucial for a successful Central European transition. One further reason to enter into close contacts with Central Europe is of a political – or perhaps even psychological – nature. Poland in particular has been uneasy over the growing power of its neighbour across the Oder and the chaos looming on the other side of the Bug. An authoritarian backlash in the former USSR might bring Central Europe back into the Russian sphere of influence. Only a few weeks before the August 1991 coup in the USSR, a document was published by the Soviet Communist Party suggesting a stronger assertion of Soviet influence in Central Europe. Since these countries are still dependent upon Soviet oil and gas, the document suggested using the 'energy weapon' in order to bring this region back in the Soviet orbit.[45] Close economic and political cooperation with the EC, with clarity on the issue of speedy membership, would assuage these worries and could make such a gloomy scenario less likely.

Early in 1990, the Commission made it abundantly clear that the association agreements with Central Europe were no automatic entrance tickets to the Community itself. During the EC Council meeting in Dublin, April 1990, no mention was even made as to their future membership.

However, Warsaw, Budapest and Prague have demanded an agreement in which it will be clearly stipulated that association will be the first step towards membership. They argued that such articles were also included in similar agreements of the EC with Greece and Turkey. Negotiations between Brussels and Central European representatives have therefore not been without friction. Andrzej Olechowski, the Polish Secretary of State at the Ministry for Foreign Economic Co-operation, argued in March 1991 that the EC proposals were 'highly unbalanced'. 'On one side, it asks Poland to commit itself to eliminate before the end of the agreement all restrictions on imports from the EC, limit and discipline the use of safeguard measures and strengthen protection afforded to intellectual property. On the other side, it offers Poland removal of import restrictions pertaining to about one half of its exports (since it excludes most of agriculture, textiles and clothing) and the assurance of GATT-consistent use of safeguards also covering only half of the products it exports. There is no government in the world which would submit such a one-sided agreement to its parliament for ratification.'[46] On 15 April 1991, the EC Foreign Ministers decided that membership of the EC could be mentioned in the Preamble to the association agreements as 'an ultimate, though not an automatic' goal. Brussels also dropped its demand for a mid-term review of the conditions for Central European membership of the EC. The EC further offered higher Central European exports of fruit, vegetables, pork and game. This would, however, not apply to cereals, beef, lamb or dairy products, which could still expect the protection of the EC's Common Agricultural Policy (CAP). Although the Mediterranean countries have objected to more Central European exports of textiles and steel, the EC also proposed to dissipate all textile tariffs over a transition period; steel import duties and quotas would be phased out over five years. However, since all bids of the EC excluded free access to the Community market for their main agricultural products, no agreement could be reached. The Polish Minister of Agriculture argued: 'We very well know that the EEC market is practically inaccessible to us'. The Polish negotiator further maintained: 'We would not like to think that Europe does not want us; such a situation would have a negative impact on public opinion and on reform';[47] 'We are increasingly worried and annoyed with the arrogance with which the European Community is acting in agriculture'.[48]

The Soviet coup of 19 August 1991 considerably strengthened the Central European negotiation position, since the short-lived Communist backlash in Moscow once more illustrated the political and economic homelessness of the countries of the former Warsaw Pact. Directly after the coup, the Hungarian President, Jozsef Antall, inquired with the Commission about the completion of the association agreements; Delors argued that 'It's no good making fine speeches with a sob in your voice on Sunday and then on Monday opposing the trade concessions enabling those countries to sell their goods and improve their standards of living'.[49] Vaclav Havel also understood the situation when he maintained that 'It seems to me that our efforts aimed at joining Western Europe might paradoxically be stepped up by this sad event'.[50] In a coordinated effort, the three Central European leaders sent letters to all the EC members on 23 August, urging for a rapid conclusion of the association agreements.[51] In response to these queries, the Commission promised to formulate new, far-ranging proposals for the Europe accords. However, after the coup's quick breakdown, the EC Council failed to come up with concrete concessions. Only after one month of bickering did the Commission table a compromise which proved to be acceptable to all sides. However, the Central Europeans only very reluctantly approved it, knowing that this was the most 'generous' offer they could possibly hope for. The EC would increase its meat imports from Central Europe by 10 per cent a year (for each of five years), simultaneously reducing its tariffs by 60 per cent over three years. However, not much of the extra meat is likely to enter the Community market, since it was agreed that any meat the states of the former USSR was going to buy from Central Europe with EC money would be subtracted from the quota. Somewhat cynically, this 'triangular' solution will therefore not result in increased economic ties between Central and Western Europe, but between Central Europe and the ex-USSR; it also promised to perpetuate the Community's protectionist agricultural policy. On 16 December 1991, the agreements were signed and are now awaiting ratification in the European Parliament and the parliaments of the EC member states and Central Europe.[52]

10.5 Towards a new European divide?

It is acknowledged that the association arrangements are of major importance for attracting western investments to Central Europe since they will imply at least partially guaranteed access to the EC market. In their present form, these agreements will certainly improve access to the EC for Central European products. It is also likely that Central European exports to the West will increase. The question is, however, whether these accords offer enough? It is clear that without the hard currencies earned from exports to the EC, Japan or the United States, Central Europe cannot afford to buy the essential modern technology which is expected to modernize their industrial plants. Hard currency is also necessary to pay for the imports of energy from Russia. The basic thrust of Brussels' dilemma was cogently formulated by the Hungarian Minister for International Economic Relations, Béla Kádár, who argued that the EC's 'security interests' would best be served by 'offering better market access' and 'encouraging the flow of technologies and direct capital'.[53] Western scholars generally agree. Lawrence H. Summers, chief economist at the World Bank, argued that 'The key is the promise of joining Europe in an economic sense, by providing them an opportunity to trade freely with the nations of Western Europe'. C. Fred Bergsten similarly maintained that 'These countries need market access to expand trade and not be dependent on a dole from the West'.[54] However, the traditional gap between 'will and wallet' has made it far from easy to accomplish this goal.[55]

This is exactly the point where Brussels' 'philanthropy' reaches its outer limits: the Central European countries are considered potential competitors by the Community member states. Hungarian and Polish agricultural products have not been given a warm welcome in the already overcrowded internal market; nor were steel and textiles. Nevertheless, the EC is well aware that the Central Europeans should not be confronted with another policy of economic containment, only a few years after their successful anti-Communist revolutions. With the question of steel and textile exports now largely solved, agriculture is destined to remain an irritant in the field of EC-Central European economic cooperation. That agriculture tends to form a major stumbling-block was also indicated by the troublesome GATT negotiations. The Uruguay Round was broken off in early December 1990, since the EC and the United States failed to reach agreement over the level of the Community's subsidies to its farmers; Brussels is still not prepared fundamentally to restructure its Common Agricultural Policy. France, Ireland, Belgium and Luxembourg in particular have been fierce opponents of any reform of the CAP. The Community's farming pressure group (COPA),[56] has argued that EC farmers have already been hurt by the increase of imports of agricultural products from Central Europe and the unification of Germany.

It must also be said that the worries of West European farmers are justified. Recent research has revealed that the comparative advantage for Hungarian agricultural products has increased considerably. Over the period of 1970-87, the following Hungarian products have boosted their competitive edge vis-à-vis the EC: some textile and clothing products, fresh and frozen meat, unmilled maize, other unmilled cereals, prepared breakfast food, fruit and vegetable juices, pig and poultry fat, pulpwood, animal materials, mineral jelly, sunflower seed oil and drawn, blown, cast and rolled glass.[57] Along similar lines, the Polish foreign trade enterprise Animex has calculated that, if there were no EC tariff barriers, exports of meat and meat products to the Community would rise by 50 per cent. It was argued that the 'aid from the EC which is so often reported is in fact a drop in the ocean by comparison with what the Community could do for Poland by improving access to its markets'.[58] Likewise, Hungarian economists complain about the Community's web of non-tariff barriers, its many licenses, seasonal tariffs, Community surveillance, quotas and its Common Customs Tariff.[59] They also fear that further enlargement of the EC with the current EFTA-states will result in trade diversion, to the detriment of the Central European countries. But that is not all. As Alfred Tovias has argued: 'Among the measures of the EC-1992 programme there is one which is likely to have detrimental effects on

Hungary's exports of agricultural exports: the doubling of the EC structural funds until 1992. It may reduce export opportunities of Hungary's producers of fruit, vegetables and spices, since one of the guiding principles of the fund is to promote the diversification of production in Southern Europe away from products where the degree of EC-sufficiency is already high.'[60] For 1993, 14 billion ECU have been reserved for the structural funds in Greece, Ireland, Portugal and Spain. Since the pattern of exports of these EC countries overlaps with that of Hungary and Poland, this will reduce the latter's export opportunities.

10.6 Lack of money or lack of political will?

All this seems to indicate that one of the major arguments against Central European EC membership and improved access of agricultural products is a practical one: the EC might simply not be rich enough. In other words, the political will to earmark sufficient financial resources for the East might be insufficient since the budgetary obligations of the 1992 initiative are already overburdening many EC states. Without doubt, Central European membership would lead to internal tensions, for example when regional and development funds would have to be shifted from the southern flank of the EC to the East. As said, some 14 billion ECU have been reserved for the structural funds in Greece, Ireland, Portugal and Spain for 1993 (and a new 'cohesion fund' is planned for 1994). One can imagine what huge amounts of money would have to be reserved in order to bring the former Communist countries to the level of economic development of the EC. In his speech to the European Parliament, in January 1990, Delors pointed out that if similar aid criteria were applied to both the underdeveloped areas of the EC and the Central European countries, the EC annual budget should be expanded with an additional sum of approximately US$ 17 billion.[61] One other indication of the vast sum needed to level up the Central European economies has been the costs of German reunification. In the Spring of 1990, it was rumoured that several EC funds would have to pay some three to four billion ECU – on a yearly basis – to the former GDR. Much can be learned from the fact that even the richest and economically healthiest member of the EC – the FRG – seems to have difficulties with the incorporation of the richest and economically healthiest member of the former CMEA.

But there are not only financial difficulties lying ahead. As William Pfaff has argued: 'economic and fiscal integration assumes parallel economic policies in countries at roughly the same level of industrial development. For this reason, a single currency is feasible today only for the core EC states, all of them already part of the European Exchange Rate Mechanism.'[62] Jürgen Nötzold has also maintained that 'The second step of the Delors Plan to create an economic and monetary union will make great demands on economic and monetary policy. New members will have to adopt the common rules, the *acquis communautaire*. So the obstacles for membership candidates already are very high, but will get even higher.'[63] With recent research indicating that Czechoslovakia, Hungary and Poland have only 56, 42, and 27 per cent of income per head in comparison with the average Dutchman, Central Europe has a long way to go in economic development.[64] Countries like Spain, Portugal and Italy might also encounter major obstacles in participating in the EC's monetary union. What is more, other prospective members like Austria, Sweden, Finland and Switzerland traditionally pursue a neutralist course, which might hamper a coherent Community foreign policy.[65] As a result, European integration will most likely be characterized by a 'variable geometry', with 'multiple speeds' on economic, political and security matters. The growing prospect of a two-speed drive to economic and monetary union within the current Twelve may give us just a glimpse of the much less homogeneous arrangements in a future enlarged Community. It is obvious that this Europe *à la carte* will not live up to the federalist notions of many Brussels policy-makers. It is also very unlikely that Jacques Delors' 'Bruges formula' – which asserts that cooperation with Central Europe should lead to further integration within the EC[66] – will be followed. Much will also depend upon the ratification process of the Maastricht Treaty. The Treaty will have to be renegotiated in order to make it acceptable for all twelve member states, making it likely that a European integration process *à la carte* will be the highest attainable.

Another closely related problem of Central European entry concerns the ensuing institutional reforms within the EC. In early April 1991, Jacques Delors announced that the Commission would develop a blueprint before the end of 1992 for the new institutional structure of a Community of about 20 to 24 members. This will be essential, since in the unlikely case that Hungary, Czechoslovakia and Poland are soon accepted as new members, countries like Austria, Turkey, Sweden, Norway, Finland and perhaps even Cyprus and Malta, will also have to be admitted. With the demise of the USSR and Yugoslavia a large number of successor states are eager to conclude association agreements in preparation for eventual full membership. During his visit to the Baltic countries, Commission Vice-President Frans Andriessen argued that the EC was willing to strengthen its ties with these three former Soviet Republics;[67] in October 1991, the EC Commission proposed first generation agreements with the possibility of replacing them as soon as possible with fully fledged association agreements.[68] Similar promises have also been made to the Ukraine and Slovenia.[69] This increase of members will have significant consequences for policy-making procedures within the EC. Pascal Lamy, Delors' top aid, has argued that enlargement of the current EC Twelve beyond two or three extra members would make the Community 'unwieldy and diffuse'.[70] Moreover, as Helen Wallace has reminded us, 'the architects of the EC simply did not need to address the question whether their model was appropriate for a European community of 20 to 30 rather diverse members'.[71]

Most Community officials are unduly optimistic on this point. Frans Andriessen has argued, in September 1991: 'It is quite clear that the present institutional structure of the EC is not conceived for a Community of 24 members or more ... Ideally, we should change the [Community's] institutional structure first and then tackle enlargement. Now we shall have to do both together.'[72] It is undisputed that it will be impossible to make decisions by unanimity in a Council of 24 ministers, and an executive body of some 30 Commissioners would be a liability. The procedure of unanimity will become unpracticable and majority voting on all issues will have to become the general rule in order to avoid the stagnation of decision-making. It has therefore been suggested that a smaller managing sub-body of the full, enlarged Council could be set up which would be composed of a permanent membership for Germany, Great Britain, France and Italy (and perhaps Spain), with some (perhaps three) rotating members representing the other EC-countries.[73] Such an arrangement will, however, fall badly in the smaller member states.[74] This will in turn lead to fears among the current Twelve that the new, and poor, Central European members could impede EC policy-making by forming blocking minorities. In this way, they could barter huge chunks of structural and regional aid in return for their votes in Community organs. This is where the financial and the political arguments against Central European membership converge. One closely related problem would be the number of votes of the new members in the Council. Should Hungary get as many votes as the Netherlands, or as Luxembourg? Should a country like Malta get its own Commissioner? These are extremely thorny political questions which are not easily answered.

All in all, the EC's security dilemma looms large, whereas short-term economic interests have until now overshadowed long-term political concerns. The association agreements have set a first but very tentative step in the right direction. The disputed issues of Central European market access and entry into the Community during the year of negotiations over the Europe agreements have also laid bare the delicate predicaments in the relationship between Brussels and the East. One of the main problems will be the EC's lack of financial resources and/or the lack of political will and vision among the EC's member states which will put a serious brake upon the process of integrating both parts of Europe. We have already argued that the successful deepening of the European Community is also not assured.[75] If further economic, monetary and political integration between the Twelve were to come to a halt for one reason or the other, the EC would lose its attraction for the East as a model of cooperation and prosperity. The EC is therefore confronted with the difficult task of sustaining the 'high-tech' nature of its integration effort *without* excluding its Central European neighbours. As Zbigniew Brzezinski argued in 1990: 'It will be critically important to the success of the entire agenda for Western Europe's political integration to be accelerated further. That integration must serve as the cornerstone of any eventually wider European commonwealth and as an attractive, and badly needed, example of successful multilateral cooperation for the Central Europeans and Russians.'[76]

In the final chapter of this book we will examine the chances for the EC of sustaining its integrationist momentum and its opportunities for its relations with Central Europe and the former Soviet Union from a more theoretical perspective.

11. Epilogue: Discord and Collaboration in the 1990s

Only a uniting Europe that could look at the whole of its fragmented past would be able to will a future. But how can it emerge, if its members have neither the drive nor the necessary incentives to transcend themselves into Europe?

Stanley Hoffmann, 'Fragments Floating in the Here and Now', *Dædalus*, vol.108, no.1 (Winter 1979), p.26.

11.1 'All's Well That Ends Well?'

This book has examined the economic and political relations between the European Community and the East. We have argued that West European integration has not been a logical and rational linear process, advancing from economic and political discord to a peaceful and prosperous European Union. We have maintained that the institutions of the ECSC and the EC have been established under the aegis of American hegemony and under conditions of global bipolarity. In the first chapters we have seen that the Cold War did not only help to set off West European integration, but that it has also determined which nations could join that process and which nations could not. The specific conditions which the United States have attached to economic assistance under the Marshall Plan have helped the Six to overcome major obstacles of collective action and have provided the basic first steps towards closer cooperation in the economic field. We have further seen that on several occasions the conditions of bipolarity have dampened internal conflicts within the EC, conflicts which could have seriously hampered the integration process. However, in several fields the member states have *not* been able to achieve closer cooperation, whereby the lack of coordination in the areas of export credits and foreign policy stands out. The Neo-realist analysis on which this book has been largely based has provided several important insights where the basic causes and mechanisms of West European integration are concerned. Applying Neo-realist arguments, this book has mainly focused upon the structural background of West European integration. This theory has proved powerful in explaining the origins and initial development of the European Community and it has proved helpful in analysing the EC's economic and political relations with the 'Other Europe'. It has also gone a long way in clarifying the background of the 1992 initiative, and has pointed out that the changes in the international system (most notably the decline of American hegemony, the demise of the Soviet Union and the ensuing shift towards multipolarity) have provided the EC with the opportunity to enhance its role and authority. However, we have to turn to the unit-level of the different West European states in order to explain why and how the EC member states have also *seized this opportunity*, and how they have actively stimulated the process of integration by means of new and innovative policy initiatives.

Just as we started this study with the assumption that things could have been different, we will end with rejecting the postulate that 'all's well that ends well'. This is not to say that the prospects for further integration and collaboration in Europe are poor. It is only to indicate that after some four decades of stability and predictability, the cards of the European balance of power have been reshuffled, which has ushered in a period of volatility. In this concluding chapter we will examine the prospects for discord and collaboration in the Europe of the 1990s. We will meditate upon the main ideas which have been launched by both pessimistic and optimistic observers of Europe's future into the next millennium. By doing so we will touch upon the two major theoretical currents within the study of International Relations: Neo-realism and Neo-liberal institutionalism, which have already been introduced in Chapter 1. We will argue that Neo-realist analysis has proved valuable in explaining and understanding international politics during the Cold War; it has also proved useful in aiding an understanding of structural change by considering the differences and modifications in the distribution of capabilities among the constituent units. The question which remains unanswered, however, is whether the recent return to multipolarity will inevitably result in instability and insecurity, something which the Neo-realist theory suggests. In this chapter we will argue that this is not *necessarily* the case, and that the institutionalized nature of international – and more particularly West European – politics, is likely to assure a significant level of political and economic cooperation.

11.2 Bipolarity, multipolarity and stability

With the demise of the Soviet Union and the relative decline of the United States' economic and political power, the post-war international system of bipolarity has clearly given way to a multipolar one. Whereas bipolarity by definition is characterized as a system wherein two Great Powers dominate, multipolarity is generally defined as a system with five or more Great Powers. Neo-realist observers have maintained that Cold War bipolarity has provided the circumstances for stability and peace, and that the shift towards multipolarity will, *ipso facto*, mean a return to instability and hence increase the likelihood of conflict and discord. Among the most prominent spokesmen of this pessimistic view has been John Mearsheimer, who has argued that collaboration will prove to be much more difficult now that the traditional bipolar system has become a thing of the past.[1]

There have, of course, also been a great number of optimistic observers. Among them is Francis Fukuyama, who has provided a rosy scenario for Europe's and the world's future, devoid of the conflicts which have for decades ensued from the East-West controversy. Optimists like Fukuyama maintain that multipolarity is not a recipe for conflict but that, with the collapse of Communism, the prospect for some form of collective security system might become more realistic. This, in turn, is expected to provide for a more peaceful and righteous world order. In the mid-1960s, theorists like Karl W. Deutsch and J. David Singer had already maintained that 'as the system moves away from bipolarity toward multipolarity, the frequency and intensity of war should be expected to diminish ... both in the short and the long run the instability of tight bipolar systems appears to be substantially greater.'[2] In the context of this argument, the nineteenth-century Concert of Europe has received renewed attention from several scholars.[3] During the period 1815 to 1854, Great Britain, Prussia, Russia, Austria and France had maintained the peace amongst themselves by constructing a regime of mutual consultation on important political matters. With the return to multipolarity, it has been argued, the experiences of the Concert of Europe should be taken as a model for the political architecture of Europe in the 1990s. Before we elaborate further upon these predictions and scenarios, let us first examine the grounds on which the arguments for the stability of bipolar and multipolar systems have been based. Since we are most interested in the role of the European Community, we will focus especially upon the role of alliances and institutions.

Kenneth Waltz has argued that bipolarity has many advantages over multipolarity and that the former provides stability and predictability whereas the latter will result in instability and insecurity. Waltz has maintained that in a bipolar world there are no peripheries: both Great Powers are concerned with all conflicts and sources of instability all over the globe, since this might result in a significant gain or loss for either of them. 'Because this is so,' Waltz has argued, 'the powers in a bipolar world promptly respond to unsettling events. In a multipolar world dangers are diffused, responsibilities unclear, and definitions of vital interests easily obscured ... In a multipolar world, who is a danger to whom is often unclear; the incentive to regard all disequilibrating changes with concern and respond to them with whatever effort may be required is consequently weakened.'[4] Applying Waltz's analysis to the alliances in Europe would suggest that conflicts within the European Community and NATO on the one hand, and within the former CMEA and former Warsaw Pact on the other hand, will now no longer be restrained by the two Great Powers. There are two main reasons for this assumption: (1) since there is now no clear-cut demarcation of the respective spheres of influence between the two Great Powers and (2) since both Great Powers lack the economic and political capabilities to pacify emerging conflicts. Several examples already seem to support this argument. Armed conflicts in several (former) Soviet Republics and Yugoslavia, for instance, have resulted from the sudden collapse of the stable Cold War stalemate in Europe. The further consequence of this systemic change might be the rise of what Samuel Huntington has called 'praetorian systems' in Central Europe, wherein 'social forces confront each other nakedly; no political institutions, no corps of professional political leaders are recognized or accepted as the legitimate intermediaries to moderate group conflict. Equally important, no agreement exists among the groups as to the legitimate and authoritative methods for resolving conflicts.'[5] The chance that these praetorian systems might arise in the former Communist countries is especially great if the economic reforms were to be unsuccessful, and if the political and security vacuum in Central Europe were maintained. This might result in a fragmented Europe in which anarchy will triumph.

But change is not restricted to the East. Under current conditions of multipolarity, Neo-realists would argue, policy-making within the European Community will also change considerably. The nature of these changes is still unclear, but some clues might be found in previous studies of the formation and dynamics of alliances from a Neo-realist perspective (for example the work of Glenn Snyder and Stephen Walt). Studying alliance theory is important in order to come to grips with the challenges which the EC will face in the years ahead. This book has reaffirmed Glenn Snyder's assertion that 'Alliance formation is a much simpler process in a bipolar than in a multipolar system. Who allies with whom is much less a matter of choice and more a matter of systemic determination.'[6] But, as he maintains, once an alliance has been formed, a so-called 'alliance security dilemma' will develop along the same lines as the traditional security dilemma which we have introduced in Chapter 10. When the chips are down, each state has to choose between cooperation or 'abandonment' of the alliance. Under conditions of bipolarity, abandonment will be highly unlikely. During the Cold War, membership of NATO and the EC could not easily be exchanged for affiliation with the Warsaw Pact and the CMEA, whereas several neutral and former Communist countries have now applied for membership of the western alliances. The different nature of alliances under bipolarity and multipolarity can be summarized as follows:

> in bipolarity, the identity of friends and foes and the definition of interests is largely a consequence of the structure of the system; alliances register but do not create interests; interests are clear and relatively unchanging, and are shared in high degree among allies. In multipolarity, enmity and amity are not determined by structure

but by conflicts of particular interests and a systemically induced compulsion to align with others to escape the dangers of isolation; alignments create interests to some degree; interests are often ambiguous but are potentially or actually intense; interests tend to be changeable, reflecting changing alignments, and are imperfectly shared among allies.[7]

Alliance management under bipolarity is therefore relatively easy, since the structure of the system provides few incentives and practical opportunities for abandonment; under multipolarity this will become a much more reasonable option.

Besides 'abandonment', states within an alliance also face the opposite risk of 'entrapment'. Entrapment occurs, says Glenn Snyder, 'when one [state] values the preservation of the alliance more than the cost of fighting for the ally's interests ... Thus, the greater one's dependence on the alliance and the stronger one's commitment to the ally, the higher the risk of entrapment.'[8] In a multipolar system, alliance management becomes much more difficult since abandonment, realignment (or de-alignment) are realistic options, whereas a strong commitment to the alliance is not encouraged since a 'strategy of strong commitment and support will have the undesired effect of reducing [the state's] bargaining leverage over the ally'.[9] Short of outright abandonment, the usual options of bargaining, balancing and bandwagoning will make up the rest of the policy menu for the members of the alliance.[10] However, coercive bargaining (which employs threats to destroy common interests in order to achieve one's own goal in an alliance-conflict), will probably dominate accommodative bargaining (whereby one's own interests are sacrificed in order to achieve a common goal within the alliance), since both the chances for abandonment and entrapment are enhanced. In short, Neo-realist theory would suggest that under conditions of multipolarity, alliance management within the European Community is likely to become more difficult.

Before examining the risks of abandonment and entrapment within the EC, the forms which this might take, as well as the consequences for the process of European integration at large, we will first discuss the Neo-liberal institutionalist argument which argues that the (alliance) security dilemma may be ameliorated by regimes and institutions.

11.3 Neo-liberal institutionalism and the EC in the 1990s

Neo-realists argue that states dwell in an anarchic, self-help environment in which they are time and again confronted with new security dilemmas. Alliances, they contend, are no solution to this problem since there too the security dilemma arises; alliances and institutions are never absolutely solid, whatever the content of the written Treaties among states. Mearsheimer has argued that European politics is therefore likely to go 'back to the future', since multipolarity is apt to give rise to the Balkanization of Europe, the proliferation of nuclear weapons and the escalation of international conflicts due to hypernationalism. Others, like Robert O. Keohane and Jack Snyder, have argued contrariwise that the existence of solid international regimes and institutions in the 1990s sharply contrasts with the lack of such arrangements during the unstable interbellum. They therefore maintain that Europe is unlikely to go 'back to the future', but that collaboration and the process of integration might be sustained even without a clear-cut Soviet threat and without American hegemony. What particularly interests us here is whether the horror-scenario à la Mearsheimer will apply to the European Community, or whether this might be averted by the further institutionalization of European economic and political cooperation?

It is important to add that Neo-liberal institutionalist theory accepts the value of systemic analysis, but that it can be distinguished from Neo-realism by its emphasis on the effects of international institutions and regimes on state behaviour. Robert Keohane, for example, has accepted the thesis that bipolarity has helped to construct many contemporary regimes and institutions, among others the European Community. However, in his book *After Hegemony*, he has made a clear case for the argument that 'Cooperation is possible after hegemony not only because shared interests can lead to the creation of regimes, but also because the conditions for maintaining international regimes are less demanding than those required for creating them'.[11] Keohane thereafter suggests that the lag between the decline of bipolarity and the (possible) disruption of international regimes and international institutions might 'be quite long and the "inertia" of the existing regimes relatively great'.[12] This might lead us to expect that multipolarity will not necessarily disrupt collaboration within the EC. The question nevertheless remains: why would this be the case?

Neo-liberal institutionalists generally identify four main reasons why structures of cooperation – i.e. regimes and institutions – can be maintained without hegemony and therefore have a chance to survive under conditions of multipolarity. Institutions and regimes (1) increase the level of information (and limit asymmetries in information) among states which reduces uncertainty about states' intentions; (2) increase the costs of 'abandonment', since they will have installed mechanisms and procedures for punishing 'defectors'; (3) encourage issue-linkage, log-rolling and the making of side-payments by states since they facilitate arrangements and reduce the transaction costs of the negotiation of international agreements; and (4) affect states' definition of their own interests. The fourth point is a crucial one, and perhaps therefore one which is most clearly in conflict with Neo-realist thinking on this issue. After assuming that regimes and institutions change the context within which states make their decisions based upon self-interest, Neo-liberal institutionalists take the next step by claiming that these regimes might under some circumstances even be necessary to the effective pursuit of a state's interests.

Pursuing this line of thought, it follows that the European Community does not have such a bleak future, since 'In a world political economy characterized by growing interdependence, [regimes and institutions] may become increasingly useful for governments that wish to solve common problems and pursue complementary purposes without subordinating themselves to hierarchical systems of control'. In short: 'Institutions are necessary ... in order to achieve *state* purposes',[13] and are therefore likely to play a pivotal role in facilitating collaboration among states, not only in post-Cold War Europe, but most likely in the world at large.

Along similar lines, Jack Snyder has applied this way of thinking to the role of the EC in averting anarchy and conflict in the Europe of the 1990s. Adopting the Neo-liberal institutionalist argument that institutions provide frameworks for collaboration, Jack Snyder has maintained that 'The most effective scheme would gradually integrate reforming Soviet bloc states into the European Community'.[14] Western Europe would thereby extend its successful international institutions and regimes towards the East and would thus fill the vacuum which has resulted from the rising political participation and the still weak government institutions in the former Communist countries. This, he argues, would be essential in order to prevent the emergence of praetorian societies in Central Europe. Snyder further suggests that the EC would be the most appropriate context for managing the New German Question, and that a cooperative, Pan-European security regime could arrange for the rights and responsibilities of ethnic and religious minorities. By proscribing a dose of regimes and institutions for this wide range of looming ills in the Europe of the 1990s, Neo-liberal institutionalism claims to have found the panacea for discord and conflict in the maintenance and extension of existing cooperative frameworks, based not on assumptions like harmony and economic interdependence, but on the egoism and rationality of states. This last aspect should be particularly stressed, since cooperation is not expected to result from a liberal harmony of interests, but from the fact that existing regimes and institutions will be able to facilitate collective action and interstate bargaining. This is a far cry from the optimistic Fukuyama thesis, and equally far removed from the Functionalist assumptions of spill-over. By applying the basic framework of Neo-realist thinking, Neo-liberal institutionalist theory is able to explain international change by looking at the transformation of the international system, without, however, adopting the a-historical hypothesis that a multipolar system is *necessarily* less stable than a bipolar one. The nineteenth-century Concert of Europe has already been a notable exception.[15]

Before we make a concluding examination as to the prospects for discord and collaboration in the Europe of the 1990s, we must ask one last question concerning the Neo-liberal institutionalist emphasis on the virtue of cooperation and stability. Although we are used to value order and cooperation highly, the question must nevertheless be asked whether cooperation among states is *necessarily* a good thing in itself? As E. H. Carr had pointed out in the late-1930s: 'What matters is that ... supposedly absolute and universal principles were not principles at all, but the unconscious reflexions of national policy based on a particular interpretation of national interests at a particular time'.[16] In the previous chapter we have already seen that Brussels is now confronted with the difficult choice between speeding up further economic and political integration ('deepening'), and absorbing new member states ('widening'). We have argued that on several points both options are incompatible, since deepening the EC will raise the threshold for prospective member states, whereas widening is expected to aggravate the predicaments of alliance management which are likely to occur under multipolarity. In this respect, it may be clear. that successful alliance management within the Community could be detrimental to the Central European countries' prospects for closer economic ties with the EC. The continuation of the basic structure of the EC's Common Agricultural Policy, for example, may be valued by several current EC member states and may be considered as a positive outcome of cooperation among the Twelve. However, the resulting lack of market access will be highly damaging for the transformation process of the Central European economies. Further cooperation within the EC on economic, monetary, political and security issues might give rise to a Europe which will behave as an independent international actor. However, excluding the Central European countries from this process is likely to give free reign to instability in this region and to the emergence of praetorian systems. Although this does not mean that the Neo-liberal institutionalist emphasis on regimes and institutions is invalid – or immoral – it nevertheless implies that collaboration does not in *all* cases generate optimal results for *all* states. Without doubt, continued integration of the EC without taking into account the economic, political and security requirements of Central Europe, would not ameliorate Brussels' (economic) security dilemma, but would even exacerbate it.

11.4 Discord and collaboration, or the significance of grins without cats

With the break-up of the Soviet Union as a unitary state and the reunification of Germany, the European balance of power has been altered significantly. The emerging multipolar system now comprises two Great Powers who have lost considerably in power and prestige due to the breakdown of the Cold War order: France and the USSR (Russia); there is also one clear-cut winner: Germany. Whereas Germany has now achieved its main possession goal, France has witnessed its main milieu goals go up in thin air; Russia has emerged as a weak state with its economy in a shambles and is now saddled with the political and economic burdens which have accompanied all Great Powers during the process of decolonization.

We have seen that Neo-realism and Neo-liberal institutionalism have quite different things to say about the consequences which this redistribution of capabilities among these nations will have for the European balance of power and for the prospects of discord, collaboration and economic and political integration. We have also seen that Neo-realists argue that alliance management within the European Community will become more complicated than during the previous decades. Since the 1960s and 1970s have certainly not been devoid of internal conflicts, this does not promise much good for the years ahead. Alliance theory has identified several mechanisms of state behaviour with which we may become familiar in the years to come. EC member states now have several options. First, they may 'abandon' the European Community. Although this does not seem a very likely choice in the light of the vested interests which all member states have in cooperation within the EC-framework, it will become very probable that several members will refuse (or are not accepted by others) to cooperate on several issues of further integration. Among the Twelve, there will be a number of states that will opt out on (or are excluded from), for instance, the establishment of the EMU, or far-going collaboration in the area of foreign policy and security. Several strict criteria have been devised for countries wishing to enter the EMU, among others concerning national budget deficits, debts and currency stability. For several reasons, countries like Italy, Greece and Great Britain – just to name a few – are unlikely to be among the EC members that will form the core of vanguard nations within the European Union.

But the main bother will be the new role of Germany. Now that Germany has released itself from the burden of national partition, it has gained self-confidence and has become less dependent upon the cooperative attitude of other EC member states in order to achieve its foreign policy goals. For this reason the future of the traditional Paris-Bonn axis is in doubt; Germany no longer needs France in order to strengthen its case. Many West European observers have asked the crucial question whether a united Germany will still have the same interests in the European Community as the old Federal Republic?[17] As *The Economist* formulated it in March 1992: 'For decades Germans yearned for a united Europe as a semi-substitute for their own defeated, divided and occupied fatherland. They thought the aim so self-evident, in stark contrast to the British and to a lesser extent the French, that they really debated only the means. German unity has started to change that ... it is slowly waking up to the fact that it has more options than it used to.'[18] This concern that Bonn's commitment to the cause of European integration might gradually wane, is genuine and sensible. Germany will in the future perhaps have difficulties in relinquishing its newly found freedom in the foreign policy area, especially when German influence in the East will be enhanced. The Czechoslovak Minister of Foreign Affairs, Jiri Dienstbier, warned (in May 1990) that Germany might become the new regional hegemon: '[The vacuum in the East] will perhaps be filled soon economically by a strong united Germany, and in view of the glaring inequality to the detriment of the East European countries in economic respects, that filling could display undeniably neo-colonial traits'.[19] And, as Reinhard Rode pointed out: 'The picture of the Soviet communist hegemon could rapidly fade from sight in Eastern Europe, replaced by that of the market hegemon Germany. The dependence of these countries on Germany could in fact become very heavy. From the standpoint of a reborn nationalism, they could well criticize Germany either in the case of a "silent economic penetration" by German interests, or in the far worse case of being neglected by those interests.'[20]

There is also a certain *Angst* – or one could perhaps better say *Grande Peur* – that the renewed economic and political ties with Russia will result in a continuous upgrading of these countries' common interests. French analysts and high-ranking policy-makers in particular have hinted at the possible return of German-Russian concordance and the consequences this might have for the development of the EC. Michel Debré, former Prime Minister under de Gaulle, argued in November 1989: 'Against the background of current events and particularly the end of the Berlin Wall, we have to see the epoch that can be discerned for the future as that of a new Rapallo'.[21] The (former) French Defence Minister Jean-Pierre Chevènement, argued a few months later: 'There is an ancient understanding between the [German and Russian] peoples that has taken on various forms, from Catherine II to Bismarck. In our century there have been new examples of it: everyone will recall Rapallo or the Hitler-Stalin pact.'[22] Paradoxically, this fear of a German detachment from the EC will only increase Bonn's influence within the Community, which might in turn give rise to further concern of German dominance within Western Europe. In short, it is not difficult to envisage quite a number of inter-alliance conflicts which might occur, conflicts which will certainly present major challenges for the strength, vitality and flexibility of the institutional framework of the European Community.

The second option would be a policy of strong support and commitment to further integration within the EC. Among the current Twelve, France and the Benelux countries are especially likely to commit themselves full-heartedly to an expansion of the EC's power, mainly as a means to contain Germany. Strong support for the EC and the cause of European integration does, however, weaken one's bargaining position since other EC members will know that they can count on being supported, which will make them less influenceable and less likely to budge during an alliance conflict. Strong commitment will also foreclose a nation's options of realignment, whereas a strategy of weak commitment has the desirable consequence that the option of realignment is kept open.[23] This mechanism might prove especially advantageous for Great Powers like Germany and Great Britain (and in the future perhaps even France), who might threaten with abandonment and realignment in order to strengthen their bargaining position within the EC.

The central question is whether this Neo-realist account of the EC member states' options is a realistic one, or whether the Neo-liberal institutionalist analysis will hold? Or, as Michael Binyon formulated it in early 1990: 'Can 1992 survive the revolutions in Eastern Europe? Have the sudden changes and ... German unification thrown into disarray the Single Market programme and halted the momentum of West European integration?'[24] This question will be difficult to answer and there will be no quick and easy solutions to the problems which the European Community will face in the coming years. The existing frameworks of cooperation in Western Europe are valuable for achieving a minimum level of cooperation, and there is no doubt that western policy-makers are fully aware of the impact which these frameworks will have. The need to strengthen the existing institutions was among the topics most often discussed directly after the fall of the Berlin Wall. French President Mitterrand maintained in December 1989: 'it would be wise to develop, strengthen and accelerate the structures of the [European] Community before taking any further steps. The Community acted on most countries in the East that are on the road to freedom and democracy like a breakwater and a magnet. Had it not been there, things would not have happened the same way. There would have been a rapid approach to European anarchy, such as we knew before the 1914 War.'[25] Despite strains within the Community, the fact is generally acknowledged that the maintenance of the EC is of major importance for Europe's stability and prosperity. Abandonment of the EC-alliance will therefore not be probable in the near future, since all member states have come to realize that obstructing European integration within the EC would be extremely costly. As Arthur Stein has argued perceptively: 'The institution may be required again in the future, and destroying them because of short-term changes may be very costly in the long run. Institutional maintenance is not, then, a function of a waiving of calculation; it becomes a factor in the decision calculus that keeps short-term calculations from becoming decisive.'[26]

Although nothing can be said with much certainty, it is likely that the momentum of economic and political integration will be sustained, even without the necessary external incentives. However, integration will probably not go beyond the level which has most recently been achieved with the draft Maastricht Treaty. Recent problems with the ratification of the Maastricht Treaty in the member states, combined with the difficulties which are involved in coming to a Community budget for the mid-1990s, seem to support this statement. After the Danish decision to reject the Treaty on 2 June 1992, the eleven member states defiantly proclaimed their determination to press on with the ratification process. The Danish decision did, however, plunge the EC into a major and unprecedented constitutional crisis, putting just another question mark over its momentum behind further economic, monetary and political integration. After the dust had settled, it soon become clear that the integration process had to shift in a markedly lower gear. This resulted in increased emphasis on the principle of 'subsidiarity', an axiom indicating that the EC should only take action on issues which cannot be better and more effectively dealt with on a national (or sub-national) level. The half-hearted support of the French people in the referendum of 20 September, and the withdrawal of the British pound sterling from the ERM, have all added to the uncertainty concerning the future of the Maastricht Treaty.[27]

The Danish decision may also delay the entry of new members to the EC by preventing the accession negotiations with countries like Austria, Finland, Sweden and Switzerland which had been planned for January 1993. Since this 'first wave' of prospective EC members has now been delayed, this will also stall the entry of the Central European 'second wave'. This does nevertheless leave unimpeded the fact that further alignment of the Central European countries with the European Community is to be encouraged for the reasons we have spelled out above. However, the changes which this will require in the institutional arrangements of the Community, as well as the financial implications of enlargement, will provoke even more tensions within the EC.

Some of the problems which now keep European policy-makers awake at night closely resemble those which emerged after World War I and World War II. However, whereas the Europe of 1919 and 1946 was devoid of clear-cut frameworks of cooperation, Europe now has an institution which might be strong enough to contain the basic centrifugal tendencies of states. Under these circumstances, Neo-liberal institutionalist concepts – which are closely linked to the Grotian tradition of international society – are now more likely to apply to European politics than strict Neo-realist concepts, which start from the Hobbesian view of international politics as a state of war. In short: interstate cooperation in Europe and collaboration within the EC might be sustained, even without a Soviet threat and without United States' hegemony. This situation may remind us of the strange adventures of Alice in Wonderland, where the Cheshire cat's grin could be seen even when the cat itself had been long gone: '"Well! I've often seen a cat without a grin," thought Alice; "but a grin without a cat! It's the most curious thing I ever saw in all my life!"'

Notes

Notes to Chapter 1

1. Francis Fukuyama, 'The End of History?', *The National Interest*, no.16 (Summer 1989), and Fukuyama, *The End of History and the Last Man* (London: Hamish Hamilton, 1992).
2. Stanley Hoffmann, 'The Case for Leadership', *Foreign Policy*, no.81 (Winter 1990-1), p.20.
3. There have been several exceptions. For instance, EC member Ireland has not been a member of NATO, whereas CMEA member Romania has not fully participated within the Warsaw Pact. France has also not participated within the military structure of NATO since 1966.
4. Quoted in Robert S. Jordan and Werner J. Feld, *Europe in the Balance. The Changing Context of European International Politics* (London, Boston: Faber and Faber, 1986), p.80.
5. Robert O. Keohane and Stanley Hoffmann, 'Institutional Change in Europe in the 1980s', in Keohane and Hoffmann (eds.), *The New European Community. Decisionmaking and Institutional Change* (Boulder: Westview Press, 1991), pp.9, 10.
6. See Robert O. Keohane, *International Institutions and State Power. Essays in International Relations Theory* (Boulder: Westview Press, 1989), and Jack Snyder, 'Averting Anarchy in the New Europe', in Sean M. Lynn-Jones (ed.), *The Cold War and After. Prospects for Peace. An International Security Reader* (Cambridge, Mass.: The MIT Press, 1991). See also Joseph S. Nye, Jr., 'Neorealism and Neoliberalism', *World Politics*, vol.40, no.2 (1988).
7. Robert O. Keohane, *After Hegemony. Cooperation and Discord in the World Political Economy* (Princeton, NJ: Princeton University Press, 1984), p.14.
8. Ernst B. Haas, *The Uniting of Europe. Political, Social and Economic Forces, 1950-1957* (London: Stevens, 1958), and Leon N. Lindberg and Stuart A. Scheingold, *Europe's Would-Be Polity. Patterns of Change in the European Community* (Englewood Cliffs, NJ: Prentice-Hall, 1970).
9. Haas, *Uniting of Europe*, p.16.
10. See on this issue the articles by Michael Doyle, 'Kant, Liberal Legacies, and Foreign Affairs', *Philosophy and Public Affairs*, vol.12 (Summer and Fall 1983), and Doyle, 'Liberalism and World Politics', *American Political Science Review*, vol.80, no.4 (December 1986).
11. As Paul Taylor has argued in 1989: 'The student of the EC in the 1980s ... needs to return to the writings of a group of scholars – the neofunctionalists – whose writings have for many years been unfashionable'. See Paul

Taylor, 'The New Dynamics of EC Integration in the 1980s', in Juliet Lodge (ed.), *The European Community and the Challenge of the Future* (London: Pinter, 1989), p.23.

12. Waltz, *Theory of International Politics* (New York: McGraw-Hill, 1979), p. 72.

13. Waltz, *Theory of International Politics*, p.65.

14. Barry Buzan, Morton Kelstrup, Pierre Lemaitre, Elzbieta Tromer and Ole Wæver, *The European Security Order Recast. Scenarios for the Post-Cold War Era* (London: Pinter, 1990), p.13.

15. Waltz, *Theory of International Politics*, pp.70-1.

16. The classical study on collective action is Mancur Olson, *The Logic of Collective Action* (Cambridge, Mass.: Harvard University Press, 1963). Jon Elster has argued that a 'group has a collective action problem if it is better for all if some do it than if nobody does, but better for each not to do it. It may or may not be better for all if all do it than if nobody does. And it may or may not be best if all do it. To *cooperate* is to act against one's self-interest in a way that benefits all if some, or possibly all, act in that way.' Elster, *Nuts and Bolts for the Social Sciences* (Cambridge: Cambridge University Press, 1989), p.126.

17. Stephen D. Krasner, 'Structural Causes and Regime Consequences: Regimes as Intervening Variables', in Krasner (ed.), *International Regimes* (Ithaca and London: Cornell University Press, 1983), p.2.

18. See John Lewis Gaddis, *The Long Peace. Inquiries into the History of the Cold War* (New York: Oxford University Press, 1987).

19. In a more broader sense, the European Community makes up the prototype of what Hedley Bull and Adam Watson have labelled an 'international society', namely 'a group of states (or, more generally, a group of independent political communities) which not merely form a system, in the sense that the behaviour of each is a necessary factor in the calculations of the others, but also have established by dialogue and consent common rules and institutions for the conduct of their relations, and recognize their common interests in maintaining their arrangements'. H. Bull and A. Watson (eds.), *The Expansion of International Society* (Oxford: Oxford University Press, 1984), p.1.

20. Keohane, *After Hegemony*, p.13.

21. Keohane, *After Hegemony*, p.50.

22. Jack Snyder in Lynn-Jones (ed.), *Cold War and After*, p.106.

23. See Charles A. Kupchan and Clifford A. Kupchan, 'Concerts, Collective Security, and the Future of Europe', *International Security*, vol.16, no.1 (Summer 1991), pp.124-5.

24. John J. Mearsheimer, 'Back to the Future. Instability in Europe After the Cold War', in Lynn-Jones (ed.), *Cold War and After*, pp.142, 183-4.

25. Buzan *et al.*, *European Security* (1990), p.25.

26. Waltz, *Man, the State and War. A Theoretical Analysis* (New York: Columbia University Press, 1959), p.232.

27. Keohane and Hoffmann, *New Europe*, p.3.

28. Kenneth N. Waltz, 'Reflections on *Theory of International Politics*: A Response to my Critics', in R. Keohane (ed.), *Neorealism and Its Critics* (New York: Columbia University Press, 1986), pp.343-4.

Notes to Chapter 2

1. 'I pushed this [half-sheet of paper] across to Stalin, who had by then heard the translation. There was a slight pause. Then he took his blue pencil and made a large tick upon it, and passed it back to us. It was all settled in no more time than it takes to set down.' Winston Churchill, *Triumph and Tragedy* (Boston: Houghton Mifflin, 1953), pp.227-8.

2. It was agreed that 'the three governments will jointly assist the people in any European liberated state or former Axis satellite state in Europe where in their judgement conditions require (a) to establish conditions of internal peace; (b) to carry out emergency measures for the relief of distressed people; (c) to form interim governmental authorities broadly representative of all democratic elements in the population and pledged to the earliest possible establishment through free elections of governments responsive to the will of the people; and (d) to facilitate where necessary the holding of such elections'.

3. Bennett Kovrig, *The Myth of Liberation. East-Central Europe in U.S. Diplomacy and Politics Since 1941* (Baltimore and London: The Johns Hopkins University Press, 1973), p.5.

4. Quoted in Daniel Yergin, *Shattered Peace. The Origins of the Cold War and the National Security State* (Boston: Houghton Mifflin Company, 1977), p.63.

5. See Milovan Djilas, *Conversations With Stalin* (New York: Harcourt, Brace & World, Inc., 1962), p.114.

6. See for instance P. M. R. Stirk, 'The Preconditions of European Integration: Observations of the Years 1918-1945', in W. A. F. Camphuis and C. G. J. Wildeboer-Schut (eds.), *Europese Eenwording in Historisch Perspectief. Factoren van Integratie en Desintegratie* (Zaltbommel: Europese Bibliotheek, 1991).

7. Such as the Food and Agricultural Organization (1945), the Economic Commission of Europe (1947) and the World Health Organisation (1948). The ECE especially was of potential use. Its stated purpose was 'to initiate and participate in measures for facilitating concerted action for the economic reconstruction of Europe, for raising the level of European economic activity and for maintaining and strengthening the economic relations of the European countries both among themselves and other countries of the world'. The ECE has mainly played a role as one of the few forums for discussion on economic issues between East and West during the Cold War (see Chapter 7.2).

8. Stephen E. Ambrose, *Rise to Globalism. American Foreign Policy Since 1938* (Harmondsworth: Penguin Books, 1986), p.75.

9. Barbara Ann Chotiner and John W. Atwell, 'Soviet Occupation Policy Toward Germany, 1945-1949', in Hans A. Schmitt (ed.), *U.S. Occupation in Europe After World War II* (Lawrence: Regents Press of Kansas, 1978), p.50.

10. For an analysis of these changing attitudes on the basis of shifting belief systems, see Deborah Welch Larson, *Origins of Containment. A Psychological Explanation* (Princeton, NJ: Princeton University Press, 1985).

11. Max Beloff, *The United States and the Unity of Europe*, (London: Faber and Faber, 1963), pp.3-4.
12. *Ibid.*
13. Quoted in John W. Young, *Britain, France and the Unity of Europe. 1945-1951* (Leicester: Leicester University Press, 1984), p.37.
14. See for commentary on the latter documents: Frank Roberts, *Dealing With Dictators. The Destruction and Revival of Europe 1930-70* (London: Weidenfeld & Nicolson, 1991), especially Chapter 14. For a general overview of the major American documents, see Th. H. Etzold and J. L. Gaddis (eds.), *Containment: Documents on American Policy and Strategy. 1945-1950* (New York: Columbia University Press, 1978).
15. J. M. Jones, *The Fifteen Weeks (February 21–June 5, 1947)* (New York: Harcourt, Brace & World, 1955), pp.221-2.
16. Ernst H. van der Beugel, *From Marshall Aid to Atlantic Partnership. European Integration as a Concern of American Foreign Policy* (Amsterdam, London, New York: Elsevier Publishing Company, 1966), p.56.
17. Quoted in Richard Mayne, *The Recovery of Europe. From Devastation to Unity* (London: Weidenfeld and Nicolson, 1970), pp.110-12, 133. Later Zhdanov argued: 'The expansionist efforts of the USA are carried out today in the Truman doctrine and the Marshall plan. Though they differ in form, both documents are actually the expression of the same policy, that is to say in both documents one and the same American claim to the enslaving of Europe is presented.' Quoted in Max Jansen and Johan K. de Vree, *The Ordeal of Unity. The Politics of European Integration Since 1945* (Bilthoven: Prime Press, 1988), p.68.
18. Quoted in Walter L. Hixson, *George F. Kennan. Cold War Iconoclast* (New York: Columbia University Press, 1989), p.55. See also Van der Beugel, *From Marshall Aid to Atlantic Partnership*, p.43.
19. George F. Kennan, 'The Marshall Plan and the Future of Europe', *Transatlantic Perspectives*, no.17 (Winter 1988), p.5.
20. Paul-Henri Spaak, *The Continuing Battle. Memoirs of a European 1936-1966* (London: Weidenfeld and Nicolson, 1971), p.191.
21. Mayne, *The Recovery of Europe*, p.113.
22. Michael J. Hogan, *The Marshall Plan. America, Britain, and the Reconstruction of Western Europe, 1947-1952* (Cambridge: Cambridge University Press, 1987), p.427.
23. Van der Beugel similarly argues that 'From the moment of the launching of the Marshall Plan, it became apparent that European integration was a major objective of American foreign policy ... It pursued this aim primarily within the framework of its stand against communist aggression.' *From Marshall Aid to Atlantic Partnership*, p.215.
24. Karl W. Deutsch, S. A. Burrell *et al.*, *Political Community and the North Atlantic Area* (Princeton, NJ: Princeton University Press, 1957), p.5.
25. Adam Ulam, *Expansion and Coexistence* (New York: Praeger, 1968), p.447.
26. Quoted in Gunnar Adler-Karlsson, *Western Economic Warfare, 1947-1967* (Stockholm: Almquist and Wicksell, 1968), p.158.
27. William Diebold, Jr., 'East-West Trade and the Marshall Plan', *Foreign Affairs*, vol.26, no.4 (July 1948), p.717. Diebold himself still thought that

Moscow would not yet be prepared to stop East-West trade, since this would have major repercussions for East-West political relations.

28. Diebold, Jr., 'East-West Trade', p.713.
29. See Joseph Rothschild, *Return to Diversity. A Political History of East Central Europe Since World War II* (New York: Oxford University Press, 1989), p.96.
30. Apart from the early years, Cominform has never had much influence in European politics and was brought to a quiet end by Khrushchev, in 1956.
31. Quoted in Mayne, *The Recovery of Europe*, p.133.
32. Resolution of the Political Commission of the Congress of Europe, The Hague. Reprinted in S. Patijn (ed.), *Landmarks in European Unity. 22 Texts on European Integration* (Leyden: A. W. Sijthoff, 1970), pp.36-41.
33. Hungarian membership of the Council of Europe, in 1990, was generally considered the first and necessary step to 'join Europe', and also towards a much desired future entry into the European Community.
34. In 1961, the OEEC was transformed to become the Organisation for Economic Co-operation and Development (OECD). European countries were joined by the United States and Canada as full members, as well as by the European Community as an 'observer'.
35. Lincoln Gordon, 'The Organization for European Economic Cooperation', *International Organization*, vol.10, no.11 (February 1956).
36. Leon Hurwitz, *The European Community and the Management of International Cooperation* (New York: Greenwood Press, 1987), p.14.
37. In October 1949, the newly established Federal Republic of Germany (FRG) entered the OEEC.
38. See Joris J. C. Voorhoeve, *Peace, Profits and Principles. A Study of Dutch Foreign Policy* (Leiden: Martinus Nijhoff, 1985), pp.153-72.
39. Halvard M. Lange, 'European Union: False Hopes and Realities', *Foreign Affairs*, vol.28, no.3 (April 1950) p.441. Walter Hallstein argued at the same time that 'Der entscheidende Grund für die Überlegenheit anderer Wirtschaftsräume, die nach Menschenzahl und Produktionskapazität mit Kontinentaleuropa vergleichbar sind, zeigt, daß, was uns mangelt, ein großer einheitlicher Binnenmarkt ist, wie er bei den Amerikaner und den Sowjetrussen vorhanden ist'. Hallstein, *Europäische Reden* (Stuttgart: Deutsche Verlags-Anstalt, 1979), p.104.
40. Paul Reynaud, 'The Unifying Force for Europe', *Foreign Affairs*, vol.28, no.2 (January 1950), p.257.
41. Paul-Henri Spaak, 'The Integration of Europe: Dreams and Realities', *Foreign Affairs*, vol.29, no.1 (October 1950), p.99.
42. The speech of Schuman is quoted in Patijn (ed.), *Landmarks in European Unity*, pp.47-53.
43. Simon Bulmer and William Paterson, *The Federal Republic of Germany and the European Community* (London: Allen & Unwin, 1987), p.6.
44. Waltz, *Theory of International Politics*, p.71.
45. Anthony Eden, *Full Circle* (London: Cassell, 1960), p.363.
46. Waltz, *Theory of International Politics*, p.171.
47. Quoted in Arnold J. Zurcher, *The Struggle to Unite Europe. 1940-58* (New York: New York University Press, 1958), p.6.

48. Bronislaw Geremek has also argued that 'Our return to Europe means a return to freedom and democracy'. Quoted in Bronislaw Geremek, Ivan Klima, and György Konrád, *Warschau – Praag – Boedapest. Hoe Cultuur Overleefde* (Rotterdam: Universitaire Pers Rotterdam, 1990), p.20.

Notes to Chapter 3

1. See Arie Bloed, *The External Relations of the Council for Mutual Economic Assistance* (Dordrecht: Martinus Nijhoff, 1988), Chapter 2.
2. Peter Calvocoressi, *World Politics Since 1945* (New York: Longman, 1982), p.123.
3. See for an argument that the CMEA has been an instrument of Soviet hegemony: Werner Gumpel, 'Der Rat für Gegenseitige Wirtschaftshilfe als Instrument sowjetischer Hegemonie', *Osteuropa*, vol.26, no.11 (November 1976).
4. Quoted in Peter Marsh, 'The Integration Process in Eastern Europe 1968 to 1975', *Journal of Common Market Studies*, vol.14, no.4 (June 1976), p.333. Jansen and De Vree have also maintained that the establishment of 'the Warsaw Pact and the greater rôle of Comecon in Eastern Europe since about the middle fifties reflected a relative weakening of the Soviet Union, or strengthening of the East European countries, rather than the other way around'. Jansen and De Vree, *Ordeal of Unity*, p.71.
5. See Reynaud, 'The Unifying Force for Europe', p.256.
6. Quoted in Bloed, *External Relations of the CMEA*, pp.478.
7. Quoted in Philip J. Funigiello, *American-Soviet Trade in the Cold War* (Chapel Hill and London: The University of North Carolina Press, 1988), p.38.
8. Hendrik Roodbeen, *Trading the Jewel of Great Value. The Participation of The Netherlands, Belgium, Switzerland and Austria in the Western Strategic Embargo*, unpublished Ph.D. thesis, Department of Political Science, Leiden University (January 1992).
9. See Adler-Karlsson, *Western Economic Warfare* (1968); Funigiello, *American-Soviet Trade*; and Marie-Hélène Labbé and Peter van Ham, 'The West European Approach Towards COCOM', in Gary K. Bertsch, Heinrich Vogel, and Jan Zielonka (eds.), *After the Revolutions. East-West Trade and Technology Transfer in the 1990s* (Boulder: Westview Press, 1991).
10. Marshall D. Shulman, 'The Communist States and Western Integration', *International Organization*, vol.17, no.2 (1963), p.660.
11. See Christopher Layton, 'Europe, Road to Co-existence', *Journal of Common Market Studies*, vol.3, no.3 (1964-5), p.274, and Werner J. Feld (ed.), *The Foreign Policies of West European Socialist Parties* (New York: Praeger Publishers, 1978).
12. Dennis Healey, MP, 'The Crisis in Europe', *International Affairs* (London) vol.38, no.2 (April 1962), p.145. Although clearly not rejecting West European integration, Charles Ransom has argued that 'It is reasonable to assume that the more closely co-ordinated the EEC states

become the more likely it is that the Eastern states will respond by presenting a common front, inevitably dominated by the USSR, but the member-states of the EEC are unlikely to allow their internal policies and objectives to be determined to any major degree by considerations of their possible effects upon the organisation and policies of Eastern Europe'. *The European Community and Eastern Europe*, p.97. Similar arguments were aired as late as 1986. Then Günther Gaus argued that the EC was 'the pillar on which the western part of the European divide is based', and that Brussels was practising 'European division-politics'. Quoted in Gerd Langguth, 'Deutschland, die EG und die Architektur Europas', *Aussenpolitik*, vol.42, no.2 (1991), p.136.

13. Quoted in Neill Nugent, *The Government and Politics of the European Community* (London: Macmillan, 1989), p.32.

14. See Howard Bliss (ed.), *The Political Development of the European Community. A Documentary Collection* (Waltham, Mass.: Blaisdell, 1970), p.43.

15. See, for example, Jansen and De Vree, *Ordeal of Unity*, p.117.

16. See W. W. Kulski, *De Gaulle and the World. The Foreign Policy of the Fifth French Republic* (Syracuse, New York: Syracuse University Press, 1966), p.29.

17. De Gaulle's interest in political union among the Six resulted in the report of the so-called Fouchet Committee (November 1961), which aimed at the adoption of a common foreign policy and the strengthening of the security arrangements of the member states.

18. See *Die Auswärtige Politik der Bundesrepublik Deutschland* (Köln: Verlag Wissenschaft und Politik, 1972), p.30.

19. Schreiben des Bundeskanzlers Dr. Konrad Adenauer an die Bundesminister vom 19. Januar 1956. *Auswärtige Politik der Bundesrepublik*, pp.317-8.

20. Quoted in Wolfram F. Hanrieder, *Germany, America, Europe. Forty Years of German Foreign Policy* (New Haven and London: Yale University Press, 1989), p.153.

21. *Ibid.*

22. Spaak, *Continuing Battle*, pp.157,159.

23. Jansen and De Vree, *Ordeal of Unity*, p.132.

24. Quoted in Bennett Kovrig, *Of Walls and Bridges. The United States and Eastern Europe* (New York: New York University Press, 1991), pp.67-8.

25. Commission des Questions de Politique Commerciale, Rapport au Conceil de Ministres (Deuxième session du Conseil), Luxembourg, le 29 Novembre 1952. *European Community Archives*, CEAB 5, no.77.

26. Quoted in Kovrig, *The Myth of Liberation*, pp.156-7.

27. Quoted in Kovrig, *Walls and Bridges*, p.94.

28. *The New York Times*, 27 October 1956.

29. *The New York Times*, 28 October 1956.

30. *The New York Times*, 2 November 1956.

31. *The New York Times*, 27 October 1956.

32. See the letter of the High Authority (Personnel Department), 15 February 1958. *European Community Archives*, CEAB 12, no.450.

33. *The New York Times*, 4 November 1956.
34. Michel Tatu, 'East-West Relations', in Max Kohnstamm and Wolfgang Hager (eds.), *A Nation Writ Large? Foreign-Policy Problems Before the European Community* (London: Macmillan, 1973), p.182.
35. For a short overview of the underestimated role of J. W. Beyen, see H. Ermers and J. Kragt, 'Tussen traditie en Tractaten: Minister Beyen van Buitenlandse Zaken en de Europese Integratie', *Internationale Spectator*, vol.45, no.5 (Mei 1991).
36. Quoted in Hurwitz, *European Community*, p.29.
37. Quoted in R. C. Mowat, *Creating the European Community* (New York: Basic Books, 1973), p.131.
38. D. Lasok and J. W. Bridge, *Law and Institutions of the European Communities* (London: Butterworths, 1991), p.17.
39. G. L. Goodwin, 'A European Community Foreign Policy?', *Journal of Common Market Studies*, vol.12, no.1 (September 1973), p.10.
40. Urwin, *Western Europe Since 1945*, p.247.
41. Richard Mayne, *The Recovery of Europe. From Devastation to Unity* (London: Weidenfeld and Nicolson, 1970), p.242.
42. Carl J. Friedrich, *Europe. An Emerging Nation?* (New York and Evanston: Harper & Row, 1969), p.25. Zbigniew Brzezinski's remark that 'If the basic European motivation in the late forties can be said to have been fear of Soviet aggression, in the early sixties it was self-confidence', also goes a long way in explaining the process of West European integration at that time. Brzezinski, 'Russia and Europe', *Foreign Affairs*, vol.42, no.3 (April 1964), p.437.
43. For a general discussion of these concepts, see John Pinder, 'Positive Integration and Negative Integration: Some Problems of Economic Union in the EEC', *The World Today*, vol.24 (1968), pp.88-110.
44. Stanley Hoffmann, 'Obstinate or Obsolete? The Fate of the Nation-State and the Case of Western Europe', *Dædalus*, vol.95, no.3 (Summer 1966), p.866.

Notes to Chapter 4

1. Article 6 of the ECSC Treaty stated that 'in international relations the Community shall enjoy the legal capacity it requires to perform its functions and attain its objectives'. The EEC and the Euratom Treaties also state that the Communities have legal personality.
2. See Lenin's pamphlet *Imperialism, the Highest Stage of Capitalism* (1916), and his *On the Slogan of the United States of Europe* (1915). See also David F. P. Forte, 'The Response of Soviet Foreign Policy to the Common Market, 1957-63', *Soviet Studies*, vol.19, no.3 (1968), p.374.
3. I. Lemin, 'Crisis of West European Integration and Its Political Aspects', *International Affairs* (Moscow), no.5 (May 1966), p.40.
4. How far Soviet political leaders and academic observers have had access to objective information on the economic and political developments in Western Europe is hard to assess. One must, however, not be overly

optimistic. Milovan Djilas once referred to the following anecdote: When one Yugoslav Party official (Edvard Kardelj) remarked to Stalin that West European customs unions had met with some success, the Soviet leader asked: 'For example?' 'Well, for example, Benelux,' Kardelj said cautiously. 'Here Belgium, Holland, and Luxembourg joined together.'

Stalin: 'No, Holland didn't. Only Belgium and Luxembourg. That's nothing, insignificant.'

Kardelj: 'No, Holland is included too.'

Stalin stubbornly: 'No, Holland is not.'

Stalin looked at Molotov, at Zorin, at the rest. I had the desire to explain to him that the syllable *ne* in the name Benelux came from the Netherlands, that is, the original designation for Holland, but since everyone kept still, I did too, and so it remained that Holland was not in the Benelux.' In M. Djilas, *Conversations With Stalin*, p.181.

5. Alfred Zauberman, 'The Soviet Bloc and the Common Market', *The World Today*, vol.19 (January 1963).

6. Shulman, 'Communist States and Western Integration', p.660.

7. Quoted in Gordon L. Weil, *A Foreign Policy For Europe? The External Relations of the European Community* (Bruges: College of Europe, 1970), p.40.

8. K. Petrov, 'Political Integration in Western Europe', *International Affairs* (Moscow), no.11 (November 1969), p.15.

9. The example of the EC had been imitated by several sub-regional groupings in the Third World, i.e. the Latin American Free Trade Association, the Central American Common Market, and the East African Economic Community. See on this issue Sidney Dell, *A Latin American Common Market?* (London: Oxford University Press, 1966), and Peter Robson, *Economic Integration in Africa* (London: Allen & Unwin, 1968).

10. Hans J. Morgenthau (with Kenneth W. Thompson), *Politics Among Nations. The Struggle For Power and Peace* (sixth edition, New York: Alfred A. Knopf, 1985), pp.198-9.

11. See Gerhard Wettig, 'Germany, Europe, and the Soviets', in Herbert J. Ellison (ed.), *Soviet Policy Toward Western Europe. Implications for the Atlantic Alliance* (Seattle and London: University of Washington Press, 1983), and Edwina Moreton (ed.), *Germany Between East and West* (Cambridge: Cambridge University Press, 1987).

12. Lemin, 'West European Integration', p.45.

13. D. Andreyev and M. Makov, 'The Common Market After Eleven Years', *International Affairs* (Moscow), no.1 (January 1969), p.49.

14. I. Chelnokov, 'The European Coal and Steel Community', *International Affairs* (Moscow), no.2 (February 1957), p.95.

15. Lemin, 'Western Integration', p.48.

16. *The Times*, 10 February 1967.

17. See 'Soviet Proposals for All-European Economic Cooperation', *International Affairs* (Moscow) no.4 (April 1957).

18. Quoted in Jansen and De Vree, *Ordeal of Unity*, p.272.

19. Iver B. Neumann, *Soviet Perceptions of the European Community, 1950-1988*, Norsk Utenrikspolitisk Institutt, NUPI Rapport, no.131

(July 1989), esp. pp.44-8. See also Forte, 'Soviet Foreign Policy', pp.375-6.

20. *Die Kommunisten und der Gemeinsame Markt* (Köln: Europa Union Verlag GmbH, 1968), p.18.

21. See Heinz Koehler, *Economic Integration in the Soviet Bloc* (New York: Praeger, 1965).

22. Article 238 of the Treaty of Rome stipulates that the EEC 'may conclude with a third country, a union of States, or an international organization agreements creating an association embodying reciprocal rights and obligations, joint actions and special procedures'. For an early analysis of the EEC's association policy, see Weil, *A Foreign Policy for Europe?*, Chapters 4, 5, 7, 8 and 9.

23. 'The Disorganizers of International Trade' (Editorial), *International Affairs* (Moscow), no.1 (January 1964), p.71.

24. Forte, 'Soviet Foreign Policy', p.379.

25. N. S. Khrushchev, 'Vital Questions of the Development of the World Socialist System', *Kommunist*, no.12 (1962). The complete translated text can be found in H. Hanak, *Soviet Foreign Policy Since the Death of Stalin* (London and Boston: Routledge & Kegan Paul, 1972), pp.191-203.

26. Vladislav Pavidt, 'Die westeuropäische Integration aus tschecho-slowakischer Sicht', in Hans Mayrzedt and Helmut Romé (eds.), *Die Westeuropäische Integration aus osteuropäischer Sicht. Bibliographie – Dokumentation – Kommentar* (Wien: Druck und Verlag Josef Laub, 1968), pp.130-2.

27. Forte, 'Soviet Foreign Policy', pp.381-2.

28. Peter Marsh, 'The Development of Relations Between the EEC and the CMEA', in Avi Shlaim and G. N. Yannopoulos, (eds.), *The EEC and Eastern Europe* (Cambridge: Cambridge University Press, 1978), p.27.

29. Neil McInnes once noted the legend that the USSR decided to live with the Common Market and has given orders to the Western Communists to work within the European institutions, in order to build some sort of supranational *socialist* state. See McInnes, 'The Communist Parties of Western Europe and the EEC', *The World Today*, vol.30 (February 1974), p.80.

30. See A. J. K. Webb, 'The Evolution of the Attitude of the Italian Communist Party Towards the European Economic Community', *Millennium: Journal of International Studies*, vol.13, no.1 (Spring 1984), pp.48-9, and H. Timmerman, 'Die italienischen Kommunisten und ihre außenpolitische Konzeption. Ein Jugoslawien des Westens?', *Europa-Archiv*, no.21 (1971). That the Soviet leaders did not give up their efforts to hamper West European integration became clear when Khrushchev suggested to the Italian Minister of Foreign Affairs (Summer 1964) that Rome should expand its trade with the East and leave the EEC. He argued that economic integration of West European states was contrary to nature, since their economic structures were similar. See Rolf Sannwald, 'Die sowjetischen Ansichten über die europäische Integration', in Mayrzedt and Romé (eds.), *Westeuropäische Integration*, p.127.

31. John Maslen, 'The European Community's Relations with the State-Trading Countries 1981-1983', in F. G. Jacobs (ed.), *Yearbook of European Law* (Oxford: Clarendon Press, 1984), p.330.
32. Charles F. G. Ransom, 'The Common Market and Eastern Europe', in Peter Stingelin (ed.), *The European Community and the Outsiders* (Don Mills, Ontario: Longman Canada Ltd., 1973), p.142.
33. Quoted in *Die Kommunisten und der Gemeinsame Markt*, p.19. The Hungarian Prime Minister, Jenö Fock, argued that his country was in principle willing to take up relations with the EEC, mainly because Hungary was losing millions of dollars due to the Community tariffs. *Frankfurter Allgemeine Zeitung*, 26 February 1968.
34. Forte, 'Soviet Foreign Policy', p.385.
35. See George Schöpflin, 'The EEC and Eastern Europe', *European Community* (London), no.10 (October 1968), p.3.
36. Bonn broke off diplomatic relations with Yugoslavia in 1957, when Tito had decided formally to recognize the GDR.
37. *Le Monde*, 25 May 1965.
38. *Die Welt*, 27-28 May 1965.
39. *Pravda*, 6 March 1968. Translated in *Current Digest of the Soviet Press* (hereafter *CDSP*), vol.20, no.12, p.3.
40. Miriam Camps, *Britain and the European Community 1955-1963* (Princeton, NJ: Princeton University Press, 1964).
41. Quoted in Neumann, *Soviet Perceptions* (1989), p.50.
42. *Ibid*, p.51.
43. Quoted in Jansen and De Vree, *Ordeal of Unity*, pp.197-8.
44. Zinovev, 'Der Widerspruchsknoten hat sich noch fester zugezogen', *TASS*, 30.1.63. Quoted (in German) in Johann Karat, 'Sowjetunion und Europäische Gemeinschaften', *Aussenpolitik*, vol.23, no.7 (1972), p.396.
45. See Uwe Kitzinger, *Diplomacy and Persuasion. How Britain Joined the Common Market* (London: Thames and Hudson, 1973), and Kitzinger, *Britain and the EEC. Past and Present* (London: Macmillan, 1983).
46. *Izvestia*, 13 November 1969. *CDSP*, vol.21, no.46, p.7.
47. N. Yuryev, 'Economic Integration and Western Blocs', *International Affairs* (Moscow), no.10 (October 1971), p.44.
48. *Izvestia*, 21 March 1971, *CDSP*, vol.22, no.12, p.20.
49. Marsh, 'Integration Process', p.315.
50. Charles Ransom also argued: 'The early successes of the EEC most probably encouraged the revitalization of CMEA in the mid-1950's and has perhaps helped to inspire the new approach to integration within that organization'. Ransom, 'The Common Market and Eastern Europe', p.157.
51. Hannes Adomeit, 'Soviet Perceptions of Western European Integration: Ideological Distortion or Realistic Assessment?', *Millennium: Journal of International Studies*, vol.8, no.1 (Spring 1979), p.6.
52. Michael Kaser, *Comecon* (London: Oxford University Press, 1965), pp.75-6, 93.
53. *Nepszabadzag*, 24 February 1968. Quoted in Frans A. M. Alting von Geusau, *Beyond the European Community* (Leyden: A. W. Sijthoff, 1969), p.149.

54. A Polish journal argued, in August 1971, that the West European integration process 'means that a speeding up of the rate of our integration is not only in the interest of the socialist countries alone but also in the interest of economic equilibrium in Europe as a whole, so that the two large community areas should develop more or less side by side and could establish between each other, natural and even necessary ties of trade and co-operation'. Quoted in Marsh, 'The Development of Relations Between the EEC and the CMEA', p.34.

55. Werner Feld, 'The Utility of the EEC Experience for Eastern Europe', *Journal of Common Market Studies*, vol.8, no.3 (1969-70), pp.254-6.

56. *Comprehensive Programme for the Further Extension and Improvement of Co-operation and the Development of Socialist Integration by the CMEA Member-Countries*, CMEA Secretariat, Moscow, 1971.

57. Quoted in Marsh, 'Integration Process', p.323.

58. Quoted in Ransom, 'The Common Market', p.147.

59. *Pravda*, 21 March 1972. In late December 1972, Brezhnev remarked on this similar topic: 'Is it possible to find a basis for some form of business relations between these intergovernmental trade and economic organizations now existing in Europe – between the CMEA and the Common Market? The answer is probably yes, if the states that are members of the Common Market refrain from all attempts at discrimination against the other side and if they promote the development of national bilateral ties and all-European cooperation.' *Pravda*, 22 December 1972.

Notes to Chapter 5

1. See on this issue Peter van Ham, *Western Doctrines on East-West Trade. Theory, History and Policy* (New York: St. Martin's Press, 1992).

2. See Lasok and Bridge, *Law and Institutions*, p.449.

3. Haas, *Uniting of Europe*, p.311.

4. Haas, *Uniting of Europe*, pp.234, 283-317.

5. P. Robson, *The Economics of International Integration* (London: Allen & Unwin, 1987), p.13.

6. Lasok and Bridge, *Law and Institutions*, p.453.

7. Gerold Schmidt, 'Vollendung der Gemeinsamen Handelspolitik', *Aussenpolitik*, vol.24, no.4 (1973), pp.395-6.

8. Weil, *Foreign Policy For Europe?*, p.275.

9. Ransom, *The European Community and Eastern Europe*, p.38.

10. See Carl A. Ehrhardt, 'EWG und die Koordinierung des Osthandels', *Aussenpolitik*, vol.16, no.6 (Juni 1965).

11. Weil, *Foreign Policy For Europe?*, p.276.

12. See for instance the communication between the Italian negotiator A. Cattani and the EEC Commission on the Italian-Soviet and Italian-Polish Agreements, February 1961. *European Community Archives*, BDT 056/1980, LIB 235.

13. See for a good overview on this issue, Francis Sarre, 'Article 115 EEC Treaty and Trade with Eastern Europe', *Intereconomics*, vol.23, no.5 (September/October 1988), pp.233-40.

14. See *Handelsblatt*, 15 November 1954. See also the communication between the Royal Dutch Hoogovens N.V. and the ECSC High Authority of that year, *European Community Archives*, CEAB 4, no.480.

15. See Peter Coffey, *The External Economic Relations of the EEC* (London: Macmillan, 1976), pp.8-14.

16. Weil, *Foreign Policy for Europe?*, p.288.

17. The FRG had the Hermes Versicherungen, France the Coface (Compagnie Française pour le Commerce Extérieur), the United Kingdom the Export Credit Guarantee Department, Belgium the Office National du Ducroire, the Netherlands the Nederlandse Credietverzekeringsmaatschappij, and Italy the Instituto Mobiliare Italiano.

18. See Georges Sokoloff, *The Economy of Detente. The Soviet Union and Western Capital* (Leamington Spa: Berg, 1987).

19. Stent, *From Embargo to Ostpolitik*, p.147.

20. Council Decision of 14-15 May 1962.

21. See Ransom, *The European Community and Eastern Europe*, p.40.

22. *European Community Information Bulletin*, 'The E.E.C. and East-West Relations' (June 1971).

23. In the early-1970s, the price of oil quadrupled and large sums (an estimated US$ 70 billion in 1974 alone) were transferred from the western countries to the oil producing states. These so-called 'petrodollars' were recycled primarily through the western private banks, who in turn financed many a project in Eastern Europe and the USSR.

24. J. Wilczynski, 'Financial Relations between the EEC and the CMEA', in Shlaim and Yannopoulos (eds.), *EEC and Eastern Europe*, p.197.

25. Jacques Groothaert, 'Financial Cooperation and Countertrade', in Marc Maresceau (ed.), *The Political and Legal Framework of Trade Relations Between the European Community and Eastern Europe* (Dordrecht: Martinus Nijhoff, 1989), pp.228-9.

26. Quoted in Peter Marsh, 'Relations between the EEC and CMEA', p.43.

27. *Official Journal of the European Communities*, (hereafter *OJ*), No. C 268, 22 November 1975.

28. See Susan Senior Nello, *The New Europe. Changing Economic Relations Between East and West* (New York: Harvester Wheatsheaf, 1991), p.67.

29. Groothaert, 'Financial Cooperation', p.229.

30. For a theoretical examination of these problems, see Kenneth A. Oye (ed.), *Cooperation Under Anarchy* (Princeton NJ: Princeton University Press, 1986).

31. Joseph Grieco, 'Anarchy and the Limits of Cooperation. A Realist Critique of the Newest Liberal Institutionalism', *International Organization*, vol.42, no.3 (Summer 1988), p.498.

32. Keohane, *International Institutions*, p.10.

33. John Pinder, 'Soviet Views of Western Economic Integration', in Avi Shlaim and G. N. Yannopoulos (eds.), *The EEC and Eastern Europe* (Cambridge: Cambridge University Press, 1978), p.108.

34. See Article 39 of the Treaty of Rome.

35. Joan Pearce, 'The Common Agricultural Policy: The Accumulation of Special Interests', in Wallace, Wallace and Webb (eds.), *Policy-Making in the European Community*, pp.146-50.

36. See the Löhr Report, *European Parliament*, 22 March 1965, Doc.10.
37. Rudolf Morawitz, 'Der innerdeutsche Handel und die EWG nach dem Grundvertrag', *Europa-Archiv*, vol.28, no.10 (1973).
38. George, *Politics and Policy in the European Community*, p.115.
39. Alting von Geusau, *Beyond the European Community*, p.154.
40. EEC Council Regulation 109/70. 19 December 1969, *OJ*, 1970 L 19.
41. Christoph Sasse, 'Kooperationsabkommen und EG-Handelspolitik. Parallelität oder Konflikt', *Europa-Archiv*, vol.29, no.20 (1974).
42. EEC Council Decision 74/393, 22 July 1974. *OJ*, 1974 L 208.
43. See the Klepsch Report on EC relations with East European countries and CMEA, *EP* 425/74.
44. Article 91 of the Treaty of Rome authorizes the Commission to investigate allegations of dumping, which is generally defined as the exporting of products to foreign markets for sale at low prices, for instance in order to capture a new market, or to maintain high prices at home.
45. Lasok and Bridge, *Law and Institutions*, p.454.
46. See Francis Jacobs, 'Anti-Dumping Procedures with regard to Imports from Eastern Europe', in Maresceau (ed.), *The Political and Legal Framework*, pp.291-2.
47. See R. Denton, 'The Non-Market Economy Rules of the European Community's Anti-Dumping and Countervailing Duties Legislation', *International and Comparative Law Quarterly*, vol.36 (1987), and P. Vandoren, 'Mise en Oeuvre de la Politique Anti-dumping de la CEE contre les Importations en Provenance des Pays à Commerce d'État', *Revue du Marché Commun*, no.316 (April 1988).
48. Quoted in Jacobs, 'Anti-dumping Procedures', p.303. See also Council Regulation 864/87, *OJ* L 83, 27 March 1987, p.4.
49. Senior Nello, *The New Europe*, p.60.
50. See Carole Webb, 'Theoretical Perspectives and Problems', in Wallace, Wallace and Webb (eds.), *Policy-Making in the European Community*, p.17.
51. J. S. Nye, 'Transnational and Transgovernmental Relations', in G. L. Goodwin and A. Linklater (eds.), *New Dimensions of World Politics* (London: Croom Helm, 1975), and R. O. Keohane and J. S. Nye (eds.), *Transnational Relations and World Politics* (Cambridge: Cambridge University Press, 1971).
52. See for a forceful analysis, Richard Haass, 'The Primacy of the State ... or Revising the Revisionists', *Dædalus*, vol.108, no.4 (Fall 1979).
53. Quoted in Richard N. Cooper, 'Trade Policy is Foreign Policy', *Foreign Policy*, no.9 (Winter 1972-3), p.32.

Notes to Chapter 6

1. De Gaulle preferred setting up a political and defence organization *outside* the EC and NATO framework. Since such a new political structure was expected to circumvent the authority of the EC, as well as

weaken the United States' influence in Western Europe and harm NATO, both the FRG and the Benelux countries disapproved of de Gaulle's ideas.

2. Quoted in Jansen and De Vree, *Ordeal of Unity*, p.181.

3. For a brief overview of the process of political cooperation within the EC, see William Wallace, 'Political Cooperation: Integration Through Inter-governmentalism', in Wallace, Wallace and Webb (eds.), *Policy-Making in the European Community*. See also A. E. Pijpers, E. Regelsberger and W. Wessels (eds.), *European Political Cooperation in the 1980s. A Common Foreign Policy for Western Europe?* (Dordrecht: Martinus Nijhoff, 1988).

4. Nugent, *The Government and Politics of the European Community* (London: Macmillan, 1989), p.211.

5. Michel Tatu, 'East-West Relations', p.167.

6. John Pinder, 'A Community Policy Towards Eastern Europe', *The World Today*, vol.30 (March 1974), p.120.

7. A. Wolfers, *Discord and Collaboration. Essays on International Politics* (Baltimore and London: The Johns Hopkins University Press, 1962), pp.67-80, p.74.

8. See Guy de Carmoy, *The Foreign Policies of France, 1944-1968* (Chicago: University of Chicago Press, 1970), and D. Bahu-Leyser, *De Gaulle, les Français et l'Europe* (Paris: Presses Universitaires de France, 1981).

9. Hassner, 'The View From Paris', in Lincoln Gordon (ed.), *Eroding Empire. Western Relations with Eastern Europe* (Washington, DC: The Brookings Institution, 1987), p.189.

10. Anne-Marie LeGloannec, 'France's German Problem', in F. Stephen Larrabee (ed.), *The Two German States and European Security* (London: Macmillan, 1989).

11. Hassner, 'West European Perceptions of the USSR', *Dædalus*, vol.108, no.1 (Winter 1979), p.124.

12. See on this issue also Renata Fritsch-Bournazel, 'Frankreich. Osthandel im Spannungsfeld von Ideologie und wirtschaftlichem Zwang', in Reinhard Rode and Hanns-D. Jacobsen (eds.), *Wirtschaftskrieg oder Entspannung. Eine politische Bilanz der Ost-West Wirtschafts-beziehungen* (Bonn: Verlag Neue Gesellschaft, 1984).

13. Quoted in Zbigniew Brzezinski, 'The Soviet Bloc, the Common Market and France', in Sydney Nettleton Fisher (ed.), *France and the European Community* (n.p.: Ohio State University Press, 1964), p.157.

14. Robert Legvold, 'France and Soviet Policy', in Herbert J. Ellison (ed.), *Soviet Policy Toward Western Europe. Implications for the Atlantic Alliance* (Seattle and London: University of Washington Press, 1983), p.67.

15. Morgenthau, *Politics Among Nations*, pp.158-9.

16. Keohane, *After Hegemony*, p.54.

17. Quoted in Jansen and De Vree, *Ordeal of Unity*, p.187.

18. See Ingo Kolboom, 'Ostpolitik als deutsch-französische Herausfor-derung', *Europa-Archiv*, vol.44, no.4 (1989), and Josef Joffe, 'The Revisionists. Moscow, Bonn, and the European Balance', *The National Interest*, no.17 (Fall 1989).

19. See Ole Wæver, 'Three Competing Europes: German, French, Russian', *International Affairs* (London), vol.66, no.3 (1990), and Barry Buzan *et al.*, *European Security Order*. For an insightful study on the difference in elite opinions towards European integration and Europe's role in world politics, see Karl W. Deutsch, Lewis J. Edinger, Roy C. Macridis and Richard L. Merritt, *France, Germany and the Western Alliance. A Study of Elite Attitudes on European Integration and World Politics* (New York: Charles Scribner's Sons, 1967).

20. Brian White, 'Britain and East-West Relations', in Michael Smith, Steve Smith and Brian White (eds.), *British Foreign Policy. Tradition, Change and Transformation* (London: Unwin Hyman, 1988), p.153. See also Richard Davy, 'Überlegungen zur britischen Ostpolitik', *Europäische Rundschau*, vol.7, no.2 (1979).

21. Roger Morgan, 'Grossbritannien', in Eberhard Schulz (ed.), *Die Ostbeziehungen der Europäischen Gemeinschaft* (Wien: R. Oldenbourg Verlag, 1977), p.193.

22. Edwina Moreton, 'The View from London', in Gordon (ed.), *Eroding Empire*, p.241.

23. Roger Morgan, 'The Role of Medium Powers in World Politics: the Case of Britain', in Karl Kaiser and Roger Morgan (eds.), *Britain and West Germany. Changing Societies and the Future of Foreign Policy* (London: Oxford University Press), p.275.

24. J. F. Brown, 'The Views from Vienna and Rome', in Gordon (ed.), *Eroding Empire*, p.281.

25. Giovanni Agnelli, 'East-West Trade: A European View', *Foreign Affairs*, vol.58, no.5 (Summer 1980), pp.1024,1026.

26. Voorhoeve, *Peace, Profits and Principles*, p.131. The classical study of the Netherlands' policy in NATO is A. van Staden's *Een Trouwe Bondgenoot. Nederland en het Atlantisch Bondgenootschap* (Baarn: In den Toren, 1974). See also Ben Knapen, *De Lange Weg Naar Moskou. De Nederlandse Relatie tot de Sovjet-Unie, 1917-1942* (Amsterdam: Elsevier, 1985), and M. L. Roholl, E. Waegemans and Cees Willemsen (eds.), *De Lage Landen en de Sovjet Unie. Beeldvorming en Betrekkingen* (Amsterdam: Uitgeverij Jan Mets, 1989).

27. Bert Bomert, *Nederland en Oost-Europa. Meer Woorden dan Daden* (Amsterdam: Uitgeverij Jan Mets, 1990), p.121.

28. For a discussion of the Netherlands' role in the EC's policy towards the East, see Jan Zielonka, 'The Dutch version of *Ostpolitik*', in Alfred E. Pijpers (ed.), *The European Community at the Crossroads. Major Issues and Priorities for the EC Presidency* (Dordrecht: Martinus Nijhoff, 1992).

29. See for an overview of the economic relations between Belgium and the Soviet Union, Katlijn Malfliet, 'De Belgo-Sovjet Handelsbetrekkingen', *Studia Diplomatica*, vol.xli, no.3 (1988).

30. For a concise overview of these proposals, see Marshall D. Shulman, 'Sowjetische Vorschläge für eine europäische Sicherheitskonferenz (1966-1969)', *Europa-Archiv*, vol.24, no.19 (October 1969).

31. Klaus Mehnert, 'Sicherheitskonferenz für Europa', *Osteuropa*, vol.20, no.10 (Oktober 1970), pp.663-4. For a comprehensive overview, see Arie

Bloed (ed.), *From Helsinki to Vienna. Basic Documents of the Helsinki Process* (Dordrecht: Martinus Nijhoff, 1990).

32. A. E. Pijpers, *The Vicissitudes of European Political Cooperation. Towards a Realist Interpretation of the EC's Collective Diplomacy* (Leiden University, Department of Political Science, Ph.D. thesis, 1990), pp.128-9.

33. Although the Common Commercial Policy was not applied to the State-trading countries until the end of 1975. See Chapter 5 on this issue.

34. See *Europa-Archiv*, 21/1972, p. D 507.

35. See Otto Graf Schwerin, 'Die Solidarität der EG-Staaten in der KSZE', *Europa-Archiv*, vol.30, no.15 (1975), Götz von Groll, 'Die KSZE und die Europäische Gemeinschaft', in Jost Delbrück, Norbert Ropers and Gerda Zellentin (eds.), *Grünbuch zu den Folgewirkungen der KSZE* (Köln: Verlag Wissenschaft und Politik, 1977); Crispin Tickell, 'Neuner-Gemeinschaft und Sicherheitskonferenz', *Aussenpolitik*, vol.25, no.1 (1974); and Hans-Adolf Jacobsen, Wolfgang Mallmann and Christian Meier (eds.), *Sicherheit und Zusammenarbeit in Europa (KSZE). Analyse und Dokumentation* (Köln: Verlag Wissenschaft und Politik, 1973).

36. Henri Kissinger had considered the CSCE 'at best significant for public opinion, but certainly not as an essential component of the substantial make-up of the process of détente'. Quoted in Pijpers, *Vicissitudes of European Political Cooperation*, p.133.

37. See Ministerie van Buitenlandse Zaken van Nederland, *Conferentie over Veiligheid en Samenwerking in Europa. Helsinki, Genève, Helsinki. 1973-1975* ('s-Gravenhage, Staatsuitgeverij, 1976), p.62.

38. Pijpers, *Vicissitudes of European Political Cooperation*, p.133.

39. See 'Erklärung des Europäischen Rates vom 17. Juli 1975 über die KSZE', *Europa-Archiv*, vol.30, no.20 (1975), p. D 575.

40. Pijpers, *Vicissitudes of European Political Cooperation*, p.139.

41. Maslen, 'European Community's Relations with the State-Trading Countries 1981-1983', p.336.

42. Pijper, *Vicissitudes of European Political Cooperation*, p.141.

43. Tatu, 'East-West Relations', p.173.

44. William Wallace, 'Political Cooperation: Integration Through Inter-governmentalism', in Wallace, Wallace and Webb (eds.), *Policy-Making in the European Community*, p.379.

45. Klaus Knorr, 'International Economic Leverage and its Uses', in Klaus Knorr and Frank N. Trager (eds.), *Economic Issues and National Security* (Lawrence, Kansas: University Press of Kansas, 1977), p.116.

46. Werner Weidenfeld, 'Die Europäische Gemeinschaft und Osteuropa', *Aussenpolitik*, vol.38, no.2 (1987), p.137.

47. Jürgen Nötzold and Hendrik Roodbeen, 'The European Community and COCOM: The Exclusion of an Interested Party', in Bertsch, Vogel and Zielonka (eds.), *After the Revolutions*.

48. Wallace, 'Political Cooperation', p.393.

49. Quoted in the EC Report *Community Exports to the Soviet Union During the 'Embargo'*, 9.3.1982.

50. Quoted in Angela E. Stent, *Technology Transfer to the Soviet Union. A Challenge for the Cohesiveness of the Western Alliance* (Bonn: Europa Union Verlag, 1983) p.111.
51. Bruce W. Jentleson, 'The Western Alliance and East-West Energy Trade', in G. K. Bertsch (ed.), *Controlling East-West Trade and Technology Transfer. Power, Politics, and Policies* (Durham and London: Duke University Press, 1988), pp.329-37.
52. See Julie E. Katzman, 'The Euro-Siberian Gas Pipeline Row: A Study in Community Development', *Millennium: Journal of International Studies*, vol.17, no.1 (Spring 1988), pp.32-7.
53. See 'Gas Pipeline. Comments of the European Community as Regards the Measures taken by the U.S. Government', 12 August 1982.
54. For a further discussion, see the special issue of *Columbia Journal of Transnational Law*, vol.26, no.1 (1987), and National Academy of Sciences, National Academy of Engineering, Institute of Medicine, *Balancing the National Interest. U.S. National Security Export Controls and Global Economic Competition* (Washington, DC: National Academy Press, 1987).
55. John P. Hardt and Kate S. Tomlinson, 'Soviet Economic Policies in Western Europe', in Ellison (ed.), *Soviet Policy Toward Western Europe*, p.186.
56. Quoted in Denis Lacorne, 'From Détente 1 to Détente 2: A Comparison of Giscard's and Mitterrand's East-West Policies', in David A. Baldwin and Helen V. Milner (eds.), *East-West Trade and the Atlantic Alliance* (New York: St. Martin's Press, 1990), p.129.
57. In their study about western collaboration on East-West trade, Beverly Crawford and Stefanie Lenway have maintained that 'the relative decline of U.S. economic power, combined with Europe's conflicting goals and interests, partially explains the move from compliance to compromise'. In many ways, the pipeline dispute has illustrated the more independent course of the West European countries on East-West trade issues from the United States. The role of the EC in determining this course, has been enhanced ever since. See Crawford and Lenway, 'Decision Modes and International Regime Change: Western Collaboration on East-West Trade', *World Politics*, vol.37, no.3 (April 1985), p.385.
58. Katzman, 'Euro-Siberian Gas Pipeline Row', p.39.
59. Pijpers, *Vicissitudes of European Political Cooperation*, p.139.
60. Wayne Sandholtz and John Zysman, '1992: Recasting the European Bargain', *World Politics*, vol.42, no.1 (October 1989), and Andrew Moravcsik, 'Negotiating the Single European Act: National Interests and Conventional Statecraft in the European Community', *International Organization*, vol.45, no.1 (Winter 1991). See also Keohane and Hoffmann (eds.) *The New European Community*.
61. See Eberhard Rhein, 'Die Europäische Gemeinschaft auf der Suche nach einer gemeinsamen Außenpolitik', *Europa-Archiv*, vol.31, no.6 (1976).
62. See the interview with Emille A. Campo, *Export Magazine* (The Hague), 17 November 1990, pp.20-1.

Notes to Chapter 7

1. See Barbara Lippert, 'EC-CMEA Relations: Normalisation and Beyond', in Geoffrey Edwards and Elfriede Regelsberger (eds.), *Europe's Global Links. The European Community and InterRegional Cooperation* (London: Pinter Publishers, 1990).
2. Quoted in C. F. G. Ransom, 'The Future of EEC-COMECON Relations', *The World Today*, vol.27 (October 1971), p.441.
3. See on this issue for example Philip Hanson, 'Economic Aspects of Helsinki', *International Affairs* (London), vol.61, no.4 (Autumn 1985), and John Pinder, 'Integration in Western and Eastern Europe: Relations between the EC and CMEA', *Journal of Common Market Studies*, vol.18, no.2 (December 1979), p.114.
4. For an early assessment of the role of the ECE, see David Wightman, 'East-West Cooperation and the United Nations Economic Commission for Europe', *International Organization*, vol.11, no.1 (Winter 1957).
5. Senior Nello, *The New Europe*, p.31.
6. See Helmut Klocke, 'Der RGW und sein Verhältnis zur EWG', *Aussenpolitik*, vol.22, no.5 (1971), pp.298-9, and Hans Bräker, 'Osteuropa, die Europäische Gemeinschaft und das GATT. Zur gegenwärtigen Außenwirtschaftspolitik der Länder des RGW', *Europa-Archiv*, vol.28, no.19 (1973). See also Serge L. Levitsky, 'GATT and the State Trading', *Libertas*, no.1 (1987). For a more theoretical analysis, see Leah Haus, 'The East European Countries and GATT: The Role of Realism, Mercantilism, and Regime Theory in Explaining East-West Trade Negotiations', *International Organization*, vol.45, no.2 (Spring 1991).
7. Catherina Sokil, 'The Soviet Union and the GATT, IMF, and World Bank', in Michael Kraus and Ronald D. Liebowitz (eds.), *Perestroika and East-West Economic Relations. Prospects for the 1990s* (New York and London: New York University Press, 1990).
8. *Trouw*, 29 Oktober 1963.
9. Quoted in Sokoloff, *Economy of Detente*, p.177.
10. Aleksandr Bovin, quoted in Stanley Hoffmann, 'Détente', in Joseph S. Nye, Jr. (ed.), *The Making of America's Soviet Policy* (New Haven and London: Yale University Press, 1984), p.243.
11. Beatrice Repetzki, 'Der schwierige Dialog zwischen der EWG und den europäischen RGW-Ländern', *Osteuropa-Wirtschaft*, vol.33, no.3 (1988), p.222.
12. Robert M. Cutler, 'Harmonizing EEC-CMEA Relations: Never the Twain Shall Meet?', *International Affairs* (London), vol.63, no.2 (Spring 1987), p.263.
13. Radio Budapest, 27 January 1975 (4/1975). Quoted in Carl A. Ehrhardt, 'EWG und RGW kommen sich nur langsam näher', *Aussenpolitik*, vol.28, no.2 (1977), p.168.
14. See Ehrhardt, 'EWG und RGW', p.167.
15. For the East European textile agreements with the EC, see *The European Communities and the Countries of Eastern Europe*, External Relations

Information Document, Commission of the EC, May 1978. See also Senior Nello, *The New Europe*, pp.34-40.

16. Max Baumer and Hanns-Dieter Jacobsen, 'EC and COMECON: Intricate Negotiations Between the Two Integration Systems in Europe', in Werner Feld (ed.), *Western Europe's Global Reach* (New York: Pergamon, 1980), pp.110-24.

17. The exact content of these articles are discussed in Ilka Bailey-Wiebecke, *Die Europäische Gemeinschaft und der Rat für Gegenseitige Wirtschaftshilfe. Multilaterale Diplomatie oder Blockpolitik?* (Bern: Peter Lang, 1989), pp.67-78.

18. See *Agence Europe*, 25 February 1976.

19. See Hans-Hagen Bremer, 'Das RGW-Angebot, Nehmen Ohne Zu Geben', *EG-Magazin*, Nr.11/1976.

20. Two of the most influential studies on this subject have been Albert O. Hirschman, *National Power and the Structure of Foreign Trade* (Berkeley, Los Angeles, London: University of California Press, 1980), and David A. Baldwin, *Economic Statecraft* (Princeton, NJ: Princeton University Press, 1985).

21. Michael Shackleton, 'Fishing for a Policy? The Common Fisheries Policy of the Community', in Wallace, Wallace and Webb (eds.), *Policy-Making in the European Community*.

22. See Lasok and Bridge, *Law and Institutions*, pp.489-91.

23. For a general discussion on this issue, see Hans R. Krämer, 'Die Stellung der EWG im Bereich der Ostsee', *Europa-Archiv*, vol.34, no.8 (1979), esp. pp.222-6.

24. Marsh, 'EEC and CMEA', pp.61-5, and D. J. Driscoll and N. McKellar, 'The Changing Regime of North Sea Fisheries', in C. M. Mason (ed.), *The Effective Management of Resources* (London: Pinter Publishers, 1979), pp.156-8.

25. Cutler, 'Harmonizing EEC-CMEA Relations', p.264.

26. *Press Release*, European Commission, IP(77)221.

27. *Press Release*, European Commission, IP(77)222.

28. See the discussion paper presented by John P. Hardt and Donna Gold, 'Premises Underlying U.S. Policy on Commercial Relations With the U.S.S.R.', Committee on Foreign Relations United States Senate and Congressional Research Service Library of Congress, *The Premises of East-West Commercial Relations* (Washington, DC: US Government Printing Office, 1982), p.5.

29. See, among others, John Pinder, 'EEC and COMECON', *Survey*, no.58 (January 1966), pp.104-5.

30. The net hard-currency indebtedness of Eastern Europe grew from US$ 4 billion in 1970, to US$ 75 billion in 1982 and almost US$ 100 billion in 1989.

31. The 1971 Comprehensive Programme stated (Chapter 1, section 1, paragraph 1): 'Socialist economic integration is conducted on a purely voluntary basis, it is not accompanied by the creation of any supranational organisations and does not affect internal planning problems or the financial and accounting activities of organisations.' Article IV of the

CMEA Charter proclaimed: 'All recommendations and decisions of the Council shall be adopted only with the consent of the interested member countries of the Council, each country having the right to declare its interest in any question considered in the Council.' Quoted in Susan Senior Nello, *Recent Developments in Relations Between the EC and Eastern Europe*, European University Institute, Florence, EUI Working Paper, no. 89/381, p.2.

32. In 1971, the Commission had already maintained that 'The European Community and the Council for Mutual Economic Assistance (Comecon) are institutions with a completely different aim and structure. There is no organ like the Commission within Comecon. Whereas Comecon is in principle a coordinating body for the national production plans, the European Community has totally different tasks. This does of course not preclude contacts with both institutions; it is nevertheless necessary to see these aspects in this light.' See *Official Journal of the European Communities*, 20.2.1971, Nr. C 17/7-8.

33. The Klepsch Report (*EP* 425/74), p.22, and the Irmer Report (*EP*, 1-531/82), p.17.

34. The Schmidt Report (*EP*, 89/78), p.29.

35. See Lebahn, 'RGW und EG', p.135.

36. Cutler, 'Harmonizing EEC-CMEA Relations', p.267.

37. The Romanian leader Gheorghiu-Dej had rejected the Soviet attempt to integrate the economies of Eastern Europe within the CMEA, in 1962. Because, as Joseph Rothschild has argued: 'They feared that this new [CMEA] program would effectively cheat them of their goal of comprehensive industrialization and modernization, and relegate them once again to their traditional and resented fate of being the backward supplier of raw materials and agricultural products to more advanced economies – this time those of the Soviet Union, Czechoslovakia, and East Germany'. Rothschild, *Return to Diversity*, p.162.

38. John Pinder, in Twitchett (ed.), *Europe and the World*, p.64; Pinder, 'The Community and Comecon: What Could Negotiations Achieve?', *The World Today*, vol.33 (May 1977), p.181; and Pinder, 'Community Policy Towards Eastern Europe', p.122.

39. Sheila A. Chapman, 'The Economic Relations Between the EEC and the CMEA: A Survey of Problems and Prospects', *La Comunita Internazionale*, vol.40, terzo trimestre (1985), p.429. This argument was also made by Guido Montani, 'Europe and the CMEA: Towards a European Ostpolitik?', *The Federalist*, vol.27, no.3 (December 1985), p.177.

40. Axel Lebahn, 'RGW und EG – Faktoren des Ost-West-Handels', *Aussenpolitik*, vol.29, no.2 (1978), p.126. See also Paul Bähr, 'Handel und Händel Zwischen Ost und West', *Europa-Archiv*, 28/1973, pp.173-82.

41. W. Morawiecki, 'Actors and Interests in the Process of Negotiations Between the CMEA and the EEC', *Legal Issues of European Integration*, no.2 (1989) p.15.

42. Sophie Verny, 'CEE-CAEM: Le Problème de la Reconnaissance Mutuele', *Courier des Pays de l'Est*, no.305 (April 1985), pp.34-7. Translated as 'The EEC and CMEA. The Problem of Mutual Recognition', *Soviet and*

Eastern European Foreign Trade, vol.24, no.2 (Summer 1988), pp.6-25. See also John Maslen, 'A Turning Point: Past and Future of the European Community's Relations with Eastern Europe', *Revista di Studi Politici Internazionali*, Anno LV, no.4 (Ottobre-Dicembre 1988), and Gianluigi Giola, 'L'Ostpolitik de la Communauté européenne', *Cadmos*, Douzième année, no.45 (Printemps 1984).

43. One study has indicated that the impact of the Greek accession to the EC has resulted in an increase of the EC share in Greek trade by 25 per cent, while that of Eastern Europe fell by 50 per cent; the EC share in Greek exports rose by 18 per cent, while that of Eastern Europe fell by 43 per cent over the same period. These figures are presented in the study of G. N. Yannopoulos, 'The Impact of the European Economic Community on East-West Trade', Paper presented at a conference on *East-West Trade and Financial Relations*, European University Institute, Florence, 4-6 June 1985. Quoted in Senior Nello, *The New Europe*, p.104.

44. *The Financial Times*, 24 October 1985.

45. *International Herald Tribune*, 9-10 August 1986.

46. See Jens Hacker, 'Die Berlin-Politik der UdSSR Unter Gorbatschow', *Aussenpolitik*, vol.40, no.3 (1989), esp. pp.257-8, and Alexander Uschakow, 'Die Beziehungen Zwischen der EG und dem EGW', *Osteuropa*, vol.38 (1988).

47. Rüdiger Hütte, 'Berlin and the European Community', in *Yearbook of European Law*, no.3 (1983) (Oxford: Clarendon Press, 1984).

48. The 'Hungarian Formula' was first adopted during the bilateral negotiations between the European Community and Budapest, where both signatories had affirmed that other agreements – including the agreement of September 1971 on West Berlin – would still apply. Letters were exchanged to this effect, whereby the Community later confirmed the receipt of these letters, thereby acknowledging the validity of the territorial clause.

49. *The Financial Times*, 17 May 1988.

50. *OJ*, L 157/35.

51. *Europe Information*, 'The European Community's Relations With COMECON and Its East European Members', January 1989 (1/89) p.1.

52. *The Financial Times*, 11 November 1988.

53. *The Financial Times*, 2 April 1988.

Notes to Chapter 8

1. After the first breaches were made on 2 May 1989, the Hungarian Foreign Minister Gyula Horn, and his Austrian colleague, jointly cut the remaining barbed wire of the Iron Curtain in June of that year.

2. 1985 EC Commission White Paper, amended by the SEA, Article 8A.

3. See on this issue Wayne Sandholtz and John Zysman, '1992: Recasting the European Bargain', *World Politics*, vol.42, no.1 (October 1989).

4. See Paul Kennedy, *The Rise and Fall of the Great Powers. Economic Change and Military Conflict from 1500 to 2000* (New York: Random

House, 1987), and David P. Calleo, *Beyond American Hegemony. The Future of the Western Alliance* (London: Wheatsheaf, 1987). For a theoretical analysis see Keohane, *After Hegemony*.

5. These acronyms stand for respectively 'European Strategic Program for Research and Development in Information Technologies', 'Program on Research and Development in Advanced Communication Technology for Europe', and 'Basic Research in Industrial Technologies in Europe'.

6. Loukas Tsoukalis, 'Money and the Process of Integration', in Wallace, Wallace and Webb (eds.), *Policy-Making in the European Community*, p.116.

7. Following upon the Barre Report on the EMU (of 1969), a new Committee was established (the so-called 'Werner Group'), to formulate new proposals on the EMU. This Committee set the final goal of the EMU for 1980, including fixed exchange rates for the currencies of the EC members, full convertibility of currencies, the transfer of the main economic powers of the member states to the European Community and the creation of new monetary institutions (an EC central bank).

8. For an analysis of the EMS, see Peter Ludlow, *The Making of the European Monetary System. A Case Study of the Politics of the European Community* (London: Butterworth Scientific, 1982).

9. EEC Committee for the Study of Economic and Monetary Union (Delors Committee), *Report on Economic and Monetary Union in the European Community* (Luxembourg, 1989). See for an analysis of these issues, John T. Woolley, 'Policy Credibility and European Monetary Institutions', in Alberta M. Sbragia (ed.), *Europolitics. Institutions and Policymaking in the 'New' European Community* (Washington, DC: The Brookings Institution, 1992).

10. Sandholtz and Zysman, '1992', p.108.

11. Peter Ludlow, 'The European Commission', in Keohane and Hoffmann (eds.), *The New European Community*, p.116.

12. Ludlow, 'The European Commission', pp.113-15. See also Wolfgang Wessels, 'The EC Council: The Community's Decisionmaking Center', in Keohane and Hoffmann (eds.), *The New European Community*.

13. Quoted in Anders Aslund, 'The New Soviet Policy Towards International Economic Organisations', *The World Today*, vol.44, no.2 (February 1988), p.29.

14. See Leonard Geron, *Soviet Foreign Economic Policy Under Perestroika* (New York: Council on Foreign Relations Press, 1990), Chapter 5.

15. Thad P. Alton, 'Comparison of Overall Economic Performance in the East European Countries', in Reiner Weichhardt (ed.), *The Economies of Eastern Europe Under Gorbachev's Influence* (Brussels: NATO Colloquium, 1988).

16. See Paul Marer and Wlodzimierz Siwinski (eds.), *Creditworthiness and Reform in Poland. Western and Polish Perspectives* (Bloomington and Indianapolis: Indiana University Press, 1988).

17. Mikhail Gorbachev, *Perestroyka. New Thinking for Our Country and the World* (New York: Harper & Row, 1987), p.161.

18. Quoted in *NRC Handelsblad*, 6 July 1989 (emphasis added).

19. EC Commission, *An Ever Closer Union* (1985). Annex 2, p.337.
20. Single European Act, art 30 (1), (2) and (3) (c).
21. Quoted in *Keesing's Record of World Events* (hereafter *KRWE*), vol.34, November 1988, p.36307.
22. Quoted in *Time*, 14 November 1988.
23. Quoted in *NRC Handelsblad*, 11 January 1988.
24. See for a comprehensive overview of these West German efforts Angela Stent, *From Embargo to Ostpolitik. The Political Economy of West German-Soviet Relations 1955-1980* (Cambridge: Cambridge University Press, 1981).
25. Quoted in Labbé and Van Ham, 'The West European Approach Towards COCOM', in Bertsch, Vogel and Zielonka (eds.), *After the Revolutions*, p.51.
26. *Der Spiegel*, 12 Juni 1989 (my translation).
27. *The Financial Times*, 17 October 1988.
28. In his speech to the Council of Europe in 1989, Gorbachev had argued: 'I think that the esteemed Assembly will agree that in our age economic ties divorced from scientific and technical ties are something not quite normal. But in East-West relations these latter are to a significant degree bled white by CoCom. And if at the height of the Cold War such a practice could somehow have been justified, now many bans simply look absurd.' BBC Monitoring Service, *Summary of World Broadcasts* (hereafter BBC, *SWB*), 6 July 1989.
29. *The Washington Post*, 21 May 1989.
30. See Barry Buzan, *People, States and Fear. An Agenda for International Security Studies in the Post-Cold War Era* (New York: Harvester Wheatsheaf, 1991), especially Chapter 6.
31. *NRC Handelsblad*, 16 March 1988.
32. In his widely covered discussion with French intellectuals at the Sorbonne University in Paris (early July 1989), Gorbachev also claimed that his visions of Europe did 'coincide with those of General de Gaulle: from the Atlantic to the Urals'. BBC, *SWB*, 5 July 1989. See also *Pravda*, 6 July 1989.
33. Neil Malcolm, 'The "Common European Home" and Soviet European Policy', *International Affairs* (London), vol.65, no.4 (Autumn 1989), p.669. For an even more sceptical analysis of Gorbachev's *Westpolitik*, see Margarita Mathiopoulos, 'Gorbatschows "gemeinsames europäisches Haus", Wiederauferstehung von Wandel durch Annäherung?', *Europäische Rundschau*, vol.17, no.2 (1989).
34. BBC, *SWB*, 20 March 1989.
35. BBC, *SWB*, 6 July 1989.
36. BBC, *SWB*, 6 July 1989.
37. Giscard aired his suggestion to the Trilateral Commission in Paris, in June 1989, and in an address to the Royal Institute of International Affairs in London, in July 1989.
38. *The Financial Times*, 13 July 1989.
39. Andriessen during the debate on German Reunification in the European Parliament, 4 April 1990 (EC Commission Documentation, p.3).

40. Joffe, 'The View from Bonn', in Gordon (ed.), *Eroding Empire*, p.137.
41. Quoted in LeGloannec, 'France's German Problems', in Larrabee (ed.), *Two German States*, pp.247-8.
42. *The New York Times*, 23 September 1984.
43. Quoted in LeGloannec, 'France's German Problem', in Larrabee (ed.), *Two German States*, p.248.
44. Quoted in Walter Leisler Kiep, 'The New Deutschlandpolitik', *Foreign Affairs*, vol.63, no.2 (Winter 1984-5), p.320.
45. See for a general overview of Adenauer's political ideas and his policy towards the EC: Hans-Peter Schwarz, *Adenauer. Der Staatsmann: 1952-1967* (Stuttgart: Deutsche Verlags-Anstalt, 1991).
46. Quoted in Hassner, 'The View from Paris', in Gordon (ed.), *Eroding Empire*, p.194.
47. Roger Morgan, 'French Perspectives of the New Germany', *Government and Opposition*, vol.26, no.1 (Winter 1991), p.108.
48. Pierre Lellouche, quoted in David S. Yost, 'France in the New Europe', *Foreign Affairs*, vol.69, no.5 (Winter 1990/91), p.111.
49. John Fenske, 'France's Uncertain Progress Toward European Union', *Current History*, vol.90, no.559 (November 1991), pp.361-2.
50. BBC, *SWB*, 19 December 1989.
51. Communication from the EC Commission, *The Community and German Unification*, SEC(90) 751, 20 April 1990, p.1.
52. BBC, *SWB*, 6 December 1989.
53. Quoted in *Time*, 9 December 1991.
54. Morgan, 'French Perspectives', p.109.

Notes to Chapter 9

1. *International Herald Tribune*, 22 November 1990.
2. *International Herald Tribune*, 2 June 1989.
3. See, for instance, Jeanne Kirk Laux, *Reform, Reintegration and Regional Security. The Role of Western Assistance in Overcoming Insecurity in Central and Eastern Europe*, Working Paper 37, Canadian Institute for International Peace and Security (October 1991), p.5.
4. Frans H. J. J. Andriessen, 'The European Community and East-West Cooperation', Address at the Conference on *The Soviet Union in the 1990s*, Moscow (7-8 June 1989), mimeographed.
5. Adrian Hewitt, 'ACP and the Developing World', in Lodge (ed.), *The European Community*.
6. The G-24 are the EC Twelve, the six EFTA countries, Canada, the United States, Japan, Australia, New Zealand and Turkey.
7. Communication of the EC Commission (DG I), 'G-24 Coordination Unit', 12 March 1991.
8. See on the lessons of western aid to the Third World for the West's role in the East European reform process: Christopher Stevens and Jane Kennan (eds.), *Reform in Eastern Europe and the Developing Country Dimension* (London: Overseas Development Institute, 1992).

9. PHARE is the official acronym for 'Pologne/Hongrie: Assistance à la Reconstruction des Économies'. *Phare* is also the French word for lighthouse, which is of course an appropriate name for a programme intended to steer the Communist countries clear from the dangerous cliffs of political and economic reform.

10. *Action Plan for Coordinated Aid to Poland and Hungary*, Commission of the European Communities. Brussels, 27 September 1989. Com(89) 470.

11. *De Volkskrant*, 10 February 1990, and J. A. Schoneveld, *Het Oosteuropees Milieu: Een Verloren Zaak?* (*The East European Environment: A Lost Cause?*), unpublished MA thesis, Department of Political Science, Leiden University (March 1991).

12. United Nations Economic Commission for Europe, *Economic Survey of Europe in 1990-1991* (New York, 1991), p.74.

13. BBC, *SWB*, 19 December 1989.

14. *Agence Europe*, 30 August 1991, no.5556.

15. *International Herald Tribune*, 30 May 1989.

16. BBC, *SWB*, 7 November 1989.

17. *Wall Street Journal*, 19 September 1989.

18. Kirk Laux, *Reform, Reintegration and Regional Security*, p.10.

19. Peter van Ham, 'Western Economic Statecraft in an Era of Communist Reform. How Can the West Help?', *Bulletin of Peace Proposals*, vol.21, no.2 (June 1990), p.231.

20. *The New York Times*, 15 December 1990.

21. *Wall Street Journal*, 14 November 1989.

22. *The Financial Times*, 20 November 1989.

23. See the official declaration of Ministers of the 'Group of 24 for Economic Assistance to Poland and Hungary' (The 24), 13 December 1989.

24. *The Financial Times*, 23 November 1989.

25. John Pinder, *The European Community and Eastern Europe* (London: The Royal Institute of International Affairs/Pinter Publishers, 1991), p.33.

26. *Wall Street Journal*, 22 November 1989.

27. *Le Monde*, 27 October 1989.

28. *Wall Street Journal*, 26 October 1989.

29. *Wall Street Journal*, 14 November 1989.

30. *The Financial Times*, 24 January 1990.

31. See for an insightful study, Commission of the EC (Directorate-General for Economic and Financial Affairs), *European Economy. Economic Transformation in Hungary and Poland*, no.43 (March 1990).

32. *The Economist*, 15 July 1989.

33. *Wall Street Journal*, 9 July 1990.

34. See Overseas Development Institute (ODI) Briefing Paper (London), 'Eastern Europe and the Developing Countries', (June 1991), p.2.

35. *The Times*, 16 March 1990.

36. *International Herald Tribune*, 1 July 1990.

37. *Agence Europe*, 4 April 1991, no.54643.

38. *Frankfurter Allgemeine Zeitung*, 5 November 1990 (my translation).

39. *International Herald Tribune*, 6 July 1990.

40. *International Herald Tribune*, 9 March 1990.
41. The Hungarian Deputy Minister for International Economic Relations, Istvan Major, proposed such a free trade area, which he considered 'the logical consequence of the negotiations under way between Hungary and other countries of Eastern Europe with the European Community and EFTA', *Agence Europe*, 8-9 April 1991, no.5467.
42. Quoted in *KRWE*, vol.35 (December 1989), p.37131. See also 'Probleme der Europäischen Einigung. Die Tagung der Europäischen Rates in Straßburg im Dezember 1989', *Europa-Archiv*, vol.45, no.1, (January 10 1990), pp.D11,12.
43. Quoted in *KRWE*, vol.35 (December 1989), p.37132.
44. *The Economist*, 20 January 1990.
45. EBRD Documentation, *Organization of the European Bank for Reconstruction and Development* (October 1991), p.21.
46. *The Economist*, 17 March 1990.
47. Marvin Jackson, 'The Impact of the Gulf Crisis on the Economies of Eastern Europe', *Report on Eastern Europe* (RFE/RL Research Institute) vol.1, no.35 (31 August 1990).
48. *Eurobusiness*, April 1991, pp.32, 33.
49. Bronislav Geremek, 'Aid to East Europe: The West's Waiting Game', *European Affairs*, vol.4, no.2 (Summer 1990), p.42.
50. This criticism has, among others, been aired by the Prometheus-Europe organization. See *Agence Europe*, 12 April 1991, no.5470.
51. Stephen van Evera, 'Primed for Peace: Europe After the Cold War', in Lynn-Jones (ed.), *Cold War and After*, p.196.
52. Buzan, *et al.*, *European Security*, p.149.
53. See, for example, Snyder, 'Averting Anarchy', *passim*.
54. European Political Cooperation, *Press Release*, 'Declaration on the "Guidelines on the Recognition of New States in Eastern Europe and in the Soviet Union"', P.128/91, 16 December 1991.

Notes to Chapter 10

1. See Barry Buzan, *People, States and Fear*; Buzan, 'New Patterns of Global Security in the Twenty-First Century', *International Affairs* (London), vol.67, no.3 (1991); and Jessica Tuchman Mathews, 'Redefining Security', *Foreign Affairs*, vol.68, no.2 (Spring 1989). In his speech to the International Institute for Strategic Studies, Jacques Delors analysed the security aspects of European political and economic integration. See *Europe/Documents*, no.1699, 13 March 1991.
2. Robert Jervis, *The Meaning of the Nuclear Revolution. Statecraft and the Prospect of Armageddon* (Ithaca and London: Cornell University Press, 1989), p.53. Jervis has introduced this concept in his article 'Cooperation Under the Security Dilemma', *World Politics*, vol.30, no.2 (1978).
3. *The Financial Times*, 20 November 1989.
4. Or, as Flora Lewis has formulated it, there looms a threat of 'a fragmented Europe of tribal states'. *The New York Times*, 28 November 1990.

5. The Treaty proclaims that the EC's new common foreign and security policy 'shall include all questions related to the security of the Union, including the eventual framing of a common defence policy, which might in time lead to a common defence' (Article J.4).

6. *International Herald Tribune*, 29 July 1992.

7. For a thorough analysis of these issues, see Anna Michalski and Helen Wallace, *The European Community: The Challenge of Enlargement* (London: Royal Institute of International Affairs, European Programme Special Paper, 1992).

8. *Europa van Morgen*, 10.5.1990.

9. *Agence Europe*, 18 April 1990. Antall further remarked that 'Our strategic aim is to obtain EC membership by 1995 – after Austria, no doubt, but before all the other countries of what used to be called Eastern Europe'. *The Christian Science Monitor*, 2 August 1990, p.5.

10. *The Financial Times*, 10 April 1990.

11. BBC, *SWB*, 3 April 1991.

12. Antall warned of 'a new Welfare Wall', which 'may arise in the place of the Iron Curtain, which has now been removed'. The Polish Prime Minister, Tadeusz Mazowiecki, has maintained that 'Our common future may be darkened by the sinister clouds of the resurging conflicts of bygone days, unless the split into a rich and a poor Europe, an "A" class and a "B" class Europe, is overcome'. *The New York Times*, 21 November 1990.

13. See Michael Czinkota, 'The EC '92 and Eastern Europe: Effects of Integration vs. Disintegration', *The Columbia Journal of World Business*, vol.26, no.1 (Spring 1991), and Wolfgang Wessels, 'Deepening and/or Widening – Debate on the Shape of EC-Europe in the Nineties', *Aussenwirtschaft*, vol.46, no.2 (1991).

14. A senior Foreign Ministry official from Hungary also argued, a few days before the Maastricht Summit, that 'If deepening precludes widening, then I would be very worried. However, the two trends are not mutually exclusive.' *The Financial Times*, 9 December 1991.

15. Jérôme Monod, Pehr Gyllenhammar and Wisse Dekker, *Reshaping Europe. A Report from the European Round Table of Industrialists* (September 1991), p.48.

16. This was, for instance, argued by Belgium's Minister of Foreign Affairs, Mark Eyskens. *NRC Handelsblad*, 15 June 1991. See also Eyskens, *Van Detente Naar Entente. Gevolgen van de Implosie van het Communisme (From Detente to Entente. The Consequences of the Implosion of Communism)* (Brussels: Ministerie van Buitenlandse Zaken, January 1990), pp.13-14.

17. Tibor Palankai, *The European Community and Central European Integration. The Hungarian Case*, Occasional Paper Series no.21, Institute for East-West Security Studies, New York/Prague (1991), pp.64,66.

18. G. de Michelis, 'Reaching Out to the East', *Foreign Policy*, no.79 (Summer 1990), p.48.

19. Douglas Hurd, the British Foreign Secretary, also argued that 'It will be at least 1993 before new applications can be entertained. But after that I do

not see how the Europe of the 12 can shut the door for any length of time against fully qualified European democracies which are anxious to join, whether they are now in EFTA or in Central Europe.' *The Christian Science Monitor*, 2 August 1990, p.5. Michael Heseltine, the former UK Minister of Defence, argued differently: 'the further we widen the membership of the Community, the more we are forced to compromise by allowing for the weakness or backwardness of the economies of potential members, the more the momentum will slow. This risk of enlargement is the risk of compromise. The more the compromising, the greater the missed opportunities.' M. Heseltine, 'The EC: First Deeper, Then Wider', *European Affairs*, vol.4, no.2 (Summer 1990), p.10.

20. *The Financial Times*, 19 November 1990.
21. Major has argued that the former Communist countries should enter the EC. Even Russia and the other former Soviet Republics could, over time, join: 'It is no use saying the Community would not be the same if Russia became closely associated with it. It might have to change, but then we do not live in an unchanging world. The Community will have to change with it.' *The Financial Times*, 13 September 1991.
22. *The Economist*, 3 February 1990.
23. *The Financial Times*, 14 August 1989.
24. *International Herald Tribune*, 20 June 1991.
25. *The Financial Times*, 20 September 1991.
26. *Wall Street Journal*, 26 October 1989.
27. *Wall Street Journal*, 26 October 1989.
28. Ole Wæver, 'Three Competing Europes', p.481. See also the interview with President Mitterrand in *L'Expansion*, 17 Oct./13 Nov. 1991.
29. This proposal has also been aired by several economists from the Institut für Weltwirtschaft, University of Kiel. See 'Umweg über EFTA?', *Wirtschaftswoche*, August 4 1989; Holger Schmiedling, 'A Concept for a Pan-European Economic Integration', *European Affairs*, vol.3 (Autumn 1989); and Wojciech Kostrzewa and Holger Schmiedling, 'An EFTA Option for Eastern Europe', *Swiss Review of World Affairs*, vol.49, no.19 (January 1990).
30. *Neue Zürcher Zeitung*, 11 September 1991. In December 1991, EFTA signed cooperation agreements with Bulgaria, Rumania and the three Baltic states. *NRC Handelsblad*, 11 December 1991.
31. See Jozef M. van Brabant, *A Central European Payments Union: Technical Aspects*, Institute for East-West Security Studies, New York/ Prague, Public Policy Paper 3 (1991), p.3, and Daniel Gros, 'A Multilateral Payments Mechanism for Eastern Europe', Centre for European Policy Studies, Brussels, Working Documents no.59 (1992).
32. See K. Schumann, 'The Role of Present Co-operation Structures in the Process of European Integration', *Helsinki Monitor*, vol.2, no.3 (July 1991), p.20.
33. See Jan B. de Weydenthal, 'The Cracow Summit', *Report on Eastern Europe* (RFE/RL Research Institute), vol.2, no.43 (25 October 1991).
34. Quoted in de Weydenthal, 'Cracow Summit', p.28.
35. *Europa van Morgen*, 6.2.1991.

36. See Werner Feld, 'The Association Agreements of the European Communities: A Comparative Analysis', *International Organization*, vol.19, no.2 (Spring 1965), and William Wallace, 'Wider But Weaker: The Continued Enlargement of the EEC', *The World Today*, vol.32 (March 1976), p.106.

37. Lasok and Bridge, *Law and Institutions*, p.67.

38. C. Deubner, *Portugals Beitritt zur EG. Perspektiven und Strategien* (Bonn: Friedrich Ebert Stiftung, 1981); *European Community and Acceding Countries of Southern Europe* (West Berlin: Deutsches Institut für Entwicklungspolitik, 1979); Loukas Tsoukalis, *The European Community and its Mediterranean Enlargement* (London: Allen & Unwin, 1981); and Tsoukalis (ed.), *Greece and the European Community* (Farnborough, Hants.: Saxon House, 1979).

39. The conference was organized by the Young Europeans for Security (YES), the Studentenvereniging voor Internationale Betrekkingen, and the Stichting Vredespolitiek. *Europa van Morgen*, 21.11.1990.

40. Similar suggestions have been made by, for instance, Jack Snyder, who has argued: 'One possible solution to the contemporary [praetorian] dangers ... would be to recruit reformist Eastern regimes into the West's already well-developed supra-national political order, especially the European Community. As in the case of Spain and Greece, this would create incentives, as well as a ready-made institutional framework for acting on those incentives.' Snyder, 'Averting Anarchy in the New Europe', p.106.

41. Charles Feinstein *et al.*, *Historical Precedents for Economic Change in Central Europe and the USSR* (Credit Suisse First Boston Ltd., and Oxford Analytyca) October 1990, p.30.

42. One study on this issue concluded that 'To reach the European Community average income of 1989 by the year 2000, more than 5% growth (plus efficiency gain) would be required for Poland alone ... With a 10% growth Czechoslovakia and Hungary would even catch up with the European Community average income in the year 2000, assuming for Community income a growth rate of 3.5%.' See Daniel Gros and Alfred Steinherr, *From Centrally-Planned to Market Economies. Issues for the Transition in Central Europe and the Soviet Union* (Oxford: Brassey's, 1991), p.32. These are, of course, very optimistic growth rates, especially in the light of the recently published figures of the OECD which indicate a falling output of the Central European countries ranging from some 10 per cent in 1991 to an estimated 2.2 per cent in 1992. *The Financial Times*, 20 December 1991.

43. For an in-depth analysis, see John Pinder, '1992 and Beyond: European Community and Eastern Europe', *The International Spectator*, vol.25, no.3 (July-September 1990). See for a discussion of the general problem, Philippe Moreau Defarges, 'L'unification communautaire et les bouleversement du paysage européen', *Politique Étrangère*, vol.55, no.1 (Printemps 1990).

44. The bargaining on the association agreements between the EC Commission and Poland, Czechoslovakia and Hungary started on 21-23 December 1990, with the presentation of the negotiation positions. See also

Frans H. J. J. Andriessen, 'Change in Central and Eastern Europe. The Role of the European Community', *NATO Review*, vol.38, no.1 (February 1990), pp.5,6.

45. *The Economist*, 15 June 1991.

46. *The Financial Times*, 2 May 1991.

47. *Agence Europe*, 10-11 June 1991, no. 5509, p.7. See also *Agence Europe*, 13 July 1991, no. 5534, pp.7,8.

48. *International Herald Tribune*, 8 July 1991.

49. *The Financial Times*, 21 August 1991.

50. *Agence Europe*, 22 August 1991, no. 5550, p.3.

51. See Louisa Vinton, 'The Attempted Coup in the USSR. East European Reactions, Poland', *Report on Eastern Europe* (RFE/RL Research Institute), vol.2, no.35 (30 August 1991), pp.12, 13.

52. Josef C. Brada, 'The European Community and Czechoslovakia, Hungary, and Poland', *Report on Eastern Europe* (RFE/RL Research Institute), vol.2, no.49 (6 December 1991), and Heinz Kramer, 'Die EG und die Stabilisierung Osteuropas', *Aussenpolitik*, vol.43, no.1 (1992).

53. Béla Kádár, 'The 1992 Challenge: Responses in East-West Cooperation and in Hungary', *The International Spectator*, vol.25, no.3 (July-September 1990), p.169.

54. *International Herald Tribune*, 23 May 1991.

55. Peter van Ham, 'Brussels Verlicht Eigenbelang: De Associatie-akkoorden Tussen de EG en Centraal-Europa', *Internationale Spectator*, vol.46, no.1 (Januari 1992).

56. COPA is the acronym for Comité des Organisation Professionelles Agricoles (Committee of Professional Agricultural Associations).

57. See Alfred Tovias, 'EC-Eastern Europe: A Case Study of Hungary', *Journal of Common Market Studies*, vol.29, no.3 (March 1991), p.293.

58. BBC, *SWB*, 15 February 1990.

59. This will be of special importance since the EC members account for some 40 per cent of Hungary's trade turnover, up from 35 per cent in 1990, with the figure expected to reach 50 per cent in 1993. These figures were presented by Kádár during a visit of Andriessen in Budapest, March 1991. BBC, *SWB*, 16 March 1991.

60. Tovias, 'EC-Eastern Europe', p.304.

61. Officials of the European Community calculated that the budget of the EC would have to expand from 1.2 per cent of GDP to 1.6 per cent; a rise of one-third. *The Financial Times*, 16-17 November 1991.

62. *International Herald Tribune*, 20 June 1991.

63. J. Nötzold, 'New Tasks of the European Community with Regard to Eastern Europe', in Armand Clesse and Raymond Vernon (eds.), *The European Community After 1992: A New Role in World Politics?* (Baden-Baden: Nomos Verlagsgesellschaft, 1991), p.235.

64. Figures derived from a report from the Dutch Ministry of Economic Affairs, *Meer Zicht op Oost-Europa*, April 1991, p.4.

65. It was remarkable that in August 1989, Moscow warned Austria that its recent application to join the EC would undermine its neutrality, as was officially guaranteed under the State Treaty, signed in October 1955. *The Financial Times*, 11 August 1989.

66. In his speech to the College of Europe (Bruges), Delors argued that 'history will not wait ... History is accelerating, so we also have to accelerate.' *Agence Europe*, 18 October 1989.

67. *The Financial Times*, 5 September 1991.

68. *Agence Europe*, 17 October 1991, no.5590, p.10.

69. The EC has put forward five criteria which will determine whether the EC will recognize the requests by successor states to the USSR and Yugoslavia for recognition. *Agence Europe*, 16/17 December 1991, no.5631, p.3.

70. See *The Christian Science Monitor*, 2 August 1990, p.5. It is important to note that the question of the number of states to achieve cooperation has also received much attention from political science theorists. Although no consensus exists, most theorists have argued that cooperation will become more difficult when the number of states involved increases. Kenneth A. Oye, for example, has maintained that cooperation becomes less likely as the number of 'players' increases. He mentions three main reasons: (1) 'cooperation requires recognition of opportunities for the advancement of mutual interests, as well as policy coordination once these opportunities have been identified. As the number of players increases, transactions and information costs rise'; (2) 'as the number of players increases, the likelihood of autonomous defection and of recognition and control problems increases'; and (3) 'as the number of players increases, the feasibility of sanctioning defectors diminishes'. See Oye, 'Explaining Cooperation Under Anarchy: Hypotheses and Strategies', in Oye (ed.), *Cooperation Under Anarchy* (Princeton, NJ: Princeton University Press, 1986), pp.18-20. From this perspective, a powerful EC of 20 to 30 members will be very difficult to imagine.

71. Helen Wallace, 'The Europe that Came in From the Cold', *International Affairs* (London), vol.67, no.4 (1991), p.651. Klaus Hänsch has drafted a report on the institutional consequences of the EC's potential enlargement which has been discussed within the European Parliament's institutional committee. *Agence Europe*, 8 November 1991, no.5605, p.5.

72. *The Financial Times*, 5 September 1991. Pierre Hassner also argued: 'The only way out of this dilemma must be to *combine* broadening and deepening, to make the challenge of broadening into a reason for greater daring and energy in the direction of deepening ... I would emphasize that the success or failure of this combination holds the key to the decline or revival of both the Community and of Europe as a whole.' Hassner, 'Europe Beyond Partition and Unity: Disintegration or Reconstitution?', *International Affairs* (London), vol.66, no.3 (1990), pp.464-5.

73. See Frank Vibert, 'Making the Community Fit to Welcome New Members', *The Financial Times*, 18 September 1991.

74. It will also risk a watering-down of the cohesiveness of the European Community, transforming it into nothing more than a loosely structured 'Concert of Europe'. See on this issue Charles A. Kupchan and Clifford A. Kupchan, 'Concerts, Collective Security, and the Future of Europe', *International Security*, vol.16, no.1 (Summer 1991).

75. For a pessimistic account on the prospects for further integration within the EC, see Walter Goldstein, 'EC: Euro-Stalling', *Foreign Policy*, no.85 (Winter 1991-2).
76. *International Herald Tribune*, 9 March 1990.

Notes to Chapter 11

1. Mearsheimer, 'Back to the Future'.
2. Deutsch and Singer, 'Multipolar Power Systems and International Stability', *World Politics*, vol.16, no.3 (April 1964), pp.390,406.
3. See Kupchan and Kupchan, 'Concerts, Collective Security'; Robert Jervis, 'From Balance to Concert. A Study of International Security Cooperation', in Oye (ed.), *Cooperation Under Anarchy*; John Mueller, 'A New Concert of Europe', *Foreign Policy*, no.77 (Winter 1989-1990); K. J. Holsti, 'Governance Without Government. Polyarchy in Nineteenth-Century European International Politics', in James N. Rosenau and Ernst-Otto Czempiel (eds.), *Governance Without Government. Order and Change in World Politics* (Cambridge: Cambridge University Press, 1992); and Coral Bell, 'Why Russia Should Join NATO. From Containment to Concert', *The National Interest*, no.22 (Winter 1990/91).
4. Waltz, *Theory of International Politics*, pp.170-1. See also Waltz, 'The Stability of a Bipolar World', *Dædalus*, vol.93 (Summer 1964).
5. Samuel P. Huntington, *Political Order in Changing Societies* (New Haven: Yale University Press, 1968), p.196.
6. Glenn H. Snyder, 'Alliance Theory. A Neorealist First Cut', *Journal of International Affairs*, vol.44, no.1 (Spring/Summer 1990), p.117.
7. Glenn H. Snyder and Paul Diesing, *Conflict Among Nations. Bargaining, Decision Making, and System Structure in International Crisis* (Princeton, NJ: Princeton University Press, 1977), pp.428-9.
8. Glenn H. Snyder, 'The Security Dilemma in Alliance Politics', *World Politics*, vol.36, no.4 (July 1984), p.467.
9. Snyder, 'Security Dilemma in Alliance Politics', p.467.
10. Balancing is generally defined as allying with other states against a prevailing threat, whereas bandwagoning refers to the alignment with the source of danger. Walt has argued that states are more inclined to balance a threat than to appease it. See Stephen M. Walt, *The Origins of Alliances* (Ithaca: Cornell University Press, 1987), p.17 and passim.
11. Keohane, *After Hegemony*, p.50.
12. Keohane, *After Hegemony*, p.101.
13. Keohane, *After Hegemony*, pp.63,245.
14. Snyder, 'Averting Anarchy', in Lynn-Jones (ed.), *Cold War and After*, p.131.
15. See for the general argument: Richard B. Elrod, 'The Concert of Europe. A Fresh Look at an International System', *World Politics*, vol.28, no.2 (January 1976). Although the superiority of Neo-liberal institutionalism has been challenged by Joseph M. Grieco (see his book *Cooperation*

Among Nations. Europe, America, and Non-Tariff Barriers to Trade (Ithaca and London: Cornell University Press, 1990), Chapter 2), we will here argue that Neo-liberal institutionalism provides more persuasive arguments for the development of (West) European politics during the 1990s, than Neo-realism.

16. E. H. Carr, *The Twenty Years' Crisis, 1919-1939* (New York: Harper & Row, 1964), p.87. See also Hedley Bull, *The Anarchical Society. A Study of Order in World Politics* (London: Macmillan, 1977), Chapter 4.

17. See, for instance, Ralf Dahrendorf, in *Die Zeit*, 20 July 1990.

18. *The Economist*, 14 March 1992.

19. Quoted in Renata Fritsch-Bournazel, *Europe and German Unification* (New York/Oxford: Berg, 1992), pp.110-1.

20. Reinhard Rode, *Germany: World Economic Power or Overburdened Eurohegemon?*, Frankfurt am Main, Peace Research Institute Frankfurt, PRIF Report No. 21 (1991), p.12.

21. *Le Monde*, 14 November 1989.

22. Speech by Chevènement on 21 May 1990. Quoted in Fritsch-Bournazel, *Europe and German Unification*, p.130. In mid-December 1989, Mitterrand also argued that 'Our German friends must remember that there was a world war', a war in which France was, of course, among the victorious nations, and implying that Germany had to tone down its ambitions in Europe. See Patrick McCarthy, *France and the EC: Can a Gaullist World Power Find Happiness in a Regional Bloc?*, Occasional Paper no. 71, The Johns Hopkins University Bologna Center (February 1992), p.21.

23. See Thomas C. Schelling, *The Strategy of Conflict* (Cambridge: Harvard University Press, 1960).

24. *The Times*, 10 February 1990.

25. Press conference by President Mitterrand in Strasbourg, 9 December 1989. In his New Year's message, in late-December 1989, Mitterrand further argued: 'Either the tendencies of dissolution and fragmentation will increase and we shall find ourselves back in the Europe of 1919 – and we know what has happened thereafter – or Europe will grow together'. *La Politique Étrangère de la France, Textes et Documents*, Paris, Ministère des Affaires Étrangères (1990), p.227.

26. Arthur A. Stein, *Why Nations Cooperate. Circumstance and Choice in International Relations* (Ithaca and London: Cornell University Press, 1990), p.52.

27. See *The Economist*, 3 October 1992.

Bibliography

Adler-Karlsson, Gunnar, *Western Economic Warfare, 1947-1967* (Stockholm: Almquist and Wicksell, 1968)

Adomeit, Hannes, 'Soviet Perceptions of Western European Integration: Ideological Distortion or Realistic Assessment?', *Millennium: Journal of International Studies*, vol.8, no.1 (Spring 1979)

Agnelli, G., 'East-West Trade: A European View', *Foreign Affairs*, vol.58, no.5 (Summer 1980)

Alting von Geusau, Frans A. M., *Beyond the European Community* (Leyden: A. W. Sijthoff, 1969)

Alton, Thad P., 'Comparison of Overall Economic Performance in the East European Countries', in Reiner Weichhardt (ed.), *The Economies of Eastern Europe Under Gorbachev's Influence* (Brussels: NATO Colloquium, 1988)

Ambrose, Stephen E., *Rise to Globalism. American Foreign Policy Since 1938* (Harmondsworth: Penguin Books, 1986)

Andreyev, D., and M. Makov, 'The Common Market After Eleven Years', *International Affairs* (Moscow), no.1 (January 1969)

Andriessen, Frans H. J. J., 'The European Community and East-West Cooperation', Address at the Conference on *The Soviet Union in the 1990s*, Moscow (7-8 June 1989), mimeo.

Andriessen, Frans H. J. J., 'Change in Central and Eastern Europe. The Role of the European Community', *NATO Review*, vol.38, no.1 (February 1990)

Aslund, Anders, 'The New Soviet Policy Towards International Economic Organisations', *The World Today*, vol.44, no.2 (February 1988)

Die Auswärtige Politik der Bundesrepublik Deutschland (Köln: Verlag Wissenschaft und Politik, 1972)

Bähr, Paul, 'Handel und Händel Zwischen Ost und West', *Europa-Archiv*, vol.28 (1973)

Bahu-Leyser, D., *De Gaulle, les Français et l'Europe* (Paris: Presses Universitaires de France, 1981)

Bailey-Wiebecke, Ilka, *Die Europäische Gemeinschaft und der Rat für Gegenseitige Wirtschaftshilfe. Multilaterale Diplomatie oder Blockpolitik?* (Bern: Peter Lang, 1989)

Baldwin, David A., *Economic Statecraft* (Princeton, NJ: Princeton University Press, 1985)

Baumer, Max, and Hanns-Dieter Jacobsen, 'EC and COMECON: Intricate Negotiations between the Two Integration Systems in Europe', in Werner J. Feld (ed.), *Western Europe's Global Reach* (New York: Pergamon, 1980)

Bell, Coral, 'Why Russia Should Join NATO. From Containment to Concert', *The National Interest*, no.22 (Winter 1990/91)

Beloff, Max, *The United States and the Unity of Europe* (London: Faber and Faber, 1963)

Beugel, Ernst H. van der, *From Marshall Aid to Atlantic Partnership. European Integration as a Concern of American Foreign Policy* (Amsterdam, London, New York: Elsevier Publishing Company, 1966)

Bliss, Howard (ed.), *The Political Development of the European Community. A Documentary Collection* (Waltham, Mass.: Blaisdell, 1970)

Bloed, Arie, *The External Relations of the Council for Mutual Economic Assistance* (Dordrecht: Martinus Nijhoff, 1988)

Bloed, Arie (ed.), *From Helsinki to Vienna. Basic Documents of the Helsinki Process* (Dordrecht: Martinus Nijhoff, 1990)

Bomert, Bert, *Nederland en Oost-Europa. Meer Woorden dan Daden* (Amsterdam: Uitgeverij Jan Mets, 1990)

Bot, Bernard R., 'EEC-CMEA: Is a Meaningful Relationship Possible?', *Common Market Law Review*, vol.13 (1976)

Brabant, Jozef M. van, *A Central European Payments Union: Technical Aspects*, Public Policy Paper 3, Institute for East-West Security Studies, New York/Prague (1991)

Brada, Josef C., 'The European Community and Czechoslovakia, Hungary, and Poland', *Report on Eastern Europe* (RFE/RL Research Institute), vol.2, no.49 (6 December 1991)

Bräker, Hans, 'Osteuropa, die Europäische Gemeinschaft und das GATT. Zur gegenwärtigen Außenwirtschaftspolitik der Länder des RGW', *Europa-Archiv*, vol.28, no. 19 (1973)

Bremer, Hans-Hagen, 'Das RGW-Angebot, Nehmen Ohne Zu Geben', *EG-Magazin*, no.11 (1976)

Brown, J. F., 'The Views from Vienna and Rome', in Lincoln Gordon (ed.), *Eroding Empire. Western Relations with Eastern Europe* (Washington, DC: The Brookings Institution, 1987)

Brzezinski, Zbigniew, 'Russia and Europe', *Foreign Affairs*, vol.42, no.3 (April 1964)

Brzezinski, Zbigniew, 'The Soviet Bloc, the Common Market and France', in Sydney Nettleton Fisher (ed.), *France and the European Community* (n.p.: Ohio State University Press, 1964)

Bull, H., *The Anarchical Society. A Study of Order in World Politics* (London: Macmillan, 1977)

Bull, H., and A. Watson (eds.), *The Expansion of International Society* (Oxford: Oxford University Press, 1984)

Bulmer, Simon, and William Paterson, *The Federal Republic of Germany and the European Community* (London: Allen & Unwin, 1987)

Buzan, Barry, *People, States and Fear. An Agenda for International Security Studies in the Post-Cold War Era* (New York: Harvester Wheatsheaf, 1991)

Buzan, Barry, 'New Patterns of Global Security in the Twenty-First Century', *International Affairs* (London), vol.67, no.3 (1991)

Buzan, Barry, and Morton Kelstrup, Pierre Lemaitre, Elzbieta Tromer and Ole Wæver, *The European Security Order Recast. Scenarios for the Post-Cold War Era* (London: Pinter, 1990)

Calleo, David P., *Beyond American Hegemony. The Future of the Western Alliance* (London: Wheatsheaf, 1987)

Calvocoressi, Peter, *World Politics Since 1945* (New York: Longman, 1982)

Campo, Emille A., 'Interview', *Export Magazine* (The Hague), 17 November 1990

Camps, Miriam, *Britain and the European Community 1955-1963* (Princeton, NJ: Princeton University Press, 1964)

Carmoy, Guy de, *The Foreign Policies of France, 1944-1968* (Chicago: University of Chicago Press, 1970)

Carr, E. H., *The Twenty Years' Crisis, 1919-1939* (New York: Harper & Row, 1964)

Chapman, Sheila A., 'The Economic Relations Between the EEC and the CMEA: A Survey of Problems and Prospects', *La Comunita Internazionale*, vol.40, terzo trimestre (1985)

Chelnokov, I., 'The European Coal and Steel Community', *International Affairs* (Moscow), no.2 (February 1957)

Chotiner, Barbara Ann, and John W. Atwell, 'Soviet Occupation Policy Toward Germany, 1945-1949', in Hans A. Schmitt (ed.), *U.S. Occupation in Europe After World War II* (Lawrence: Regents Press of Kansas, 1978)

Christensen, Thomas J., and Jack Snyder, 'Chain Gangs and Passed Bucks: Predicting Alliance Patterns in Multipolarity', *International Organization*, vol.44, no.2 (Spring 1990)

Churchill, Winston, *Triumph and Tragedy* (Boston: Houghton Mifflin, 1953)

Coffey, Peter, *The External Economic Relations of the EEC* (London: Macmillan, 1976)

Commission of the EC (Directorate-General for Economic and Financial Affairs), *European Economy. Economic Transformation in Hungary and Poland*, no.43 (March 1990)

Comprehensive Programme for the Further Extension and Improvement of Co-operation and the Development of Socialist Integration by the CMEA Member-Countries, CMEA Secretariat, Moscow, 1971

Cooper, Richard N., 'Trade Policy is Foreign Policy', *Foreign Policy*, no.9 (Winter 1972-3)

Crawford, Beverly, and Stefanie Lenway, 'Decision Modes and International Regime Change: Western Collaboration on East-West Trade', *World Politics*, vol.37, no.3 (April 1985)

Cutler, Robert M., 'Harmonizing EEC-CMEA Relations: Never the Twain Shall Meet?', *International Affairs* (London), vol.63, no.2 (Spring 1987)

Czinkota, Michael, 'The EC '92 and Eastern Europe: Effects of Integration vs. Disintegration', *The Columbia Journal of World Business*, vol.26, no.1 (Spring 1991)

Davy, Richard, 'Überlegungen zur britischen Ostpolitik', *Europäische Rundschau*, vol.7, no.2 (1979)

Dell, Sidney, *A Latin American Common Market?* (London: Oxford University Press, 1966)

Denton, R., 'The Non-Market Economy Rules of the European Community's Anti-Dumping and Countervailing Duties Legislation', *International and Comparative Law Quarterly*, vol.36 (1987)

Deubner, C., *Portugals Beitritt zur EG. Perspektiven und Strategien* (Bonn: Friedrich Ebert Stiftung, 1981)

Deutsch, Karl W., and S. A. Burrell *et al.*, *Political Community and the North Atlantic Area* (Princeton, NJ: Princeton University Press, 1957)

Deutsch, Karl W., and Lewis J. Edinger, Roy C. Macridis and Richard L. Merritt, *France, Germany and the Western Alliance. A Study of Elite Attitudes on European Integration and World Politics* (New York: Charles Scribner's Sons, 1967)

Deutsch, Karl W., and J. David Singer, 'Multipolar Power Systems and International Stability', *World Politics*, vol.16, no.3 (April 1964)

Diebold, William, Jr., 'East-West Trade and the Marshall Plan', *Foreign Affairs*, vol.26, no.4 (July 1948)

Djilas, Milovan, *Conversations with Stalin* (New York: Harcourt, Brace & World, Inc., 1962)

Doyle, Michael, 'Kant, Liberal Legacies, and Foreign Affairs', *Philosophy and Public Affairs*, vol.12 (Summer and Fall 1983)

Doyle, Michael, 'Liberalism and World Politics', *American Political Science Review*, vol.80, no.4 (December 1986)

Driscoll, D. J., and N. McKellar, 'The Changing Regime of North Sea Fisheries', in C. M. Mason (ed.), *The Effective Management of Resources* (London: Pinter, 1979)

Eden, Anthony, *Full Circle* (London: Cassell, 1960)

Ehrhardt, Carl A., 'EWG und die Koordinierung des Osthandels', *Aussenpolitik*, vol.16, no.6 (June 1965)

Ehrhardt, Carl A., 'EWG und RGW kommen sich nur langsam näher', *Aussenpolitik*, vol.28, no.2 (1977)

Elrod, Richard B., 'The Concert of Europe. A Fresh Look at an International System', *World Politics*, vol.28, no.2 (January 1976)

Elster, Jon, *Nuts and Bolts for the Social Sciences* (Cambridge: Cambridge University Press, 1989)

Ermers H., and J. Kragt, 'Tussen Traditie en Tractaten: Minister Beyen van Buitenlandse Zaken en de Europese Integratie', *Internationale Spectator*, vol.45, no.5 (Mei 1991)

Etzold, Th. H., and J. L. Gaddis (eds.), *Containment: Documents on American Policy and Strategy. 1945-1950* (New York: Columbia University Press, 1978)

European Community and Acceding Countries of Southern Europe (West Berlin: Deutsches Institut für Entwicklungspolitik, 1979)

Evera, Stephen van, 'Primed for Peace: Europe After the Cold War', in Sean M. Lynn-Jones (ed.), *The Cold War and After. Prospects for Peace. An International Security Reader* (Cambridge, Mass.: The MIT Press, 1991)

Eyskens, Mark, *Van Detente Naar Entente. Gevolgen van de Implosie van het Communisme*, (Brussels: Ministerie van Buitenlandse Zaken, 1990)

Feinstein, Charles, *et al.*, *Historical Precedents for Economic Change in Central Europe and the USSR* (Credit Suisse First Boston Ltd., and Oxford Analytyca) October 1990

Feld, Werner J., 'The Association Agreements of the European Communities: A Comparative Analysis', *International Organization*, vol.19, no.2 (Spring 1965)

Feld, Werner J., 'The Utility of the EEC Experience for Eastern Europe', *Journal of Common Market Studies*, vol.8, no.3 (1969-70)

Feld, Werner J. (ed.), *The Foreign Policies of West European Socialist Parties* (New York: Praeger Publishers, 1978)

Fenske, John, 'France's Uncertain Progress Toward European Union', *Current History*, vol.90, no.559 (November 1991)

Forsyth, Murray, 'The Political Objectives of European Integration', *International Affairs* (London), vol.43, no.3 (July 1967)

Forte, David F. P., 'The Response of Soviet Foreign Policy to the Common Market, 1957-63', *Soviet Studies*, vol.19, no.3 (1968)

Friedrich, Carl J., *Europe. An Emerging Nation?* (New York and Evanston: Harper & Row, 1969)

Fritsch-Bournazel, Renata, 'Frankreich. Osthandel im Spannungsfeld von Ideologie und wirtschaftlichem Zwang', in Reinhard Rode and Hanns-D. Jacobsen (eds.), *Wirtschaftkrieg oder Entspannung. Eine politische Bilanz der Ost-West Wirtschaftsbeziehungen* (Bonn: Verlag Neue Gesellschaft, 1984)

Fritsch-Bournazel, Renata, *Europe and German Unification* (New York/ Oxford: Berg, 1992)

Fukuyama, Francis, 'The End of History?', *The National Interest*, no.16 (Summer 1989)

Fukuyama, Francis, *The End of History and the Last Man* (London: Hamish Hamilton, 1992)

Funigiello, Philip J., *American-Soviet Trade in the Cold War* (Chapel Hill and London: The University of North Carolina Press, 1988)

Fursdon, Edward, *The European Defence Community. A History* (London: Macmillan, 1980)

Gaddis, John Lewis, *The Long Peace. Inquiries into the History of the Cold War* (New York: Oxford University Press, 1987)

Galtung, Johan, *The European Community: A Superpower in the Making* (London: Allen & Unwin, 1973)

George, Stephen, *Politics and Policy in the European Community* (Oxford: Clarendon Press, 1985)

Geremek, Bronislav, 'Aid to East Europe: The West's Waiting Game', *European Affairs*, vol.4, no.2 (Summer 1990)

Geremek, Bronislav, Ivan Klima and György Konrád, *Warschau – Praag – Boedapest. Hoe Cultuur Overleefde* (Rotterdam: Universitaire Pers Rotterdam, 1990)

Geron, Leonard, *Soviet Foreign Economic Policy Under Perestroika* (New York: Council on Foreign Relations Press, 1990)

Giola, Gianluigi, 'L'Ostpolitik de la Communauté européenne', *Cadmos*, Douzième année, no.45 (Printemps 1984)

Goldstein, Walter, 'EC: Euro-Stalling', *Foreign Policy*, no.85 (Winter 1991-2)

Goodwin, G. L., 'A European Community Foreign Policy?', *Journal of Common Market Studies*, vol.12, no.1 (September 1973)

Gorbachev, Mikhail, *Perestroyka. New Thinking for Our Country and the World* (New York: Harper & Row, 1987)

Gordon, Lincoln, 'The Organization for European Economic Cooperation', *International Organization*, vol.10, no.11 (February 1956)

Gordon, Lincoln (ed.), *Eroding Empire: Western relations with Eastern Europe* (Washington, DC: The Brookings Institution, 1987)

Götz von Groll, 'Die KSZE und die Europäische Gemeinschaft', in Jost Delbrück, Norbert Ropers and Gerda Zellentin (eds.), *Grünbuch zu den Folgewirkungen der KSZE* (Köln: Verlag Wissenschaft und Politik, 1977)

Grieco, Joseph M., 'Anarchy and the Limits of Cooperation. A Realist Critique of the Newest Liberal Institutionalism', *International Organization*, vol.42, no.3 (Summer 1988)

Grieco, Joseph M., *Cooperation Among Nations. Europe, America, and Non-Tariff Barriers to Trade* (Ithaca and London: Cornell University Press, 1990)

Gros, Daniel, 'A Multilateral Payments Mechanism for Eastern Europe', Working Documents no.59, Centre for European Policy Studies, Brussels (1992)

Gros, Daniel, and Alfred Steinherr, *From Centrally-Planned to Market Economies. Issues for the Transition in Central Europe and the Soviet Union* (Oxford: Brassey's, 1991)

Groothaert, Jacques, 'Financial Cooperation and Countertrade', in Marc Maresceau (ed.), *The Political and Legal Framework of Trade Relations Between the European Community and Eastern Europe* (Dordrecht: Martinus Nijhoff, 1989)

Gumpel, Werner, 'Der Rat für Gegenseitige Wirtschaftshilfe als Instrument sowjetischer Hegemonie', *Osteuropa*, vol.26, no.11 (November 1976)

Haas, Ernst B., *The Uniting of Europe. Political, Social and Economic Forces, 1950-1957* (London: Stevens, 1958)

Haass, Richard, 'The Primacy of the State ... or Revising the Revisionists', *Dædalus*, vol.108, no.4 (Fall 1979)

Hacker, Jens, 'Die Berlin-Politik der UdSSR Unter Gorbatschow', *Aussenpolitik*, vol.40, no.3 (1989)

Hallstein, W., *Europäische Reden* (Stuttgart: Deutsche Verlags-Anstalt, 1979)

Ham, Peter van, 'Western Economic Statecraft in an Era of Communist Reform. How Can the West Help?', *Bulletin of Peace Proposals*, vol.21, no.2 (June 1990)

Ham, Peter van, 'Brussels Verlicht Eigenbelang: De Associatie-akkoorden Tussen de EG en Centraal-Europa', *Internationale Spectator*, vol.46, no.1 (Januari 1992)

Ham, Peter van, *Western Doctrines on East-West Trade. Theory, History and Policy* (New York: St. Martin's Press, 1992)

Hanak, H., *Soviet Foreign Policy Since the Death of Stalin* (London and Boston: Routledge & Kegan Paul, 1972)

Hanrieder, Wolfram F., *Germany, America, Europe. Forty Years of German Foreign Policy* (New Haven and London: Yale University Press, 1989)

Hanson, Philip, 'Economic Aspects of Helsinki', *International Affairs* (London), vol.61, no.4 (Autumn 1985)

Hanson, Philip, and Vlad Sobell, 'The Changing Relations Between the EC and the CMEA', *Radio Free Europe Research* (RAD Background Report/73), vol.14, no.17 (May 1989)

Hardt, John P., and Donna Gold, 'Premises Underlying U.S. Policy on Commercial Relations With the USSR', Committee on Foreign Relations United States Senate and Congressional Research Service Library of Congress, *The Premises of East-West Commercial Relations* (Washington, DC: US Government Printing Office, 1982)

Hardt, John P., and Kate S. Tomlinson, 'Soviet Economic Policies in Western Europe', in Herbert J. Ellison (ed.), *Soviet Policy Toward Western Europe. Implications for the Atlantic Alliance* (Seattle and London: University of Washington Press, 1983)

Hassner, Pierre, 'West European Perceptions of the USSR', *Dædalus*, vol.108, no.1 (Winter 1979)

Hassner, Pierre, 'The View From Paris', in Lincoln Gordon (ed.), *Eroding Empire. Western Relations with Eastern Europe* (Washington, DC: The Brookings Institution, 1987)

Hassner, Pierre, 'Perceptions of the Soviet Threat in the 1950s and the 1980s: The Case of France', in Carl-Christoph Schweitzer (ed.), *The Changing Western Analysis of the Soviet Threat* (London: Pinter, 1989)

Hassner, Pierre, 'Europe Beyond Partition and Unity: Disintegration or Reconstitution?', *International Affairs* (London), vol.66, no.3 (1990)

Haus, Leah, 'The East European Countries and GATT: The Role of Realism, Mercantilism, and Regime Theory in Explaining East-West Trade Negotiations', *International Organization*, vol.45, no.2 (Spring 1991)

Healey, Dennis, 'The Crisis in Europe', *International Affairs* (London), vol.38, no.2 (April 1962)

Heseltine, M., 'The EC: First Deeper, Then Wider', *European Affairs*, vol.4, no.2 (Summer 1990)

Hewett, Ed. A., *Reforming the Soviet Economy. Equality versus Efficiency* (Washington, DC: The Brookings Institution, 1988)

Hewitt, Adrian, 'ACP and the Developing World', in Juliet Lodge (ed.), *The European Community and the Challenge of the Future* (London: Pinter, 1989)

Hirschman, Albert O., *National Power and the Structure of Foreign Trade* (Berkeley, Los Angeles, London: University of California Press, 1980)

Hixson, Walter L., *George F. Kennan. Cold War Iconoclast* (New York: Columbia University Press, 1989)

Hoffmann, Stanley, 'Obstinate or Obsolete? The Fate of the Nation-State and the Case of Western Europe', *Dædalus*, vol.95, no.3 (Summer 1966)

Hoffmann, Stanley, 'Fragments Floating in the Here and Now', *Dædalus*, vol.108, no.1 (Winter 1979)

Hoffmann, Stanley, 'Détente', in Joseph S. Nye, Jr. (ed.), *The Making of America's Soviet Policy* (New Haven and London: Yale University Press, 1984)

Hoffmann, Stanley, 'The Case for Leadership', *Foreign Policy*, no.81 (Winter 1990-1)

Hogan, Michael J., *The Marshall Plan. America, Britain, and the Reconstruction of Western Europe, 1947-1952* (Cambridge: Cambridge University Press, 1987)

Holsti, K. J., 'Governance Without Government. Polyarchy in Nineteenth-Century European International Politics', in James N. Rosenau and Ernst-Otto Czempiel (eds.), *Governance Without Government. Order and Change in World Politics* (Cambridge: Cambridge University Press, 1992)

Hrbek, Rudolf, 'The EC and the Changes in Central and Eastern Europe', *Intereconomics*, vol.25, no.3 (May/June 1990)

Huntington, Samuel P., *Political Order in Changing Societies* (New Haven: Yale University Press, 1968)

Hurwitz, Leon, *The European Community and the Management of International Cooperation* (New York: Greenwood Press, 1987)

Hütte, Rüdiger, 'Berlin and the European Community', in F. G. Jacobs (ed.), *Yearbook of European Law* (Oxford: Clarendon Press, 1984)

Jackson, Marvin, 'The Impact of the Gulf Crisis on the Economies of Eastern Europe', *Report on Eastern Europe* (RFE/RL Research Institute), vol.1, no.35 (31 August 1990)

Jacobs, Francis, 'Anti-Dumping Procedures with regard to Imports from Eastern Europe', in Marc Maresceau (ed.), *The Political and Legal Framework of Trade Relations Between the European Community and Eastern Europe* (Dordrecht: Martinus Nijhoff, 1989)

Jacobsen, Hans-Adolf, Wolfgang Mallmann and Christian Meier (eds.), *Sicherheit und Zusammenarbeit in Europa (KSZE). Analyse und Dokumentation* (Köln: Verlag Wissenschaft und Politik, 1973)

Jansen, Max, and Johan K. de Vree, *The Ordeal of Unity. The Politics of European Integration Since 1945* (Bilthoven: Prime Press, 1988)

Jentleson, Bruce W., 'The Western Alliance and East-West Energy Trade', in G. K. Bertsch (ed.), *Controlling East-West Trade and Technology Transfer. Power, Politics, and Policies* (Durham and London: Duke University Press, 1988)

Jervis, Robert, 'Cooperation Under the Security Dilemma', *World Politics*, vol.30, no.2 (1978)

Jervis, Robert, 'From Balance to Concert. A Study of International Security Cooperation', in Kenneth A. Oye (ed.), *Cooperation Under Anarchy* (Princeton, NJ: Princeton University Press, 1986)

Jervis, Robert, *The Meaning of the Nuclear Revolution. Statecraft and the Prospect of Armageddon* (Ithaca and London: Cornell University Press, 1989)

Joffe, Josef, 'The View from Bonn', in L. Gordon (ed.) *Eroding Empire: Western Relations with Eastern Europe* (Washington, DC: The Brookings Institution, 1987)

Joffe, Josef, 'The Revisionists. Moscow, Bonn, and the European Balance', *The National Interest*, no.17 (Fall 1989)

John, Ieuan G., 'The Soviet Response to Western European Integration', in Ieuan G. John (ed.), *EEC Policy Towards Eastern Europe* (Westmead, Farnborough, Hants.: Saxon House, 1975)

Jones, J. M., *The Fifteen Weeks (February 21 – June 5, 1947)* (New York: Harcourt, Brace & World, 1955)

Jordan, Robert S., and Werner J. Feld, *Europe in the Balance. The Changing Context of European International Politics* (London, Boston: Faber and Faber, 1986)

Kádár, Béla, 'The 1992 Challenge: Responses in East-West Cooperation and in Hungary', *The International Spectator*, vol.25, no.3 (July-September 1990)

Karat, Johann, 'Sowjetunion und Europäische Gemeinschaften', *Aussenpolitik*, vol.23, no.7 (1972)

Kaser, Michael, *Comecon* (London: Oxford University Press, 1965)

Kaser, Michael, and C. F. G. Ransom, 'Relations with Eastern Europe', in G. R. Denton (ed.), *Economic Integration in Europe* (London: Weidenfeld and Nicolson, 1969)

Katzman, Julie E., 'The Euro-Siberian Gas Pipeline Row: A Study in Community Development', *Millennium: Journal of International Studies*, vol.17, no.1 (Spring 1988)

Kennan, George F., 'The Marshall Plan and the Future of Europe', *Transatlantic Perspectives*, no.17 (Winter 1988)

Kennedy, Paul, *The Rise and Fall of the Great Powers. Economic Change and Military Conflict from 1500 to 2000* (New York: Random House, 1987)

Keohane, Robert O., *After Hegemony. Cooperation and Discord in the World Political Economy* (Princeton, NJ: Princeton University Press, 1984)

Keohane, Robert O., *International Institutions and State Power. Essays in International Relations Theory* (Boulder: Westview Press, 1989)

Keohane, Robert O., and Stanley Hoffmann, 'Institutional Change in Europe in the 1980s', in Robert O. Keohane and Stanley Hoffmann (eds.), *The New European Community. Decisionmaking and Institutional Change* (Boulder: Westview Press, 1991)

Keohane, Robert O., and Joseph S. Nye, Jr. (eds.), *Transnational Relations and World Politics* (Cambridge: Cambridge University Press, 1971)

Khrushchev, N. S., 'Vital Questions of the Development of the World Socialist System', *Kommunist*, no.12 (1962)

Kiep, Walter Leisler, 'The New Deutschlandpolitik', *Foreign Affairs*, vol.63, no.2 (Winter 1984-5)

Kirk Laux, Jeanne, *Reform, Reintegration and Regional Security. The Role of Western Assistance in Overcoming Insecurity in Central and Eastern Europe*, Working Paper 37, Canadian Institute for International Peace and Security (October 1991)

Kitzinger, Uwe, *Diplomacy and Persuasion. How Britain Joined the Common Market* (London: Thames and Hudson, 1973)

Kitzinger, Uwe, *Britain and the EEC. Past and Present* (London: Macmillan, 1983)

Klocke, Helmut, 'Der RGW und sein Verhältnis zur EWG', *Aussenpolitik*, vol.22, no.5 (1971)

Knapen, Ben, *De Lange Weg Naar Moskou. De Nederlandse Relatie tot de Sovjet-Unie, 1917-1942* (Amsterdam: Elsevier, 1985)

Knorr, Klaus, 'International Economic Leverage and its Uses', in Klaus Knorr and Frank N. Trager (eds.), *Economic Issues and National Security* (Lawrence, Kansas: University Press of Kansas, 1977)

Koehler, Heinz, *Economic Integration in the Soviet Bloc* (New York: Praeger, 1965)

Kolboom, Ingo, 'Ostpolitik als deutsch-französische Herausforderung', *Europa-Archiv*, vol.44, no.4 (1989)

Die Kommunisten und der Gemeinsame Markt (Köln: Europa Union Verlag, 1968)

Kostrzewa, Wojciech, and Holger Schmiedling, 'An EFTA Option for Eastern Europe', *Swiss Review of World Affairs*, vol.49, no.19 (January 1990)

Kovrig, Bennett, *The Myth of Liberation. East-Central Europe in US Diplomacy and Politics Since 1941* (Baltimore and London: The Johns Hopkins University Press, 1973)

Kovrig, Bennett, *Of Walls and Bridges. The United States and Eastern Europe* (New York: New York University Press, 1991)

Krämer, Hans R., 'Die Stellung der EWG im Bereich der Ostsee', *Europa-Archiv*, vol.34, no.8 (1979)

Kramer, Heinz, 'Die EG und die Stabilisierung Osteuropas', *Aussenpolitik*, vol.43, no.1 (1992)

Krasner, Stephen D., 'Structural Causes and Regime Consequences: Regimes as Intervening Variables', in Stephen D. Krasner (ed.), *International Regimes* (Ithaca and London: Cornell University Press, 1983)

Kulski, W. W., *De Gaulle and the World. The Foreign Policy of the Fifth French Republic* (Syracuse, New York: Syracuse University Press, 1966)

Kupchan, Charles A., and Clifford A. Kupchan, 'Concerts, Collective Security, and the Future of Europe', *International Security*, vol.16, no.1 (Summer 1991)

Labbé, Marie-Hélène, and Peter van Ham, 'The West European Approach Towards COCOM', in G. K. Bertsch, H. Vogel and J. Zielonka (eds.), *After the Revolutions. East-West Trade and Technology Transfer in the 1990s* (Boulder: Westview Press, 1991)

Lacorne, Denis, 'From Détente 1 to Détente 2: A Comparison of Giscard's and Mitterrand's East-West Policies', in David A. Baldwin and Helen V. Milner (eds.), *East-West Trade and the Atlantic Alliance* (New York: St. Martin's Press, 1990)

Lange, Halvard M., 'European Union: False Hopes and Realities', *Foreign Affairs*, vol.28, no.3 (April 1950)

Langguth, Gerd, 'Deutschland, die EG und die Architektur Europas', *Aussenpolitik*, vol.42, no.2 (1991)

Lasok, D., and J. W. Bridge, *Law and Institutions of the European Communities* (London: Butterworths, 1991)

Layton, Christopher, 'Europe, Road to Co-existence', *Journal of Common Market Studies*, vol.3, no.3 (1964-5)

Lebahn, Axel, 'RGW und EG – Faktoren des Ost-West-Handels', *Aussenpolitik*, vol.29, no.2 (1978)

Lebahn, Axel, 'Alternativen in den EG-RGW Beziehungen', *Aussenpolitik*, vol.31, no.2 (1980)

LeGloannec, Anne-Marie, 'France's German Problem', in F. Stephen Larrabee (ed.), *The Two German States and European Security* (London: Macmillan, 1989)

Legvold, Robert, 'France and Soviet Policy', in Herbert J. Ellison (ed.), *Soviet Policy Toward Western Europe. Implications for the Atlantic Alliance* (Seattle and London: University of Washington Press, 1983)

Lemin, I., 'Crisis of West European Integration and Its Political Aspects', *International Affairs* (Moscow), no.5 (May 1966)

Levitsky, Serge L., 'GATT and the State Trading', *Libertas*, no.1 (1987)

Lindberg, Leon N., and Stuart A. Scheingold, *Europe's Would-Be Polity. Patterns of Change in the European Community* (Englewood Cliffs, NJ: Prentice-Hall, 1970)

Lippert, Barbara, 'EC-CMEA Relations: Normalisation and Beyond', in Geoffrey Edwards and Elfriede Regelsberger (eds.), *Europe's Global Links. The European Community and InterRegional Cooperation* (London: Pinter, 1990)

Ludlow, Peter, *The Making of the European Monetary System. A Case Study of the Politics of the European Community* (London: Butterworth Scientific, 1982)

Ludlow, Peter, *German Unification and European Unity*, Working Document no.49, Centre for European Policy Studies, Brussels (1990)

Ludlow, Peter, 'The European Commission', in Robert O. Keohane and Stanley Hoffmann (eds.), *The New European Community. Decisionmaking and Institutional Change* (Boulder: Westview Press, 1991)

Lysén, Göran, 'EEC-CMEA/Eastern Europe Legal Aspects on Trade and Co-operation', *Legal Issues of European Integration*, no.1 (1987)

McCarthy, Patrick, *France and the EC: Can a Gaullist World Power Find Happiness in a Regional Bloc?*, Occasional Paper no. 71, The Johns Hopkins University Bologna Center (February 1992)

McInnes, Neil, 'The Communist Parties of Western Europe and the EEC', *The World Today*, vol.30 (February 1974)

Maistre, Joseph de, *The Works of Joseph de Maistre* (New York: Schocken Books, 1971)

Malcolm, Neil, 'The "Common European Home" and Soviet European Policy', *International Affairs* (London), vol.65, no.4 (Autumn 1989)

Malfliet, Katlijn, 'De Belgo-Sovjet Handelsbetrekkingen', *Studia Diplomatica*, vol.xli, no.3 (1988)

Marer, Paul, and Wlodzimierz Siwinski (eds.), *Creditworthiness and Reform in Poland. Western and Polish Perspectives* (Bloomington and Indianapolis: Indiana University Press, 1988)

Marsh, Peter, 'The Integration Process in Eastern Europe 1968 to 1975', *Journal of Common Market Studies*, vol.14, no.4 (June 1976)

Marsh, Peter, 'The Development of Relations Between the EEC and the CMEA', in Avi Shlaim and G. N. Yannopoulos (eds.), *The EEC and Eastern Europe* (Cambridge: Cambridge University Press, 1978)

Maslen, John, 'The European Community's Relations with the State-Trading Countries 1981-1983', in F. G. Jacobs (ed.), *Yearbook of European Law* (Oxford: Clarendon Press, 1984)

Maslen, John, 'The European Community's Relations with the State-Trading Countries 1984-1986', in F. G. Jacobs (ed.), *Yearbook of European Law* (Oxford: Clarendon Press, 1987)

Maslen, John, 'A Turning Point: Past and Future of the European Community's Relations with Eastern Europe', *Revista di Studi Politici Internazionali*, Anno LV, no.4 (Ottobre-Dicembre 1988)

Mathiopoulos, Margarita, 'Gorbatschows "gemeinsames europäisches Haus", Wiederauferstehung von Wandel durch Annäherung?', *Europäische Rundschau*, vol.17, no.2 (1989)

Mayne, Richard, *The Recovery of Europe. From Devastation to Unity* (London: Weidenfeld and Nicolson, 1970)

Mearsheimer, John J., 'Back to the Future. Instability in Europe After the Cold War', in Sean M. Lynn-Jones (ed.), *The Cold War and After. Prospects for Peace. An International Security Reader* (Cambridge, Mass.: The MIT Press, 1991)

Mehnert, Klaus, 'Sicherheitskonferenz für Europa', *Osteuropa*, vol.20, no.10 (Oktober 1970)

Michalski, Anna, and Helen Wallace, *The European Community: The Challenge of Enlargement*, Special Paper European Programme, Royal Institute of International Affairs, London (1992)

Michelis, G. de, 'Reaching Out to the East', *Foreign Policy*, no.79 (Summer 1990)

Ministerie van Buitenlandse Zaken van Nederland, *Conferentie over Veiligheid en Samenwerking in Europa. Helsinki, Genève, Helsinki. 1973-1975* ('s-Gravenhage, Staatsuitgeverij, 1976)

Monod, Jérôme, Pehr Gyllenhammar and Wisse Dekker, *Reshaping Europe. A Report from the European Round Table of Industrialists* (September 1991)

Montani, Guido, 'Europe and the CMEA: Towards a European Ostpolitik?', *The Federalist*, vol.27, no.3 (December 1985)

Moravcsik, Andrew, 'Negotiating the Single European Act: National Interests and Conventional Statecraft in the European Community', *International Organization*, vol.45, no.1 (Winter 1991)

Morawiecki, W., 'Actors and Interests in the Process of Negotiations Between the CMEA and the EEC', *Legal Issues of European Integration*, no.2 (1989)

Morawitz, Rudolf, 'Der innerdeutsche Handel und die EWG nach dem Grundvertrag', *Europa-Archiv*, vol.28 (1973)

Moreau Defarges, Philippe, 'L'unification Communautaire et Les Bouleversement du Paysage Européen', *Politique Étrangère*, vol.55, no.1 (Printemps 1990)

Moreton, Edwina (ed.), *Germany Between East and West* (Cambridge: Cambridge University Press, 1987)

Moreton, Edwina, 'The View from London', in Lincoln Gordon (ed.), *Eroding Empire. Western Relations with Eastern Europe* (Washington, DC: The Brookings Institution, 1987)

Morgan, Roger, 'The Role of Medium Powers in World Politics: the Case of Britain', in Karl Kaiser and Roger Morgan (eds.), *Britain and West Germany. Changing Societies and the Future of Foreign Policy* (London: Oxford University Press, 1971)

Morgan, Roger, 'Grossbritannien', in Eberhard Schulz (ed.), *Die Ostbeziehungen der Europäischen Gemeinschaft* (Wien: R. Oldenbourg Verlag, 1977)

Morgan, Roger, 'French Perspectives of the New Germany', *Government and Opposition*, vol.26, no.1 (Winter 1991)

Morgenthau, Hans J. (with Kenneth W. Thompson), *Politics Among Nations. The Struggle For Power and Peace* (New York: Alfred A. Knopf, 1985)

Mowat, R. C., *Creating the European Community* (New York: Basic Books, 1973)

Mueller, John, 'A New Concert of Europe', *Foreign Policy*, no.77 (Winter 1989-90)

National Academy of Sciences, National Academy of Engineering, Institute of Medicine, *Balancing the National Interest. U.S. National Security Export Controls and Global Economic Competition* (Washington, DC: National Academy Press, 1987)

Neumann, Iver B., *Soviet Perceptions of the European Community, 1950-1988*, Norsk Utenrikspolitisk Institutt, NUPI Rapport, no.131 (July 1989)

Nötzold, Jürgen, 'New Tasks of the European Community with Regard to Eastern Europe', in Armand Clesse and Raymond Vernon (eds.), *The European Community After 1992: A New Role in World Politics?* (Baden-Baden: Nomos Verlagsgesellschaft, 1991)

Nötzold, Jürgen, and Hendrik Roodbeen, 'The European Community and COCOM: The Exclusion of an Interested Party', in G. K. Bertsch, H. Vogel, and J. Zielonka (eds.), *After the Revolutions. East-West Trade and Technology Transfer in the 1990s* (Boulder: Westview Press, 1991)

Nugent, Neill, *The Government and Politics of the European Community* (London: Macmillan, 1989)

Nugent, Neill, 'The Changes in Eastern Europe: Implications For the European Community', *European Access*, (October 1990)

Nye, Joseph S., Jr., 'Transnational and Transgovernmental Relations', in G. L. Goodwin and A. Linklater (eds.), *New Dimensions of World Politics* (London: Croom Helm, 1975)

Nye, Joseph S., Jr., 'Neorealism and Neoliberalism', *World Politics*, vol.40, no.2 (1988)

Olson, Mancur, *The Logic of Collective Action* (Cambridge, Mass.: Harvard University Press, 1963)

Oye, Kenneth A. (ed.), *Cooperation Under Anarchy* (Princeton, NJ: Princeton University Press, 1986)

Palankai, Tibor, *The European Community and Central European Integration. The Hungarian Case*, Occasional Paper Series no.21, Institute for East-West Security Studies, New York/Prague (1991)

Patijn, S. (ed.), *Landmarks in European Unity. 22 Texts on European Integration* (Leyden: A. W. Sijthoff, 1970)

Pavidt, Vladislav, 'Die westeuropäische Integration aus tschechoslowakischer Sicht', in Hans Mayrzedt and Helmut Romé (eds.), *Die Westeuropäische Integration aus osteuropäischer Sicht. Bibliographie – Dokumentation – Kommentar* (Wien: Druck und Verlag Josef Laub, 1968)

Pearce, Joan, 'The Common Agricultural Policy: The Accumulation of Special Interests', in Helen Wallace, William Wallace and Carole Webb (eds.), *Policy-Making in the European Community* (Chichester: John Wiley & Sons, 1989)

Pelkmans, Jacques, and Anna Murphy, *Catapulted Into Leadership: The Community's Trade and Aid Policies vis-à-vis Eastern Europe*, Working Document no.56, Centre for European Policy Studies, Brussels (1991)

Petrov, K., 'Political Integration in Western Europe', *International Affairs* (Moscow), no.11 (November 1969)

Pijpers, Alfred E., *The Vicissitudes of European Political Cooperation. Towards a Realist Interpretation of the EC's Collective Diplomacy* (Leiden University, Department of Political Science, Ph.D. thesis, 1990)

Pijpers, Alfred E., E. Regelsberger and W. Wessels (eds.), *European Political Cooperation in the 1980s. A Common Foreign Policy for Western Europe?* (Dordrecht: Martinus Nijhoff, 1988)

Pinder, John, 'EEC and COMECON', *Survey*, no.58 (January 1966)

Pinder, John, 'Positive Integration and Negative Integration: Some Problems of Economic Union in the EEC', *The World Today*, vol.24 (1968)

Pinder, John, 'A Community Policy Towards Eastern Europe', *The World Today*, vol.30 (March 1974)

Pinder, John, 'The Community and the State Trading Countries', in Kenneth J. Twitchett (ed.), *Europe and the World. The External Relations of the Common Market* (London: Europa Publications, 1976)

Pinder, John, 'The Community and Comecon: What Could Negotiations Achieve?', *The World Today*, vol.33 (May 1977)

Pinder, John, 'Economic Integration and East-West Trade: Conflict of Interests or Comedy of Errors?', *Journal of Common Market Studies*, vol.16, no.1 (September 1977)

Pinder, John, 'Soviet Views of Western Economic Integration', in Avi Shlaim and G. N. Yannopoulos (eds.), *The EEC and Eastern Europe* (Cambridge: Cambridge University Press, 1978)

Pinder, John, 'Integration in Western and Eastern Europe: Relations Between the EC and CMEA', *Journal of Common Market Studies*, vol.18, no.2 (December 1979)

Pinder, John, 'Economic Integration versus National Sovereignty: Differences Between Eastern and Western Europe', *Government and Opposition*, vol.24, no.3 (Summer 1989)

Pinder, John, '1992 and Beyond: European Community and Eastern Europe', *The International Spectator*, vol.25, no.3 (July-September 1990)

Pinder, John, *The European Community and Eastern Europe* (London: The Royal Institute of International Affairs/Pinter, 1991)

La Politique Étrangère de la France, Textes et Documents, Paris, Ministère des Affaires Étrangères (1990)

Ransom, Charles F. G., 'The Future of EEC-COMECON Relations', *The World Today*, vol.27 (October 1971)

Ransom, Charles F. G., *The European Community and Eastern Europe* (London: Butterworths, 1973)

Ransom, Charles F. G., 'The Common Market and Eastern Europe', in Peter Stingelin (ed.), *The European Community and the Outsiders* (Don Mills, Ontario: Longman Canada Ltd., 1973)

Repetzki, Beatrice, 'Der schwierige Dialog zwischen der EWG und den europäischen RGW-Ländern', *Osteuropa-Wirtschaft*, vol.33, no.3 (1988)

Reynaud, Paul, 'The Unifying Force for Europe', *Foreign Affairs*, vol.28, no.2 (January 1950)

Rhein, Eberhard, 'Die Europäische Gemeinschaft auf der Suche nach einer gemeinsamen Außenpolitik', *Europa-Archiv*, vol.31, no.6 (1976)

Roberts, Frank, *Dealing With Dictators. The Destruction and Revival of Europe 1930-70* (London: Weidenfeld & Nicolson, 1991)

Robson, P., *Economic Integration in Africa* (London: Allen & Unwin, 1968)

Robson, P., *The Economics of International Integration* (London: Allen & Unwin, 1987)

Rode, Reinhard, *Germany: World Economic Power or Overburdened Eurohegemon?*, PRIF Report No. 21, Peace Research Institute Frankfurt, Frankfurt am Main (1991)

Roholl, M. L., E. Waegemans and Cees Willemsen (eds.), *De Lage Landen en de Sovjet Unie. Beeldvorming en Betrekkingen* (Amsterdam: Uitgeverij Jan Mets, 1989)

Roodbeen, Hendrik, *Trading the Jewel of Great Value. The Participation of The Netherlands, Belgium, Switzerland and Austria in the Western Strategic Embargo* (Leiden University, Department of Political Science, Ph.D. thesis, 1992)

Rothschild, Joseph, *Return to Diversity. A Political History of East Central Europe Since World War II* (New York: Oxford University Press, 1989)

Royen, Christoph, 'Die EWG – Schrittmacher der osteuropäischen Integration?', *Osteuropa*, vol.22, no.9 (September 1972)

Sandholtz, Wayne, and John Zysman, '1992: Recasting the European Bargain', *World Politics*, vol.42 no.1 (October 1989)

Sannwald, Rolf, 'Die sowjetischen Ansichten über die europäische Integration', in Hans Mayrzedt and Helmut Romé (eds.), *Die Westeuropäische Integration aus osteuropäischer Sicht. Bibliographie – Dokumentation – Kommentar* (Wien: Druck und Verlag Josef Laub, 1968)

Sarre, Francis, 'Article 115 EEC Treaty and Trade with Eastern Europe', *Intereconomics*, vol.23, no.5 (September/October 1988)

Sasse, Christoph, 'Kooperationsabkommen und EG-Handelspolitik. Parallelität oder Konflikt', *Europa-Archiv*, vol.29 (1974)

Schelling, Thomas C., *The Strategy of Conflict* (Cambridge: Harvard University Press, 1960)

Schmidt, Gerold, 'Vollendung der Gemeinsamen Handelspolitik', *Aussenpolitik*, vol.24, no.4 (1973)

Schmiedling, Holger, 'A Concept for a Pan-European Economic Integration', *European Affairs*, vol.3, no.3 (Autumn 1989)

Schoneveld, J. A., *Het Oosteuropees Milieu: Een Verloren Zaak?* (Leiden University, Department of Political Science, MA thesis, 1991)

Schöpflin, George, 'The EEC and Eastern Europe', *European Community* (London), no.10 (October 1968)

Schumann, K., 'The Role of Present Co-operation Structures in the Process of European Integration', *Helsinki Monitor* (Utrecht), vol.2, no.3 (July 1991)

Schwarz, Hans-Peter, *Adenauer. Der Staatsmann: 1952-1967* (Stuttgart: Deutsche Verlags-Anstalt, 1991)

Schweisfurth, Theodor, 'Sowjetunion, westeuropäische Integration und gesamteuropäische Zusammenarbeit', *Europa-archiv*, vol.27 (1972)

Schwerin, Otto Graf, 'Die Solidarität der EG-Staaten in der KSZE', *Europa-Archiv*, vol.30 (1975)

Segbers, K., 'Migration and Refugee Movements from the USSR: Causes and Prospects', *Report on the USSR* (RFE/RL Research Institute), vol.3, no.46 (November 15 1991)

Senior Nello, Susan, *Recent Developments in Relations Between the EC and Eastern Europe*, EUI Working Paper no. 89/381, European University Institute, Florence (1989)

Senior Nello, Susan, *The New Europe. Changing Economic Relations Between East and West* (New York: Harvester Wheatsheaf, 1991)

Shackleton, Michael, 'Fishing for a Policy? The Common Fisheries Policy of the Community', in Helen Wallace, William Wallace and Carole Webb (eds.), *Policy-Making in the European Community* (Chichester: John Wiley & Sons, 1989)

Shulman, Marshall D., 'The Communist States and Western Integration', *International Organization*, vol.17, no.2 (1963)

Shulman, Marshall D., 'Sowjetische Vorschläge für eine europäische Sicherheitskonferenz (1966-1969)', *Europa-Archiv*, vol.24, no.19 (October 1969)

Skak, M., 'East Europe, the Soviet Union and Europeanization: A Challenge for the European Community', Paper presented at the 87th Annual Meeting of the American Political Science Association (29 August – 1 September 1991)

Snyder, Glenn H., 'The Security Dilemma in Alliance Politics', *World Politics*, vol.36, no.4 (July 1984)

Snyder, Glenn H., 'Alliance Theory. A Neorealist First Cut', *Journal of International Affairs*, vol.44, no.1 (Spring/Summer 1990)

Snyder, Glenn H., and Paul Diesing, *Conflict Among Nations. Bargaining, Decision Making, and System Structure in International Crisis* (Princeton, NJ: Princeton University Press, 1977)

Snyder, Jack, 'Averting Anarchy in the New Europe', in Sean M. Lynn-Jones (ed.), *The Cold War and After. Prospects for Peace. An International Security Reader* (Cambridge, Mass.: The MIT Press, 1991)

Sobell, Vlad, 'Eastern Europe and the European Community', *Report on Eastern Europe* (RFE/RL Research Institute), vol.1, no.8 (February 23 1990)

Sokil, Catherina, 'The Soviet Union and the GATT, IMF, and World Bank', in Michael Kraus and Ronald D. Liebowitz (eds.), *Perestroika and East-West Economic Relations. Prospects for the 1990s* (New York and London: New York University Press, 1990)

Sokoloff, Georges, *The Economy of Detente. The Soviet Union and Western Capital* (Leamington Spa: Berg, 1987)

Spaak, Paul-Henri, 'The Integration of Europe: Dreams and Realities', *Foreign Affairs*, vol.29, no.1 (October 1950)

Spaak, Paul-Henri, *The Continuing Battle. Memoirs of a European 1936-1966* (London: Weidenfeld and Nicolson, 1971)

Spence, David, *Enlargement Without Accession: The EC's Response to German Unification*, Discussion Paper no.36, Royal Institute of International Affairs, London (1991)

Spero, Joan Edelman, *The Politics of International Economic Relations* (New York: St. Martin's Press, 1990)

Staden, A. van, *Een Trouwe Bondgenoot. Nederland en het Atlantisch Bondgenootschap* (Baarn: In den Toren, 1974)

Stein, Arthur A., *Why Nations Cooperate. Circumstance and Choice in International Relations* (Ithaca and London: Cornell University Press, 1990)

Stent, Angela E., *From Embargo to Ostpolitik. The Political Economy of West German-Soviet Relations 1955-1980* (Cambridge: Cambridge University Press, 1981)

Stent, Angela E., *Technology Transfer to the Soviet Union. A Challenge for the Cohesiveness of the Western Alliance* (Bonn: Europa Union Verlag, 1983)

Stevens, Christopher, and Jane Kennan (eds.), *Reform in Eastern Europe and the Developing Country Dimension* (London: Overseas Development Institute, 1992)

Stingelin, Peter (ed.), *The European Community and the Outsiders* (Don Mills, Ontario: Longman Canada Ltd., 1973)

Stirk, P. M. R., 'The Preconditions of European Integration: Observations of the Years 1918-1945', in W. A. F. Camphuis and C. G. J. Wildeboer-Schut (eds.), *Europese Eenwording in Historisch Perspectief. Factoren van Integratie en Desintegratie* (Zaltbommel: Europese Bibliotheek, 1991)

Tatu, Michel, 'East-West Relations', in Max Kohnstamm and Wolfgang Hager (eds.), *A Nation Writ Large? Foreign-Policy Problems Before the European Community* (London: Macmillan, 1973)

Taylor, Paul, 'The New Dynamics of EC Integration in the 1980s', in Juliet Lodge (ed.), *The European Community and the Challenge of the Future* (London: Pinter, 1989)

Tickell, Crispin, 'Neuner-Gemeinschaft und Sicherheitskonferenz', *Aussenpolitik*, vol.25, no.1 (1974)

Timmerman, H., 'Die italienischen Kommunisten und ihre außenpolitische Konzeption. Ein Jugoslawien des Westens?', *Europa-Archiv*, vol.21 (1971)

Tomann, Horst, 'EC Internal Market: An Opportunity for CMEA Countries?', *Intereconomics*, vol.24, no.6 (November/December 1989)

Tovias, Alfred, 'EC-Eastern Europe: A Case Study of Hungary', *Journal of Common Market Studies*, vol.29, no.3 (March 1991)

Tsoukalis, Loukas (ed.), *Greece and the European Community* (Farnborough, Hants.: Saxon House, 1979)

Tsoukalis, Loukas, *The European Community and its Mediterranean Enlargement* (London: Allen & Unwin, 1981)

Tsoukalis, Loukas, 'Money and the Process of Integration', in Helen Wallace, William Wallace and Carole Webb (eds.), *Policy-Making in the European Community* (Chichester: John Wiley & Sons, 1989)

Tuchman Mathews, Jessica, 'Redefining Security', *Foreign Affairs*, vol.68, no.2 (Spring 1989)

Ulam, Adam, *Expansion and Coexistence* (New York: Praeger, 1968)

United Nations Economic Commission for Europe, *Economic Survey of Europe in 1990-1991* (New York, 1991)

Urwin, Derek W., *Western Europe Since 1945. A Short Political History* (London: Longmans, 1968)

Uschakow, Alexander, 'Die Beziehungen Zwischen der EG und dem EGW', *Osteuropa*, vol.38 (1988)

Vandoren, P., 'Mise en Oeuvre de la Politique Anti-dumping de la CEE contre les Importations en Provenance des Pays à Commerce d'État', *Revue du Marché Commun*, no.316 (April 1988)

Verny, Sophie, 'CEE-CAEM: Le Problème de la Reconnaissance Mutuele', *Courier des Pays de l'Est*, no.305 (April 1985)

Vinton, Louisa, 'The Attempted Coup in the USSR. East European Reactions, Poland', *Report on Eastern Europe* (RFE/RL Research Institute), vol.2, no.35 (30 August 1991)

Völker, E. L. M., 'Importing From East-Bloc Countries: Common Rules and Remedies for the Parties Concerned', *Legal Issues of European Integration*, no.1 (1985)

Voorhoeve, Joris J. C., *Peace, Profits and Principles. A Study of Dutch Foreign Policy* (Leiden: Martinus Nijhoff, 1985)

Wæver, Ole, 'Three Competing Europes: German, French, Russian', *International Affairs* (London), vol.66, no.3 (1990)

Wallace, Helen, *Widening and Deepening: The European Community and the New European Agenda*, Discussion Paper no.23, Royal Institute of International Affairs, London (1989)

Wallace, Helen, 'The Europe That Came in From the Cold', *International Affairs* (London), vol.67, no.4 (1991)

Wallace, William, 'Wider But Weaker: The Continued Enlargement of the EEC', *The World Today*, vol.32 (March 1976)

Wallace, William, 'Political Cooperation: Integration Through Intergovernmentalism', in Helen Wallace, William Wallace and Carole Webb (eds.), *Policy-Making in the European Community* (Chichester: John Wiley & Sons, 1989)

Walt, Stephen M., *The Origins of Alliances* (Ithaca and London: Cornell University Press, 1987)

Waltz, Kenneth N., *Man, the State and War. A Theoretical Analysis* (New York: Columbia University Press, 1959)

Waltz, Kenneth N., 'The Stability of a Bipolar World', *Dædalus*, vol.93 (Summer 1964)

Waltz, Kenneth N., *Theory of International Politics* (New York: McGraw-Hill, 1979)

Waltz, Kenneth N., 'Reflections on *Theory of International Politics*: A Response to my Critics', in Robert O. Keohane (ed.), *Neorealism and Its Critics* (New York: Columbia University Press, 1986)

Webb, A. J. K., 'The Evolution of the Attitude of the Italian Communist Party Towards the European Economic Community', *Millennium: Journal of International Studies*, vol.13, no.1 (Spring 1984)

Webb, Carole, 'Theoretical Perspectives and Problems', in Helen Wallace, William Wallace and Carole Webb (eds.), *Policy-Making in the European Community* (Chichester: John Wiley & Sons, 1989)

Weidenfeld, Werner, 'Die Europäische Gemeinschaft und Osteuropa', *Aussenpolitik*, vol.38, no.2 (1987)

Weil, Gordon L., *A Foreign Policy For Europe? The External Relations of the European Community* (Bruges: College of Europe, 1970)

Welch Larson, Deborah, *Origins of Containment. A Psychological Explanation* (Princeton, NJ: Princeton University Press, 1985)

Wessels, Wolfgang, 'The EC Council: The Community's Decisionmaking Center', in Robert O. Keohane and Stanley Hoffmann (eds.), *The New European Community. Decisionmaking and Institutional Change* (Boulder: Westview Press, 1991)

Wessels, Wolfgang, 'Deepening and/or Widening – Debate on the Shape of EC-Europe in the Nineties', *Aussenwirtschaft*, vol.46, no.2 (1991)

Wettig, Gerhard, 'Germany, Europe, and the Soviets', in Herbert J. Ellison (ed.), *Soviet Policy Toward Western Europe. Implications for the Atlantic Alliance* (Seattle and London: University of Washington Press, 1983)

Weydenthal, Jan B. de, 'The Cracow Summit', *Report on Eastern Europe* (RFE/RL Research Institute), vol.2, no.43 (25 October 1991)

White, Brian, 'Britain and East-West Relations', in Michael Smith, Steve Smith and Brian White (eds.), *British Foreign Policy. Tradition, Change and Transformation* (London: Unwin Hyman, 1988)

Wightman, David, 'East-West Cooperation and the United Nations Economic Commission for Europe', *International Organization*, vol.11, no.1 (Winter 1957)

Wilczynski, J., 'Financial Relations Between the EEC and the CMEA', in Avi Shlaim and G. N. Yannopoulos (eds.), *The EEC and Eastern Europe* (Cambridge: Cambridge University Press, 1978)

Wolfers, A., *Discord and Collaboration. Essays on International Politics* (Baltimore and London: The Johns Hopkins University Press, 1962)

Woolley, John T., 'Policy Credibility and European Monetary Institutions', in Alberta M. Sbragia (ed.), *Europolitics. Institutions and Policymaking in the 'New' European Community* (Washington, DC: The Brookings Institution, 1992)

Yannopoulos, G. N., 'The Impact of the European Economic Community on East-West Trade', Paper presented at a Conference on *East-West Trade and Financial Relations*, European University Institute, Florence, 4-6 June 1985

Yergin, Daniel, *Shattered Peace. The Origins of the Cold War and the National Security State* (Boston: Houghton Mifflin Company, 1977)

Yost, David S., 'France in the New Europe', *Foreign Affairs*, vol.69, no.5 (Winter 1990/91)

Young, John W., *Britain, France and the Unity of Europe. 1945-1951* (Leicester: Leicester University Press, 1984)

Yuryev, N., 'Economic Integration and Western Blocs', *International Affairs* (Moscow), no.10 (October 1971)

Zauberman, Alfred, 'The Soviet Bloc and the Common Market', *The World Today*, vol.19 (January 1963)

Zielonka, J., 'The Dutch version of *Ostpolitik*', in Alfred E. Pijpers (ed.), *The European Community at the Crossroads. Major Issues and Priorities for the EC Presidency* (Dordrecht: Martinus Nijhoff, 1992)

Zurcher, Arnold J., *The Struggle to Unite Europe. 1940-58* (New York: New York University Press, 1958)

Index

Learning Resources
Centre